InDesign® CS5

FOR

DUMMIES®

by Galen Gruman

WILEY

Wiley Publishing, Inc.

InDesign® CS5 For Dummies®
Published by
Wiley Publishing, Inc.
111 River Street
Hoboken, NJ 07030-5774
www.wiley.com

WILEY

About the Author

Galen Gruman is the principal at The Zango Group, an editorial and book production firm. As such, he has produced several books for Wiley Publishing and is a regular contributor to *Macworld*. He is author or coauthor of 24 other books on desktop publishing.

Gruman led one of the first successful conversions of a national magazine to desktop publishing in 1986 and has covered publishing technology since then for several publications, including *Layers Magazine;* the trade weekly *InfoWorld,* for which he began writing in 1986 and of which he is now executive editor; and *Macworld,* whose staff he was a member of from 1991 to 1998.

Dedication

To Ingall, who gives me the space as needed to write books such as this.

Author's Acknowledgments

Thanks are due to several people for making this book the best guide possible for InDesign beginners and those wanting a quick tour of the program: Jonathan Woolson was tech reviewer on previous versions of this book, and several how-to suggestions based on his production savvy also remain for your benefit. Thanks are also due to the current edition's editor, Pat O'Brien, for making the book as clear and direct as possible. The photographs you see in this book's example layouts were taken by Ingall W. Bull III (and used with permission). Last, thanks are due to the many talented people at Adobe who continue to refine InDesign to the advantage of us all.

Publisher's Acknowledgments

We're proud of this book; please send us your comments at http://dummies.custhelp.com. For other comments, please contact our Customer Care Department within the U.S. at 877-762-2974, outside the U.S. at 317-572-3993, or fax 317-572-4002.

Some of the people who helped bring this book to market include the following:

Acquisitions, Editorial, and Media Development

Project Editor: Pat O'Brien

Acquisitions Editor: Bob Woerner

Copy Editor: Debbye Butler

Technical Editor: Jonathan Woolson

Editorial Manager: Kevin Kirschner

Media Development Project Manager: Laura Moss-Hollister

Media Development Assistant Project Manager: Jenny Swisher

Media Development Associate Producers: Josh Frank, Marilyn Hummel, Douglas Kuhn, and Shawn Patrick

Editorial Assistant: Amanda Graham

Sr. Editorial Assistant: Cherie Case

Cartoons: Rich Tennant (www.the5thwave.com)

Composition Services

Project Coordinator: Patrick Redmond

Layout and Graphics: Ashley Chamberlain, Joyce Haughey

Proofreaders: Laura Albert, Susan Hobbs

Indexer: BIM Indexing & Proofreading Services

Publishing and Editorial for Technology Dummies

    Richard Swadley, Vice President and Executive Group Publisher

    Andy Cummings, Vice President and Publisher

    Mary Bednarek, Executive Acquisitions Director

    Mary C. Corder, Editorial Director

Publishing for Consumer Dummies

    Diane Graves Steele, Vice President and Publisher

Composition Services

    Debbie Stailey, Director of Composition Services

Contents at a Glance

Table of Contents

Introduction

*W*hat is Adobe InDesign, and what can it do for you? In its more than a decade in existence, InDesign has become the most powerful publishing application, one that lets you work the way *you* want to work. You can use InDesign as a free-form but manual approach to layout, or as a structured but easily revised approach. The fact that you can choose which way to work is important for both novice and experienced users because there is no single, correct way to lay out pages. Sometimes (for example, if your project is a one-time publication, such as an ad), creating a layout from scratch — almost as if you were doing it by hand on paper — is the best approach. And sometimes using a highly formatted template that you can modify as needed is the way to go. You don't need to reinvent the wheel for documents that have a structured and repeatable format, such as books and magazines.

InDesign can handle sophisticated tasks, such as glossy magazines and high-impact ads, but its structured approach to publishing also makes it a good choice for newspapers, newsletters, and books. InDesign is also a good choice for corporate publishing tasks, such as proposals and annual reports. In all cases, you can design for printing on paper or electronic distribution as Adobe Acrobat Portable Document Format (PDF) files. Plug-in software from other vendors adds extra capabilities.

Plus, you can use InDesign for interactive PDF and Flash documents that can play movies and sounds, and let users click buttons to invoke actions such as changing pages, opening files, and animating objects on the page either automatically or in response to user actions. You can also use InDesign as a starting point to create Web pages, though you'll more likely use its Web-export capabilities to convert your print documents into files that you can refine in your favorite Web editor. This support for electronic media and distribution is the new frontier for publishing, and Adobe is provisioning the first wave of settlers.

About This Book

After you get the hang of it, InDesign is quite easy to use. At the same time, it's a powerful publishing program with a strong following among the ranks of professional publishers — and the latest InDesign CS5 version is certain to reinforce that position given its many refinements, including its newfound animation capabilities and other features that make working with objects easier. Part of its success is due to the fact that its interface is like that of its sister applications, Adobe Illustrator and Adobe Photoshop, which are also components of the Adobe Creative Suite.

If you're new to InDesign, welcome! I hope you find the information in these pages exactly what you need as you get started.

Foolish Assumptions

Although this book has information that any level of layout artist or production editor needs to know to use InDesign, this book is primarily for those of you who are fairly new to the field, or who are just becoming familiar with the program. I try to take the mystery out of InDesign and give you guidance on how to create a bunch of different types of documents.

I don't assume that you've ever used InDesign (or any publishing program). But I do assume that you have a basic knowledge of Macintosh or Windows — enough to work with files and applications. And I assume that you have basic familiarity with layout design, such as knowing what pages, margins, and fonts are. But I don't expect you to be an expert in any of these areas —nor do you have to be!

How This Book Is Organized

This book contains eight parts. I also include some bonus content on the InDesignCentral Web site (www.InDesignCentral.com).

Part 1: Before You Begin

Designing a document is a combination of science and art. The science is in setting up the structure of the page: How many places will hold text, and how many will hold graphics? How wide will the margins be? Where will the page numbers appear? You get the idea. The art is in coming up with creative ways of filling the structure to please your eyes and the eyes of the people who will be looking at your document.

In this part, I tell you how to navigate your way around InDesign using the program's menus, dialog boxes, panels, and panes. I also explain how to customize the preferences to your needs.

Part II: Document Essentials

Good publishing technique is about more than just getting the words down on paper. It's also about opening, saving, adding, deleting, numbering, and setting layout guidelines for documents. This part shows you how to do all that and a lot more, including tips on setting up master pages that you can use over and over again. You also find out how to create color swatches for easy reuse in your documents.

Part III: Object Essentials

This part of the book shows you how to work with *objects:* the lines, text frames, graphics frames, and other odds and ends that make up a publication. If you've used previous versions of InDesign, pay extra attention to the CS5 version's (good) changes in how to select objects and do things like rotate them. You also discover how to apply some really neat special effects to them.

Part IV: Text Essentials

When you think about it, text is a big deal when it comes to publishing documents. After all, how many people would want to read a book with nothing but pictures? In this part, I show you how to create and manipulate text, in more ways than you can even imagine.

Part V: Graphics Essentials

Very few people would want to read a book with nothing but text, so this part is where I show you how to handle graphics in InDesign — both importing them from the outside and creating your own within InDesign.

Part VI: Getting Down to Business

InDesign is really good at handling the many kinds of documents that tend to be used in businesses, such as manuals, annual reports, and catalogs. This part shows you how to create tables, handle footnotes, create indexes, manage page numbering across multiple chapters in a book, and use text variables and cross-references to make InDesign update text as needed based on the document's current context.

Part VII: Printing, Presentation, and Web Essentials

Publishing is no longer about just the printed page. Now you can create PDF files, Web pages, and Flash files from InDesign — and each supports different kinds of interactive capabilities and media files. This part starts with the skinny on how to set up your output files, manage color, and work with service bureaus. Then it explains how to use hyperlinks in your document for both Web and PDF pages. Finally, it explains InDesign's interactive push-button, page transition effects, and animation capabilities that bring page layout into new dimensions, and then shows you how to export these interactive files to PDF and Flash formats.

Part VIII: The Part of Tens

This part of the book is like the chips in the chocolate chip cookies; you can eat the cookies without them, but you'd be missing a really good part. It's a part that shows you some important resources that can help you make the most of InDesign, as well as highlights what I think are the best of InDesign's new features.

Conventions Used in This Book

This book covers InDesign on both Macintosh and Windows. Because the application is almost identical on both platforms, I point out platform-specific information only when it's different — and that's very rare. I've used Macintosh screen shots throughout; Windows screen shots are usually identical, except for the dialog boxes to open, save, and export files — these are arranged differently on Macs and PCs (for *all* programs, not just InDesign), but the relevant options to InDesign are the same. If you're a Windows user, a quick look at Adobe's documentation, which shows Windows screens, can show you how the interfaces are nearly identical. So don't worry about them.

Here are some other conventions used in this book:

✓ **Menu commands:** They're listed like this: Window⇔Pages. That means go to the Window menu and choose the Pages option from it. In almost every case, the menu command sequences are the same for Mac and Windows users; in very few cases, they differ (such as the Preferences menu option and the Configure Plug-ins menu option), so I note these differences where they exist by putting the Mac menu sequence first and then the Windows one.

✔ **Key combinations:** If you're supposed to press several keys together, I indicate that by placing a plus sign (+) between them. Thus, Shift+⌘+A means press and hold the Shift and ⌘ keys and then press A. After you've pressed the A key, let go of all the keys. I also use the plus sign to join keys to mouse movements. For example, Alt+drag means to hold the Alt key when dragging the mouse.

Note that the Macintosh sequence comes first, followed by the Windows equivalent.

✔ **Pointer:** The small graphic icon that moves on the screen as you move your mouse is a pointer (also called a cursor when you're working with text). The pointer takes on different shapes depending on the tool you select, the current location of the mouse, and the function you are performing.

✔ **Click:** This means to quickly press and release the mouse button once. Many Mac mice have only one button, but some have two or more. All PC mice have at least two buttons. If you have a multibutton mouse, click the leftmost button when I say to click the mouse.

✔ **Double-click:** This tells you to quickly press and release the mouse button twice. On some multibutton mice, one of the buttons can function as a double-click. (You click it once, but the computer acts as if you clicked twice.) If your mouse has this feature, use it; it saves strain on your hand.

✔ **Right-click:** A feature first implemented on Windows, but present on Macs since the late 1990s, this means to click the right-hand mouse button. If your Mac has only one button, hold the Control key when clicking the mouse button to do the equivalent of right-clicking in programs that support it. Mac OS X automatically assigns the right-hand button on a multibutton mouse to the Control+click combination; if your mouse came with its own system preference, you can often further customize the button actions.

✔ **Dragging:** Dragging is used for moving and sizing items in an InDesign document. To drag an item, position the mouse pointer on the item, press and hold down the mouse button, and then slide the mouse across a flat surface.

Icons Used in This Book

So that you can pick out parts that you really need to pay attention to (or, depending on your taste, to avoid), I use some symbols, or *icons,* in this book.

When you see this icon, it means I am pointing out a feature that's new to InDesign CS5.

If you see this icon, it means that I'm mentioning some really nifty point or idea that you may want to keep in mind as you use the program.

This icon lets you know something you'll want to keep in mind. If you forget it later, that's fine; but if you remember it, it will make your InDesign life a little easier.

Even if you skip all the other icons, pay attention to this one. Why? Because ignoring it can cause something really, really bad or embarrassing to happen, like when you were sitting in your second-grade classroom waiting for the teacher to call on you to answer a question, and you noticed that you still had your pajama shirt on. I don't want that to happen to you!

This icon tells you that I am about to pontificate on some remote technical bit of information that may help explain a feature in InDesign. The technical info will definitely make you sound impressive if you memorize it and recite it to your friends.

What You're Not to Read

If you see any text in this book that has this icon next to it, feel free to skip right over to the next paragraph. This icon alerts you to geeky information that you don't need to know to use InDesign. I just couldn't help giving you a little extra-credit information in case you were a budding geek like me.

Where to Go from Here

If you're a complete beginner, I suggest you read the book's parts in the order I present them. If you haven't used InDesign before but you have used other layout programs, do read Part I first to get in the InDesign frame of mind, and then explore other parts in any order you want. If you *have* used InDesign before, peruse them in any order you want, to see what's changed.

As you gain comfort with InDesign, you'll be surprised how much you can do with it. And when you're ready to discover more, take advantage of the wealth of resources out there to go the next level. The InDesignCentral Web site (www.InDesignCentral.com) can help you do that.

Part I

Before You Begin

The 5th Wave

By Rich Tennant

"The odd thing is he always insists on using the latest version of InDesign."

In this part . . .

You have your copy of InDesign, and you'd like some basic information on how to get started, right? Well, you've come to the right place. This part helps you sail smoothly through InDesign and gives you a general idea of what InDesign can do. I explain the layout approaches you can take, as well as how to set up InDesign to work the way you work.

Along the way, you find out how to navigate the plethora of panels, menus, tools, and shortcuts that can seem overwhelming at first, but which soon become second nature as you gain experience using the program. Welcome aboard!

Chapter 1

Understanding InDesign Ingredients

*S*tarting to use a new software application is not unlike meeting a new friend for the first time. You take a long look at the person, maybe ask a few questions, and begin the process of becoming acquainted. (If you're not new to InDesign but are new to the CS5 version, it's like seeing a friend you haven't seen in a while — you observe any changes and catch up on what's happened in the meantime.)

Just as it's worthwhile to find out the likes and dislikes of a new friend, it's also worth your time to wrap your head around InDesign's unique style and approaches. When you do so, you'll find it much easier to start using InDesign to get work done.

This chapter explains where to look in InDesign for the features and capabilities you need to master. (For a quick look at what's new to version CS5, check out Chapter 26.) I introduce you to the process that InDesign assumes you use when laying out documents, describe the unique interface elements in the document window, survey the most commonly used tools, and explain how InDesign packages much of its functionality through an interface element called a *panel*.

Understanding Global and Local Control

The power of desktop publishing in general, and InDesign in particular, is that it lets you automate time-consuming layout and typesetting tasks while at the same time letting you customize each step of the process according to your needs.

What does that mean in practice? That you can use *global* controls to establish general settings for layout elements, and then use *local* controls to modify those elements to meet specific requirements. The key to using global and local tools effectively is to know when each is appropriate.

Global tools include

- General preferences and application preferences (see Chapter 2)
- Master pages and libraries (see Chapter 5)
- Character and paragraph styles (see Chapter 13)
- Table and cell styles (see Chapter 18)
- Object styles (see Chapter 9)
- Sections and page numbers (see Chapter 4)
- Color definitions (see Chapter 6)
- Hyphenation and justification (see Chapter 14)

Styles and master pages are the two main global settings that you can expect to override locally throughout a document. You shouldn't be surprised to make such changes often because although the layout and typographic functions that styles and master pages automate are the fundamental components of any document's look, they don't always work for all the specific content within a publication. (If they did, who'd need human designers?!)

Local tools include

- Frame tools (see Part III, as well as Chapter 16)
- Character and paragraph tools (see Chapters 14 and 15)
- Graphics tools (see Part V)

Keep your bearings straight

A powerful but confusing capability in InDesign is something called a *control point*. InDesign lets you work with objects from nine different reference points — any of the four corners, the middle of any of the four sides, or the center — such as when positioning the object precisely or rotating the object. You choose the active reference point, or control point, in the Control panel or Transform panel, using the grid of nine points arranged in a square.

By default, InDesign uses the central reference point as the control point, which is great for rotating an object, but can lead to confusion when you enter in the X and Y coordinates to place it precisely. That's because most people use the upper-left corner of an object when specifying its coordinates, not the center of the object. Be sure to change the control point to the upper-left reference point whenever entering X and Y coordinates in the Control or Transform panels.

How do you change the control point? That's easy: Just click the desired reference point in that preview grid. The control point will be black, whereas the other reference points will be white.

Choosing the right tools for the job

Depending on what you're trying to do with InDesign at any given moment, you may or may not immediately know which tool to use. If, for example, you maintain fairly precise layout standards throughout a document, using master pages is the way to keep your work in order. Using styles is the best solution if you want to apply standard character and paragraph formatting throughout a document. When you work with one-of-a-kind documents, on the other hand, designing master pages and styles doesn't make much sense — it's easier just to format elements as you create them.

For example, you can create *drop caps* (large initial letters set into a paragraph of type, such as the drop cap that starts each chapter in this book) as a character option in the Character panel, or you can create a *paragraph style* (formatting that you can apply to whole paragraphs, ensuring that the same formatting is applied each time) that contains the drop-cap settings and then apply that style to the paragraph containing the drop cap. Which method you choose depends on the complexity of your document and how often you need to perform the action. The more often you find yourself taking a set of steps, the more often you should use a global tool (like character and paragraph styles) to accomplish the task.

Fortunately, you don't need to choose between global and local tools while you're in the middle of designing a document. You can always create styles from existing local formatting later. You can also add elements to a master page if you start to notice that you need them to appear on every page.

Specifying measurement values

Another situation in which you can choose between local or global controls is specifying measurement values. Regardless of the *default measurement unit* you set (that is, the measurement unit that appears in all dialog boxes and panels), you can use any unit when entering measurements in an InDesign dialog box. For example, if the default measurement is picas, but you're new to publishing and are more comfortable working in inches, go ahead and enter measurements in inches.

InDesign accepts any of the following codes for measurement units. (Chapter 2 explains how to change the default measurements.) Note that the *x* in the following items indicates where you specify the value, such as **2i** for 2 inches. It doesn't matter whether you put a space between the value and the code: Typing **2inch** and typing **2 inch** are the same as far as InDesign is concerned:

- *x*i or *x* inch or *x*" (for inches)
- *x*p (for picas)
- *x*pt or 0p*x* (for points)
- *x*px (for pixels)
- *x*c (for ciceros, a European newspaper measurement)
- *x*ag (for agates, an American newspaper measurement)
- *x*cm (for centimeters)
- *x*mm (for millimeters)

What to do when you make a mistake

InDesign is a very forgiving program. If you make a mistake, change your mind, or work yourself into a complete mess, you don't have to remain in your predicament or save your work. InDesign offers several escape routes. You can

- **Undo your last action by choosing Edit⇨Undo (⌘+Z or Ctrl+Z).** (You can't undo some actions, particularly actions such as scrolling that don't affect any items or the underlying document structure.) You can undo multiple actions in the reverse order in which they were done by

repeatedly choosing Edit⇨Undo (⌘+Z or Ctrl+Z); each time you undo, the preceding action is undone.

- **Redo an action you've undone by choosing Edit⇨Redo (Shift+⌘+Z or Ctrl+Shift+Z).** Alternatively, choosing Undo and Redo is a handy way of seeing a before/after view of a particular change. As with an undo action, you can redo multiple undone actions in the reverse of the order in which they were undone.

InDesign CS5 adds the capability to specify measurements in pixels, as part of its newfound capability to create "Web-intent" documents in addition to the traditional "print-intent" ones, as Chapter 3 explains.

You can enter fractional picas in two ways: in decimal format (as in **8.5p**) and in picas and points (as in **8p6**). Either of these settings results in a measurement of 8½ picas. (A pica contains 12 points.)

Discovering the Document Window

In InDesign, you spend lots of time working in document windows — the "containers" for your documents. Each document, regardless of its size, is contained within its own document window.

The best way to get familiar with the InDesign document window is by opening a blank document. Simply choosing File➪New➪Document (⌘+N or Ctrl+N) and clicking OK opens a new document window. Don't worry about the settings for now — just explore.

Figure 1-1 shows all the standard elements of a new document window. I won't bore you by covering interface elements that are standard to all programs. Instead, the rest of this section focuses on InDesign-specific elements.

Rulers

Document windows display a horizontal ruler across the top and a vertical ruler down the left side. As shown in Figure 1-1, the horizontal ruler measures from the top-left corner of the page across the entire spread, and the vertical ruler measures from the top to the bottom of the current page. These rulers are handy for judging the size and placement of objects on a page. Even experienced designers often use the rulers while they experiment with a design.

Both rulers display increments in picas unless you change the measurement system for each ruler in the Units & Increments pane of the Preferences dialog box. Choose InDesign➪Preferences➪Units & Increments (⌘+K) or Edit➪Preferences➪Units & Increments (Ctrl+K) to open the Preferences dialog box. Your choices include inches, picas, points, pixels, decimal inches, ciceros, agates, millimeters, and centimeters.

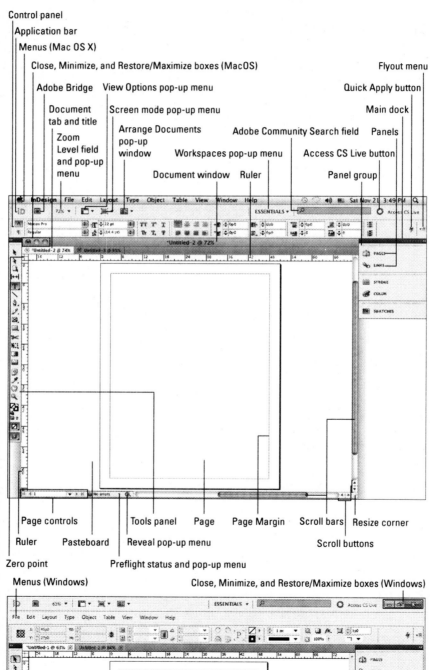

Control panel
Application bar
Menus (Mac OS X)
Close, Minimize, and Restore/Maximize boxes (MacOS)
Flyout menu
Adobe Bridge
View Options pop-up menu
Quick Apply button
Document tab and title
Screen mode pop-up menu
Main dock
Zoom Level field and pop-up menu
Arrange Documents pop-up window
Adobe Community Search field
Panels
Workspaces pop-up menu
Access CS Live button
Document window   Ruler
Panel group

ESSENTIALS
Access CS Live

Figure 1-1:
The document window is where you work on documents. Bottom: The Windows 7 version differs in its Close, Minimize, and Restore/Maximize controls.

Page controls
Tools panel   Page   Page Margin   Scroll bars   Resize corner
Ruler   Pasteboard   Reveal pop-up menu   Scroll buttons
Zero point   Preflight status and pop-up menu
Menus (Windows)   Close, Minimize, and Restore/Maximize boxes (Windows)

ESSENTIALS   Access CS Live

If you change the ruler measurement system when no documents are open, the rulers in all new documents will use the measurement system you selected. If a document is open when you make the change, the rulers are changed only in that document.

You can also create your own measurement system by choosing Custom. Most people should ignore this option, but sometimes it can make sense, such as setting the ruler to match the line spacing, so that you can measure number of lines in your ruler.

If your computer has a small monitor and the rulers start to get in your way, you can hide them by choosing View➪Hide Rulers (⌘+R or Ctrl+R). Get them back by choosing View➪Show Rulers (⌘+R or Ctrl+R).

Zero point

The point where the rulers intersect in the upper-left corner of the page is called the *zero point*. (Some people call it the *ruler origin*.) The zero point is the starting place for all horizontal and vertical measurements.

If you need to place items in relation to another spot on the page (for example, from the center of a spread rather than from the left-hand page), you can move the zero point by clicking and dragging it to a new location. Notice that the X: and Y: values in the Control panel update as you drag the zero point so that you can place it precisely.

If you change the zero point, it changes for all pages or spreads in the document. You can reset the zero point to the upper-left corner of the left-most page by double-clicking the intersection of the rulers in the upper-left corner.

If you move the zero point, all the objects on the page display new X: and Y: values even though they haven't actually moved. Objects above or to the left of the zero point will show negative X: and Y: values, and the X: and Y: values of other objects will not relate to their actual position on the page or spread.

You can lock the zero point, making it more difficult to accidentally change it. Control+click (Mac) or right-click (Windows) the ruler origin and choose Lock Zero Point from the menu that appears. (The Unlock Zero Point command is right there as well, so you can just as easily unlock it.) Locking the zero point is a good idea because it will remind anyone working on your document that you prefer that they not fiddle with the zero point.

Pasteboard

The white area that surrounds the page is called the *pasteboard*. It's a work-space for temporarily storing objects. The pasteboard above and below each page or spread is an inch deep. The pasteboard at both left and right of a page or spread is just as wide as the page. For example, a spread composed of two 8-inch-wide pages has 8 inches of pasteboard to the left and 8 inches of pasteboard to the right, plus 1 inch of pasteboard above and 1 inch below.

You can set your own preferred height and width of the pasteboard. To do so, open the Guides & Pasteboard pane of the Preferences dialog box and choose a new value for the Horizontal Margins and/or Vertical Margins field. (Choose InDesign➪Preferences➪Guides & Pasteboard [⌘+K] or Edit➪Preferences➪Guides & Pasteboard [Ctrl+K] to open the Preferences dialog box.)

Application frame and bar

With the application frame, Mac users can put all the InDesign elements in their own container so that they *don't* float freely and other applica-tions don't peek through. You show the application frame by choosing Window➪Application Frame — doing so makes InDesign for Mac behave like InDesign for Windows. (By default, the application frame is turned *off* in InDesign for Mac.)

Conversely, Windows users can choose Window➪Application Frame to *hide* the application frame so that InDesign for Windows looks like InDesign for Mac. (By default, the application frame is turned *on* in InDesign for Windows.)

The Application Frame menu command is a *toggle,* hiding the application frame if it's visible and showing it if it's hidden. You see a check mark next to the menu option if the application frame is visible. (InDesign uses the same toggling indicator in other menus.)

Above the Control panel is the application bar, which offers easy access to other Adobe applications, such as Bridge, and access to controls over vari-ous view options. It appears by default if the application frame is enabled. When the application frame is hidden, you can show or hide the application bar by choosing Window➪Application Bar.

The application bar has several handy elements. From left to right:

> ✔ The first element is the set of quick-access buttons to Bridge and other Adobe software.
>
> ✔ The second element is the Zoom Level field and pop-up menu.

✔ The third element is the View Options pop-up menu, which lets you hide and show frames boundaries, hidden characters, grids, and other such visual aids from one handy location. These options previously existed but only in a variety of scattered menu options (where they also remain).

✔ The fourth element, the Screen Mode pop-up menu, duplicates the Screen Mode feature at the bottom of the Tools panel (explained later in this chapter).

✔ The fifth element, the Arrange Documents pop-up menu, gives you fast access to InDesign's controls over how document windows are arranged (covered later in this chapter).

✔ The sixth element, the Workspaces pop-up menu, gives you quick access to the workspaces you've defined (as described in the "Working with Panels, Docks, and Workspaces" section, later in this chapter).

✔ The seventh element is the Adobe Community Search menu, which you can use to find help from the Adobe community forums on the Web.

✔ At the far right is the new Access CS Live button, which opens up Adobe's extra-cost subscription services such as multiuser screen sharing and multiuser design review in your browser.

Pages and guides

Pages, which you can see on-screen surrounded by black outlines, reflect the page size you set up in the New Document dialog box (File➪New➪Document [⌘+N or Ctrl+N]). If in your document window it looks like two or more pages are touching, you're looking at a *spread*.

InDesign uses nonprinting guides, lines that show you the position of margins and that help you position objects on the page. *Margins* are the spaces at the outside of the page, whereas *columns* are vertical spaces where text is supposed to go by default. Magenta lines across the top and bottom of each page show the document's top and bottom margins. Violet lines show left and right columns (for single-page documents) or inside and outside columns (for spreads).

You can change the location of margin and column guides by choosing Layout➪Margins and Columns. You can create additional guides — such as to help you visually align objects — by holding down your mouse button on the horizontal or vertical ruler and then dragging a guide into the position you want.

Page controls

If you feel like flipping through pages of the document you're creating, InDesign makes it easy with page-turning buttons and the Page field and pop-up menu. Controls for entering prefixes for the page numbers of sections, and for indicating absolute page numbers in a document that contains multiple sections, are also handy. (An *absolute page number* indicates a page's position in the document, such as +1 for the first page, +2 for the second page, and so on.)

At the bottom left of the document window is a combined Page page-number field and pop-up menu encased by two sets of arrows. These arrows are page-turning buttons that take you to, from left to right, the first page, the preceding page, the next page, and the last page. Just click an arrow to get where you want to go.

You can also jump directly to a specific document page or master page in several ways:

- Highlight the current number in the page number field (by selecting it with your cursor), enter a new page number or master-page name, and press Return or Enter.
- Use the Go to Page dialog box (⌘+J or Ctrl+J), enter a new page number or a master-page name, and press Return or Enter.
- Choose the desired page from the Page pop-up menu.
- You can also use the Pages panel to navigate your document, as Chapter 4 explains.

Opening Multiple Document Windows

If you like to work on more than one project at once, you've come to the right program. InDesign lets you open several documents at once. It also lets you open multiple windows simultaneously for individual documents. A large monitor (or having multiple monitors connected) makes this multiwindow feature even more useful. By opening multiple windows, you can

- **Display two (or more) different pages or spreads at once.** You still have to work on the documents one at a time, but no navigation is required — you have only to click within the appropriate window.
- **Display multiple magnifications of the same page.** For example, you can work on a detail at high magnification in one window and display the entire page — and see the results of your detail work — at actual size in another window.

✔ **Display a master page in one window and a document page based on that master page in another window.** When you change the master page, the change is reflected in the window in which the associated document page is displayed.

Document windows are by default accessed through a set of tabs below the Control panel, though as I explain later, you can also work with them as a series of free-floating windows.

When multiple windows are open, you activate a window by clicking on a window's title tab or anywhere within its window. Also, the names of all open documents are displayed at the bottom of the Window menu. Choosing a document name from the Window menu brings that document to the front. If multiple windows are open for a particular document, each window is displayed (they're displayed in the order in which you created them) in the Window menu.

To show multiple windows on-screen at once, first make them free-floating by choosing Window⇨Float All in Window. Then choose either

✔ Window⇨Arrange⇨Tile

When you choose the Tile command, all open windows are resized and displayed side by side.

✔ Window⇨Arrange⇨Cascade

When you choose the Cascade command, the windows overlap each other so that each title bar is visible.

You can also use one of the window-layout options in the Arrange Documents pop-up menu's options in the application bar. How they display will depend on the option you chose.

To put all these windows back into their regular tabs so that only one document window is visible on-screen at a time, choose Window⇨Arrange⇨ Consolidate All Windows or choose the Consolidate All Windows option (the single-window icon) in the Arrange Documents pop-up menu in the application bar.

To close all windows for the currently displayed document, press Shift+⌘+W or Ctrl+Shift+W. To close all windows for all open documents, press Option+Shift+⌘+W or Ctrl+Alt+Shift+W.

Not only do you get separate document windows for each open document, but you can also create multiple windows for an individual document so that you can see different parts of it at the same time. To open a new window for the active document, choose Window⇨Arrange⇨New Window (or use the New Window option in the new Arrange Documents pop-up menu in the application bar). The new window is displayed in its own tab or free-floating window, depending on whether you've enabled Open Documents as Tabs in the Interface pane of the Preferences dialog box (InDesign⇨Preferences⇨Interface [⌘+K] or Edit⇨Preferences⇨Interface [Ctrl+K]).

You can tell that a document window shows a different view of an existing document by looking at the name of the document in the window's title. At the end of the document name will be a colon (:) followed by a number. Newsletter.indd:1 would be the document's first window, Newsletter.indd:2 would be its second window, and so on.

Tooling around the Tools Panel

You can move the InDesign Tools panel (see Figure 1-2) — the control center for 32 of InDesign's 33 tools, as well as for 13 additional functions — by clicking and dragging it into position. The Tools panel usually appears to the left of a document.

The one tool not directly accessible from the Tools panel is the Marker tool. But you can switch to it from the Eyedropper tool by holding Option or Alt. (Chapter 6 explains its use.)

To discover each tool's "official" name, hover the mouse pointer over a tool for a few seconds, and a tool tip will appear (see Figure 1-2), telling you the name of that tool. If the tool tips don't display, make sure that the Tool Tips pop-up menu is set to Normal or Fast in the Interface pane of the Preferences dialog box (choose InDesign⇨Preferences⇨Interface [⌘+K] or Edit⇨Preferences⇨Interface [Ctrl+K]).

Tools panel includes tools for creating and manipulating the objects that make up your designs. The tools in the Tools panel are similar to those in other Adobe products (such as Photoshop, Illustrator, and Dreamweaver).

You don't need to worry about all the tools, so in the text that follows I highlight just those that you'll need to know to start using InDesign. You'll likely come across the other tools as you work on specific tasks, so I cover those tools in the chapters that introduce those functions.

The small arrow in the lower-right corner of some tools is a pop-out menu indicator. A tool that displays this arrow is hiding one or more similar tools. To access these "hidden" tools, click and hold a tool that has the pop-out menu indicator, as shown in Figure 1-2. You can also Control+click or right-click a tool to see the "hidden" tools. When the pop-out displays, click one of the new tools.

InDesign adds two tools: the Page tool (see Chapter 4) and the Gap tool (see Chapter 10). It drops the Position tool. Also, you can get more detail on any tool and how to use it by going to the new Tool Hints panel (choose Window⇨ Utilities⇨Tool Hints); it shows options for whatever tool you then select.

Rectangular frame tool

Pencil tool

Pen tool

Line tool

Type tool

Gap tool

Page tool

Direct Selection tool

Selection tool

Rectangle tool
Scissors tool
Free Transform tool
Gradient tool
Gradient Feather tool
Note tool
Eyedropper tool
Hand tool
Zoom tool

Swap fill and Stroke

Fill

Stroke

Default Fill and Stroke

Select Container

Select Contents

Apply options

Screen Mode options

Marker tool

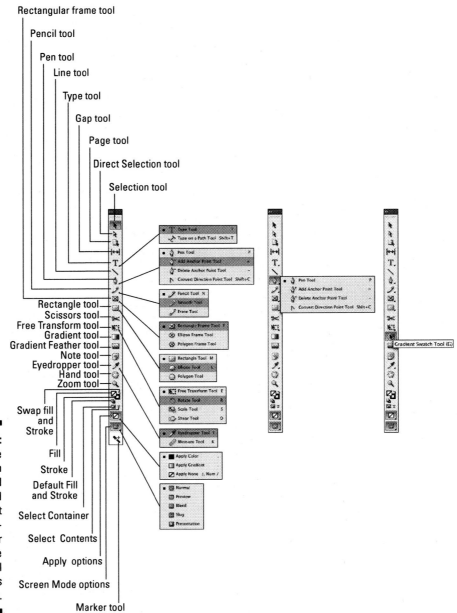

Figure 1-2: The InDesign Tools panel (left) and its pop-out tools (center). Hover the mouse over a tool to see its name (right).

Using the Selection tools

To work with objects, you have to select them. InDesign provides two tools to do that, letting you select different aspects of objects.

Selection tool

The Selection tool is perhaps the most-used tool in InDesign. With the Selection tool, you can select objects on the page and move or resize them. You may want to think of this tool as the Mover tool because it's the only tool that lets you drag objects around on-screen.

After you've selected the Selection tool, here's how it works:

- ✔ **To select any object on a document page,** click it. If you can't seem to select it, the object might be placed by a master page (a preformatted page used to format pages automatically), or the object might be behind another object.

- ✔ **To select an object placed by a master page,** press Shift+⌘ or Ctrl+Shift while you click.

- ✔ **To select an object that is completely behind another object,** ⌘+click it or Ctrl+click it. For graphics frames, you can also click the "doughnut hole" icon — formally called the *content grabber* — that appears over the center of an object when you hover over any portion of it.

The content grabber is new to InDesign CS5. You can turn it off and on by choosing View⇨Extras⇨Show/Hide Content Grabber.

Direct Selection tool

The Direct Selection tool is what you use to work on the contents of a frame, not the frame itself. For example, you can use the Direct Selection tool to select individual handles on objects to reshape them or to move graphics within their frames.

Here's how the Direct Selection tool works:

- ✔ **To select an object to reshape it,** click the object to display anchor points on the edges (the anchor points are hollow handles that you can select individually, as shown in Figure 1-3). You can drag the anchor points to reshape the object.

- ✔ **To select objects placed by a master page,** Shift+⌘+click or Ctrl+Shift+click, as with the Selection tool. The Direct Selection tool lets you easily select objects behind other objects and select items within groups.

- ✔ **To move a graphic within its frame,** click inside the frame and drag the graphic. The new content grabber is also available when using the Direct

Selection tool, making it easier to select and move graphics in frames that are overlapped by others.

✔ **To move a frame but leave the graphic in place,** click an edge of the frame and drag it.

Using the Type tool

A very frequently used tool, the Type tool lets you enter, edit, and format text. The Type tool also lets you create rectangular text frames.

Here's how the Type tool works:

✔ **To create a rectangular text frame,** click and drag; hold the Shift key to create a perfect square.

✔ **To begin typing or editing text,** click in a text frame or in any empty frame and type away.

I explain stories and threaded text frames in Chapter 11.

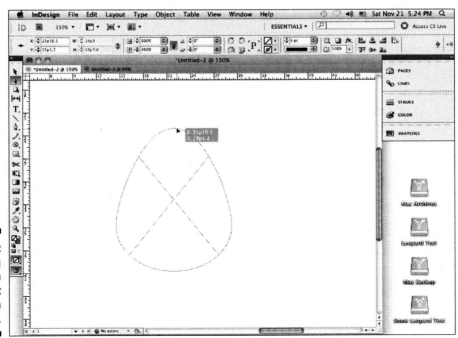

Figure 1-3:
Reshaping
an item with
the Direct
Selection
tool.

Using the object-creation tools

InDesign has a bunch of tools for creating shapes. Part V covers them in more depth, but you should know about a few of them now because they create objects that can contain either text or graphics. Plus, you can also use them to draw your own shapes that you then color or otherwise embellish in your layout. Here's what you need to know:

- ✓ **Pen tool:** With the Pen tool, you can create simple illustrations. You use the Pen tool, which is modeled after the pen tools in Illustrator and Photoshop, to create paths (both open, such as lines, and closed, such as shapes) consisting of straight and curved segments. Give it a try — it's fun! (Chapter 7 explains how to use the tool.)

- ✓ **Type tool:** The Type tool lets you draw rectangular text frames, as well as type text inside them.

- ✓ **Line tool:** The Line tool lets you draw freestanding lines (paths) on your page. After selecting this tool, simply click and drag the mouse to draw the line. Holding the Shift key while you click and drag constrains the line angle to 45-degree increments, which is useful for creating straight horizontal and vertical lines.

- ✓ **Frame and shape tools:** InDesign has three frame tools (Rectangle Frame, Ellipse Frame, and Polygon Frame) and three shape tools (Rectangle, Ellipse, and Polygon). The frame and shape tools are redundant because both frames and shapes can hold text or graphics or be empty.

Because the frame and shape tools really do the same thing, you might use the frame tool when creating frames that will have their content added later. Why? Because the frames appear with a big X through them, making them easier to spot when looking for frames to fill. The shape tools create frames without that X, so it's easier to overlook them.

To create a rectangle or ellipse, choose the appropriate tool, click somewhere in the document window, and drag the mouse to another location. The rectangle or ellipse fills the area. But creating a polygon works differently, as Chapter 7 explains.

Using the navigation tools

Several tools, described in the following list, help you navigate your document so that you can move around your pages, move your pages around the screen, and change the degree of magnification to see just part of a page or to see several pages at once.

✔ **Hand tool:** The Hand tool lets you move a page around to view different portions of it or another page entirely. After selecting the Hand tool, click and drag in any direction. You can access the Hand tool temporarily without actually switching tools by pressing Option+spacebar or Alt+spacebar.

For a quick way to pan through your document, make sure that the Hand tool is active. Then click and hold the mouse. InDesign will zoom out and display a red rectangle. If you move the mouse, InDesign stops zooming and instead lets you move the rectangle to a new area of focus. Let go to have InDesign display that part of the document back at the original zoom setting. If the autozoom is too fast, you can use the up and down arrow keys instead to manually move through various zoom levels. And if you decide you've navigated some place you didn't mean to, just press Esc — as long as the mouse is still pressed — to start over.

✔ **Zoom tool:** With the Zoom tool, you increase and decrease the document view scale. You can highlight a specific area on a page to change its view, or you can click on-screen to change the view scale within InDesign's preset increments, which is the same as pressing ⌘+= or Ctrl+= to zoom in.

✔ **Screen Mode buttons:** At the very bottom of the Tools panel is the Screen Mode button, which by default shows the Normal mode as active. Its pop-out menu has four additional options: Bleed, Slug, Preview, and Presentation. The Normal screen mode shows rulers, frame edges, document margins, page boundaries, guides, text flow indicators, and all the other visual cues that InDesign displays to help you identify various kinds of objects. The Preview mode shows you just the pages and their content, without these onscreen indicators, so you can see what the reader will ultimately see. The Bleed mode is a variation of the Preview mode that shows any objects that *bleed* (extend) beyond the page boundaries, whereas Slug mode is a variation of the Preview mode that shows the space reserved for information such as crop marks and color separation names used in final output. (The View menu also has a Screen Mode submenu that lets you access these modes.)

The new Presentation mode is also a variation of the Preview mode, except that even the InDesign menus and document window disappear, so all you see is the layout. Furthermore, you can go through the layout as if it were a slideshow, such as to show the layout comps to a client. Click the mouse or press → to advance to the next spread, and Shift+click or right-click the mouse or press ← to go to the previous spread. You can also press Home to go to the first spread and End to go to the final spread. Press Esc to return to your previous screen mode.

If your Tools panel displays in two columns, you get two screen mode buttons at the bottom of the panel: Normal and Preview. In that case, Preview Mode has a pop-out menu that also has the Presentation, Bleed, and Slug options. To toggle between single-column and two-column views of the Tools panel, click the collapse icon (>> or <<, depending on how many columns are displayed) at the top of the panel.

Using contextual menus

InDesign's contextual menu interface element is very useful. By Control+clicking or right-clicking the document, an object, elements listed in a panel (such as a list of files or styles), the rulers, and so on, you can display a menu of options for modifying whatever it is you clicked. InDesign provides a lot of options this way, and using the contextual menus to access InDesign functions is often easier than hunting through the many regular menu options and panels.

Working with Panels, Docks, and Workspaces

InDesign has so many controls and features that its designers have long ago stopped relying on menu commands to access them all. Instead, most of InDesign's features are presented as sort of miniature dialog boxes, called *panels,* that are "windows" of readily accessible options to consider when working in InDesign.

Working with panels

Panels provide an interactive method of working with features, one that lets you access the controls quickly. In many cases, panels offer the only method for performing many tasks. Figure 1-1, earlier in this chapter, shows the panels that appear on-screen by default. Note that you can access all panels — except Quick Apply and Tabs — via the Window menu, whether or not the panel is displayed on-screen at the moment.

Panels typically have three — but sometimes four — controls:

✔ All panels but the Access CS Live, Attributes, Background Tasks, CS News and Resources, Kuler, Pathfinder, Script Label, Story, Tool Hints, and Tools panels have a flyout menu, which provides a pop-up menu of controls relevant to that panel.

✔ Any *active panel* — meaning it's displayed in front of any others in its panel group so that you can actually modify its settings — has a close control to remove the panel from the panel group. This control isn't a way to switch to another panel in that panel group — to do that, just click the tab of the panel you want to work with. (If you remove a panel by mistake, go to the Window menu to open it again.)

✔ Any active panel has a collapse control (the >> icon). For panels in the dock, clicking that icon collapses it back into the dock. For panels not in the dock (that is, for *floating panels*), collapsing them shrinks the panel to a much smaller size to get them out of the way. When collapsed, these panels will have a << icon to expand them again. (The Tools panel is an exception: Clicking the >> icon changes it to a two-column layout, while clicking the << icon changes it to a one-column layout.)

✔ *Some* panels have an expand/collapse control, which looks like a caret (^) above a down-facing caret. Click the control to show more or fewer options. (If all options are displayed, clicking the control will shorten the panel and hide some of the advanced options; if only the basic options are displayed, clicking the control lengthens the panel and shows all the options.)

Panels new to InDesign CS5 are

✔ The Access CS Live, CS News and Resources, and CS Review panels (which relate to extra-cost online services from Adobe not covered in this book)

✔ The Animation, Background Tasks, Media, Object States, Preview, and Timing panels, which are part of InDesign CS5's new multimedia capabilities (see Chapter 24)

✔ The Mini Bridge and Tool Hints panels covered in this chapter

✔ The Track Changes panels (see Chapter 12)

To better suit your working style, you can drag panels by their tabs to move them from one panel group to another, drag them out of a dock so that they're free-floating, or drag them into a dock so that they're no longer free-floating. The dock feature lets you keep panel groups in one contained area, which helps keep the interface from getting too cluttered. But you're not forced to work this way: You can still drag panels outside the main dock so that they're free-floating on-screen.

Not all panels display in the main dock; less-used panels, such as Data Merge, show up in a free-floating panel group when you open them via the Window menu. Of course, you can always add such panels to the main dock if you use them a lot.

All but three panels have a tab, which contains its name, to help you select the desired panel without having to go to the Window menu. The three special panels (without tabs) are the Tools, Control, and Quick Apply panels. Unlike the rest of InDesign's panels, they can't be grouped with other panels, so you don't need a tab to select them. Also, note that the Quick Apply panel is the only one not available via the Window menu; instead, use the lightning-bolt icon to open it from the Control panel and several other panels; you can also choose Edit⬡Quick Apply (⌘+Return or Ctrl+Enter).

To quickly select a panel, just click its tab from its open panel group. When a panel is active, its controls have the following characteristics:

- ✔ **To display and select an option,** click a pop-up menu or an iconic button; the changes take effect immediately.

- ✔ **To place a new value in a field,** highlight the value that's already in the field and enter the new value. Note that fields accept values in all supported measurement systems, as described in the "Specifying measurement values" section, earlier in this chapter. To implement the new value, press Shift+Return or Shift+Enter. To get out of a field you've modified, leaving the object unchanged, press Esc.

- ✔ **To increase or decrease the value in the field,** use the clickable up and down arrows where available.

- ✔ **To use math to perform changes,** enter calculations in the field. You can add, subtract, multiply, and divide values in fields by using the following operators: +, −, * (multiply), and / (divide). For example, to reduce the width of a frame by half, type **/2** after the current value in the Width field. Or, to increase the length of a line by 6 points, you can type **+6** next to the current value in the Length field. You can also use percentages in fields, such as 50%, which adjusts the current value by that percentage.

As with the tools, if you make sure that Tool Tips is set to Normal or Fast in the Interface pane of the Preferences dialog box (choose InDesign⬡ Preferences⬡Interface [⌘+K] or Edit⬡Preferences⬡Interface [Ctrl+K]), you'll get some ideas as to what the panel iconic buttons and fields do.

If panels are getting in your way, you can make them all disappear by pressing Tab — as long as the Type tool is not active and the text cursor is active within a text frame, of course. Press Tab to get your panels back.

Working with docks

Docks have controls to collapse and expand them. Click the double-arrow iconic button at a dock's upper corner to collapse or expand the dock. You can also resize the main dock by dragging its resize handle. Figure 1-4 shows the dock controls and what they look like when expanded and collapsed.

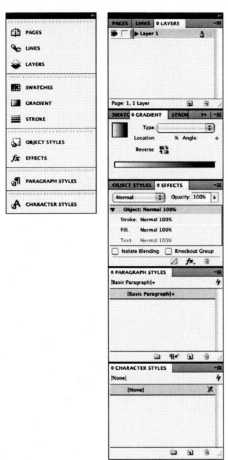

Figure 1-4:
The collapsed dock is the default (left), but you can expand it (right).

Working with workspaces

Although you can rearrange InDesign's panels to suit your needs, rearranging again and again as you switch from one task to another can be a real chore. For example, you may open several of the table- and text-oriented panels when working on text, but then close them and open the graphics- and positioning-oriented panels when refining layout placement.

That's why InDesign lets you create *workspaces,* which are essentially memorized panel collections. Display the panels you want, where you want them, and create a new workspace by choosing Window⇨Workspace⇨New

Workspace. (Note that this menu option has been called Save Workspace in previous versions.) Give the workspace a name that makes sense, such as Text Panels. That workspace is now available via Window➪Workspace➪ *workspace name,* automatically displaying just those saved panels in their saved locations.

Not only can you save workspaces, but you can also tell InDesign to save any menu customizations made along with the currently opened selection panels into that workspace. (Chapter 2 covers menu customization.)

Working with the Mini Bridge

Adobe's Bridge application lets you manage project files across the Adobe Creative Suite, as well as get preview information on files and their attributes (such as color depth for image files).

Bridge is mostly used by Photoshop users, but you might find it useful for perusing project files or searching for files based on metadata attributes such as color model.

The new Mini Bridge panel in InDesign CS5 lets you use Bridge's file navigation and information capabilities without leaving InDesign.

To navigate to files on your computer from Mini Bridge, start by turning on the Panel Bar view; click the Panel View icon (it looks like a page) and select Panel Bar. Now you can navigate your files in Mini Bridge. You can also drag files right into InDesign from Mini Bridge.

Surveying the Menus

Although InDesign relies heavily on its panels to present its rich capabilities, it also uses traditional menus. In some cases, you can use menus instead of panels; in others, you must use a menu command; in still others, you must use a panel (such as for the data merge and object alignment features).

InDesign for Windows has nine menus, while InDesign for Macintosh has ten:

- ✔ **InDesign (Macintosh only):** This menu contains the Preferences menu, where you set much of InDesign's behavioral defaults. You can also configure plug-ins (now called *extensions*) here. Other functions are standard for all Mac programs, including hiding and quitting the program. Note that none of these menu items' functions are available in panels.

- ✔ **File:** This menu is where you open, create, save, close, export, and set up documents and books; where you import text and graphics; where you print documents and prepare them for commercial printing; and where you set basic user information. Note that none of these menu items' functions are available in panels, except for the Preflight feature.

✔ **Edit:** This menu lets you cut, copy, and paste elements; edit, spell-check, and do search-and-replace operations across entire stories and set up story for the InCopy add-on program; adjust and manage color settings; set up and change keyboard shortcuts and menu preferences; apply various styles to selected objects and text; and undo and redo recent actions. In Windows, you also set preferences and quit the program from this menu. Note that these menu items' functions, except for Quick Apply, aren't available in panels.

✔ **Layout:** With this menu, you add, delete, rearrange, and navigate pages; change margins and guides; automatically resize a page and its objects; set up page numbering and sections; and create and format tables of contents. Note that these menu options' functions — except for the Pages, page-navigation, and Numbering & Section Options menus — aren't available in panels.

✔ **Type:** With this menu, you adjust typographic attributes such as size and font, insert special characters, work with footnotes, work with layout notes; add placeholder text; and control the on-screen display of special characters such as spaces. Note that the Find Font, Change Case, Type on a Path, Document Footnote Options, Text Variables, Insert Character, Fill with Placeholder Text, Tabs, and Show Hidden Characters menu items' functions aren't available through panels.

✔ **Object:** You use this menu to change the shape, size, location, and other attributes of objects, such as frames and lines; apply special effects to objects; insert multimedia effects such as buttons; and control how fast the screen redraws when you make changes. Note that the Text Frame Options, Anchored Object, Corner Options, Clipping Path, and Convert Shape menu items' functions aren't available through panels.

✔ **Table:** Use this menu to create, change, and format tables and cells. Note that this menu's functions *are* available through panels.

✔ **View:** This menu lets you control the display of your document, from zoom level to whether guides, rulers, and frame edges appear. Note that none of these menu items' functions, except for Screen Mode and the zoom controls, are available in panels.

✔ **Window:** This menu is where you manage the display of document windows and panels, as well as where you set up and work with workspaces. The window display and workspace functions aren't available via panels.

✔ **Help:** Use this menu to access InDesign's help system and manage product activation and registration. In Windows, this menu also lets you manage plug-ins. Note that none of these menu items' functions are available in panels.

Chapter 2

Making InDesign Work Your Way

*I*t's safe to say that the nice people who created InDesign did their best: They put their heads together and made educated guesses about how most people would like to work and, in doing so, established defaults for various settings in the program. When you're just starting out, simply sticking with the default settings and seeing how they work for you isn't a bad idea. But after you become more familiar with InDesign and start putting it through its paces, you can change default preferences, views, and measurements, making them better suited to your way of working.

Preferences are program settings that dictate how InDesign will act in certain instances. InDesign provides extensive preference settings for everything from how objects appear on-screen to how text is managed for spelling and hyphenation.

Setting InDesign to work your way is easy, and this chapter explains how. I promise not to numb you by covering every single option. Instead, I focus on just those preferences you're likely to change. As for the rest, feel free to explore their effects after you're more comfortable using InDesign.

Setting Document Preferences

Preferences are settings that affect an entire document — such as what measurement system you use on rulers, what color the guides are, and whether substituted fonts are highlighted. To access these settings, open the Preferences dialog box by choosing InDesign➪Preferences➪*desired pane name* (⌘+K) or Edit➪Preferences➪*desired pane name* (Ctrl+K).

When you open the Preferences dialog box using the keyboard shortcut (⌘+K or Ctrl+K), InDesign automatically opens the General pane, as shown in Figure 2-1. To access one of the other 17 preferences panes, just click its name from the list at the left of the dialog box.

InDesign has two methods for changing preferences: You can change preferences when no documents are open to create new settings for all future documents, or you can change preferences for the active document, which affects only that document. Either way, after you've changed the desired preferences settings, just click OK to save those settings.

You can't reverse changes to preferences after the fact by using the Undo command (Edit➪Undo [⌘+Z or Ctrl+Z]). If you change your mind about a preference setting, reopen the Preferences dialog box and change the setting again.

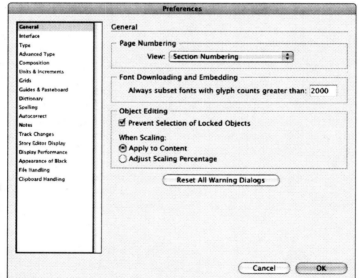

Figure 2-1:
The General pane of the Preferences dialog box.

Type preferences

The Type pane of the Preferences dialog box includes settings that affect character formats, controls whether you use typographer's quotes, and manages how text appears on-screen. You're likely to adjust these settings, so here's a quick review of the main ones:

✔ If Use Typographer's Quotes is checked, InDesign inserts the correct typographer's quotes (often called *curly quotes*) for the current language in use whenever you use quotation marks. For example, for U.S. English, InDesign inserts typographic single quotes (' ') or double quotes (" ") rather than straight quotes. For French, Catalan, Polish, and other languages, InDesign inserts guillemets (« »).

✔ Check Triple Click to Select a Line if you want to be able to select an entire line of text by triple-clicking it.

✔ When the Apply Leading to Entire Paragraph box is checked, changes to *leading* (the space between lines) apply to the entire paragraph, as opposed to the current line. In most cases, you want the leading to be applied to all paragraphs, so checking this box is a good idea.

✔ Adjust Spacing Automatically When Cutting and Pasting Words, which is checked by default, will add or delete spaces around words when you cut and paste.

✔ When Font Preview Size is checked, menus let you preview how your font choice looks before you actually select it. The pop-up menu at the right of the check box lets you select the size of the preview.

✔ The options in the Drag and Drop Text Editing section of the Type pane control whether you can drag and drop text selections within a document. By default, Enable in Story Editor is checked and Enable in Layout View is unchecked, which means that you can drag and drop text in the Story Editor but not when working on a layout. You'll probably want to check them both.

✔ The options in the Smart Text Reflow section of the Type pane tell InDesign how to create new pages if the text you are placing takes more room than the number pages already in your document (see Chapter 11).

The Advanced Type pane includes additional typographic settings. In the Character Settings section of the Advanced Type pane, you control precisely how superscript, subscript, and small-caps characters are placed and sized:

✔ The Size fields let you specify the percentages to which superscript and subscript characters are reduced (or even enlarged). The default is 58.3 percent, but you can enter a value between 1 and 200 percent. I prefer 60 or 65 percent, depending on the type size and font.

✔ The Position fields let you specify how much to shift superscript characters up and subscript characters down. The default is 33.3 percent, but you can enter a value between –500 percent and 500 percent. I prefer 30 percent for subscripts and 35 percent for superscripts. Note that negative values move text in the opposite directions: down for superscripts and up for subscripts. The percentage is relative to the top of a lowercase letter (the *x height*) for superscripts and to the baseline for subscripts.

✔ The Small Cap field lets you specify the scale of Small Caps characters in relation to the actual capital letters in the font. The default is 70 percent, but you can enter a value between 1 percent and 200 percent.

The Clipboard Handling pane includes one text-oriented preference: Use the When Pasting Text and Tables from Other Applications setting to choose how formatting is handled when you paste textual objects from other applications. The default is Text Only, which means that you want copied text to look exactly like the existing text in your InDesign layout. The All Information option retains the original formatting when you paste the text into InDesign.

Composition preferences

Preferences in the Composition pane do two things:

✔ Highlight potential problems on-screen while you're working

✔ Establish the behavior of text wrap in certain situations

Highlighting potential problems

The Highlight check boxes control whether InDesign calls attention to possible typesetting problems by drawing a highlighter pen effect behind the text. All are unchecked by default unless indicated otherwise in the descriptions that follow:

✔ Keep Violations highlights the last line in a text frame when it can't follow the rules specified in the Keep Options dialog box in the Paragraph panel's flyout menu (Type⇨Paragraph [Option+⌘+T or Ctrl+Alt+T]), as explained in Chapter 14. For example, if the Keep Options settings require at least three lines of text in the text frame, but only two lines fit and thus bump all the text in a frame to the next text frame in the chain, the Keep Options rules are violated, and the last line of text is highlighted.

✔ When H&J Violations is checked, InDesign uses three shades of yellow (the darker the shade, the worse the problem) to mark lines that may be too loose or too tight due to the combination of spacing and hyphenation settings. (H&J refers to hyphenation and justification.) Chapter 14 covers this topic, too.

✔ Custom Tracking/Kerning, if checked, highlights custom tracking and kerning (essentially, anywhere you overrode the defaults) in a bluish green. Chapter 15 covers kerning and tracking in more detail.

✔ Substituted Fonts, which is checked by default, uses pink highlights to indicate characters in fonts that aren't available and thus for which

InDesign has substituted a different font. For output purposes, it's important that you have the correct fonts, so you typically want to leave this option checked.

✔ Substituted Glyphs highlights, in pink, any *glyphs* (special characters) that were substituted. This substitution usually occurs when you have multiple versions of the same font, with different special characters in each version. For example, a file that uses the euro (€) currency symbol may have been created in the newest version of a font, but a copy editor working on the same file may have an older version of the font that is missing the euro symbol. If uncorrected, the printed symbol may not be what you expected, even if it looks right on-screen.

Setting text-wrap rules

The three options in the Text Wrap area affect how text flows (wraps) around images and other frames:

✔ Selecting the Justify Text Next to an Object check box overrides any local justification settings to make text wrapping around an object justified. The text will smoothly follow the object's shape, rather than keep any ragged margins that can make the wrap look strange. This option comes into play when you wrap *ragged* (left-aligned or right-aligned) text around objects.

✔ Skip by Leading, if checked, uses the text's leading to determine how much space follows an object around which text wraps. This effect is used only if you choose the Jump Object text-wrap option in the Text Wrap panel (Window➪Text Wrap [Option+⌘+W or Ctrl+Alt+W]).

✔ Text Wrap Only Affects Text Beneath, if checked, causes only text below (behind) an object to wrap around that object.

Chapter 17 covers text wrap in detail.

Measurement preferences

The Units & Increments pane is where you choose the measurement systems for positioning items.

Ruler Units area

The Ruler Units area affects three things: the zero point (by page, by spread, or by the spine), the measurement system displayed on the horizontal and vertical rulers in the document window, and the default values in fields used for positioning objects.

Typographic terminology 101

Publishing tools like InDesign use specialized terms, some of which appear in the Preferences dialog box:

- **Baseline:** This term refers to the invisible line that text sits on in each line. Except for a few characters like *g* and *p* that poke below it, all characters rest on this baseline.

- **Kerning:** This refers to an adjustment of the space between two letters. You kern letters to accommodate their specific shapes. For example, you probably would use tighter kerning in the letter pair *to* than in *oo* because *to* looks better if the *o* fits partly under the cross of the *t.*

- **Leading:** This term, also called line spacing, refers to the space from one baseline to another.

- **Tracking:** Tracking determines the overall space between letters within a word.

The Origin pop-up menu determines the zero point (typically, the upper-left corner of the page) for object positions. If you choose Page, the positions of objects are relative to each page's upper-left corner. If you choose Spread, the positions of objects are relative to the current spread's upper-left corner. If you choose Spine, objects' positions are relative to the binding spine of each spread — the very top and center of where the two pages meet.

With the Vertical and Horizontal pop-up menus, you specify one measurement system for the horizontal ruler and measurements, and the same or different measurement system for the vertical ruler and measurements. For example, you might use points for horizontal measurements and inches for vertical measurements.

With the new Text Size and Stroke pop-up menus, you specify the default measurement to be used for text and strokes (the outlines of frames and text).

To specify the measurement systems you want to use, choose an option from the Horizontal pop-up menu and from the Vertical pop-up menu. You have the following options:

- **Points:** A typesetting measurement equal to ½₂ of an inch (or ½₂ of a pica). To enter values in points, type a **p** before the value or **pt** after the value (for example, **p6** or **6 pt**).

- **Picas:** A typesetting measurement equal to ⅙ of an inch. To enter values in picas, type a **p** after the value (for example, **6p**).

You can combine measurements using both picas and points. Keeping in mind that 1 pica is equal to 12 points, you can enter 1½ picas as either **1.5p** or **1p6**.

✔ **Inches:** An English measurement system that is divided into 16ths. To enter values in inches, type **i**, **in**, **inch**, or **"** after the value. For example, **3i**, **3in**, **3 inch**, and **3"** are all read by InDesign as "3 inches."

✔ **Inches decimal:** Inches divided into 10ths on the ruler rather than 16ths. To enter values in inches decimal, include a decimal point as appropriate and type **i**, **in**, **inch**, or **"** after the value.

✔ **Agates:** Typically used in newspapers, an agate is ¹⁄₁₄ of an inch, usually the depth of a line in the small type of classified ads, stock tables, and sports statistics boxes. To enter values in agates, type **ag** after the value — for example, **10ag**.

✔ **Pixels:** Typically used for Web pages and other on-screen documents, a pixel is the dot on a computer monitor that is the smallest element visible; the thousands of pixels on-screen at their various colors make up the image. To enter values in agates, type **px** after the value — for example, **10px**.

✔ **Millimeters:** A metric measurement that is ¹⁄₁₀ of a centimeter. To enter values in millimeters, type **mm** after the value, such as **14mm**.

✔ **Centimeters:** A metric measurement that is about ⅓ of an inch. To enter values in centimeters, type **cm** after the value, as in **2.3cm**.

✔ **Ciceros:** A European typesetting measurement that is slightly larger than a pica. To enter values in ciceros, type **c** after the value — for example, **2c**.

✔ **Custom:** This option lets you set a custom number of points as your measurement unit, placing a labeled tick mark at every point increment you specify. You get to customize the number of tick marks between the labeled marks by entering a value in the Points field. For example, if you enter **12** in the field, you get a tick mark at each pica because a pica contains 12 points. A good way to use this option is if you need to have the rulers show tick marks at whole-line increments; in that case, if your leading is 8 points, you'd set the Custom field to **8**.

Keyboard Increments area

The Keyboard Increments area lets you customize the way the keyboard arrow keys work. You can use the arrow keys to move selected objects right, left, up, or down. You can also use the arrow keys and other keyboard shortcuts to change some text formatting. The options are

✔ **Cursor Key field:** When you select an object with the Selection tool or the Direct Selection tool, you can move it up, down, left, or right by using the arrow keys on the keyboard. By default, the item moves 1 point with each key press. You can change the increment to a value between 0.001 and 8p4 (1.3888 inches). If you use a document grid, you can change the increment to match the grid lines.

✔ **Size/Leading field:** The value in this field specifies by how many points the leading or font size is increased or decreased when done with keyboard commands. You can enter a value between 0.001 and 100 (the default is 2).

✔ **Baseline Shift field:** To shift the baseline of highlighted text up or down, you can click in the Baseline Shift field on the Character panel and then click the up or down arrow on the keyboard. The default for the Baseline Shift increment value is 2 points, which you can change to any value between 0.001 and 100.

✔ **Kerning field:** To kern text with keyboard commands, you position the cursor between two letters and then press Option+→ or Alt+→ to increase kerning, and press Option+← or Alt+← to decrease kerning. By default, each press changes kerning by $\frac{1}{50}$ of an em — shown on-screen as $\frac{20}{1000}$ em. You can change this value to anything between 1 and 100, in increments of $\frac{1}{1000}$ of an em. (An *em* is a space the width of a capital *M,* a commonly used space in professional typography.)

Document defaults

InDesign lets you change the default page size, margins, and columns in new documents; the default attributes of guides; and the way layouts are adjusted. You don't modify these settings in the Preferences dialog box; instead, to modify document defaults, first make sure that no documents are open and then choose the following:

✔ **File➪Document Setup (Option+⌘+P or Ctrl+Alt+P):** The Document Setup dialog box lets you change the default settings in the New Document dialog box for the Intent, Number of Pages, Start Page #, Page Size, Facing Pages, and Master Text Frame, as well as for bleeds and slugs if you click the More Options button.

✔ **Layout➪Margins and Columns:** The Margins and Columns dialog box lets you change the default settings in the New Document dialog box for the Margins and Columns areas.

✔ **Layout➪Ruler Guides:** This command opens the Ruler Guides dialog box where you adjust the View Threshold and Color for all new guides.

✔ **Layout➪Layout Adjustment:** The Layout Adjustment dialog box lets you resize entire layouts and modify how they are resized.

If you're unhappy with the preferences and defaults you've established, you can revert InDesign to all its default settings. To revert all preferences and defaults, press Control+Option+Shift+⌘ or Ctrl+Alt+Shift when launching InDesign.

Working with stored preferences

Some preferences in InDesign are stored in files that you can share with other users, so the preferences can be consistently used in a workgroup. These preferences include keyboard shortcut sets, color swatch libraries, document setups, workspaces, and scripts.

Some of these stored preferences — such as document setups and printing setups — are called *presets,* and the files that store them reside in the Presets folder within the InDesign application folder. When you save a preset, InDesign automatically updates the presets file. You can then copy that preset file to another user's Presets folder.

To create presets, look for menu items with the word *preset* in them — examples are Adobe PDF Presets, Document Presets, and Print Presets in the File menu; and Transparency Flattener Presets in the Edit menu. Also look for the Save Preset option in some dialog boxes. To use a preset, look for a pop-up menu with the word *preset* in them in dialog boxes; for example, you would use the Document Preset pop-up menu in the New Document dialog box to create a new document using a specific preset's settings.

InDesign has other types of stored preferences whose settings are also stored in separate files, also stored in the Presets folder. But you won't see options labeled *Presets* in the InDesign user interface to work with them. These stored preferences include Keyboard Shortcuts, Menus, and Color Profiles options in the Edit menu and the Workspace option in the Window menu. You can share these settings by copying them to other users' Presets folders.

Another kind of preference is typically stored as part of a document: master pages, text variable, color swatches, and the various types of text, stroke, and object styles available through a series of panels. These preferences can be imported from other documents using the Load command in the various panels' flyout menus and in some dialog boxes. Most presets — such as document presets, print presets, trap presets, and Adobe PDF presets — can also be loaded and saved this same way. In addition, you can save color swatches to files to be shared with other Adobe applications using a Save Swatches command in the Swatches panel's flyout menu.

Modifying Defaults for Text and Objects

When you create a new document, start typing, or create a new object, your work conforms to default settings. You can change these settings. For example, by default, a new document is always letter-sized, but if you design only posters, you can change the default.

You may need to work with InDesign for a while to figure out which settings you prefer. When you identify a problem — for example, you realize that you always end up changing the inset for text frames — jot down a note about it or close all documents right then. When no documents are open, change the setting for all future documents.

Text defaults

When you start typing in a new text frame, the text is formatted with default formats and attributes. You can also choose to show invisible characters such as spaces and tabs by default; otherwise, you need to manually activate character visibility in each text-heavy document. To modify text defaults:

- ✔ **Choose default options for character formats** such as Font Family, Font Size, and Leading from the Character panel. Choose Type➪Character (⌘+T or Ctrl+T).

- ✔ **Choose defaults for paragraph formats,** such as alignment, indents, spacing, and so on, from the Paragraph panel. Choose Type➪Paragraph (Option+⌘+T or Ctrl+Alt+T).

- ✔ **Choose defaults for the [Basic Paragraph] style,** which is what all unstyled imported text, as well as text entered in a new text frame in InDesign, will use. Choose Type➪Paragraph Styles (⌘+F11 or Ctrl+F11).

- ✔ **Activate Optical Margin Alignment.** Choose Type➪Story. This option adjusts the left position of characters along the left margin to make the left edges look more pleasing, by letting the top of a *T*, for example, hang slightly to the left of the margin, even if that means the characters aren't strictly aligned. (Because optical margin alignment works best for display type rather than body type, it's unlikely that you'll activate optical margin alignment as your default setting.)

- ✔ **Show Hidden Characters** is a good thing to activate if you always end up turning on Show Hidden Characters when you're editing a document. Choose Type➪Show Hidden Characters (⌘+Option+I or Ctrl+Alt+I), or choose Hidden Characters from the View Options pop-up menu in the application bar. *Hidden characters* are spaces, tabs, and so on that print "blank" but that you may want to see on-screen to make sure that you have the right character in use. InDesign has a unique on-screen symbol for every kind of space, tab, indent-to-here, and other such "blank" characters.

Object defaults

When you create new objects, they're based on default settings. For example, you can specify how text wraps around objects. To modify object defaults, use the following commands:

- ✔ **Specify the default Columns, Inset Spacing, First Baseline, and Ignore Text Wrap settings** for new text frames using the Text Frame Options dialog box. Choose Object➪Text Frame Options (⌘+B or Ctrl+B).

✔ **Choose defaults for the [Normal Graphics Frame] and [Normal Text Frame] styles,** which are what all new frames created in InDesign will use. Choose Window➪Object Styles (⌘+F7 or Ctrl+F7).

✔ **Specify how text will wrap around all new objects.** Choose Window➪Text Wrap (⌘+Option+W or Ctrl+Alt+W).

✔ **Choose a style for the corners of all new frames except those created with the Type tool.** Choose Object➪Corner Options.

✔ **Specify the default attributes of clipping paths imported into graphics frames.** Choose Object➪Clipping Path➪Options (Option+Shift+⌘+K or Ctrl+Alt+Shift+K).

✔ **Specify other default properties of objects.** For example, if all objects you create are stroked (framed), specify a weight in the Stroke panel. Choose Window➪Stroke (⌘+F10 or Ctrl+F10), Window➪Color➪Swatches (F5), Window➪Color➪Gradient, or Window➪Attributes.

✔ **Specify the default number of sides and the inset for the first new polygon in a new document.** Double-click the Polygon or Polygon Frame tool to open the Polygon Settings dialog box (there is no menu command or keyboard shortcut).

Modifying Defaults for Views

InDesign provides controls for several view attributes, including zoom level, frame boundaries, and grids.

The application bar contains the Zoom Level field, which shows the current zoom percentage. You can type in a new value any time. Immediately to its right is the Zoom Level pop-up menu, which also lets you change the document's view. The view can be between 5 percent and 4,000 percent in 0.01-percent increments.

If you use a MacBook Air, a 2008-or-newer-model MacBook Pro, a 2009-or-newer-model MacBook, or a Mac with a Magic Mouse, you can use gestures on its Multi-Touch trackpad (first introduced in the iPhone) to zoom in or out. For example, use the pinch gesture (two fingers moving closer) to zoom in and the expand gesture (two fingers moving apart) to zoom out, or use the two-finger twist gesture to rotate an object.

Likewise, you can use the pinch, expand, and rotate gestures on a Windows 7 PC that has a touchscreen. To turn off gesture support within InDesign for your Mac or PC, deselect Multi-Touch Gestures in the Interface pane of the Preferences dialog box.

You can also control which layout visual aids display, using options in the View menu.

For example, if you prefer not to view the edges of frames, you can hide them. Similarly, you can hide the visual indicators for the threads indicating which frames flow to and from the selected text frame.

If you want to start with a document-wide grid (see Chapter 10), you can. Settings you can modify in the View menu include

- **Show the links between text frames.** Choose View⇨Extras⇨Show Text Threads (Option+⌘+Y or Ctrl+Alt+Y).

- **Hide the edges of frames.** Choose View⇨Extras⇨Hide Frame Edges (Control+⌘+H or Ctrl+H).

- **Hide the horizontal and vertical ruler.** Choose View⇨Hide Rulers (⌘+R or Ctrl+R).

- **Hide margin, column, and layout guides.** Choose View⇨Grids & Guides⇨Hide Guides (⌘+; [semicolon] or Ctrl+; [semicolon]).

- **Hide smart grids.** Choose View⇨Grids & Guides⇨Smart Guides (⌘+U or Ctrl+U).

- **Show the baseline grid established in the Grids pane of the Preferences dialog box.** Choose View⇨Grids & Guides⇨Show Baseline Grid (Option+⌘+' or Ctrl+Alt+').

- **Show the document-wide grid established in the Grids pane of the Preferences dialog box.** Choose View⇨Grids & Guides⇨Show Document Grid (⌘+' or Ctrl+').

InDesign has another place to set view settings: In the Pages panel's flyout menu, choose View⇨Show/Hide Master Items. When you choose Show Master Items, any objects on the currently displayed document page's master page are displayed. When you choose Hide Master Items, master objects on the currently displayed page are hidden. This command is page-specific, so you can show or hide master objects on a page-by-page basis.

Adding Default Colors and Styles

If you're a creature of habit, you may find yourself creating the same colors, paragraph styles, character styles, table styles, and object styles over and over again. Save yourself some steps by creating these features when no documents are open; when you do so, the features will be available to all future documents.

To set up these often-used items, use the New command in the flyout menus for the following panels: Swatches (F5), Character Styles (Shift+⌘+F11 or Ctrl+Shift+F11), Paragraph Styles (⌘+F11 or Ctrl+F11), Table Styles (no short-cut), Cell Styles (no shortcut), and Object Styles (⌘+F7 or Ctrl+F7). You can also use the flyout menus' Load commands to import colors and styles from existing documents instead of creating them from scratch.

Chapter 6 covers color swatches, Chapter 9 covers object styles, Chapter 13 covers character and paragraph styles, and Chapter 18 covers table and cell styles in more detail.

Part II
Document Essentials

"Are you using that 'clone' tool again?!"

In this part . . .

The reader sees your text and images, but as a layout artist, you know a lot more is going on behind the scenes. Your documents contain all sorts of elements — the publishing equivalent of the girders and beams and so on of a building — that are essential to delivering the final text and graphics. This part covers those document essentials, showing you how to work with the document files, pages, layers, templates, libraries, and sections — the basic organizing elements and containers. You also find out how to create colors that you can use over and over again.

Chapter 3

Opening and Saving Your Work

In This Chapter

▶ Creating a new document

▶ Opening documents

▶ Saving and exporting documents

▶ Exporting document content

▶ Recovering information after a crash

You're eager to create a new document and get started with InDesign. So you launch InDesign, create or open a new document, and begin working. Right? Wrong, sort of. You can just plunge in, but you're best served if you have an idea before you start of what you want to accomplish. That way, you won't be staring at a blank screen with no brilliant ideas in mind.

After you have an idea of what you want to do, you need to create the document that will hold those brilliant ideas. InDesign lets you apply those ideas from the very start of creating the document and also lets you make changes later on, as you refine your ideas.

This chapter shows you the basics of working with document files, from creating and opening them to saving them.

Setting Up a New Publication

After you launch InDesign, you have two options: You can choose File➪Open (⌘+O or Ctrl+O) to open a previously created document or template, or you can choose File➪New➪Document (⌘+N or Ctrl+N) to create a new document.

Creating a new document is where all the fun is because you get to create something yourself, from scratch. Here's how to create a new document:

1. Choose File⇨New⇨Document (⌘+N or Ctrl+N).

The New Document dialog box appears, as shown in Figure 3-1. It's here that you make many up-front decisions about how you want your new document set up — page size, number of pages, number of columns, and margin width. Although you're free to change your mind later, you'll save yourself time and potential headaches by sticking with the basic page parameters you establish in the New Document dialog box.

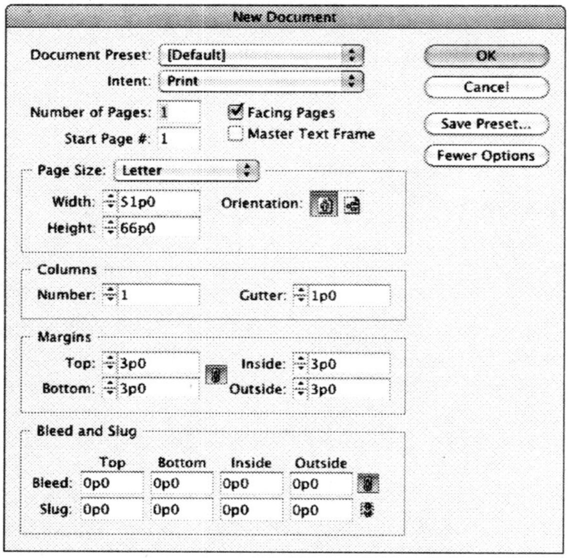

Figure 3-1:
The New Document dialog box establishes the basic framework for your pages.

New Document dialog box:

Document Preset: [Default]
Intent: Print
Number of Pages: 1   ☑ Facing Pages
Start Page #: 1   ☐ Master Text Frame
Page Size: Letter
Width: 51p0   Orientation: ▯ ▭
Height: 66p0

Columns
Number: 1   Gutter: 1p0

Margins
Top: 3p0   Inside: 3p0
Bottom: 3p0   Outside: 3p0

Bleed and Slug

	Top	Bottom	Inside	Outside	
Bleed:	0p0	0p0	0p0	0p0	
Slug:	0p0	0p0	0p0	0p0	

Buttons: OK, Cancel, Save Preset..., Fewer Options

2. If your document is intended to be printed, choose Print from the Intent pop-up menu; otherwise, choose Web.

This option changes the default measurements used for your document: pixels for Web pages, inches or picas, or whatever you set in the Units & Increments pane of the Preferences dialog box, as Chapter 2 explains. This option also changes the default page size (Letter if you choose Print, 800 × 600 if you choose Web). No matter which option you pick, all tools and menu options are available throughout InDesign, and you can print the document or export it for on-screen viewing.

3. If you know exactly how many pages your publication will have, enter the number in the Number of Pages field.

If you don't know for sure, you can easily add or delete pages later. Just guesstimate.

 4. **Decide whether to lay out your documents in a spread or as separate pages.**

 Here are a few pointers:

 - If you're creating a multipage publication that will have a spine, such as a book, catalog, or magazine, select Facing Pages.

 - If you're creating a one-page document, such as a business card, an ad, or a poster, don't select Facing Pages.

 - Some publications, such as flip charts, presentations, and three-ring bound documents, have multiple pages but use only one side of the page. For such documents, don't check Facing Pages, either.

 5. **If you know the starting page number for your document, enter the number in the Start Page # field.**

 Even if you don't know but you do know the document will start on a left-hand page (assuming it's a facing-pages document), enter **2** so the document starts on a left-hand page. (Chapter 4 covers page numbering in more detail.)

 6. **If you want to flow text from page to page in a multipage document, such as a book or a catalog, check Master Text Frame.**

 If you check this box, InDesign automatically adds a text frame to the document's master page and to all document pages based on this master page. Checking this option saves you the work of creating a text frame on each page and manually threading text through each frame. (See Chapter 11 for more information about using master text frames.)

 7. **In the Page Size area, you can choose one of the predefined sizes from the pop-up menu.**

 8. **Specify margin values in the Margins area.**

 If Facing Pages is checked, Inside and Outside fields are available in the Margins area. Designers often specify larger inside margins for multi-page publications to accommodate the fold at the spine. If Facing Pages isn't checked, Left and Right fields replace the Inside and Outside fields. You can also specify margin values by clicking the up/down arrows associated with the fields.

 9. **To specify how many columns your pages have, enter a value in the Columns field.**

 You can also specify the number of columns by clicking the up/down arrows associated with the Column field.

 10. **Specify a gutter distance in the Gutter field.**

 The *gutter* is the space between columns. You can also specify a gutter width value by clicking the up/down arrows associated with the Gutter field.

11. **Click the More Options button to access the Bleed and Slug area of the New Document dialog box.**

    Clicking the More Options button provides options to set bleed and slug areas, as shown earlier in Figure 3-1. (Note that the button then changes to Fewer Options.)

    A *bleed area* is a margin on the outside of the page for objects you want to extend past the edge of the page — you want them to extend at least ⅛ inch so that if the paper shifts during printing, no white space appears where the image should be (touching the edge of the page).

    The *slug area* is an area reserved for printing crop marks, color plate names, and other such printing information — some output devices will cut these off during printing unless a slug area is defined. For both bleed and slug areas, you can set the top, bottom, left, and right margins independently.

12. **Click OK to close the New Document dialog box.**

    Your new, blank document appears in a new document window.

 You can bypass the New Document dialog box by pressing Shift+⌘+N or Ctrl+Shift+N. When you use this method, the most recent settings in the New Document dialog box are used for the new document.

Opening documents

Opening documents with InDesign is pretty much the same as opening documents with any program. Simply choose File➪Open (⌘+O or Ctrl+O), select the document you want to work on, and then click the Open button. But InDesign offers a few options for opening documents that you don't find in every program. For example, you can

✔ **Open more than one document at a time.** Just select multiple documents in the Open a File dialog box.

✔ **Open a copy of a document instead of the original.** This option keeps the original file from being overwritten accidentally — very helpful if you're making several variations of one document.

✔ **Open a template under its own name.** This setting makes editing templates easier than it is with other programs, specifically QuarkXPress.

✔ **Open documents created with Versions 6.0, 6.5, and 7.0 of PageMaker and Versions 3.3, 4.0, and 4.1 of both QuarkXPress and QuarkXPress Passport.** Unfortunately, you can't open files created in later versions of QuarkXPress (or in any version of Microsoft Publisher) unless you buy a separate utility from Markzware. (Go to www.InDesignCentral.com for a link to these utilities.)

To open an InDesign file (any version from 1.0 to CS5), follow these steps:

1. **Choose File⇨Open (⌘+O or Ctrl+O).**

2. **Locate and open the folder that contains the documents you want to open.**

   Select a single filename or hold down the ⌘ or Ctrl key and select multiple filenames.

   On a Mac, the Open a File dialog box displays all files in a supported file format with a filename extension. The dialog box includes a Preview pane that displays a thumbnail version of the selected file or, more commonly, its icon. Use All Documents in the Enable pop-up menu to display files without the expected filename extensions (typically, those transferred or copied from a computer running Mac OS 9).

   In Windows, the Open a File dialog box will display any supported file formats that have a supported filename extension. Use All Formats in the Files of Type pop-up menu to display files with no filename extensions. (Typically, these files are created on an older version of the Mac OS.) The Files of Type pop-up menu offers several options: PageMaker 6.0–7.0 files, QuarkXPress 3.3–4.1 files, InDesign files, InDesign Markup (IDML), InDesign CS3 Interchange (INX), Adobe PDF Creation Settings Files, and All Formats. Choose any of these options to display a specific file format in the file list. (The Adobe PDF Creation Settings Files option is for experts, so don't worry about it for now.)

3. **Select Open Normal at the bottom of the dialog box to open the original version of the document or a copy of a template; click Open Original to open the original version of the document or of a template; click Open Copy if you just want to open a copy of it.**

   In Windows, the options are labeled simply Normal, Original, and Copy and appear under the Open As label.

   When you open a copy of a document, it's assigned a default name (Untitled-1, Untitled-2, and so on).

   Chapter 5 covers templates.

4. **Click Open to close the dialog box and open the selected files.**

   Each document you opened appears in a separate document window. The page and view magnification used when the document was last saved is also used when you open the document. (Chapter 2 covers document views.)

Opening foreign formats

One of InDesign's hallmarks is its capability to open documents from other programs and convert them into InDesign documents. You can open documents created in PageMaker 6.0, 6.5, and 7.0 as well as QuarkXPress and QuarkXPress Passport 3.3, 4.0, and 4.1.

But beware: InDesign's capability to open a foreign-format file doesn't mean you get a perfect translation. The other programs' formats and capabilities are so different from InDesign's that you should expect to spend time cleaning up the converted files by hand. In some cases, you may find that the amount of cleanup work is greater than if you simply re-create the document from scratch in InDesign — don't panic. And be happy when your documents convert effortlessly.

The good news is that InDesign will alert you to any import issues of PageMaker and QuarkXPress files with a dialog box that appears after the import is complete.

Saving documents

When you open a new document, it's assigned a default name — Untitled-1, Untitled-2, and so on — and the first page is displayed in the document window. At this point, you're like a painter in front of a blank canvas. You can work on your layout without giving it a name, but you're better off giving it a name by saving it as soon as possible so that you don't lose any changes to a power outage or other system problem.

The second group of commands in InDesign's File menu — Close, Save, Save As, Save a Copy, and Revert — provide options for saving the active (front-most) document. Here's a rundown of what each command does:

- ✔ **Close** (⌘+W, or Ctrl+W or Ctrl+F4) closes the active document. If the document has never been saved or if it has been changed since it was last saved, a dialog box lets you save, close without saving, or cancel and return to the document.

  To close multiple windows at once, use the shortcuts Option+Shift+⌘+W or Ctrl+Alt+Shift+W.

- ✔ **Save** (⌘+S or Ctrl+S) saves changes you've made to the active document since you last saved. (If you choose Save for a document that hasn't yet been saved, the Save As dialog box appears.)

- ✔ **Save As** (Shift+⌘+S or Ctrl+Shift+S) lets you save a copy of the active document using a different name (or with the same name in a different folder). When you choose Save As — and when you choose Save for an unsaved document — the Save As dialog box appears. This dialog box lets you create or choose a folder for the document, as well as name the document.

✔ **Save a Copy** lets you create a copy of the active document in a different (or in the same) folder using a different (or the same) name. When you use the Save a Copy command, the original document remains open and retains its original name. It differs from Save As only in that it keeps the original document open.

✔ **Revert** undoes all changes you've made to a document since you last saved it.

Exporting document content

InDesign's Save commands (Save, Save As, and Save a Copy) let you save documents and templates in InDesign's native file format. But the Export command (File⇨Export [⌘+E or Ctrl+E]) lets you save the stories — and in some cases stories and whole layouts — from InDesign documents in several formats: InDesign Markup (a format that lets InDesign CS4 and some specialty programs open a file created in InDesign CS5), Rich Text Format (RTF), Text Only, InDesign Tagged Text, Encapsulated PostScript (EPS), Portable Document Format (PDF), JPEG, Flash Player animation (SWF), and Flash project (FLA).

InDesign CS5 lets you export print and interactive versions of PDF files:

✔ The new interactive option provides a simpler dialog box that gives you just the controls over interactive features such as buttons (see Chapter 24).

✔ The print option gives you a dialog box that provides many export options, as Chapter 22 explains.

Note that when exporting a file, you need to choose a format from the Format menu (Mac) or Save as Type menu (Windows).

Here are your format options in more detail:

✔ **InDesign Markup (IDML) format:** This file-exchange format can be opened only by InDesign CS5, InDesign CS4, or custom software designed to handle this format.

✔ **Word-processing formats:** If you place the text cursor into a story, you can export its text (select a range of text if you want to export only that selection) into one of two formats: RTF, for import into word processors with only basic formatting retained; and Text Only, for import into word processors that don't support RTF (with Text Only, note that no formatting is retained).

You can save only one text file at a time. If you need to export several stories from the same document, you must do so one at a time.

✔ **InDesign Tagged Text format:** If text is selected via the Type tool, you can save the story in the InDesign Tagged Text format for editing in a word processor and later reimporting into InDesign with all formatting retained.

✔ **Production formats:** If text or a frame is selected via the Type tool or the Direct Selection tool, you can save the document — not just the story — in EPS or print PDF formats for use by prepress tools and service bureaus or for import into other applications as pictures.

✔ **Online formats:** If text or a frame is selected via the Type tool or the Direct Selection tool, you can save the document — not just the story — in XML format for use in online database-oriented, content-management systems. (XML is an advanced feature not covered in this book.) You can save as a specific page, spread, or text selection into JPEG files for use as online graphics.

✔ **Multimedia formats:** You can export your document to interactive PDF and to two Adobe Flash formats: the SWF play-only format and the FLA format that lets you further work on the file in Adobe Flash Professional.

Two separate options are available for the entire document (no matter what tool is active) or for whatever objects are selected. One is File➪Export For➪Dreamweaver, which lets you export InDesign layouts to the structured HTML format for use in Web creation programs such as (but not limited to) Adobe Dreamweaver. The other is File➪Export For➪EPUB, which lets you create a special type of online multimedia document, called an e-book. Chapters 23 and 24 explain the basics for these two types of documents. Note that the Export For➪EPUB option was called Export for Digital Editions in InDesign CS4.

Recovering from Disaster

When you work on InDesign documents, make sure that you follow the first rule of safe computing: Save early and often.

InDesign includes an automatic-recovery feature that protects your documents in the event of a power failure or a system crash. As you work on a document, any changes you make after saving it are stored in a separate, temporary file. Under normal circumstances, each time you choose Save, the information in the temporary file is saved to the document file. The data in the temporary file is important only if you aren't able to save a document before a crash. (A word of warning: Although InDesign's automatic-recovery feature is a nice safety net, you should still be careful to save your work often.)

If you suffer a system crash, follow these steps to recover your most recent changes:

1. **Relaunch InDesign or, if necessary, restart your computer and then launch InDesign.**

2. **If automatic-recovery data is available, InDesign automatically opens the recovered document and displays the word "Recovered" in the document's title bar.**

   This "Recovered" indicator lets you know that the document contains changes that weren't included in the last saved version.

3. **If you want to save the recovered data, choose File⇨Save (⌘+S or Ctrl+S).**

   "Recovered" is removed as part of the filename, and InDesign asks whether you want to overwrite the old file.

   Overwriting the old file is easier than using File⇨Save As (Shift+⌘+S or Ctrl+Shift+S) and entering a name — unless you do want to save a copy of the file in case you want to go back to the old version later. If you want to use the last saved version of the document (and disregard the recovered data), close the file (File⇨Close [⌘+W or Ctrl+W]) without saving and then open the file (File⇨Open [⌘+O or Ctrl+O]).

Sometimes, InDesign can't automatically recover the documents for you. Instead, it gives you the choice of recovering any files open during a crash or power outage, saving the recovery data for later, or deleting the recovery data. You typically want to recover the files immediately.

Chapter 4

Discovering How Pages and Layers Work

*I*t's a rare InDesign user who creates only one-page documents. Even if you spend your time working on business cards, ads, and posters, you probably produce at least a few multipage documents. And if you create newsletters, newspapers, books, catalogs, or any other such multipage publications, you must know how to add pages to your document, move pages around if you change your mind, and delete unneeded pages. InDesign also lets you divide multipage documents into independently numbered sections.

As documents grow in size, getting around can be a real drag — on your time, that is. The longer you spend getting to the page you want, the less time you have to work on it. Fortunately, InDesign provides several navigation aids that make it easy to move around on a page or in a document.

Understanding the Pages Panel

The Pages panel is where you do most of your page actions, so you get to know it better as you use InDesign more.

If you intend to create a multipage document, you want to display the Pages panel (Window⇨Pages [⌘+F12 or Ctrl+F12]), shown in Figure 4-1, because it provides the controls that let you add pages (both document and master), delete and move pages, apply master pages to document pages, and navigate through a document.

For more information about using the Pages panel to work on master pages, see Chapter 5.

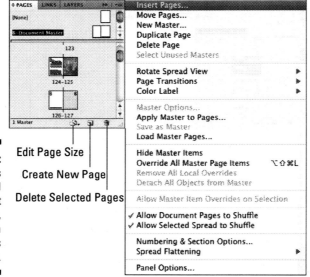

Figure 4-1:
The Pages panel and its flyout menu, showing a facing-pages document.

Edit Page Size

Create New Page

Delete Selected Pages

Keep in mind that the overwhelming majority of multipage documents are facing-pages publications, such as books, catalogs, and magazines. Some exceptions are flip charts and three-hole-punched publications printed on only one side. In this chapter, the figures show examples of a facing-pages document. If you create a single-sided multipage document, the techniques are the same as for facing-pages documents, but the icons in the Pages panel show only single-sided page icons. (The icons aren't dog-eared.)

Adding pages

A document can contain as many as 9,999 pages — more than anyone would ever want to have in one file. In general, try to break up long publications into logical pieces. For example, if you're creating a book, it's a good idea to create separate documents for the front matter, each chapter, the index, and any other parts (appendixes and so on). Also, if you're producing a long document, you want to take advantage of master pages (see Chapter 5), which save you the work of building each page from scratch.

When you create a multipage document, you're free to add however many pages you want. But be careful: Even though InDesign will let you create a seven-page newsletter, in real life, printed facing-page publications always have an even number of pages — usually a multiple of 4 and often a multiple of 16 — because of the way printers arrange multiple pages on a single sheet of paper before folding and cutting them into the final document.

Here's how to add pages to a document:

1. **If it's not displayed, open the Pages panel by choosing Window⊏⊃Pages (⌘+F12 or Ctrl+F12).**

2. **From the Pages panel's flyout menu, choose Insert Pages.**

3. **In the Pages field, type the number of pages you want to add.**

4. **Select an option from the Insert pop-up menu: After Page, Before Page, At Start of Document, or At End of Document.**

   Be careful: If you've already started working on page 1, for example, make sure that you add new pages *after* page 1. Otherwise, it won't be page 1 anymore, and you'll have to move the objects you already created.

5. **Type a page number in the field next to Insert or use the arrows to increase or decrease the value in one-page increments.**

6. **From the Master pop-up menu, select the master page you want to apply to the new pages.**

7. **When you're finished, click OK to close the dialog box.**

InDesign offers a faster way to add and manipulate pages if you don't happen to have the Pages panel already open: Choose Layout⊏⊃Pages and then select the appropriate option, such as Add Pages, from the submenu. The resulting dialog boxes match those accessed from the Pages panel.

If you want to quickly add just one page after the current page, click Layout⊏⊃Pages⊏⊃Add Page (Shift+⌘+P or Ctrl+Shift+P).

You can also add new pages or spreads one at a time at the end of a document by clicking the Create New Page iconic button at the bottom of the Pages panel. (Spreads are added if a spread is selected in the Pages panel.) When you use this method, the master page applied to the last document page is applied to each new page. Pages are added after the currently selected page in the panel.

You can also click and drag a master page icon (or both pages in a facing-pages spread to add a spread) from the top of the Pages panel to add a page using a master page's settings (use the [None] page for a plain page) between any pair of document page spreads or to the right of the last document spread. If a vertical bar appears when you release the mouse button, the spread is placed between the spreads on either side of the bar. If a vertical bar doesn't appear between document page spreads when you release the mouse button, the new spread is placed at the end of the document.

When you insert an uneven number of new pages into a facing-pages document, existing pages are automatically changed from left-hand pages to right-hand pages, and vice versa. You can prevent this change for selected spreads by first selecting them in the Pages panel and then clicking Keep Spread Together in the flyout menu. You may opt for this approach for a spread, such as a two-page table, that you don't want to have broken apart when other pages are added or deleted. Of course, for proper printing, you may need to move that spread when you're done adding or deleting pages so that it follows a complete spread.

Selecting pages

InDesign offers several choices for selecting pages from a document, so you can move, delete, copy, or otherwise manipulate them:

- ✔ Click a page's icon in the Pages panel to select it.
- ✔ To select both pages in a spread, the easiest way is to click a spread's page numbers to select both pages.
- ✔ To select a range of pages, you can click a page icon or spread number beneath it and then Shift+click another page icon or spread number.
- ✔ To select multiple, noncontiguous pages, hold down the ⌘ or Ctrl key and click page icons or spread numbers.

InDesign shows a preview image of your pages in the Pages panel. You can control the display by choosing Panel Options from the panel's flyout menu. In the Panel Options dialog box, select the desired icon size and make sure that Show Thumbnails is checked. You can also set separate view settings for master pages.

Copying pages

You can copy pages from one document to another by clicking and dragging the page icons from the source document's Pages panel to the target document's Pages panel. Any master pages associated with the copied document pages are copied as well.

You can also duplicate the current spread within the current document by clicking Duplicate Spread from the Pages panel's flyout menu or by choosing Layout⇨Pages⇨Duplicate Spread.

Deleting pages

The fastest way to delete selected pages is to click and drag them to the pane's Delete Selected Pages button (the trashcan icon) or simply click the Delete Selected Pages button.

Moving pages within documents

To move a page within a document, drag its icon between two spreads or between the pages of a spread inside the Pages panel. A vertical bar indicates where the selected page will be placed. Release the mouse button when the vertical bar is where you want to move the page. To move a spread, drag the page numbers beneath the icons (rather than the page icons themselves).

InDesign automatically scrolls the Pages panel's pages as you move pages up or down.

Alternatively, you can select the pages you want to move in the Pages panel and then choose Move Pages from the Pages panel's flyout menu. (If you don't want to work through the Pages panel, you can also choose Layout⇨Pages⇨Move Pages.) In that dialog box, you can specify where to move the pages: after a specific page, before a specific page, at the beginning of the document, or at the end of the document.

Although you can move pages around in a document, do so only with great care — if at all. Generally, if you want to move the objects on one page to another page, it's safer to cut (Edit⇨Cut [⌘+X or Ctrl+X]) or copy (Edit⇨Copy [⌘+C or Ctrl+C]) the objects than to move the page, which can cause subsequent pages to shuffle.

What's the big deal about shuffling? Shuffling will move pages around to make space for the moved page, which can move what had been left-hand pages to the right-hand side of the spread and vice versa. If you have different alignments on left and right pages — such as having page numbers on the outside of pages — this shuffling can wreak havoc with that alignment.

If you absolutely must move a single page, it's safer to move its spread. (Of course, if you're working on a single-sided facing-page document, shuffling isn't an issue.)

Moving pages among documents

You can also copy or move pages to other documents. Select the page in the Pages panel and then drag its icon to the document you want to copy or move it to. (You'll need to have that other document window accessible by having it displayed in a tiled view, as described in Chapter 1.) The Insert Pages dialog box then appears, giving you a choice of where to insert the page in the new document as well as whether to copy or move the page into the new document. To move a page rather than copy it, be sure to check the Delete Pages After Inserting option.

Alternatively, you can copy or move pages among documents by choosing Layout⇨Pages⇨Move Pages or by choosing Move Pages from Pages panel's flyout menu, either of which opens the Move Pages dialog box. Here, you also can select the destination (at which page number to insert the new pages) and which document you want to move the page into via the Move To pop-up menu. (The document must be open to display in that pop-up menu.) To move a page rather than copy it, be sure to check the Delete Pages After Moving option.

Figure 4-2 shows both the Insert Pages and Move Pages dialog boxes.

Figure 4-2:
The Insert Pages dialog box (top) and the Move Pages dialog box (bottom).

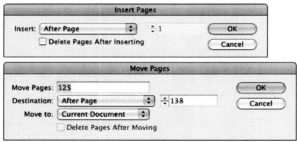

Applying custom page sizes

You can change the size of individual pages in InDesign. Follow these steps:

1. **In the Pages panel, select the pages or master pages whose size you want to change.**

   You can ⌘+click or Ctrl+click additional pages to have them all selected.

2. **Click the Edit Page Size iconic button at the bottom of the Pages panel, and choose the desired page size from the menu that appears.**

   If you choose Custom Page Size, the Custom Page Size dialog box appears; in it, you specify the page width and height, as well as orientation and click OK to apply it. (Note that the Pages panel won't show the relative height of pages, just the relative width.)

3. **If you want to save this page size for future use, enter a name for it in the Name field before you click OK, then click Add to save it; then click OK to apply it.**

Keep in mind that having multiple page sizes in your document can cause problems when the document is printed, especially for larger pages, as the output device may crop the larger pages within the confines of the document's default page size. Coordinate use of mixed pages sizes with your service bureau or production staff — they may prefer that odd-size pages be in their own documents, or at least want a heads-up so they can output those pages separately.

Working with Page Numbers

By default, pages are numbered automatically starting at 1 or whatever you set in the Start Page # field of the New Document dialog box, but you can change the page numbering from Arabic numerals to Roman numerals or letters, as well as change the Start page to something other than 1.

To do so, select the first page in the document in the Pages panel and choose Layout⇨Numbering & Sections or choose Numbering & Section Options from the Pages panel's flyout menu. You get the dialog box shown in Figure 4-3. (If the current page isn't the first page in the document and if a section hasn't been applied to this page previously, the dialog box is called New Section. Its options are identical.)

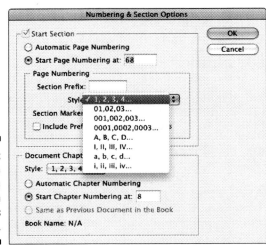

Figure 4-3: The Numbering & Section Options dialog box.

To change the initial page number, select the Start Page Numbering At option and type a new starting page number in its field. To change the page numbering style from the default of Arabic numerals (1, 2, 3, 4 . . .), use the Style pop-up menu and choose from I, II, III, IV . . . ; i, ii, iii, iv . . . ; A, B, C, D . . . ; a, b, c, d . . . ; 01, 02, 03, 04, . . . ; 001, 002, 003, 004, . . . ; and 0001, 0002, 0003, 0004, ...

Working with starting pages

InDesign starts a document on a right-hand page if it starts with an odd-numbered page, and it starts a document on a left-hand page if it starts with an even-numbered page.

If you didn't enter a starting page number in the Start Page # field of the New Document dialog box (see Chapter 3), you can set it in the nearly identical Document Setup dialog box (File⇨Document Setup [Option+⌘+P or Ctrl+Alt+P]). Entering an even number causes InDesign to make the document start on a left-hand page.

Or you can set the starting page number in the Pages panel's Numbering & Section Options dialog box shown in Figure 4-3 (again, entering an even number causes InDesign to make the document start on a left-hand page). Enter the desired page number in the Start Page Numbering At field:

You may not want to assign a starting page number (for example, if the starting page number is unknown because the number of pages that precede this document is unknown and you let the book feature determine the page numbers later). In this case, deselect Start Section in the Numbering & Section Options dialog box.

See Chapter 21 for more information on the book feature and long-document creation.

Dividing a document into sections

Some long documents are divided into parts that are numbered separately. For example, the page numbers of book introductions often use Roman numerals, while standard Arabic numerals are used for the body of the book. If the book has appendixes, you can apply a separate numbering scheme to these pages. In InDesign, such independently numbered parts are referred to as *sections*.

A multipage document can contain as many sections as you want. (A section has to contain at least one page.) If each section of a document uses a different page layout, you probably want to create a different master page for each section. Here's how to create a section:

1. **If it's not displayed, open the Pages panel by choosing Window⇨Pages (⌘+F12 or Ctrl+F12).**

2. **Click the icon of the page where you want to start a section.**

3. **Choose Numbering & Section Options from the panel's flyout menu.**

   If you've selected the document's first page, the Numbering & Section Options dialog box appears (refer to Figure 4-3). Otherwise, the identical New Section dialog box appears. By default, the Start Section option is selected. Leave it selected.

   You can also create a section starting at the current page in your document by choosing Layout⇨Numbering & Section Options.

4. **In the Section Prefix field, type up to eight characters that identify the section in the page-number box at the lower-left corner of the document window.**

   For example, if you type **Sec2**, the first page of the section will be displayed as Sec2:1 in the page-number box. This prefix won't appear as part of the actual page numbers when you print — it's really just a way for you to keep track of sections while you work.

5. **From the Style menu, choose the Roman numeral, Arabic numeral, or alphabetic style you want to use for page numbers.**

6. **For Page Numbering, select the Automatic Page Numbering option if you want the first page of the section to be one number higher than the last page of the preceding section.**

   The new section will use the specified style; the preceding section may use this style or another style.

7. **Select the Start Page Numbering At option and type a number in the accompanying field to specify a different starting number for the section.**

   For example, if a book begins with a section of front matter, you could begin the body section of a book on page 1 by choosing Start At and typing **1** in the field. If you select Continue from Previous Section, the first page of the body section begins one number higher than the numeral on the last page of the front matter.

8. **In the Section Marker field, type a text string that you can later automatically apply to pages in the section.**

   You may want to enter something straightforward like **Section 2** or, if the section is a chapter, the name of the chapter.

   You can insert the section marker name so that it prints in folios, chapter headings, and story text by choosing Type⇨Insert Special Character⇨Markers⇨Section Marker. This technique is a great way to get a chapter name (if you use it as the section marker) in your folio or to have cross-references in text to a section whose name might later change. (A *folio* is the collection of a page number, magazine or chapter name, section name, or issue date, and so on that usually appears at the top or bottom of pages.)

9. **Click OK to close the dialog box.**

When you create a section, it's indicated in the Pages panel by a small black triangle over the icon of the first page in the section. (If you move the mouse pointer over the black triangle, the name of the section appears.) The page-numbering scheme you specify is reflected in the page numbers below the page icons. When you begin a section, it continues until the end of the document or until you begin a new section.

By default, the Pages panel displays section numbers beneath the icons of document pages. If you want to display absolute page numbers — the first page is page 1 and all other pages are numbered sequentially — you can do so by choosing InDesign⇨Preferences⇨General (⌘+K) or Edit⇨Preferences⇨General (Ctrl+K). Then choose Absolute Numbering from the General pane's View pop-up menu.

Removing a section start

If you decide that you want to remove a section start, navigate to the page that begins the section, choose Numbering & Section Options from the Pages panel's flyout menu, or choose Layout⇨Numbering & Section Options, and deselect the Section Start option. That's it! The pages in the former section remain, but their numbering now picks up from the previous pages.

Navigating Documents and Pages

Moving from page to page in a long document and scrolling around a large or magnified page are among the most common tasks you perform in InDesign. The more time you spend navigating to the page or page area you want to work on, the less time you have to do the work you need to do. Like most trips, the less time you spend between destinations, the better.

Navigating with the Pages panel

For navigating through the pages of a document, the Pages panel (Window⇨ Pages [⌘+F12 or Ctrl+F12]) offers the fastest ride.

When the Pages panel appears, you can use it to quickly move from page to page in a multipage document and to switch between displaying master pages and document pages. To display a particular document page, double-click its icon. The selected page is centered in the document window. To display a master spread, double-click its icon in the lower half of the panel. (Note that you can reverse the order of master pages and regular pages in the Pages panel by choosing the Panel Options option in the flyout menu.)

The Fit Page in Window command (View⇨Fit Page in Window [⌘+0 or Ctrl+0]) and Fit Spread in Window command (View⇨Fit Spread in Window [Option+⌘+0 or Ctrl+Alt+0]) let you enlarge or reduce the display magnification to fit the selected page or spread in the document window. Related view options are View⇨Fit Spread in Window (Option+⌘+0 or Ctrl+Alt+0) and View⇨Entire Pasteboard (Option+Shift+⌘+0 or Ctrl+Alt+Shift+0). (Note that the shortcuts use the numeral *0*, not the letter *O.*)

Navigating with the menus and shortcuts

The oldest way to navigate pages in InDesign is via the Page-turning buttons, pop-up menu, and field at the bottom left of the document window, as described in Chapter 1.

InDesign also offers several menu commands and keyboard shortcuts to quickly navigate your layout, as Table 4-1 details.

Table 4-1	Page Navigation Menus and Shortcuts		
Navigation	*Menu Sequence*	*Macintosh Shortcut*	*Windows Shortcut*
Go to first page	Layout⇨First Page	Shift+⌘+Page Up	Ctrl+Shift+PgUp
Go back one page	Layout⇨Previous Page	Shift+Page Up	Shift+PgUp
Go forward one page	Layout⇨Next Page or Layout⇨Go Forward	Shift+Page Down or ⌘+Page Down	Shift+PgDn or Ctrl+keypad PgDn
Go to last page	Layout⇨Last Page	Shift+⌘+Page Down	Ctrl+Shift+PgDn
Go to last page viewed	Layout⇨Go Back	⌘+Page Up	Ctrl+keypad PgUp
Go forward one spread	Layout⇨Next Spread	Option+Page Down	Alt+PgDn
Go back one spread	Layout⇨Previous Spread	Option+Page Up	Alt+PgUp
Go to a specific page	Layout⇨Go to Page	⌘+J	Ctrl+J

Using the navigator

You can use the navigator to move among pages: With the Hand tool selected, click and hold the mouse button to zoom and then move the mouse to move through the document's pages, as shown in Figure 4-4. Release the mouse when you're at the desired location. You'll be put back to the original zoom level. Figure 4-4 shows the navigator in action.

If the autozoom is too fast, you can use the up and down arrow keys instead to manually move through various zoom levels. And if you decide you've navigated some place you didn't mean to, just press Esc — as long as the mouse button is still pressed — to start over.

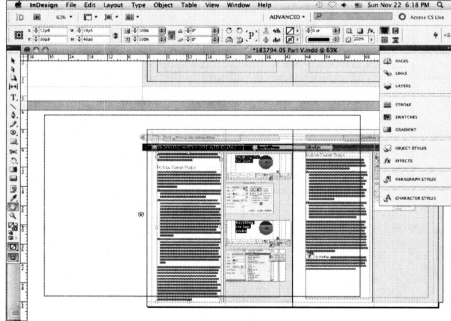

Figure 4-4:
The navigator lets you zoom in and move among pages via the mouse.

Adjusting Page Layouts and Objects

If you've ever created and worked with a document all the way to the finishing touches and then discovered that the page size was wrong from the beginning, you know the meaning of frustration. Manually adjusting the size and placement of all the objects in a document is an ugly chore — one you want to avoid at all costs. However, should the unthinkable happen — you have to modify the size, orientation, or margins of a document that is partially or completely finished — InDesign can automatically resize and reposition objects when you change its basic layout.

For example, maybe you created a magazine for an American audience that subsequently needs to be converted for publication in Europe. Most newsletters in the United States use letter-sized pages ($8\frac{1}{2} \times 11$ inches), while in Europe the standard page size for such publications is A4 (210×297 mm), which is slightly narrower and slightly taller than U.S. letter size. Of course, you have to change *color* to *colour, apartment* to *flat,* and so on, but you also have to both squeeze (horizontally) and stretch (vertically) every item on every page to accommodate the A4 page's dimensions.

Using the Layout Adjustment command

The Layout Adjustment command (Layout⇨Layout Adjustment) gives you the option of turning this chore over to InDesign, which automatically adjusts object shape and position according to the new page size, column guides, and margins.

The Layout Adjustment dialog box lets you turn layout adjustment on or off and specify the rules used to adjust objects when you change page size or orientation, margins, or columns. To adjust a layout, follow these steps:

1. **Choose Layout⇨Layout Adjustment to display the Layout Adjustment dialog box.**

2. **Select the Enable Layout Adjustment option to turn on the feature; deselect it to turn it off.**

3. **In the Snap Zone field, type the distance within which an object edge will automatically snap to a guideline when layout adjustment is performed.**

4. **Select the Allow Graphics and Groups to Resize option if you want InDesign to resize objects when layout adjustment is performed.**

   If you don't select this option, InDesign will move objects but not resize them (the preferred option, so you don't get awkward sizes).

5. **Select the Allow Ruler Guides to Move option if you want InDesign to adjust the position of ruler guides proportionally according to a new page size.**

   Generally, ruler guides are placed relative to the margins and page edges, so you probably want to select this option.

6. **Select the Ignore Ruler Guide Alignments option if you want InDesign to ignore ruler guides when adjusting the position of objects during layout adjustment.**

   If you think that objects might snap to ruler guides that you don't want them to snap to during layout adjustment, select this option. If selected, InDesign will still snap object edges to other margin and column guides.

7. **Select the Ignore Object and Layer Locks option to let InDesign move locked objects (either objects locked directly via Object⇨Lock [⌘+L or Ctrl+L] or objects that reside on a locked layer).**

   Otherwise, locked objects aren't adjusted.

8. **When you're done, click OK to close the dialog box.**

The Layout Adjustment feature works best when you don't have much work for it to do. Otherwise, it usually creates more work than it saves. For example, the switch from a U.S. letter-sized page to an A4-sized page is a relatively minor change, and the layout adjustments will probably be barely noticeable. But if you decide to change a tabloid-sized poster into a business card in midstream, well, you're probably better off starting over.

Here are a few things to keep in mind if you decide to use InDesign's Layout Adjustment feature:

✔ If you change page size, the *margin widths* (the distance between the left and right margins and the page edges) remain the same.

✔ If you change page size, column guides and ruler guides are repositioned proportionally to the new size.

✔ If you change the number of columns, column guides are added or removed accordingly.

✔ If an object edge is aligned with a guideline before layout adjustment, it remains aligned with the guideline after adjustment. If two or more edges of an object are aligned with guidelines, the object is resized so that the edges remain aligned with the guidelines after layout adjustment.

✔ If you change the page size, objects are moved so that they're in the same relative position on the new page.

✔ If you used margin, column, and ruler guides to place objects on pages, layout adjustment will be more effective than if you placed objects or ruler guides randomly on pages.

✔ Check for text reflow when you modify a document's page size, margins, or column guides. Decreasing a document's page size can cause text to overflow a text frame whose dimensions have been reduced.

✔ Check *everything* in your document after the adjustment is complete. Take the time to look over every page of your document. You never know what InDesign has actually done until you see it with your own eyes.

If you decide to enable layout adjustment for a particular publication, you may want to begin by using the Save As command (File⇨Save As [Shift+⌘+S or Ctrl+Shift+S]) to create a copy. That way, if you ever need to revert back to the original version, you can simply open the original document.

Using the Page tool

You can quickly make several adjustments to pages using the Pages tool. When selected, the Control panel changes to offer the tools shown in Figure 4-5. These tools are available elsewhere in InDesign — typically in the Layout menu or the Pages panel — so their availability in the Control panel is really just a convenience.

With the Page tool selected, select one or more pages in your document or in the Pages panel, and then choose an option from the Control panel:

✔ Change the Y coordinate to move the selected pages up or down relative to the others in the spread. You might do this to align a half-height page to the bottom of the adjacent page rather than to the top or middle, for example.

You can also drag a page up or down using the mouse to change its Y coordinate. If multiple pages are selected, dragging the mouse moves only the first selected page.

✔ Change the page size by selecting a different size from the unnamed pop-up menu at center (the current page size is shown).

✔ Change the page orientation by clicking the Landscape or Portrait iconic button (the current orientation's button will be highlighted).

When using these Control panel adjustments, you can also control how the pages' objects are handled as the pages are adjusted:

✔ If selected, the Enable Layout Adjustment option moves and resizes objects to the new page size and/or orientation, as explained in the "Adjusting Page Layouts and Objects" section, earlier in this chapter.

✔ If selected, the Show Master Page Overlay option displays the master page over the adjusted pages so you can see the differences between them.

✔ If selected, the Objects Move with Page option moves the pages' objects if you adjust the page's Y coordinate.

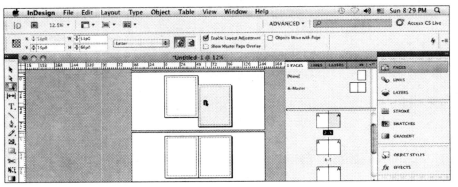

Figure 4-5:
The Control
panel when
the Page
tool is
selected,
and a docu-
ment whose
second
page is
repositioned.

Using Layers

If you've ever seen a series of clear plastic overlays in presentations, under-standing layers is easy. In one of those old overhead presentations, the teacher may choose to start with one overlay containing a graphic, add another overlay with descriptive text, and then add a third overlay con-taining a chart. Each overlay contained distinct content, but you could see through each one to the others to get the entire message. InDesign's layers are somewhat like these overlays, letting you isolate content on slices of a document. You can then show and hide layers, lock objects on layers, rear-range layers, and more.

You can use layers in the following situations (and in many others):

✔ **A project with a high-resolution background image:** For example, a background such as a texture may take a long time to redraw. You can hide that layer while designing other elements, and then show it occa-sionally to see how it works with the rest of the design.

✔ **A document that you produce in several versions:** For example, a pro-duce ad may have different prices for different cities, or a clothing cata-log may feature different coats depending on the climate in each area. You can place the content that changes on separate layers, and then print the layers you need.

✔ **A project that includes objects you don't want to print:** If you want to suppress printout of objects for any reason, the only way you can do it is to place them on a layer and hide the layer. You can have a layer that's used for nothing but adding editorial and design comments, which can be deleted when the document is final. (Even though InDesign sup-ports nonprinting notes, they can be inserted only into text, so having a design-comments layer is still useful to be able to make annotations for frames, images, and other nontextual elements.)

✔ **A publication that is translated into several languages:** Depending on the layout, you can place all the common objects on one layer and then create a different layer for each language's text. Changes to the common objects need to happen only once — unlike creating copies of the original document and flowing the translated text into the copies, which you'd need to do for each language's version.

✔ **To ensure folios and the like are never overprinted:** By placing standard elements, such as folios (the document's page numbers, running headings, and so on), on their own layer, they're uppermost in the layer stack. This order ensures that they're never accidentally obscured by other objects.

✔ **To help text print properly over transparent elements:** Layers are also useful to isolate text above other objects with transparency effects. This isolation avoids text *rasterizing* (conversion to a bitmapped graphic) during output to plate or film — something that can make the text quality look poor.

Layer basics

Each document contains a default layer, Layer 1, which contains all your objects until you create and select a new layer. Objects on the default layer — and any other layer for that matter — follow the standard *stacking order* of InDesign. (What's the stacking order? Well, the first object you create is the backmost, the last one you create is the frontmost, and all the other objects fall somewhere in between. This order is how InDesign knows what to do with overlapping objects.)

Like the clear plastic overlays, the order of the layers also affects the stacking order of the objects. Objects on the bottom layer are behind other objects, and objects on the top layer are in front of other objects. For example, for a business card, the Default layer would contain the business card's standard graphics and the main text. An additional layer would contain a different set of contact information — in separate text frames — for a different person. Each new person would have his information on his own new layer. Each layer has its own color, and frames will display in that color if frame edges are visible. (Choose View⇨Extras⇨Show Frame Edges [Control+⌘+H or Ctrl+H.])

Although people often compare layers to plastic overlays, one big difference exists: Layers aren't specific to individual pages. Each layer encompasses the entire document, which doesn't make much difference when you're working on a one-page ad but makes a significant difference when it comes to a 16-page newsletter. When you create layers and place objects on them, you must consider all the pages in the document.

The Layers panel (choose Window⇨Layers [F7]) is your gateway to creating and manipulating layers (see Figure 4-6).

Layer icon (indicates the layer the object is on)

Pen icon (indicates the active layer)

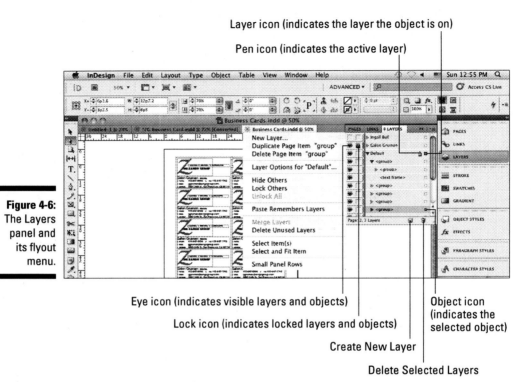

Figure 4-6:
The Layers
panel and
its flyout
menu.

Eye icon (indicates visible layers and objects)

Lock icon (indicates locked layers and objects)

Object icon (indicates the selected object)

Create New Layer

Delete Selected Layers

Working with layers

Each document contains a default layer, Layer 1, that contains all the objects you place on master pages and document pages. You can create as many layers as you need. After you create a new layer, it's activated automatically so that you can begin working on it.

Creating a layer

The Layers panel (choose Window➪Layers [F7]) provides several methods for creating new layers. It doesn't matter which document page is displayed when you create a layer because the layer encompasses all the pages in the document. To create a layer, do one of the following:

✓ **To create a new layer on top of all existing layers,** click the New Layer button on the Layers panel to open the New Layer dialog box. The layer receives the default name of Layer *x*.

✔ **To create a layer above the selected layer,** ⌘+click or Ctrl+click the New Layer button. The layer receives the default name of Layer *x*.

✔ **To create a new layer on top of all existing layers but customize its name and identifying color,** Option+click or Alt+click the New Layer iconic button, or choose New Layer from the Layers panel's flyout menu. Use the New Layer dialog box to specify options for the layer.

Customizing layers

You can customize the name, identifying color, guides, and lock status of objects on a new or existing layer. If you choose to customize the layer when you create it (by Option+clicking or Alt+clicking the New Layer iconic button or by choosing New Layer from the Layers panel's flyout menu), the New Layer dialog box appears. If you choose to customize an existing layer, double-click it to display the Layer Options dialog box. (You can also choose Layer Options for *Layer Name* from the flyout menu on the Layers panel.)

Whether you're using the New Layer dialog box shown in Figure 4-7 or the nearly identical Layer Options dialog box, the options all work the same:

✔ **Name field:** Type a descriptive name for the layer. For example, if you're using layers for multilingual publishing, you might have a United States English layer, a French layer, and a German layer. If you're using layers to hide background objects while you're working, you might have a Background Objects layer.

✔ **Color pop-up menu:** Choose a color from the menu. A layer's color helps you identify which layer an object is on. The color appears to the left of the layer name in the Layers panel and appears on each object on that layer. The color is applied to frame edges, selection handles, bounding boxes, text ports, and text wraps. By default, InDesign applies a different color to each new layer, but you can customize it to something meaning-ful for your document and workflow.

✔ **Show Layer check box:** Selected by default, this control lets you specify whether objects on a layer display on-screen. Hidden layers also don't print. The Show Layer option has the same effect as clicking the eye icon on the Layers panel.

✔ **Lock Layer check box:** Deselected by default, this option lets you con-trol whether objects on a layer can be edited. You can lock a layer that contains boilerplate text or a complex drawing that you don't want altered. Locking and unlocking layers is easy, so you can lock one layer while focusing on another and then unlock it. Select Lock Layer if you don't want to be able to select items and modify them. For example, in a document containing multiple versions of text on different layers, you can lock the layer containing background images and other objects that stay the same. The Lock Layer option has the same effect as clicking the lock icon on the Layers panel. The Layers panel's flyout menu contains additional locking options to, for example, unlock all layers and lock all layers except the active one.

When you lock an object to a page (by choosing Object⇨Lock [⌘+L or Ctrl+L]), the object's position stays locked regardless of its layer's lock status.

✔ **Print Layer check box:** Selected by default, this option lets you control whether the layer prints or exports to PDF. You can use this option for a layer containing design comments, for example. (In previous versions of InDesign, deselecting Show Layer also prevented the layer from printing. That remains true, but now you can control whether unhidden layers print or not as well.) You can also override whether nonprinting layers print in the Print dialog box, as explained in Chapter 22.

✔ **Suppress Text Wrap When Layer Is Hidden check box:** Deselected by default, this option prevents text wrapping around the layer's objects when the layer is hidden. Be sure to select this option when you use multiple layers for variations of the same content, such as multilingual text or different contacts for business cards. Otherwise, your layer's text can't display because it's wrapping around a hidden layer with an object of the same size in the same place.

✔ **Show Guides check box:** This check box lets you control the display of guides that were created while the selected layer was active. When selected, as it is by default, you can create guides while any layer is active and view those guides on any layer. When deselected, you can't create guides. Any guides you create while that layer is active aren't displayed, but you can still see guides that you created while other layers were active. Note that when guides are hidden entirely (choose View⇨Grids & Guides⇨Hide Guides or ⌘+; [semicolon] or Ctrl+; [semicolon]), this command has no apparent effect.

✔ **Lock Guides check box:** This option works similarly to Show Guides in that it affects only the guides that you created while the layer is active. When deselected, as it is by default, you can move guides on any layer for which Lock Guides is deselected. When selected, you can't move guides created while that layer was active. You can, however, move guides on other layers for which Lock Guides is deselected. Note that when all guides are locked (choose View⇨Grids & Guides⇨Lock Guides or Option+⌘+; [semicolon] or press Ctrl+Alt+; [semicolon]), this command has no apparent effect.

You can select multiple layers and customize them all at once. However, because each layer must have a different name, the Name field isn't available in the Layer Options dialog box when multiple layers are selected.

Working with objects on layers

Whether you're designing a magazine template from the ground up or modifying an existing ad, you can isolate specific types of objects on layers. You can create objects on a layer, move objects to a layer, or copy objects to a layer.

The *active layer* is the one on which you're creating objects — whether you're using tools, importing text or graphics, clicking and dragging objects in from a library, or pasting objects from other layers or other documents. A pen icon to the right of a layer's name means it's the active layer. Although more than one layer can be selected at a time, only one can be active. To switch the active layer to another layer, click to the right of the layer name that you want to be active; the pen icon moves, making that the new active layer. Keep in mind that to activate a layer, it must be visible.

InDesign CS5's Layers panel now works like Illustrator's and Photoshop's: You can hide and reveal the objects on each layer, as well as hide and reveal the individual objects within a group on each layer. Thus, you can also lock individual items and rearrange the stacking order of objects within a layer (see Chapter 10).

To see the objects (including groups) in a layer, or the objects within a group, click the reveal control (the right-facing triangle icon to the left of the layer name). It turns into the hide control (the down-pointing triangle icon), which if clicked hides the layer's or group's objects and turns back into the reveal control.

You can change the default names assigned to groups and objects by clicking the name in the Layers panel, waiting for a second, clicking it again, and then entering your preferred name.

Selecting objects on layers

Regardless of the active layer, you can select, move, and modify objects on any visible, unlocked layer. You can even select objects on different layers and manipulate them.

The Layers panel (choose Window➪Layers [F7]) helps you work with selected objects in the following ways:

✔ To determine which layer an object belongs to, match the color on its bounding box to the color that appears to the left of a layer name.

✔ To determine which layers contain active objects, look to the right of the layer names. A small square — the layer icon — to the right of a layer name indicates that you have selected an object on that layer. Another small square — the object icon — to the right of an object name indicates that you have selected that specific object.

✔ To select all the objects on a layer, Option+click or Alt+click the layer's name in the Layers panel. The layer must be active, unlocked, and visible. (Likewise, Option+click or Alt+click an object within a group to select all the objects in that group.)

To select master-page objects as well as document-page objects on a layer, you need to Option+Shift+click or Alt+Shift+click the layer name.

Placing objects on layers

To place objects on a layer, the layer must be active as indicated by the pen icon. Anything you copy, import, or create in InDesign goes on the active layer.

When you create objects on master pages, they're placed on the default layer and are therefore behind other objects on document pages. To create objects on master pages that are in front of other objects, place the objects on a different layer while the master page is displayed.

You can cut and paste objects from one page to another, but have the objects remain on their original layer — without concern about the active layer. To do so, be sure the Paste Remembers Layers check box is selected in the Layers panel's flyout menu before choosing Edit⇨Paste (⌘+V or Ctrl+V).

Moving objects to different layers

When an object is on a layer, it isn't stuck there. You can copy and paste objects to selected layers, or you can move them by using the Layers panel. When you move an object to a layer, it's placed in front of all other objects on a layer. To select multiple objects, remember to Shift+click them and then move them in one of the following ways:

✔ **Paste objects on a different layer.** First cut or copy objects to the Clipboard. Activate the layer on which you want to put the objects and then use the Paste command (by choosing Edit⇨Paste [⌘+V or Ctrl+V]). This method works well for moving objects that are currently on a variety of layers.

✔ **Move objects to a different layer.** Click and drag the object icon for the selected objects (to the right of a layer's name) to another layer. When you use this method, it doesn't matter which layer is active. However, you can't move objects from several different layers to the same layer using this method. (If you select multiple objects that reside on different layers, dragging the box moves only objects that reside on the first layer on which you selected an object.) Also, you can't move individual objects within a group to another layer; you have to move the group instead.

✔ **Move objects to a hidden or locked layer.** Press ⌘ or Ctrl while you click and drag the selected objects' object icon.

✔ **Copy rather than move objects to a different layer.** Press Option or Alt while you click and drag the selected objects' object icon.

✔ **Copy objects to a hidden or locked layer.** Press Option+⌘ or Ctrl+Alt while you drag the selected objects' object icon.

Manipulating entire layers

In addition to working on objects and their layer positions, you can also select and manipulate entire layers. These changes affect all the objects on the layer — for example, if you hide a layer, all its objects are hidden; if you move a layer up, all its objects appear in front of objects on lower layers. Functions that affect an entire layer include hiding, locking, rearranging, merging, and deleting. You work on entire layers in the Layers panel.

The active layer containing the pen icon is always selected. You can extend the selection to include other layers the same way you multiple-select objects: Shift+click for a continuous selection and ⌘+click or Ctrl+click for a noncontiguous selection.

When working with the Layers panel, InDesign CS5 gives you much richer control when manipulating layers than the groups and objects within them. In the Layers panel, you can simply hide/unhide, lock/unlock, and change the stacking order for objects, as well as move objects to other layers.

Rearranging layers

Each layer has its own front-to-back stacking order, with the first object you create on the layer being its backmost object. You can modify the stacking order of objects on a single layer by using the Arrange commands on the Object menu. (New to InDesign CS5, you can also drag the objects within and among layers in the Layers panel.) Objects are further stacked according to the order in which the layers are listed in the Layers panel. The layer at the top of the list contains the front-most objects, and the layer at the bottom of the list contains the back-most objects.

If you find that all the objects on one layer need to be in front of all the objects on another layer, you can move that layer up or down in the list. In fact, you can move all currently selected layers up or down, even if the selection is noncontiguous. To move layers, click the selection and drag it up or down. When you move layers, remember that layers are document-wide, so you're actually changing the stacking order of objects on all the pages.

Combining layers

When you're just discovering the power of layers, you can create a document that is unnecessarily complex (for example, you may have put each object on a different layer and realized that the document has become too difficult to work with). The good news is that you can also merge all the layers in a document to *flatten* it to a single layer. To flatten all layers, follow these steps:

1. **Select the *target layer* (the layer where you want all the objects to end up) by clicking it.**

2. **Select the *source layers* (the layers that contain the objects you want to move) in addition to the target layer.**

3. **Shift+click or ⌘+click or Ctrl+click to add the source layers to the selection.**

   Make sure that the target layer contains the pen icon and that the target and source layers are all selected.

4. **Choose Merge Layers from the Layers panel's flyout menu.**

   All objects on the source layers are moved to the target layer, and the source layers are deleted.

When you merge layers, the stacking order of objects doesn't change, so the design looks the same, but with one notable exception: If you created objects on a layer while a master page was displayed, those objects go to the back of the stacking order with the regular master-page objects.

Deleting layers

If you carefully isolate portions of a document on different layers and then find that you don't need those portions of the document, you can delete the layer. For example, if you have a United States English and an International English layer and you decide that you can't afford to print the different versions, you can delete the unneeded layer. You can also simplify a document by deleting layers that you don't end up using.

When you delete layers, all the objects on the layer throughout the document are deleted.

Using the Layers panel, you can delete selected layers in the following ways:

- ✔ Click and drag the selection to the Delete Selected Layers iconic button.
- ✔ Click the Delete Selected Layers iconic button. The currently selected layers are deleted.
- ✔ Choose Delete Layer from the Layers panel's flyout menu.

If any of the layers contain objects, a warning reminds you that they'll be deleted. And, of course, the ubiquitous Undo command (choose Edit⇨Undo [⌘+Z or Ctrl+Z]) lets you recover from accidental deletions.

To remove all layers that don't contain objects, choose Delete Unused Layers from the Layers panel's flyout menu.

Chapter 5

The Joys of Reuse

*U*nless you enjoy continually reinventing the wheel, you'll want to take full advantage of the features that InDesign offers to help you work more productively. After you make some important decisions about elements in your document that will repeat, page after page, in the same spot (such as page numbers, graphics, headers and footers, and so on), you want to set up mechanisms that make the process simple.

Fewer activities in life are less rewarding than doing the same job over and over, and publishing is no exception. Fortunately, InDesign includes some valuable features that let you automate repetitive tasks. In this chapter, I focus on three of them: templates, master pages, and libraries.

Building and Using Templates

A *template* is a prebuilt InDesign document that you use as the starting point for creating multiple versions of the same design or publication. For example, if you create a monthly newsletter that uses the same basic layout for each issue, but with different graphics and text, you begin by creating a template that contains all the elements that are the same in every issue — placeholder frames for the graphics and text, guidelines, and so on.

Creating templates

Creating a template is very similar to creating a document. You create character, paragraph, and object styles, master pages, repeating elements (for example, page numbers), and so on. The only thing you don't add to a template is actual content.

Most often, you create a template after building the first iteration of a document. After you have that document set up the way you like, you simply strip out the content (that first issue's stories and graphics in your newsletter example) and save it as a template.

Here are the steps for creating a template:

1. **Choose File⇨Save As (Shift+⌘+S or Ctrl+Shift+S) to display the Save As dialog box.**

2. **Choose a folder and specify a name for the file.**

3. **Choose InDesign CS5 Template in the Format pop-up menu (Mac) or Save As Type pop-up menu (Windows).**

4. **Click Save to close the Save As dialog box and save the template.**

If you're designing a template that will be used by others, you may want to add a layer of instructions. When you're ready to print a document based on the template, simply hide the annotation layer. (See Chapter 4 for more information about working with layers.)

If you didn't know better, you might think that a template is exactly the same as a regular InDesign document. It is, with one major exception: A template is a bit more difficult to override. When you open a template, InDesign actually opens a copy and provides that copy a default name (Untitled-1, Untitled-2, and so on). The first time you choose File⇨Save (⌘+S or Ctrl+S), the Save As dialog box appears, so you can give it a real name.

Modifying templates

As you use a template over time, you may discover that you forgot to include something — perhaps a paragraph style, a repeating element on a particular master page, or an entire master page. To modify a template, you have two options:

✔ Open it as a normal file, make your changes, and then choose File⇨Save As (Shift+⌘+S or Ctrl+Shift+S) to save it again as a template (using the same name to overwrite the original template). To open a file as a normal file, be sure that Open Normal (Mac) or Normal (Windows) — the default option — is selected at the bottom of the Open a File dialog box.

✔ Open it as an original file (see Chapter 3), make your changes, and then choose File⇨Save (⌘+S or Ctrl+S) to save it again as a template. To open a file as an original file, be sure that Open Original (Mac) or Original (Windows) is selected at the bottom of the Open a File dialog box. Forgetting to select this option is easy, so most people end up using the preceding technique to resave the template.

Creating documents from templates

You can easily create a document from a template: Just open a template file and save it with a new name, making sure that InDesign CS5 Document — the default option — is selected in the Format pop-up menu (Mac) or Save As Type pop-up menu (Windows). Work on your document and continue to save changes normally.

Building and Using Master Pages

A *master page* is a preconstructed page layout that you can use to create new pages — it's the starting point for document pages. Typically, master pages contain text and graphic elements, such as page numbers, headers, footers, and so on, which appear on all pages of a publication. Master pages also include guidelines that indicate page edges, column boundaries, and margins, as well as other manually created guidelines to aid page designers in placing objects. By placing items on master pages, you save yourself the repetitive work of placing the same items one by one on each and every document page.

Don't confuse master pages with templates. Think of a master page for use within a document; with master pages, you can apply consistent formatting to document pages when desired, and you can have multiple master pages in a document so that you can easily format different kinds of pages. By contrast, a template is simply a document that, when you save it, you must provide a new name. Templates contain document pages, master pages, color swatches, style sheets — the entire file. You use templates for documents you want to reuse as a whole, such as each month's edition of a newsletter or each new title in a book series.

It may surprise you to know that every InDesign document you create already contains a master page, called A-Master. Whether you use the default master page or create and use additional master pages depends on what kind of document you want to create. If it's a single-page document, such as a flier or an ad, you don't need master pages at all, so you can just ignore them. However, if you want to create a document with multiple pages — a brochure or booklet, for example — master pages save time and help ensure consistent design.

Creating a new master page

When you're ready to create a new master page, here's what you do:

1. **If the Pages panel isn't displayed, choose Windows⇨Pages (⌘+F12 or Ctrl+F12).**

   The Pages panel is covered in more detail in Chapter 4.

2. **From the Pages panel's flyout menu, choose New Master.**

   You can also hold Option+⌘ or Ctrl+Alt and click the Create New Page iconic button at the bottom of the panel. The New Master dialog box appears.

3. **In the Prefix field, specify a one-character prefix to attach to the front of the master page name and display on associated document page icons in the Pages panel.**

   The default will be a capital letter, such as *A*.

4. **In the Name field, give your new master page a name.**

   It's a good idea to use a descriptive name, such as `Title Page`.

5. **To base the new master page (the *child*) on another master page (the *parent*), choose the parent master page from the Based on Master pop-up menu.**

6. **In the Number of Pages field, enter the number of pages you want to include in the master spread.**

   For a document with a single-page design, enter **1**; if the document will have facing pages, enter **2**.

7. **Click OK to save the page and close the dialog box.**

Your new master page appears in the document window. The name of the master page appears in the Page Number field in the bottom-left corner of the document window. To make changes to a master page's attributes, simply click its icon at the top of the Pages panel, choose Master Options from the panel's flyout menu, and then change settings in the Master Options dialog box.

Note that you can move master pages to be at the bottom of the Pages panel — rather than at the top — by choosing Panel Options from the flyout menu and enabling the Pages on Top option.

When you're building a master page, you should think more about the overall structure of the page than about details. Keep the following in mind:

- ✔ **To build a document with facing pages,** create facing-page master spreads. The facing pages are somewhat like mirror images of each other. Typically, the left-hand master page is for even-numbered document pages, and the right-hand master page is for odd-numbered document pages.

- ✔ **To have page numbers automatically appear on document pages,** add a page number character on each page of your master spreads by drawing a text frame with the Type tool where you want the page number to appear and then choosing Type⇨Insert Special Character⇨Markers⇨ Current Page Number (Option+⌘+N or Ctrl+Alt+N). The prefix of the master page (A, B, C, and so on) appears on the master page, but the actual page number is what appears on document pages. Don't forget to format the page number on the master page so that page numbers will look the way you want them to in the document.

- ✔ **Specify master page margins and columns** by first making sure that the page is displayed in the document window and then choosing Layout⇨Margins and Columns. The Margins and Columns dialog box is displayed. The controls in this dialog box let you specify the position of the margins, the number of columns, and the *gutter width* (space between columns).

You can place additional guidelines on a master page — as many custom guidelines as you want (see Chapter 10.)

Basing one master page on another

Some publications benefit from having more than one master page. If you're building a document with several pages that are somewhat similar in design, it's a good idea to start with one master page and then use it as a basis for additional master pages.

For example, if the brochure you're working on uses both two-column and three-column page layouts, you can create the two-column master spread first. (Be sure to include all repeating page elements.) You can then create the three-column master page spread, basing it on the two-column master, and simply specify different column formats. The child master page will be identical to the parent except for the number of columns. If you later change an element on the original master page, the change will apply automatically to the child master page.

When you create a new master page, the New Master dialog box provides the option to base it on an existing master page. To help you keep things straight, when you base a master page on another master page, InDesign displays the prefix of the parent page on the icon of the child page.

If you base a master spread on another master spread, you can still modify the *master objects* (that is, the objects inherited from the parent master) on the child master page. As with regular document pages, you have to Shift+⌘+click or Ctrl+Shift+click the object inherited from a parent master to release it before you can edit it on a child master.

Basing a master spread on a document spread

You may be talented enough to create an effective spread, one that is so handsome that you want to create a master page from it to use on future documents. Simply highlight the spread by clicking the page numbers below the relevant page icons in the Pages panel and choose Save as Master from the Pages panel's flyout menu. The new master is assigned a default name and prefix. To change any of its attributes, click its name in the Pages panel and then choose Master Options from the flyout menu.

Duplicating a master spread

Create a copy of a master spread by selecting its icon and then choosing Duplicate Master Spread from the Pages panel's flyout menu or simply by dragging its icon onto the Create New Page button at the bottom of the panel. Note that if you duplicate a master spread, the duplicate loses any parent/child relationships.

Importing a master page

Sometimes, another document has a master page that you'd like to use in your current layout. InDesign lets you import those master pages: Just choose Load Master Pages from the Pages panel's flyout menu, select the source document in the dialog box that appears, and click Open. InDesign will import all master pages from that document into your current one. (Sorry, there's no way to select specific master pages.)

If any of the imported master pages have the same name as your current document's master pages (such as the default name A-Master), a dialog box will appear giving you the choice of replacing the current master pages with the imported ones that use the same name or of renaming the imported master pages, so you keep what you have and add the imported ones. InDesign does the renaming for you.

Note that InDesign will also alert you if the imported master pages use different dimensions than the current document's pages. It won't adjust the imported pages, so some items may appear off the page if the imported master page has larger dimensions than the current document.

Deleting a master page

To delete a master page, select its name and then choose Delete Master Page from the Pages panel's flyout menu. You can also drag the master icon to the Delete Pages iconic button at the bottom of the Pages panel.

So what happens when you delete a master page on which document pages are based? Don't worry — your document pages are unchanged, though they no longer have a master page. (In the Pages panel, the page icons won't display the letter of a master page in their upper outside corners.)

You can remove a master page from a specific document page without removing the master page from your document (and thus other pages) by applying the [None] master page to the document page using the process described in the next section.

Applying a master page to document pages

After you build a master page, you can apply it to new or existing document pages. (See Chapter 4 for information about adding and removing document pages.) For documents with facing pages, you can apply both pages of a master spread to both pages of the document spread, or you can apply one page of a master spread to one page of the document spread. For example, you can apply a master page with a two-column format to the left-hand page of a document spread and apply a master page with a three-column format to the right-hand page.

To apply a master page to a document page, select the name or icon of the master page in the top part of the Pages panel and then drag it onto the icon of the document page you want to format. When the target document page is highlighted (framed in a black rectangle, as shown in the left side of Figure 5-1), release the mouse button. If both document pages are highlighted, and if you're applying a master page to the document, both sides of the master spread are applied to the document spread.

Figure 5-1 shows these techniques: At upper left, I am applying a single page of a master spread to a document page using the mouse. At upper right, I am applying both pages of a master spread to a document spread using the mouse. At bottom, I'm using the Apply Master dialog box to apply a master page to selected pages.

Figure 5-1:
Top left:
Applying
master
pages to
document
pages.
Top right:
Applying
master
spreads to
document
spreads.
Bottom:
The Apply
Master
dialog box.

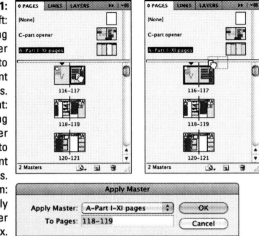

You can also apply a master page to the currently displayed pages by choosing Layout⇨Pages⇨Apply Master to Pages.

Changing master items on document pages

As you work on a document page that's based on a master, you may find that you need to change, move, or delete a master object. Any change you make to a master object on a local page is referred to as a *local override.*

Whenever you remove a master object from a document page, you sever the object's relationship to the master-page object for that document page only. If you subsequently move or modify the object on the master page, it won't affect the deleted object on the document page — it remains deleted on that particular document page.

The Show/Hide Master Items command in the Pages panel's flyout menu lets you show or hide master objects on document pages.

To change a master object on a document page, you must first select it, which can be a bit tricky. To select a master object on a document page, hold down Shift+⌘ or Ctrl+Shift when you click the object with one of the selection tools. (You can also Shift+⌘+drag or Ctrl+Shift+drag to select multiple master objects within the selection marquee.) After you select a master object on a document page, you can modify it just as you would objects that aren't part of a master page.

If you modify one or more master objects on a document page and then decide you want to revert to using the original master objects, you can remove the local overrides. To do so, display the document page that contains the master objects you've modified, select the objects, and then choose Remove Selected Local Overrides from the Pages panel's flyout menu. If no objects are selected, the command name changes to Remove All Local Overrides. If the selected spread doesn't have any modified master objects, the command isn't available.

Sometimes, you don't want people to have the capability to override a master page object. InDesign gives you a way to block such overrides: With the master page open and any objects selected that you don't want to be overridden, deselect Allow Master Item Overrides on Selection in the Pages panel's flyout menu. With this option deselected, someone else won't be able to override the selected master page objects on any document pages using them — unless, of course, the person reselects the Allow Master Item Overrides on Selections option.

Building and Using Libraries

An InDesign *library* is a file — similar in some ways to a document file — where you can store individual objects (graphics, text, and so on), groups and nested objects, ruler guides, and grids (see Chapter 10). After an item is in a library, every time you need a copy, you simply drag it out of the library.

Creating a library

Creating a library is easy. Follow these steps:

1. **Choose File⇨New⇨Library.**

   The New Library dialog box appears, with essentially the same options as the Save As dialog box (see Chapter 3).

2. **Choose a location in which to save the library.**

3. **Give the library a name.**

4. **Click OK.**

You can create as many libraries as you want and store them wherever is most convenient, including on a networked server so that other InDesign users can share them. You can also open libraries created on a Mac from a Windows computer, and vice versa.

Right after you create a new library, you see an empty library panel group. Each library that you create or open will appear as its own panel within that panel group, with its name displayed in its tab, as shown in Figure 5-2. To add items to the library, you simply drag them to the desired panel.

Here is an explanation of some of the controls and commands shown in Figure 5-2:

- ✔ The numbers in the lower-left corner of the panel indicate the number of items currently displayed in the pane and the number of items in the library.

- ✔ The Library Item Information iconic button displays the Item Information dialog box, as does the Library Item flyout menu option. Here, you can give each library item a name, a type (for example, image or text), and a description. Later, you can search for library items based on these attributes.

- ✔ The Show Library Subset iconic button displays a dialog box that lets you locate and display items that meet certain search criteria, as does the Show Subset flyout menu option.

- ✔ The Delete Library Item iconic button lets you delete highlighted items in the library, as does the Delete Item(s) flyout menu option.

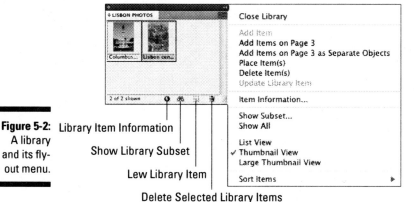

Figure 5-2: A library and its fly-out menu.

Library Item Information

Show Library Subset

Lew Library Item

Delete Selected Library Items

Why you'll love snippets

InDesign has a neat option called *snippets* that lets you take pieces of your document and create a file that other InDesign users can bring into their documents, preserving all formatting and effects applied to them. Snippets in InDesign CS4 and CS5 have the filename extension .idms; snippets in InDesign CS3 have the filename extension .inds — InDesign CS5 can work with both types.

Snippets are sort of like libraries, with a key exception: Each snippet is a separate file, so they're not as easy or as convenient as libraries when you have lots of document pieces that you want to share or make available for reuse. So snippets are best for sharing specific elements on an as-needed basis, whereas libraries are better for having, well, a library of standard, shared elements. For example, a snippet is a great way to give another designer a specific element, such as a masthead or a formatted photo, for use in her own documents — especially by e-mail, because snippets are easily shared as file attachments. By contrast, a library is meant to keep in one place a bunch of objects you intend to use over and over again.

The process of creating snippets is easy: Select the objects and drag them outside your document window onto the Mac or Windows desktop or into a folder. InDesign automatically creates the snippet file containing those objects and their formatting. You can also select the objects you want to make the snippet from and choose File⇨Export (⌘+E or Ctrl+E); choose InDesign Snippet from the Format pop-up menu (Mac) or Save As Type pop-up menu (Windows), select the destination folder, and then click Save.

You can then send that snippet to other users on storage drives, via e-mail, or over the network — like any other file.

To use the snippet in another document, just drag the snippet into your document window. That's it!

Putting items into a library

You can place individual items, such as text and graphics frames, into a library. You can also place multiple selected objects, groups, nested frames, ruler guides, guidelines, and all items on a document page.

To add items to a library:

✔ Select one or more items and then drag them into an open library panel. (Open an existing library by choosing File⇨Open [⌘+O or Ctrl+O].)

✔ Select one or more items and then choose Add Item from the flyout menu of an open Library panel.

✔ Choose Add All Items on Page from the flyout menu of an open Library panel to add all items on the current page or spread as *one library item*.

> Choose Add All Items on Page as Separate Objects to add each object on the page in one step as *separate library items.*
>
> ✔ Select one or more items, and then click the New Library Item iconic button at the bottom of an open Library panel.

If you hold down the Option or Alt key when adding an item to a library, the Item Information dialog box is displayed. This dialog box lets you add searchable attributes to the library item.

If you import a graphic into a document and then place a copy of the graphic into a library, the path to the original graphics file is saved, as are any transformations you've applied to the graphic or its frame (scale, rotation, shear, and so on). If you save text in a library, all formatting, including styles, is retained.

If tool tips are turned on for InDesign and you hover the mouse over a library item, a tool tip appears with its item name. (If you didn't specify a name for the item in the Item Information dialog box, the item name is the filename if the item is a graphic or otherwise is Untitled.) Chapter 1 explains how to turn on tool tips.

Tagging library items

A library can hold as many items as you want. As a library grows, locating a particular item can become increasingly difficult. To make InDesign library items easier to find, tag them with several searchable attributes.

To tag a library element, follow these steps:

1. **Select the library element, and then choose Item Information from the library panel's flyout menu.**

   You can also display the Item Information dialog box by double-clicking a library item or by clicking once on a library item and then clicking the Library Item Information iconic button at the bottom of the library panel. (It's the *i* in a circle.)

2. **Specify a Name, Object Type, and/or Description.**

   In the Description field, use a few words that describe the object so that you can easily find it later.

3. **Click OK to close the dialog box and return to the document.**

Searching for library items

You can search for library items based on the information specified in the Item Information dialog box. For example, if you place several different icons into a library that includes many other items, and if you use the term *icon* in the Name or Description field, a search of these fields that includes "icon" will find and display those items stored in your library.

Follow these steps to search a library:

1. **Choose Show Subset from a library panel's flyout menu or click the Show Library Subset iconic button at the bottom of the panel.**

2. **Decide whether to search the entire library or only the items currently displayed in the page and select the appropriate radio button.**

3. **In the Parameters area, choose the Item Information category you want to search from the first pop-up menu.**

   Your choices are Item Name, Creation Date, Object Type, and Description.

4. **If you chose Item Name or Description as the category, from the next pop-up menu, choose Contains if you intend to search for text contained in the chosen category; choose Doesn't Contain if you want to exclude items that contain the text you specify.**

   The Object Type category's options are Equal and Not Equal, while the Creation Date category's options are Greater Than, Less Than, Equal, and Not Equal.

5. **If you chose Item Name or Description as the category, in the Parameter's area text-entry field type the word or phrase you want to search for (if you selected Contains in Step 4) or exclude (if you selected Doesn't Contain).**

   If you chose Creation Date as the category, enter the date in *mm/dd/yy* format in the text-entry field. If you chose Object Type as the category, choose the type of object in the pop-up menu.

6. **Add more search criteria by clicking the More Choices button; reduce the number of search criteria by clicking Fewer Choices.**

   You can create up to five levels of search criteria. If you select two or more levels of search criteria, you will be able to choose whether to display items that match all search criteria (by selecting Match All) or to display items that match any of the search criteria (by selecting Match Any One).

7. **Click OK to conduct the search and close the dialog box.**

The library items that match the search criteria are displayed in the panel (unless no items matched the search criteria). To display all items after conducting a search, choose Show All from the Library panel's flyout menu.

Deleting items from a library

To delete a library item, drag its icon to the trashcan icon at the bottom of the panel or select the item and then choose Delete Item(s) from the library panel's flyout menu. You can select a range of items by clicking the first one and then Shift+clicking the last one. You can select multiple, noncontiguous items by holding down the ⌘ or Ctrl key and clicking each icon.

Copying library items onto document pages

After an item is in a library, you can place copies of that library item into any document or into another library. To place a copy of a library item onto the currently displayed document page, drag the item's icon from the library panel onto the page. As you drag, the outline of the library item is displayed. Release the mouse button when the outline of the item is positioned where you want it to end up. You can also place a library item onto a document by clicking its icon and then choosing Place Item(s) from the flyout menu.

Copy an item from one library to another by dragging its icon from the source library panel onto the target library panel. To move (rather than copy) an item from one library to another, hold down the Option or Alt key when dragging and dropping an item between libraries.

Managing library panels

You can close an individual library panel by clicking its close box or choosing Close Library from its flyout menu. You can close all libraries at once by clicking the panel group's close box.

You can move panels into their own panel groups by dragging their tab outside their current panel groups. Likewise, you can combine library panels by dragging them by their tabs into another panel group (including those that contain non-library panels).

Chapter 6

Working with Color

In This Chapter

▶ Creating and modifying colors

▶ Setting up tints

▶ Constructing gradients

▶ Managing swatches

▶ Applying colors, tints, and gradients

*Y*ou see the world in glorious color. Yet not all publications take advantage of that fact, typically for budget reasons. But when you do have color available, take advantage of it: It brings a visual dimension that taps into brains, creating a level of raw visual interest unmatched by anything else.

To take advantage of human beings' color hot buttons, InDesign offers the ability to create and apply colors in many creative ways. But even if you can't use color in every document, some of the techniques described here — especially for tints and gradients — can help a staid black-and-white document get new panache through shades of gray.

Working with Colors

InDesign comes with only ten predefined colors: black, registration (black on each negative for the printing press), paper (white), none (transparent), cyan, magenta, yellow, red, green, and blue. You'll likely want to add a few of your own.

If your chose Print as the document intent in the New Document dialog box (see Chapter 3), the colors are set to the CMYK color model and have names based on their CMYK values (so cyan is C=100 M=0 Y=0 K=0, containing 100 percent cyan and 0 percent of the other three process colors, and green is C=75 M=5 Y=100 K=0, containing 75 percent cyan, 5 percent magenta, 100 percent yellow, and 0 percent black). If you chose Web as the document intent, the colors are set to the RGB color model and have the names RGB Cyan, RGB Green, and so forth.

Creating color swatches

Before you can apply any colors — whether to bitmap images or to layout elements, such as strokes, text, frames, and shapes — you must first define the colors in the Swatches panel (Window⇨Color⇨Swatches [F5]). You can also import colors from other Adobe programs and from some color images.

No matter how you define colors, you have a couple of decisions to make first:

✔ Do you want to create your own color by mixing basic colors, such as red, green, and blue (called RGB and typically used for documents like Web pages and PDF files displayed on-screen); or cyan, yellow, magenta, and black (called CMYK, or *process colors,* and typically used for printing presses and by inkjet printers)?

✔ Do you want to use a color from an ink maker like Pantone or Toyo? These colors — called *spot colors* — are typically used as an extra ink on your professionally printed document, but can also be converted to the standard four-process colors and so are handy when you know the color you want when you see it.

How do you tell what kind of color a specific swatch is? Look at the icons to the right of the swatch name. For example, in Figure 6-1, you can see that Pantone DS 2-1 C is a process color (the gray square) defined as CMYK (the square made up of four triangles) and set to 32 percent tint.

All the color-creation tools in InDesign support both process and spot colors, and all have access to the predefined colors like Pantone and Toyo as well as to the free-form color pickers for mixing CMYK or RGB colors. If you plan to print the color on its own plate, you need to use a predefined color so that you know the printer can reproduce it. If you plan to color-separate a color into the four CMYK plates, it doesn't matter whether you use a predefined color or make one of your own. One advantage to using a predefined color is that it's easy to tell other designers what the color is; another is that you'll get very close matches if you start with a predefined color and then end up having it color-separated in some documents and kept as a spot color in others.

All colors in the Swatches panel receive a unique name and are tracked by InDesign. Each color is available to be used on any object in your document, with no risk of having slightly different variants. Plus, you can modify a swatch and ensure that all objects using that swatch are updated. You can also delete a swatch and tell InDesign which color to use in its place. Furthermore, when you print, you have control over how each color is handled (whether it's printed to its own plate, whether it's printed at all, and whether you need to make any adjustments to its ink density or screening angle). Figure 6-1 shows the Swatches panel.

InDesign CS5 adds Stroke and Fill iconic buttons to the Control panel, as well as pop-up menus for each. If you click either pop-up menu, the mini-Swatches panel appears, offering the same capabilities as the regular Swatches panel. Figure 6-1 shows the Control panel's Fill and Stroke controls as well as the mini-Swatches panel.

If no document is open when you create, edit, or delete colors, the new color palette becomes the default for all future documents.

To create your own color, go to the Swatches panel and select New Color Swatch from the flyout menu. The New Color Swatch dialog box, shown in Figure 6-2, appears.

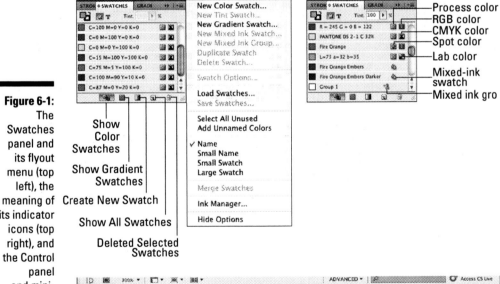

Figure 6-1:
The Swatches panel and its flyout menu (top left), the meaning of its indicator icons (top right), and the Control panel and mini-Swatches panel (bottom).

Show Color Swatches

Show Gradient Swatches

Create New Swatch

Show All Swatches

Deleted Selected Swatches

Process color
RGB color
CMYK color
Spot color
Lab color
Mixed-ink swatch
Mixed ink gro

Figure 6-2:
Two examples of the New Color Swatch dialog box, each using a different color mode.

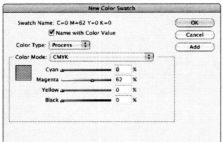

Now follow these steps:

1. **In the Swatch Name field, give your color a name that describes it, such as Lemon Yellow or Blood Red.**

   To do so, uncheck the Name with Color Value option. (If left checked, InDesign names the color for you based on its color values; see an example at the top of the left-hand example in Figure 6-2.) Note that this option is not available for swatch-based colors such as Pantone — you can't change their names (that would confuse the printer as to what ink to use).

2. **In the Color Type pop-up menu, choose from Process or Spot.**

3. **In the Color Mode pop-up menu, choose the mixing system or swatch library (both are considered to be *color models*) you'll use:**

   - **CMYK:** Cyan, magenta, yellow, and black are the colors used in professional printing presses and many color laser printers.

   - **RGB:** Red, green, and blue are the colors used on a computer monitor, for CD-based or Web-based documents, and for some color printers.

   - **Lab:** Luminosity, *A* axis, *B* axis, is a way of defining colors created by the international standards group Commission Internationale de l'Éclairage (the CIE, which translates to *International Commission on Illumination* in English).

   - **A swatch-based model:** Sets of premixed colors from various vendors, including ANPA, DIC, Focoltone, HKS, Pantone, Toyo Ink, and Trumatch, for print documents, as well as a Web-specific set and sets specific to Windows and Mac OS X for on-screen documents.

   - **Other Library:** InDesign also has the Other Library option from which you can select any color, tint, or gradient swatch library file in the old Adobe Illustrator 8 format. (You can't use Illustrator's patterned swatches, but don't worry if the swatch file contains them: InDesign will simply ignore them.)

4. **For the CMYK, RGB, and Lab models, use the sliders to create your new color; for the swatch-based models, scroll through the lists of colors and select one.**

   A preview appears in the box on the left.

5. **If you want to create multiple colors, click Add after each color definition and then click Done when you're finished; to create just one color, click OK instead of Add.**

   You can also click Cancel to abort the current color definition.

The most popular swatch libraries used by North American professional publishers are those from Pantone, whose Pantone Matching System (PMS) is the de facto standard for most publishers in specifying spot-color inks. The Pantone swatch libraries come in several variations, of which InDesign includes 13. Most of the time, you'll use one of the following four:

✔ **Pantone Process Coated:** Use this library when you color-separate Pantone colors and your printer uses the standard Pantone-brand process-color inks. (These colors reproduce reliably when color-separated, while the other Pantone swatch libraries' colors often don't.)

✔ **Pantone Solid Coated:** Use this library when your printer will use actual Pantone inks (as spot colors) when printing to coated paper stock.

✔ **Pantone Solid Matte:** Use this library when your printer will use actual Pantone inks (as spot colors) when printing to matte-finished paper stock.

✔ **Pantone Solid Uncoated:** Use this library when your printer will use actual Pantone inks (as spot colors) when printing to uncoated paper stock.

Color swatches based on the CMYK colors — such as Focoltone, Pantone Process, and Trumatch — will accurately color-separate and thus print accurately on a printing press because a printing press uses the CMYK colors. Other swatches' colors often don't color-separate accurately because they're supposed to represent special inks that may have added elements like metals and clays designed to give metallic or pastel appearances that simply can't be replicated by combining cyan, magenta, yellow, and black. Similarly, some colors (like several hues of orange and green) can't be accurately created using the CMYK colors.

The bad way to create colors

Many people try to use the Color panel (Window⇨Color⇨Color [F6]) to define colors, which can be a mistake. At first, you may not realize that you can create colors from the Color panel. It shows a gradation of the last color used and lets you change the tint for that color on the current object. But if you go to its flyout menu and choose a color model (RGB, CMYK, or Lab), you get a set of mixing controls.

So what's the problem? Colors created through the Color panel won't appear in your Swatches panel, so they can't be used for other objects. They're called *unnamed colors* because they don't appear in the Swatches panel, but may be used by objects in a document, which can cause problems when you print. (Adobe added them to InDesign to be consistent with how Illustrator defines colors — a foolish consistency.)

Fortunately, you can prevent unnamed colors: If you go to the Color panel and modify a color

without thinking about it, choose Add Unnamed Colors from the Swatches panel's flyout menu to add all unnamed colors to the Swatches panel. Of course, if you forget to do so, you have an unnamed color, so it's best to think *Swatches panel* when you think about adding or editing colors instead of the more obvious *Color panel.* Even better, close the Color panel so that you're not tempted to use it in the first place.

Similarly, don't use this InDesign feature: the capability to create unnamed colors by double-clicking the Stroke and Fill iconic buttons on the Tools panel, using a Photoshop-style color picker. If you use this feature, you can rectify the unnamed-color sin by adding any colors created this way to the Swatches panel by using the Swatches panel's Add Unnamed Colors menu item. Otherwise, you run the same risk as creating colors through the Color panel.

Using Kuler colors

There's a Web site out there that lets users share palettes of colors they've created. The idea is to give people with little fashion sense sets of colors that work well together. InDesign lets you tap into these colors and add them to your Swatches panel, using the Kuler panel (Window⇨Extensions⇨Kuler).

You go to the Browse pane in the Kuler panel and choose from the color swatch palettes — called *themes* — already there. You can use the unlabeled pop-up menus at the top and the search field to narrow down your choices. Click one you want and then click the Add Selected Theme to Swatches iconic button at the bottom right of the panel. Repeat for each theme you want to copy.

You can create your own themes in the Create pane (as well as edit an existing theme; click the Create Theme in Create Pane iconic button in the Browse pane to do so). The options are mostly for expert users, but the principles aren't too hard: For each of the five color swatches, use the color wheel to select new values or drag its current color (the circles) to a new location on the wheel. Click the Add Selected Theme to Swatches iconic button at the bottom right of the panel. You can also save the themes and upload them to the Kuler site for other users to enjoy.

Figure 6-3 shows both the Browse and Create panes of the Kuler panel.

Remove This Color from the Theme

Brightness slider

Add a New Color to This Theme

Affect the Other Colors in the Theme Based on a Harmony

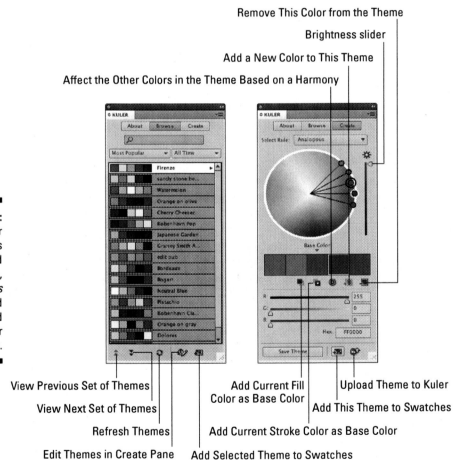

Figure 6-3:
The Kuler panel opens predefined color sets, or *themes* (left), and creates and shares your own (right).

View Previous Set of Themes

View Next Set of Themes

Refresh Themes

Edit Themes in Create Pane

Add Current Fill Color as Base Color

Add Current Stroke Color as Base Color

Add Selected Theme to Swatches

Upload Theme to Kuler

Add This Theme to Swatches

Creating mixed colors

InDesign offers another type of color: mixed-ink color. Essentially, a mixed-ink color combines a spot color with the default process colors (cyan, magenta, yellow, and black) to create new color swatches. For example, you can combine 100 percent Pantone Yellow with 10 percent Deep Brown to get a darker version of yellow (called a *duotone,* though InDesign doesn't limit you to mixing spot colors with just black, as traditional duotones do).

To create a mixed-ink swatch, add a spot color swatch if none exists and then follow these steps:

1. **Choose New Mixed Ink Swatch from the Swatches panel's flyout menu.**

   The New Mixed Ink Swatch dialog box appears, as shown in Figure 6-4.

2. **Select the percentages of the spot color and any or all of the default process colors you want to mix and give the new color a name.**

3. **Click Add to add another mixed-ink swatch based on the current spot color.**

   If you're creating just one color, click OK instead of Add. You can click Cancel to abort the current mixed-ink color definition.

4. **Click OK when you're finished.**

Figure 6-4:
The New Mixed Ink Swatch dialog box lets you mix a selected spot color with any or all of the default process colors to create new shades and variations.

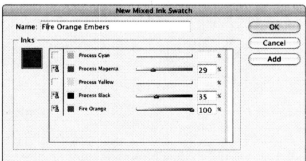

New Mixed Ink Group, a related option in the Swatches panel's flyout menu, lets you create a set of colors from the same mix. You get to set the initial percentage of each color you want in the mix and the final value, as well as how many increments of each color you want. InDesign then takes all this information and creates a bunch of color swatches that combine each of the colors at each level so that you get a whole range of colors. The idea is to get a set of related colors created for you, such as a set of blue-green hues that range from light aqua to dark marine. Experiment with this expert feature to see what it can do for you.

Defining Tints

A _tint_ is simply a shade of a color. InDesign lets you create such tints as separate color swatches — like any other color — so they're easy to use for multiple items. The process is easy. Follow these steps:

1. **In the Swatches panel, select a color from which you want to create a tint.**

2. **Using the Swatches panel's flyout menu, select New Tint Swatch.**

   The New Tint Swatch dialog box, shown in Figure 6-5, appears.

3. **Click and drag the slider to adjust the tint or type a value in a field on the right.**

4. **Click Add to create another tint from the same base color, and then click OK when you're finished.**

   If you're adding a single tint, you don't need to click Add; just click OK when done.

Figure 6-5:
The New Tint Swatch dialog box lets you define colors; a nearly identical dialog box named Swatch Options lets you edit them.

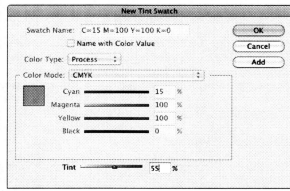

Click Cancel if you change your mind about the current tint. Any new tint will have the same name as the original color and the percentage of shading, such as Sky Blue 66%.

You can create a tint from a tint, which can be confusing. Fortunately, InDesign goes back to the original color when letting you create the new tint. Thus, if you select Sky Blue 66% and move the slider to 33%, you get a 33 percent tint of the original Sky Blue, not a 33 percent tint of the Sky Blue 66% (which would be equivalent to a 22 percent tint of the original Sky Blue).

You modify and delete tint swatches like any other color swatch, using the Swatches panel's flyout menu.

You can also apply tints to objects without creating a separate swatch for each tint. After applying the color (described in the "Applying swatches" section, later in this chapter), select the object and change the value in the Tint field of the Swatches panel or use its pop-up menu's predefined tint values. Easy as pie!

Working with Gradients

A long-popular design technique is the gradient (also called a *blend* or *graduated fill*), which blends two or more colors in a sequence, going smoothly from, say, green to blue to yellow to orange. InDesign has a powerful gradient-creation feature that lets you define and apply gradients to pretty much any object in InDesign, including text, lines, frames, shapes, and their outlines (strokes).

Creating gradient swatches

In the Swatches panel, where you define colors and tints, you can also define gradients. Just select the New Gradient Swatch option in the flyout menu. You get the dialog box shown in Figure 6-6. The first two options are straightforward, but the rest of the controls are tricky, so pay close attention:

To create new gradients, follow these steps:

1. **Type a name for the gradient in the Swatch Name field.**

   Picking a name is a bit more difficult than naming a color, but use something like "Blue to Red" or "Bright Multihue" or "Logo Gradient" that has a meaning specific to the colors used or to its role in your document.

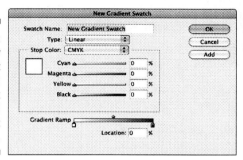 

Figure 6-6:
The New Gradient Swatch dialog box (left) and Gradient panel (right).

2. **In the Type pop-up menu, choose Linear or Radial.**

   A linear blend goes in one direction, while a radial blend radiates out in a circle from a central point.

3. **Select a stop point — one of the squares at the bottom of the dialog box on either end of the gradient ramp (the gradient ramp shows the gradient as you define it).**

   The stop points essentially define the start color (the stop point on the left) and the end color (the stop point on the right). With a stop point selected, you can now define its color.

4. **In the Stop Color pop-up menu, choose what color model you want to use — select from CMYK, RGB, Lab, and Swatches — for the selected stop point.**

   The area directly beneath the pop-up menu changes accordingly, displaying sliders for CMYK, RGB, or Lab, or a list of all colors from the Swatches panel for Swatches, depending on which model you choose.

5. **Create or select the color you want for that stop point.**

   If you selected Swatches in the Stop Color pop-up menu, you can select the [Paper] swatch — essentially, transparency or no color — as a stop point in a gradient. (Note that you may have to scroll through the list of swatches to find it; it's near the top of the swatch list.) You can also click and drag swatches from the Swatches panel to the gradient ramp.

6. **Repeat Steps 3 to 5 for the other stop points (you can have several).**

   Note that the color models for the two stop points don't have to be the same — you can blend from a Pantone spot color to a CMYK color, for example. (If a gradient mixes spot colors and process colors, InDesign converts the spot colors to process colors.)

You now have a simple gradient. But you don't have to stop there. Here are your other options:

- You can change the rate at which the colors transition by sliding the location controls (the diamond icons) at the top of the gradient ramp.

- You can create additional stop points by clicking right below the gradient ramp. By having several stop points, you can have multiple color transitions in a gradient. (Think of them like tab stops in text — you can define as many as you need.) You delete unwanted stop points by clicking and dragging them to the bottom of the dialog box.

Notice that a location control appears between each pair of stop points — that means each pair can have its own transition rate.

When you create a new gradient, InDesign uses the settings from the last one you created. If you want to create a gradient similar to an existing one, click that existing gradient before selecting New Gradient Swatch from the flyout menu. InDesign copies the selected gradient's settings to the new one, which you can then edit. For example, you would first click a linear gradient and then select New Gradient Swatch to create a radial version of that existing linear gradient.

The Swatches panel shows the actual gradient next to its name. The pattern also appears in the Fill iconic button or Stroke iconic button in the Tools panel if that gradient is currently selected as a fill or stroke, as well as in the Gradient button in that panel, whether or not it's currently applied as a fill or stroke.

Understanding the Gradient panel

Just as it does with unnamed colors, InDesign lets you create *unnamed gradients* — gradients that have no swatches. Unlike unnamed colors, you can use these to your heart's content because all colors in a gradient are converted to process colors and/or use defined spot-color swatches — so no unnamed colors are in their output. The process is pretty much the same as creating a gradient swatch (covered in the preceding section, "Creating gradient swatches"), except that you select an object and then open the Gradient panel (Window➪Color➪Gradient), shown in Figure 6-6. In that panel, you select a stop point and then choose a color to apply to it by clicking a color in the Swatches panel or in the Color panel. You create and adjust stop points here just as you do when defining a gradient swatch.

The difference? You can reuse gradients in the Swatches panel, whereas you can't reuse gradients applied through the Gradient panel. But you can add them to the Swatches panel by Control+clicking or right-clicking the gradient in the Tools panel's Fill or Stroke iconic button and then choosing Add to Swatches in the contextual menu that appears.

The Gradient panel can also manipulate gradient swatches: After you apply a linear gradient — whether via a gradient swatch or as an unnamed gradient — you can change the angle of the gradient, rotating the gradient within the object. Just type the desired degree of rotation in the Angle field to rotate the gradient's direction by the value. Negative values rotate counterclockwise, whereas positive values rotate clockwise.

Note that you can't rotate a radial gradient because it's circular and, thus, any rotation has no effect. That's why InDesign grays out the Angle field for radial gradients.

But you can still adjust the location of a radial gradient — as well as that of a linear gradient — by using the Gradient tool in the Tools panel. After applying a gradient to an object, select the Gradient tool and draw a line in the object, as shown in Figure 6-7:

✔ For a linear gradient, the start point of your line corresponds to where you want the first stop point of the gradient to be; the end point of the line corresponds to the last stop point. The length of the line determines how stretched or compressed the gradient is, while the starting point of the line determines how much the gradient is offset within the object. Also, the angle at which you draw the line becomes the angle for the gradient.

✔ For a radial gradient, the line becomes the start and end point for the gradient, in effect offsetting it.

Figure 6-7:
At left: The Gradient tool in use. At right: The Gradient Feather tool in use.

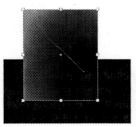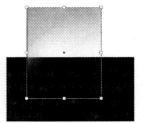

 The Gradient Feather tool — accessed through the Gradient tool's pop-out menu or via the shortcut Shift+G — acts just like the Gradient tool except that it starts with transparency as the initial "color," as shown in Figure 6-7. See Chapter 8 for more on gradient feather and other lighting effects.

Managing Swatches

When you create colors, tints, and gradients, don't go overboard and make too many. You'll also find that different documents have different colors, each created by different people, and you'll likely want to move colors from one document to another. InDesign provides basic tools for managing colors in and across documents.

Editing swatches

Modifying a swatch to change its settings is simple: Just double-click it in the Swatches panel. (You can also choose Swatch options from the Swatches panel's flyout menu.) The Swatch options dialog box appears, a clone of the New Color Swatch, New Tint Swatch, or New Gradient Swatch dialog box (based on what kind of swatch you double-clicked).

The New Swatch and the Swatch Option dialog boxes do have a slight difference: The Swatch Option dialog boxes include the Preview option, which lets you see your changes in a selected object (if it's visible on-screen, of course) as you make changes in the Swatch Options dialog box.

Copying swatches

To duplicate a swatch so that you can create a new one based on it, use the Duplicate Swatch option in the Swatches panel. The word *copy* is added to the name of the new swatch. You edit it — including its name — as you would any swatch.

When selecting swatches for deletion or duplication, you can ⌘+click or Ctrl+click multiple swatches to work on all of them at once. Note that Shift+clicking selects all swatches between the first swatch clicked and the swatch that you Shift+click, whereas ⌘+click or Ctrl+click lets you select specific swatches in any order and in any location in the panel.

Deleting swatches

InDesign makes deleting swatches simple: Just select the color, tint, or gradient in the Swatches panel. Then choose Delete Swatch from the flyout menu or click the trashcan iconic button at the bottom of the Swatches panel.

Well, that's not quite it. You then get the Delete Swatch dialog box, which lets you either assign a new color to anything using the deleted swatch (the Defined Swatch option) or leave the color on any object that is using it but delete the swatch from the Swatches panel (the Unnamed Swatch option). (As explained in this chapter's sidebar "The bad way to create colors," you should avoid unnamed colors so don't choose the Unnamed Swatch option.)

If you delete a tint and replace it with another color, any object using that tint will get the full-strength version of the new color, not a tint of it. Likewise, if you delete a color swatch that you've based one or more tints on, those tints will also be deleted if you replace the deleted swatch with an unnamed swatch. However, if you delete a color swatch and replace it with a defined swatch, any tints of that deleted swatch will retain their tint percentages of the replacement-defined swatch.

InDesign offers a nice option to quickly find all unused colors in the Swatches panel: the flyout menu's Select All Unused option. With this option, you can delete all the unused colors in one fell swoop. Note that you don't get the option to assign each deleted color separately to another color in the Delete Swatch dialog box — they all are replaced with the color you select or are made into unnamed colors. Because no object uses these colors, choosing Unnamed Swatch in essence is the same as replacing them with a color using the Defined Swatch option.

If you delete a swatch and replace it with an unnamed swatch, you can recapture that deleted swatch later by choosing the Add Unnamed Colors menu item in the Swatches panel's flyout menu.

Importing swatches

A quick way to import specific colors from another InDesign document or template is to click and drag the colors from that other file's Swatches panel into your current document or template.

You can import colors from other Creative Suite programs from which you have saved Adobe Swatch Exchange color library files, choosing Load Swatches from the Swatches panel's flyout menu. You can also import swatches directly from other InDesign documents. From the resulting dialog box, navigate to the file that contains the colors you want to import, select that file, and click Open.

When you import color swatches from other documents or Adobe Swatch Exchange files, InDesign brings in *all* the colors. You can't choose specific colors to import.

Sampling colors

You may wonder how you can use colors in your imported graphics for which InDesign can't find any swatch information, such as in TIFF files or photos embedded in a PDF file. As you may expect, InDesign provides a way to capture these colors: the Eyedropper tool. Here's how it works:

1. **In the Tools panel or Swatches panel, choose the Fill iconic button or Stroke iconic button.**

   It doesn't really matter which button you use unless you'll immediately create a shape or enter text after capturing the desired color; in that case, choose whichever aspect you'll want the new object or text to have the color applied to.

2. **Select the Eyedropper tool and then click the graphic where the desired color is used.**

   The Fill or Stroke iconic button now has that color. (If the Eyedropper tool isn't visible in the Tools panel, look for the Measure tool and then click and hold down its icon to get the pop-up menu that lets you select the Eyedropper tool.)

3. **The Eyedropper tool changes to the Marker tool.**

   Any object you select with the Marker tool will have the color applied to its fill or stroke, depending on whether the Fill or Stroke iconic button is active. Note that you can switch between the Eyedropper and Marker tools to select different colors and apply them by holding the Option or Alt key to get the Eyedropper tool back and then releasing it to switch to the Marker tool.

4. **To add the new, unnamed color to the Swatches panel, Control+click or right-click the Fill iconic button or Stroke iconic button (whichever has the captured color) and choose Add to Swatches from the contextual menu that appears.**

   Now you can edit and apply the captured color like any other color swatch.

The following figure shows a composite image that highlights the Eyedropper tool at left (in the area behind the horse) and the Marker tool at right (over the thick framing line).

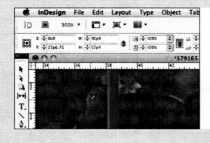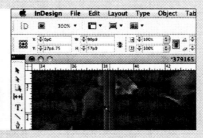

Also, when you import a graphic file in PDF or EPS format, any named colors (swatches) in that file are automatically added to the Swatches panel.

You can also use the new Kuler panel to import sets of color swatches. (For more on that topic, see the section "Using Kuler colors," earlier in this chapter.)

Exporting swatches

You can do more than import swatches. InDesign also lets you save swatches into color library files for use by other Creative Suite users. Just select the colors you want to save and then choose Save Swatches from the Swatches panel's flyout menu. You are asked to give the color library file a name before you save it.

InDesign doesn't include mixed-ink colors when you save swatches for use by other Creative Suite programs. Any selected such swatches are simply ignored.

Applying Swatches

Applying colors, tints, and gradients to objects in InDesign is quick work. Select the object and then click the Formatting Affects Text button or Formatting Affects Container iconic button in the Swatches or Gradient panel as appropriate. If you're using the Swatches panel, click the appropriate swatch; if you're using the Gradient panel, adjust the gradient as desired.

When it comes to coloring graphics in InDesign, you can apply color and tints to grayscale and black-and-white bitmapped images, such as those in the TIFF and Photoshop formats. But you can't color vector-based graphics (such as those in the Illustrator and EPS formats) or color bitmapped images.

Another way to apply colors, tints, and gradients is by selecting the object and using the Formatting Affects Text, Formatting Affects Content, Fill, or Stroke iconic buttons near the bottom of the Tools panel to define what part of the object you want to color. You can use the Swatches or Gradients panels to select a swatch or pick the last-used color and gradient from the Apply Color and Apply Gradient iconic buttons, also near the bottom of the Tools panel.

For tints, you can use a tint swatch, or you can simply apply a color from the Swatches panel and enter a tint value in the panel's Tint field.

When applying color to text, you can apply it to all the text in the frame by using the Formatting Affects Text iconic button (which is what the Formatting Affects Contents iconic button is renamed when you select text) or to specific text by highlighting that text with the Type tool.

You can also apply color as part of your character and paragraph styles in the Character Color pane when creating or editing styles. See Chapter 13 for more on styles, and Chapters 14 and 15 for more on text formatting.

You can also apply colors and tints to gaps in strokes. Open the Stroke panel by choosing Window➪Stroke (⌘+F10 or Ctrl+F10), then select a color in the Gap Color menu (if you don't see this option in the Stroke panel, select Show Options from the panel's flyout menu).

Part III
Object Essentials

"Needlepoint my foot! This is InDesign. What I can't figure out is how you got the pillow cases into your printer."

In this part . . .

The rubber really hits the road when you've got your basic layout structure in place. Now you can focus on the meat of your documents: the objects that contain your text and graphics. It's amazing all the objects you can create — from simple rectangles to complex curves. And it's equally amazing all the things you can do to objects, such as rotate them, color and align them, and apply special effects, such as drop shadows and directional feathers. And you can even save a lot of these settings so that you can apply them consistently to other objects later — a real timesaver that also ensures quality results.

Note that you can apply most of these effects to objects whether or not they already contain their graphics and text — so if you're a really structured kind of person, you'll probably create your basic object containers first, apply your effects to them, and then bring in the text and graphics. But if you're more free-form in your approach, you'll likely bring in all your text and graphics, and then start arranging the objects that contain them to produce your final layout. That's fine. Either way, you just apply the techniques in this part while doing so.

Chapter 7

Adding Essential Elements

* *

In This Chapter

▶ Creating frames and shapes

▶ Making lines and paths

▶ Working with text shapes and paths

▶ Using strokes

* *

*T*he fundamental components of any layout are its objects. This chapter explains how to create these building blocks: frames, shapes, lines, and paths, as well as the strokes you apply to them.

Working with Frames and Shapes

An *object* is a container that can (but doesn't have to) hold text or graphics, as well as display attributes such as color, strokes, and gradients. When an object contains an imported graphic or text, or if an object is created as a placeholder for a graphic or text, it's referred to as a *frame* in InDesign. Otherwise, it's called a *shape*.

The difference between frames and shapes is artificial. Because a shape can easily become a frame simply by placing text or graphics into it, it's easiest to think of shapes and frames as the same thing. I tend to use the word "frame" to mean either frames or shapes.

Designing pages in InDesign is largely a matter of creating and modifying frames and shapes, as well as modifying the text and graphics that the frames contain.

Creating frames and shapes

As Figure 7-1 shows, the Tools panel contains several tools for creating both shapes and frames:

✔ **The Rectangle, Ellipse, and Polygon shape tools:** The Ellipse and Polygon tools are available through the pop-up menu that appears if you click and hold on the Rectangle tool.

✔ **The Rectangle Frame, Ellipse Frame, and Polygon Frame tools:** The Ellipse Frame and Polygon Frame tools are available through the pop-up menu that appears if you click and hold on the Rectangle Frame tool.

✔ **The Type tool:** You can use this tool to create rectangular text frames in addition to letting you work with text.

Figure 7-1:
The frame- and shape-creating tools in the Tools panel, as well as the other tools to create and manipulate lines and paths.

Type tool
Line tool
Pencil tool

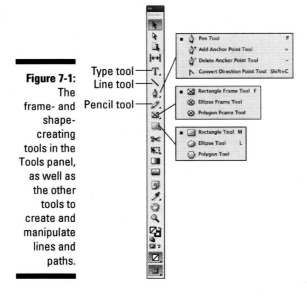

Here's how to create a frame (or shape):

1. **Select the desired tool from the Tools panel.**

2. **Optionally, set up the polygon's number of sides and the depth of its spikes.**

   To do so, double-click the tool you're using (Polygon or Polygon Frame) so the Polygon Settings dialog box appears. Figure 7-2 shows that dialog box and example starburst. Adjust the number of sides and their depth (the Star Inset field) as desired, and then click OK. If you don't adjust the polygon's settings and instead just begin drawing on as in the next steps, InDesign will use the last-used settings for the selected tool.

3. **Move the mouse pointer anywhere within the currently displayed page or on the pasteboard.**

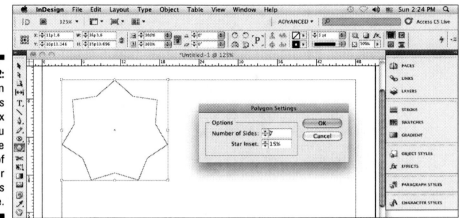

4. **Click and drag in any direction.**

   As you drag, a cross-hair pointer appears in the corner opposite your starting point; a colored rectangle indicates the boundary of the frame. (The color is blue for objects on the default layer; objects on other layers have those layers' respective colors. See Chapter 4 for more on layers.) You can look at the width and height values displayed in the Control panel or the Transform panel as you drag to help you get the size you want. Holding down the Shift key as you drag limits the tool to creating a frame or shape within a square bounding box.

5. **When the frame is the size and shape you want, release the mouse button.**

Pretty easy, huh? At this point, you can begin typing in the frame, paste text or a graphic into it, or import a text or a graphics file, as Chapters 10 and 16 explain.

If you create a text frame with the Type tool, be sure not to click in an existing text frame when your intention is to create a new one. If you click within an existing frame when the Type tool is selected, the flashing cursor appears, and InDesign thinks you want to type text.

InDesign CS5 lets you create multiple frames at the same time, using a new capability that Adobe calls *gridified frame creation*. While dragging the mouse to create a frame, press the → key to add an additional frame horizontally (a new "column") or the ↑ key to add an additional frame vertically (a new "row"). Each time you press → or ↑, you add another column or row of frames. Press ← to delete a column and ↓ to delete a row.

As Figure 7-3 shows, when you release the mouse, InDesign creates a grid of frames, all with the same shape and size. If you're creating text frames, all the text frames in such a grid are automatically threaded for text flow. The thread follows the order you dragged the mouse when creating the frame: If you dragged from upper left to lower right, the thread starts at the leftmost text frame in the top row and continues to each adjacent text frame, then continues at the leftmost text frame in the next row, and so on.

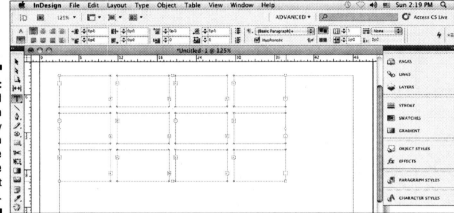

Figure 7-3:
The gridified
frame-creation
capability
lets you
create
multiple
frames at
once.

When any of the frame-creation tools is selected, you can create as many new frames as you want. Simply keep clicking, dragging, and releasing. After you create a graphics frame, you can modify it (without changing tools) by adding a border or a colored background or by applying any of the effects — such as rotation, shear, and scale — in the Control panel. You can also move or resize a graphics frame, but you have to switch to the Selection tool or the Direct Selection tool to do so. Chapter 8 explains how to resize, move, delete, and otherwise manipulate frames and other objects.

Reshaping frames and shapes

Sometimes, a frame or shape needs to be more than resized or moved. It needs to be reshaped. InDesign makes it easy to change an object's shape:

✔ The simplest way is to select an object with the Direct Selection tool and then drag any of the handles or frame edges. Notice how the frame's shape actually changes, as shown in Figure 7-4.

✔ To change a shape more radically, choose the desired shape from Object➪Convert Shape's submenu. Your choices are Rectangle, Rounded Rectangle, Beveled Rectangle, Inverse Rounded Rectangle, Ellipse, Triangle, Polygon, Line, and Orthogonal Line. (Note that if you choose Polygon, InDesign will use whatever the last polygon settings were, which you can see by double-clicking the Polygon or Polygon Frame tool. Also, if you try to convert a text frame into a line, InDesign will abort the action, telling you it can't do the conversion.)

✔ You can manually edit a shape by adding or removing anchor points — the points in a shape's edges that you can adjust, as described in the next section.

If you're working with frames that contain graphics, InDesign CS5 has a quick way to switch from the Selection tool to the Direct Selection tool: Just click the content grabber (the doughnut shape at the frame's center when you hover the mouse over the frame). If the content grabber does not display, turn it on by choosing View➪Extras➪Show Content Grabber. Note that in InDesign CS5 double-clicking a frame no longer switches between the Selection and Direction Selection tools.

Figure 7-4:
After creating a frame (left), reshape it by dragging its handle with the Direct Selection tool (right).

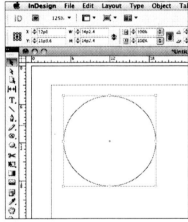
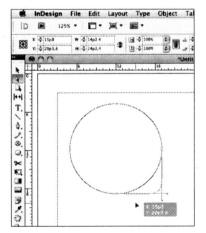

Creating Lines and Paths

When you're drawing the old-fashioned way, with pen and paper, you typically use one tool to draw straight lines, curved lines, and free-form objects. InDesign is less flexible, using different tools for different kinds of lines. InDesign lets you create straight lines with the Line tool and zigzag lines, curved lines, and free-form shapes with the Pen and Type on a Path tools. (Those nonstraight lines and free-form shapes are called *paths* in InDesign.) Figure 7-1, earlier in this chapter, shows these tools on the Tools panel.

Drawing a straight line

Although not as flashy or versatile as shapes and paths, lines can serve many useful purposes in well-designed pages. For example, you can use plain ol' vertical rules to separate columns of text in a multicolumn page or the rows and columns of data in a table. Dashed lines are useful for indicating folds and cut lines on brochures and coupons. And lines with arrowheads are handy if you have to create a map or a technical illustration.

Follow these steps to draw a simple, straight line:

1. **Select the Line tool (or press \).**
2. **Move the pointer anywhere within the currently displayed page or on the pasteboard.**
3. **Click and drag the mouse in any direction.**

   As you drag, a thin, blue line appears from the point where you first clicked to the current position of the cross-hair pointer. Holding down the Shift key as you drag constrains the line to a horizontal, vertical, or 45-degree diagonal line.

4. **When the line is the length and angle you want, release the mouse button.**

   Don't worry too much about being precise when you create a line. You can always go back later and fine-tune it.

When you release the mouse button after creating a line, the line is active. As illustrated in Figure 7-5, if the Selection tool was previously selected, the line appears within a rectangular bounding box, which contains eight resizing handles. If the Direct Selection tool was previously selected, moveable anchor points appear at the ends of the line. In either case, you have to choose the right tool if you want to change the shape or size of the bounding box or the line:

✔ The Selection tool lets you change the shape of the line's bounding box (which also changes the angle and length of the line) by dragging any of the resizing handles.

✔ The Direct Selection tool lets you change the length and angle of the line itself by moving anchor points on the frame.

As long as the Line tool is selected, you can create as many new lines as you want. Simply keep clicking, dragging, and releasing.

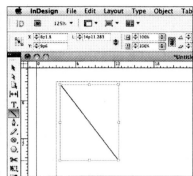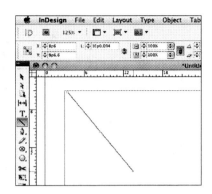

Figure 7-5:
A line
selected
with the
Selection
tool (left)
and the
Direct
Selection
tool (right).

When you create a line, it takes on the characteristics specified in the Stroke panel (Window⇨Stroke [⌘+F10 or Ctrl+F10]), covered in the "Applying strokes" section later in this chapter. When you first open a document, the default line width is 1 point. If you want to change the appearance of your lines, double-click the Line tool and adjust the Weight setting in the Stroke panel that appears. If you make this adjustment when no document is open, all new documents will use the new line settings.

Understanding paths

Paths are a lot more complex than lines, so you need to understand some of the theory behind paths so that you can create and manipulate them more easily.

Every object you create with InDesign's object-creation tools is a *path*. Regardless of the tool you use to create a path, you can change its appearance by modifying any of four properties that all paths share:

- **Closure:** A path is either open or closed. Straight lines created with the Line tool and curved and zigzag lines created with the Pen tool are examples of open paths. Basic shapes created with the Ellipse, Rectangle, and Polygon tools and free-form shapes created with the Pen and Pencil tools are examples of closed shapes. A *closed free-form shape* is an uninterrupted path with no end points.

- **Stroke:** If you want to make a path visible, you can apply a stroke to it by selecting it with a selection tool, entering a Weight value in the Stroke panel (Window⇨Stroke [⌘+F10 or Ctrl+F10]), and selecting a color from the Swatches panel (see Chapter 6). (An unselected, unstroked path isn't visible.)

✔ **Fill:** A color, color tint, or gradient applied to the background of a path is called a *fill*. You apply fills by using the Swatches panel.

✔ **Contents:** You can place a text file or a graphics file in any path except a straight line. When a path holds text or a graphic, the path functions as a frame. Although InDesign can place text or graphics in an open path, placing text and pictures in closed paths is far more common than placing them in open paths. In addition to putting text inside paths, you can also have text on the path itself, following its shape, as Chapter 17 explains.

No matter how simple or complicated, all paths are made up of the same components. Figure 7-6 shows the parts that make up a path:

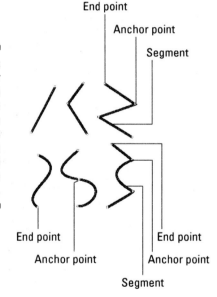

Figure 7-6:
Anchor points between line segments can be corner (top) or smooth (bottom).

End point

Anchor point

Segment

End point

Anchor point

End point

Anchor point

Segment

✔ A path contains one or more straight or curved *segments*.

✔ An anchor point is located at each end of every segment. The anchor points at the ends of a closed path are called *end points*. When you create a path of any kind, anchor points are automatically placed at the end of each segment. After you create a path, you can move, add, delete, and change the direction of corner points.

✔ InDesign has two kinds of anchor points: *smooth points* and *corner points*. A smooth point connects two adjoining curved segments in a continuous, flowing curve. At a corner point, adjoining segments — straight or curved — meet at an angle. The corners of a rectangular path are the most common corner points.

✔ A *direction line* runs through each anchor point and has a handle at both ends. You can control the curve that passes through an anchor point by dragging a direction line's handles, as I explain a little later on.

Drawing your own paths

Even if you're an artistic master with a piece of charcoal or a No. 2 pencil, you need to practice with the Pen tool for a while before your drawing skills kick in. The good news is that after you get comfortable using the Pen tool, you can draw any shape you can imagine. (Of course, if you can't draw very well in the first place, using the Pen tool won't magically transform you into a master illustrator!) If creating a free-form path is new terrain for you, start simply and proceed slowly.

When creating paths, use as few anchor points as possible. As you become more comfortable creating free-form paths, you should find yourself using fewer anchor points to create paths.

For an easy way to draw free-form shapes, use the Pencil tool. This tool simply traces the movement of your mouse (or pen tablet) as you move it, much like a pencil works on paper. Although not as exact as the Pen tool, the Pencil tool creates Bézier curves that you can later edit. Note that the Pencil tool is not meant for creating straight lines — unless you're capable of drawing perfectly straight lines by hand, that is.

Straight and zigzag lines

Follow these steps to draw lines with straight segments, such as a zigzag:

1. **Select the Pen tool.**

2. **Move the Pen pointer to where you want to start your line segment.**

3. **Click and release the mouse button.**

   Make sure that you don't drag before you release the mouse button.

   An anchor point appears; it looks like a small, filled-in square.

4. **Move the Pen pointer to where you want to place the next anchor point.**

5. **Click and release the mouse button.**

   InDesign draws a straight line between the two anchor points. The first anchor point changes to a hollow square, and the second anchor point is filled in, which indicates that it's the active anchor point.

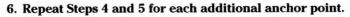
6. **Repeat Steps 4 and 5 for each additional anchor point.**

To reposition an anchor point after you click the mouse button but before you release it, hold down the spacebar and drag. Otherwise, you need to select it with the Direct Selection tool after you finish drawing the line and then click and drag it to its new location.

7. **To complete the path, press Enter or Return, ⌘+click or Ctrl+click elsewhere on the page, or simply choose another tool.**

If you ⌘+click or Ctrl+click, the Pen tool remains active, so you can continue creating new paths.

Curved lines

Knowing how to draw zigzag lines is fine (see preceding section), but chances are, you want to draw curved shapes as well. The basic process is similar to drawing straight segments, but drawing curved paths (technically, *Bézier paths*) is more complicated and will take you some time to get the hang of.

If you want to draw a continuously curvy path that contains no corner points and no straight segments, you should create only smooth points as you draw. Here's how:

1. **Select the Pen tool.**

2. **Move the Pen pointer to where you want to start the curve segment.**

3. **Click and hold down the mouse button.**

The arrowhead pointer appears.

4. **Drag the mouse in the direction of the next point you intend to create, and then release the mouse button.**

As you drag, the anchor point, its direction line, and the direction line's two handles are displayed, as shown in Figure 7-7.

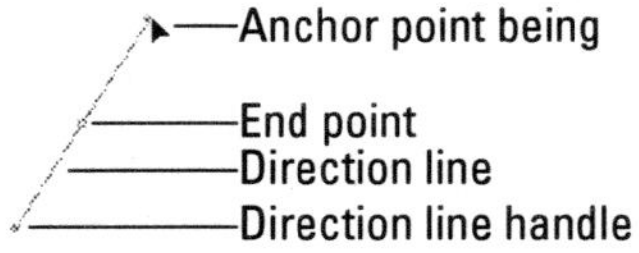

Figure 7-7:
To create a smooth point, click and hold the mouse and drag in the direction of the next point.

—Anchor point being
—End point
—Direction line
—Direction line handle

How smooth and corner points work

Bézier paths have two kinds of points to join segments: corner and smooth.

The two segments that form a smooth point's direction line work together as a single, straight line. When you move a handle, the line acts like a teeter-totter; the opposite handle moves in the opposite direction. If you shorten one of the segments, the length of the other segment doesn't change. The angle and length of direc-tion lines determine the shape of the segments with which they're associated.

A corner point that connects two curved seg-ments has two direction lines: a corner point that connects two straight segments has no direction lines; and a corner point that connects a straight and curved segment has one direc-tion line. If you drag a corner point's direction line, the other direction line, if there is one, isn't affected.

If you hold down the Shift key as you drag, the angle of the direction line is limited to increments of 45 degrees.

5. **Move the Pen pointer to where you want to place the next anchor point — and end the first segment — and then drag the mouse.**

   If you drag in roughly the same direction as the direction line of the pre-ceding point, you create an S-shaped curve; if you drag in the opposite direction, you create a C-shaped curve.

6. **When the curve between the two anchor points looks how you want it to look, release the mouse button.**

   Alternatively, when you want to connect curved segments to corner points (shown in Figure 7-8), move the Pen pointer to where you want to place the next anchor point — and end the first segment — and then press and hold Option or Alt as you click and drag the mouse. As you drag, the anchor point's handle moves, and the direction line changes from a straight line to two independent segments. The angle of the direc-tion line segment that you create when you drag the handle determines the slope of the next segment.

7. **Repeat Steps 5 and 6 for each additional desired curved segment.**

8. **To complete the path, ⌘+click or Ctrl+click elsewhere on the page or simply choose another tool.**

   If you ⌘+click or Ctrl+click, the Pen tool remains active, so you can create new paths.

   You can also complete the path by clicking the first point you created, which creates a closed path.

If you create two open paths that you want to join together into one path, you can do so in InDesign by selecting the two paths and then choosing Object➪Paths➪Join. InDesign usually joins the two closest points with a straight line, but it sometimes joins the last point of the first path and the first point of the second path.

Do note that if you try to join a text path with a regular path, the text will be deleted if it's the second path selected. If you join two text paths, the second path's text will also be deleted. Finally, if you select three or more paths and choose Object➪Paths➪Join, nothing will happen.

Figure 7-8:
Three corner points join four curved segments.

Closed paths

A *closed path* is simply a path that ends where it began. When it comes to creating closed paths with the Pen tool, the process is exactly the same as for creating open paths (such as curved lines and zigzag lines), as explained in the "Curved lines" and "Straight and zigzag lines" sections, earlier in this chapter, with one difference at the end:

- ✔ To create a straight segment between the end point and the last anchor point you created, click and release the mouse button.

- ✔ To create a curved segment, click and drag the mouse in the direction of the last anchor point you created and then release the mouse button.

Just like an open path, a closed path can contain straight and/or curved segments and smooth and/or corner anchor points. All the techniques explained earlier in this chapter for drawing lines with curved and straight segments and smooth and corner points apply when you draw closed paths.

You can also, of course, edit and adjust your curves in InDesign, but doing so requires some more expertise with drawing tools such as those in Adobe Illustrator and is beyond the scope of this book. Check out *Illustrator CS5 For*

Dummies by Ted Alspach or *Adobe InDesign CS5 Bible* by Galen Gruman (both by Wiley Publishing) for more details.

Blurring the Lines between Text and Graphics

InDesign lets you create shapes out of text, as well as make text run along a path — blurring the boundary between text and graphics.

Converting text to shapes

If you want to use the shape of a letter or the combined shapes of several letters as a frame for text or a graphic, you could test your skill with the Pen tool and create the letter shape(s) yourself. But getting hand-drawn characters to look just the way you want them to can take lots of time. A quicker solution is to use the Create Outlines command to convert text characters into editable outlines. The Create Outlines command is particularly useful if you want to hand-tweak the shapes of characters, particularly at display font sizes, or place text or a graphic within character shapes.

If all you need to do is apply a stroke or fill to characters within text, you don't have to convert the characters into outlines. Instead, simply highlight the characters and use the Stroke panel (Window➪Stroke [⌘+F10 or Ctrl+F10]) and Swatches panel (Window➪Color➪Swatches [F5]) to change their appearance. This way, you can still edit the text. (Strokes are covered later in this chapter.)

When you use the Create Outlines command, you have the choice of creating an inline compound path that replaces the original text or an independent compound path that's placed directly on top of the original letters in its own frame. If you want the text outlines to flow with the surrounding text, create an inline compound path. If you want to use the outlines elsewhere, create an independent compound path.

To convert text into outlines, follow these steps:

1. **Use the Type tool to highlight the characters you want to convert into outlines.**

   Generally, this feature works best with large font sizes.

2. **Choose Type➪Create Outlines (Shift+⌘+O or Ctrl+Shift+O — that's the letter *O*, not a zero).**

   If you hold down the Option or Alt key when you choose Create Outlines (or if you press Shift+Option+⌘+O or Ctrl+Alt+Shift+O), a compound path is created and placed in front of the text. In this case, you can use either of the selection tools to move the resulting compound path. If you don't hold down Option or Alt when you choose Create Outlines, an inline compound path is created. This object replaces the original text and flows with the surrounding text.

After you create text outlines, you can modify the paths the same as you can modify hand-drawn paths. You can also use the transformation tools, the Control panel (Window⇨Control [Option+⌘+6 or Ctrl+Alt+6]), and the Transform panel (Window⇨Transform) to change the appearance of text outlines. But you can't edit text after converting it to outlines.

Additionally, you can use the Place command (File⇨Place [⌘+D or Ctrl+D]) or the Paste Into command (Edit⇨Paste Into [Option+⌘+V or Ctrl+Alt+V]) to import text or a graphic into the frames created by converting text to graphics.

Making text follow a path

InDesign lets you have text follow any open or closed path, such as a line or frame. Simply select the path or shape with the Type on a Path tool, which is available from the Type tool's pop-up menu. Now start typing (or paste or place) your text.

After you enter the text and format it with font, size, color, and so on, you can apply special effects to it using the Type on a Path Options dialog box, accessed by choosing Type⇨Type on a Path⇨Options.

You can also double-click the Type on a Path tool to open the Type on a Path Options dialog box.

Figure 7-9 shows the dialog box and several examples of its formatting. In the dialog box:

- ✔ Use the Effect pop-up menu to choose a visual effect.
- ✔ Use the Align pop-up menu to choose what part of the text is aligned (baseline, center, ascender, or descender).
- ✔ Use the To Path pop-up menu to choose whether to align to the center, bottom, or top of the path.
- ✔ Flip the text by selecting the Flip option.
- ✔ Change the text's spacing by entering a value in the Spacing field (positive numbers space out the text, while negative ones contract it).

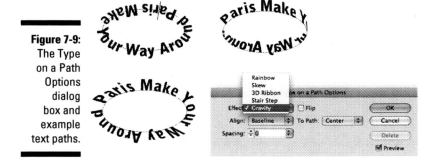

Figure 7-9:
The Type
on a Path
Options
dialog
box and
example
text paths.

Applying Strokes

All objects have a stroke with a width of 0 built in, so you never have to add strokes. But to use them, you need to modify them so that they have some thickness onto which you can apply attributes, such as colors and gradients.

Setting stroke appearance

The Stroke panel is where you give the stroke its width, as well as apply the type of stroke and other attributes. Follow these steps:

1. **Select either of the selection tools and click the object whose stroke you want to modify, or select the Type tool and select the text whose stroke you want to modify.**

2. **If the Stroke panel isn't displayed, show it by choosing Window⇨Stroke (⌘+F10 or Ctrl+F10).**

   Figure 7-10 shows the panel.

Figure 7-10:
The Stroke
panel (left)
and the
Swatches
panel (right).

3. **To change the width of the stroke, enter a new value in the Weight field.**

   You can also change the Weight value by choosing a new value from the field's pop-up menu or by clicking the up and down arrows. (Each click increases or decreases the stroke by 1 point.)

4. **Set the Miter Limit.**

   The default of 4 is fine for almost all frames. You rarely need to use this feature, so don't worry about it.

5. **Click any of the three Cap iconic buttons to specify how dashes will look if you create a dashed stroke (covered in Step 9).**

   Experiment with them in your objects to see which looks best for your situation. (This option is not available for text.)

6. **Click any of the three Join iconic buttons to specify how corners are handled.**

   Again, experiment with these buttons to see what works best for you.

7. **Choose an Align Stroke option.**

   The default is the first button, Align Stroke to Center, which has the stroke straddle the frame. You can also choose Align Stroke to Inside, which places the entire thickness inside the frame boundary, or Align Stroke to Outside, which places the entire thickness outside the frame boundary. (The Align Stroke to Inside button is not available for text.)

8. **Unless you're working with text, you can choose end points for your strokes by using the Start and End pop-up menus.**

   End points appear only on lines and other open paths, not on rectangles, ellipses, or other closed-loop shapes.

9. **To create a dashed line instead of a solid line, choose an option from the Type pop-up menu.**

   These options are also available from the Control panel. Note they are not available for text selections.

   Choose from 18 types of predefined dashes and stripes. The Gap Color and Gap Tint fields at the bottom of the Stroke panel also become active, to let you choose a color and tint for the gaps in dashes and stripes.

After you have a visible stroke, you want to color it. Here's how:

1. **Select either of the selection tools and click the frame to which you want to add a stroke, or select the stroked text with the Type tool.**

2. **Click the Stroke iconic button in the Swatches panel, Control panel, or Tools panel.**

3. **Click a color, tint, or gradient from the Swatches panel; or click one of the boxes at the bottom of the Tools panel, which let you use (from left to right) the last-selected color, last-selected gradient, or None.**

(The None option removes the stroke's color, tint, or gradient.)

For information about adding colors to the Swatches panel and applying colors to objects, see Chapter 6.

Creating stroke styles

InDesign lets you create custom strokes, known as *stroke styles,* in any of three types: dashed, dotted, and striped. To create custom dashes or stripes, choose the Stroke Styles option in the Stroke panel's flyout menu. In the resulting Stroke Styles dialog box, you can create new strokes, edit or delete existing ones, and import strokes from a stroke styles file, which you create by saving a document's strokes as a separate file for import into other documents. Stroke style files have the filename extension .inst.

Note that you can't edit or delete the seven default stripe patterns shown in the Stroke Styles dialog box, nor can you edit or delete the default dash patterns — they're not even available in the dialog box. When you edit or create a stroke pattern, you get the New Stroke Style dialog box, shown in Figure 7-11. In the Name field, enter a name for your stroke. In the Type pop-up menu, you can choose to create (or convert a stripe you're editing to) a dashed, dotted, or striped stroke.

For dashes, you can resize the dash component by dragging the down-pointing triangle at the end of the dash in the ruler section. You can add dash segments by simply clicking the ruler and dragging a segment to the desired width. Or you can use the Start and Length fields to manually specify them. The Pattern Length field is where you indicate the length of the segment that will be repeated to create a dashed line.

Adding fills

The option to add a stroke to any shape becomes even more powerful when combined with the option to fill any shape with a color or tint. For example, adding a fill to a text frame is an effective way to draw attention to a sidebar.

Adding a fill to a shape is much like adding a stroke, and the options available for specifying color and tint are identical. The only difference is that you click the Fill iconic button in the Tools panel, Control panel, or Swatches panel rather than the Stroke iconic button.

When working with text, you can also set a color or gradient as its fill using the Fill iconic buttons.

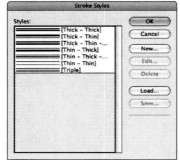

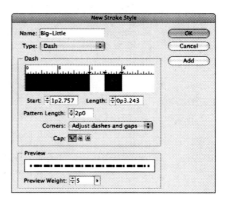

In the Corners pop-up menu, you tell InDesign whether to adjust how the dashes and gaps are handled at corners; the default is Adjust Dashes and Gaps, a setting you should keep — it will make sure that your corners have dash segments that extend along both sides of the corner, which looks neater. (Your other options are Adjust Dashes, Adjust Gaps, and None.) You can also choose a cap style and the stroke weight. The preview section of the pane lets you see your dash as you create or edit it.

For dots, you get a similar dialog box as for dashes. The Start and Length fields disappear, replaced with the Center field that determines where any added dots are placed on the ruler. (The initial dot, shown as a half-circle, starts at 0 and can't be moved or deleted.) The Caps field is also gone.

To delete a dash or dot segment, just drag it to the left, off the ruler.

For stripes, you also get a similar dialog box. The principle is the same as for dashes: You create segments (in this case, vertical, not horizontal) for the stripes by dragging on the ruler. However, the stripes version of the dialog box expresses its values in percentages because the actual thickness of each stripe is determined by the stroke weight — the thicker the stroke, the thicker each stripe is in the overall stroke.

In all three versions of the New Stroke Style dialog box, you click Add to add the stroke to your document, and then you can create a new stroke. When you're done creating strokes, click OK. (When editing a stroke, the Add button won't be available.)

Be sure to use the Preview Weight slider shown in Figure 7-11. This slider is available in all three versions of the New Stroke Style dialog box. It lets you increase or decrease the preview size so that you can better see thin or small elements in your stroke.

Chapter 8

Manipulating Objects

⁕ ⁕

In This Chapter

▶ Resizing, moving, and deleting objects

▶ Hiding objects' display

▶ Keeping objects from printing

▶ Rotating, shearing, and flipping objects

▶ Changing object attributes

▶ Applying special effects

⁕ ⁕

*F*rames, shapes, lines, and paths are the building blocks of your layout. But as anyone who ever played with Legos or Tinkertoys knows, it's how you manipulate the building blocks that results in a unique creation, whether it be a Lego house, a Tinkertoys crane, or an InDesign layout.

InDesign provides a lot of control over layout objects so that you can create really interesting, dynamic publications suited to any purpose. In this chapter, I explain the controls that apply to all objects.

This chapter focuses on various effects and actions that apply to any frame or path. Chapter 17 covers actions specific to graphics frames. Chapter 7 explains how to add frames, shapes, lines, and paths in the first place. Chapter 10 explains how to align objects and precisely position them.

Selecting Objects

Before you can manipulate an object, you have to select it so that InDesign knows what you want to work on. To select an object (rather than its contents), use the Selection tool. Selected items display their item boundary (a rectangle that encompasses the object), as well as eight small resizing handles (one at each of the four corners and one midway between each side of the item boundary).

To select an individual object, just click it with the Selection tool. To select multiple objects, you have several options:

- ✔ Click the first object and Shift+click each additional object.

- ✔ Click and drag the mouse to create a selection rectangle (called a *marquee*) that encompasses at least part of each desired object. When you release the mouse, all objects that this marquee touches are selected.

- ✔ Choose Edit⇨Select All (⌘+A or Ctrl+A) to select all objects on the current spread.

If an object is on a master page and you're working on a document page, you must Shift+⌘+click or Ctrl+Shift+click the object to select it. How do you know whether an object is on a master page? Easy: If you try to select it by clicking and it doesn't become selected, it must be on a master page.

InDesign CS5 automatically shows an object's frame edges as you move your mouse over it. (A dashed frame indicates a group of objects.) The frame edges disappear when you move the mouse past the object.

To have frame edges always display, choose View⇨Extras⇨Show Frame Edges (Control+⌘+H or Ctrl+H) to see object edges if they aren't already visible.

These options are pretty easy, but it can get tricky when you want to select objects that overlap or are obscured by other objects. (See Chapter 10 for more details on object stacking.) So how do you select them?

The easiest way — if the frame contains a graphic — is to use the new content grabber, the doughnut-like icon that appears over the center of a frame as you hover the Selection tool over it. Each frame is automatically selected as you hover over it. Figure 8-1 shows the content grabber. (If the content grabber doesn't appear, choose View⇨Extras⇨Show Content Grabber.) If you click the content grabber itself, the Selection tool becomes the Direct Selection tool and the graphic frame's contents are selected.

Another selection method, which works for any object, is to use the Select Previous Object or Select Next Object iconic buttons in the Control panel. (If you Shift+click either button, InDesign jumps past four objects and selects the fifth one. If you ⌘+click or Control+click either button, InDesign selects to the bottommost or topmost object, respectively.) Note that the buttons don't display when the default Essentials workspace is in use; they do appear in the Advanced workspace, and you can turn them on individually by modifying the Control panel's appearance. (Choose Customize from its flyout menu and then go to the Object section to turn on the Select Container & Content option.)

If you use the Select Previous Object or Select Next Object iconic buttons and reach the top or bottom of the object stack, InDesign cycles back. For example, if you reach the topmost object and click Select Previous Object, InDesign moves to the bottommost object.

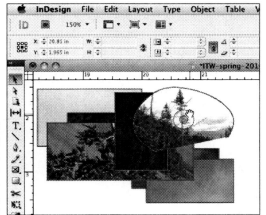

Figure 8-1:
The content grabber (the doughnut-like icon).

Another way to select buried objects is by using the Select submenu option in the Object menu.

The first four options in the Select submenu let you select another object relative to the currently selected object:

- ✔ First Object Above (Option+Shift+⌘+] or Ctrl+Alt+Shift+]) selects the topmost object.
- ✔ Next Object Above (Option+⌘+] or Ctrl+Alt+]) selects the object immediately on top of the current object.
- ✔ Next Object Below (Option+⌘+[or Ctrl+Alt+[) selects the object immediately under the current object.
- ✔ Last Object Below (Option+Shift+⌘+[or Ctrl+Alt+Shift+[) selects the bottommost object.

If no objects are selected, InDesign bases its selection on the order in which the objects were created, the topmost object being the one that was most recently created.

You can also access these four selection options by Control+clicking or right-clicking an object and choosing the Select menu from the contextual menu that appears.

The Select submenu has four other options:

- ✔ If you select an object's content (text or graphic), choose Object➪ Select➪Container to choose the frame or path. Using this option is the same as selecting the object with the Selection tool.

- ✔ If an object has content (text or graphic) and you select it, choose Object➪Select➪Content to choose the content within the object. This option is basically the same as selecting the frame with the Direct Selection tool.

- ✔ If you select an object in a group of objects by using the Direct Selection tool, choose Object➪Select➪Previous Object in Group to navigate to the previous object in the group.

- ✔ Similarly, if you select an object in a group of objects by using the Direct Selection tool, choose Object➪Select➪Next Object in Group to navigate to the next object in the group.

The order in which the objects were created determines what is "previous" or "next" in a group.

The Control panel also provides iconic buttons to select the next or previous object, as well as to select the content or container (frame). These last two buttons appear only if you've selected a group. The buttons for selecting the next or previous object appear only if you're using the Direct Selection tool, while the buttons for selecting the content or container appear whether you're using the Selection or Direct Selection tool. (Yes, this interface approach is very confusing!) Figure 8-2 shows the buttons.

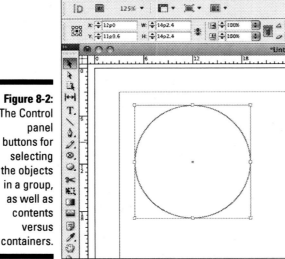

Figure 8-2:
The Control panel buttons for selecting the objects in a group, as well as contents versus containers.

To deselect objects, just click another object, an empty part of your page, or the pasteboard. To deselect individual objects after you've selected multiple objects, Shift+click those you want to deselect.

The Direct Selection tool lets you select any of the individual anchor points (and direction handles of free-form shapes and curved lines) on an object. If you use the Direct Selection tool to click an object that has a bounding box, the shape within is selected, and the bounding box is deselected. You use this tool to work on the contents independently of its container frame. You can also move a graphic within its frame by clicking within the object (see Chapter 17).

Resizing and Scaling Objects

Two closely related features are resizing and scaling. What's the difference? *Resizing* affects just the container — the frame or path — whereas *scaling* affects both the container and its contents.

Resizing objects

You resize objects in pretty much the same way you move them: by using the mouse for inexact sizes or the Control panel for precise sizes.

To resize an object with the mouse, click and drag one of the frame's (or path's) handles with the Selection tool. (Hold the Shift key as you drag to maintain the proportions of the frame.) Drag a corner handle to resize both the width and height or a side handle to resize just the height or width. This method leaves the contents' size unchanged but changes the size of the frame or path.

InDesign shows you the new dimensions as you scale an object via the mouse, with an information box that pops up near the control point you're dragging.

You can also enter new values in the W: and H: fields (for *width* and *height*) of the Control panel. This action also doesn't change the contents' size.

Remember those reference points for positioning an object from Chapter 1? They come into play for resizing objects as well. Basically, the object will grow or shrink starting from the selected reference point, called the *control point*. So if the upper-left reference point is selected and you enter greater W: and H: values, the object will add the extra width to the right and the extra height below. But if you choose the center reference point, it will grow on both sides as well as on the top and bottom, spreading the extra size evenly.

Another way to resize a frame — this method doesn't apply to paths — is to choose Object⇨Fitting⇨Fit Frame to Content (Option+⌘+C or Ctrl+Alt+C). For a graphic, this action makes the frame the same size as the graphic itself. For text, it increases or decreases the depth of the text frame to match the depth of the text; it doesn't widen or narrow the frame.

Double-clicking one of a frame's four handles — the squares at the midpoints of each side — resizes the frame to the content in that axis. For example, double-clicking the left or right handles fits the frame to the contents' width, while double-clicking the top or bottom handle fits the frame to the contents' height. Likewise, double-clicking a corner handle resizes the frame in both directions.

Scaling objects

InDesign offers several ways to *scale* an object, resizing both its contents and its frame (or path):

✔ Enter percentage values in the Scale X Percentage and Scale Y Percentage fields of the Control panel and Transform panel. If the icon to the right of these fields shows a solid chain, adjusting one field automatically adjusts the other by the same percentage, creating proportional resizing. If the icon shows a broken chain, the two dimensions are resized independently, distorting the contents. Click the iconic button to toggle between the unbroken chain and broken chain icons.

✔ You can also scale an object using the mouse. Select the object with the Selection tool, make sure that the desired control point is active to control where the scaling operation starts, and then select the Scale tool. Now drag the mouse away from the object to enlarge it or into the object to reduce it. Objects scaled this way are scaled unproportionally; to scale the object proportionally, hold the Shift key when moving the mouse. (You can also use the Free Transform tool in the same way.)

✔ For graphics frames, use the content-fitting options in the Object menu and Control panel, described in Chapter 17.

Moving Objects

The easiest way to move an object is by using the mouse. With the Selection tool, click an object and drag it to a new location. When you release the mouse, the object is deposited in the new location.

If you want to more precisely move an object, you can enter specific X: and Y: coordinates in the Control panel and Transform panel, as explained in Chapter 10.

Be sure to select the correct reference point to be used as the control point when entering coordinates. The little squares at the top left of the Control panel and Transform panel represent the object's *reference points* (corners, side midpoints, and center). Click a reference point to make it the control point (it turns black, the others turn white); all coordinates are now based on this point.

Deleting Objects

Alas, not all the objects you create survive all the way to the final version of your publication. Some wind up on the cutting room floor. You can always move an object to the pasteboard if you're not sure whether you want to get rid of it altogether. (Objects on the pasteboard don't print.) But when it's time to ax an object, oblivion is just a keystroke or two away.

If you delete a text or graphics frame or path, the contents are removed as well as the frame.

Here's how to delete objects: Using any selection tool, select the object or objects you want to delete and then press the Delete key or Backspace key. You can also delete a selected item by choosing Edit⇨Clear.

Choosing Edit⇨Cut (⌘+X or Ctrl+X) also removes a selected object. However, in this case, a copy of the object is saved to the Clipboard, and you can paste it elsewhere (by choosing Edit⇨Paste [⌘+V or Ctrl+V]) until you cut or copy something else, or you shut down your computer.

Preventing Objects from Printing

InDesign lets you prevent a specific object from printing. To do so, select the object with the Selection or Direct Selection tool, open the Attributes panel (Window⇨Output⇨Attributes), and then select the Nonprinting check box. (The other settings in this panel duplicate stroke settings, covered in Chapter 7.)

You use this feature for comments and other elements that should not print but that the designer needs to have visible on-screen. Another approach to nonprinting objects is to place them all on a layer and make the entire layer nonprinting, as explained in Chapter 4.

Hiding Objects

InDesign CS5 lets you hide objects in your layout, which also prevents them from printing. To hide an object, select it and choose Object➪Hide or press ⌘+3 or Ctrl+3. To show hidden objects, choose Object➪Show All on Spread or press Option+⌘+3 or Ctrl+Alt+3.

You can show hidden objects only if you are working on the spread they are hidden on. There is no way to show all hidden objects throughout your layout. How do you know a spread has hidden objects? The Show All on Spread menu option is black (available) if the current spread has hidden objects and grayed out (unavailable) if the spread that does *not* have hidden objects.

Transforming Objects

InDesign offers several tools and methods for transforming objects. I discuss resizing, scaling, and moving earlier in this chapter, but you can also take advantage of several other useful transformation tools, including rotating, shearing (skewing), flipping, and reshaping.

Rotating is just spinning an object around. Shearing is a little more complicated: *Shearing* skews an object (slanting it in one direction) while also rotating the other axis at the same time.

Regardless of whether you use the mouse or numeric controls to apply rotation and/or shearing to graphics, you first need to follow these steps:

1. **Select the Selection tool.**

2. **Click the object you want to modify.**

3. **If you want, change the object's control point.**

   By default, the control point is the upper-left corner of a frame or shape. You can change the control point by clicking one of the little black boxes — the reference points — in the upper-left corner of the Control panel.

4. **Choose the appropriate tool — Rotate, Shear, or Free Transform — or use the flip options in the Control panel.**

   Figure 8-3 shows the Tools panel and Control panel iconic buttons for these controls.

Rotate 90° Clockwise

Rotate 90° Counterclockwise

Rotation Angle   Flip and rotation indicator

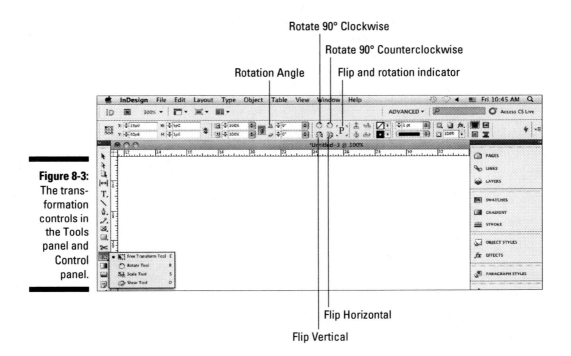

Flip Horizontal

Flip Vertical

Figure 8-3:
The trans-
formation
controls in
the Tools
panel and
Control
panel.

If you hold down the Option or Alt key before and while moving and object, InDesign copies the object and then moves that copy. If you start rotating or resizing, or otherwise transforming an object and then hold Option or Alt, InDesign applies the transformation to a copy. (If you hold Option or Alt first, InDesign opens a dialog box that lets you enter in the new values, such as for scaling or rotating, and choose Copy to apply the new attributes to a copy of the object.

Rotating objects

InDesign CS5 lets you rotate objects using the Selection tool: After selecting the object, move the mouse pointer to any area just outside any corner to get a curved double-arrow pointer. Now drag the mouse to rotate the object. (Holding down the Shift key while dragging limits rotation increments to mul-tiples of 45 degrees.) For graphics frames, you can rotate the graphic (but not the frame) the same way using the Direct Selection tool.

You can also use the Rotate tool after selecting an object: Click and drag a selected object to rotate it.

To change the center of rotation, such as to a corner, select the desired control point representing that corner, side, or the centerpoint in the Control panel or Transform panel before rotating the object. If you use the Rotate tool, you can drag the rotation point (it appears as a cross-hair pointer) wherever you want to get a custom rotation point.

For more precise rotation, use the Control panel. You can change the angle of a selected object by entering a value in the Rotation Angle field. If you choose to enter a value in the Rotation Angle field, positive values rotate the selected item counterclockwise around the control point; negative values rotate it clockwise.

Or you can choose one of the predefined angles from the Rotation Angle field's pop-up menu, or choose any of the three rotation options — Rotate 180°, Rotate 90° CW, and Rotate 90° CCW — in the Control panel's flyout menu.

If you choose one of these flyout menu options, the current angle of the selected object is added to the applied angle. For example, if you choose Rotate 90° CCW (counterclockwise), an object that's currently rotated 12 degrees will end up with a rotation angle of 102 degrees.

However you rotate an object, the flip-and-rotation indicator in the Control panel — the big *P* — will show the selected object's current rotation. It also shows the selected object's flip status (covered later in this chapter.).

To "unrotate" an object, enter a Rotation Angle value of **0**.

Sometimes, rotated objects — especially those containing text — can be hard to edit in the regular view of a page. InDesign thus lets you rotate a spread so that you can view it at 90-, 180-, and 270-degree views — in addition to the standard 0-degree view, of course. Note that the actual spread isn't rotated, just its appearance in InDesign; it still prints correctly. Note the rotation icon that appears in the Pages panel to the right of the rotated spread.

You can rotate a spread's view in two ways:

✔ Choose View⇨Rotate Spread, and then choose the desired rotation amount from the submenu.

✔ Select the desired spread for which to rotate its view in the Pages panel, and then choose Rotate Spread View and the desired rotation amount from the submenu.

To set the view back to normal, choose the Clear Rotation option in the submenu.

Shearing objects

With the Shear tool selected, click and drag a selected object to shear it. (Holding down the Shift key constrains the selected object's rotation value to increments of 45 degrees.) If you drag the mouse in a straight line parallel with one set of edges (such as the top and bottom), you skew the graphic (just slant it in one direction). But if you move the mouse in any other direction, you slant the object's edges closest to the direction that you move the mouse the farthest and rotate the rest of the graphic. Give it a few tries to see what happens.

As with other functions, you can also use the Control panel for more precise control. Just enter a Shear X Angle value in the Control panel or choose a predefined value from the field's pop-up menu. Positive shear values slant an object to the right (that is, the top edge of the object is moved to the right), whereas negative values slant an object to the left (the bottom edge is moved to the right). You can enter shear values between 1 and 89 (although values above 70 cause considerable distortion).Note that when you use the Shear tool, you change the selected object's angle of rotation *and* skew angle simultaneously. If you use the mouse, you can in effect get different skew and rotation angles based on how you move the mouse, but if you use the Control panel, both the skew and rotation will have the same angles applied.

To "unshear" an object, enter a Shear X Angle value of **0**.

Flipping objects

The Object menu has two flipping commands: Object⇨Transform⇨Flip Horizontal and Object⇨Transform⇨Flip Vertical. They're also available in the Control panel as iconic buttons (refer to Figure 8-3).

Using the Free Transform tool

Advanced users will like the Free Transform tool. When you select this tool, InDesign lets you scale, rotate, and resize — but not shear — selected objects — as follows:

✔ If you click within the frame, you can move the object by dragging it.

✔ If you select a frame handle (whether corner or midpoint), you can resize the object by dragging.

✔ Finally, if you move the mouse close to a frame handle, you see a curved arrow, which indicates that you can rotate the object around that object's center point.

Having a tool that does more than one thing can be confusing, but once you get the hang of it, it sure beats constantly changing tools!

These controls let you make a mirror image of a selected object and its contents. If you choose Flip Horizontal, the graphic is flipped along a vertical axis (that is, the right edge and left edge exchange places); if you choose Flip Vertical, the object is flipped upside down. (You're not making a flipped copy of the select object, but actually flipping the selected object.)

As with other tools, the invisible line over which an object is flipped is based on what reference point is currently active as the control point for that object.

The Control panel displays the current object's flip status. (Look for the large *P* in the panel when an object is selected; it's to the right of the two flip buttons.) The *P* changes appearance so that it's flipped the same way as the selected object.

Repeating transformations

Whatever transformations you use, you can apply them repeatedly. InDesign remembers the effects that you apply to frames via the Control panel, Transform panel, and transform tools. Choose Object⇨Transform Again⇨Transform Again (Option+⌘+3 or Ctrl+Alt+3) to repeat the last transformation on the selected object. (It can be a different object than you last applied a transformation to.)

Or choose Object⇨Transform Again⇨Transform Sequence Again (Option+⌘+4 or Ctrl+Alt+4) to apply all recent transformations to a selected object. That sequence of transactions stays in memory until you perform a new transformation, which then starts a new sequence, so you can apply the same transformation to multiple objects.

Two other transform-again options are available through the Object⇨ Transform Again menu option's submenu: Transform Again Individually and Transform Sequence Again Individually. You use these options on groups; they work like the regular Transform Again and Transform Sequence Again options but apply any effects to each object individually within the group. For example, applying Transform Again to a group rotates the entire group as if it were one unit, but choosing Transform Again Individually rotates each object in the group separately, not the group as a unit. Try it and see exactly what it does!

Replacing Object Attributes

A really painstaking task in any layout is going through it to fix formatting to frames, lines, or other objects once the design standards have changed. InDesign has a very handy way to apply object formatting consistently to objects — the object styles feature described in Chapter 9 — but even if you use these styles, you'll still have local formatting applied to at least some objects.

That's where the Object pane of the Find/Replace dialog box comes in, letting you replace attributes throughout your document, no matter what they're applied to. Figure 8-4 shows that pane.

Here's how it works:

1. **Open the Find/Change dialog box by choosing Edit⇨Find/Change (⌘+F or Ctrl+F), and then go to the Object pane.**

2. **Select the desired object attributes and click OK when you're done.**

   To do so, click the Specify Attributes to Find iconic button to the right of the Find Object Format list. In the dialog box that appears (see Figure 8-5), select the attributes to search (choose one category at a time from the list at left and then set the desired parameters in the pane that appears) and click OK when you're done.

   Highlight an attribute in the list and click the Clear Object Find Format Settings iconic button — the trashcan icon — if you want to remove an attribute from your search. (This dialog box is nearly identical to the New Object Style dialog box covered in Chapter 9.)

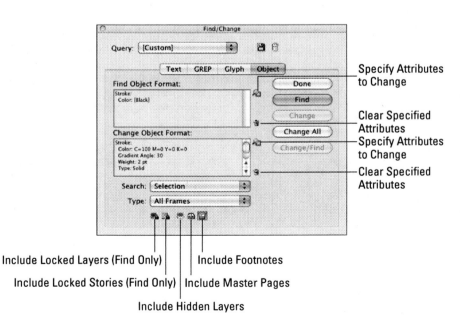

Figure 8-4: The Find/ Change dialog box's Object pane (upper left) and its Find Object Format dialog box (lower right).

Include Locked Layers (Find Only)
Include Locked Stories (Find Only)
Include Hidden Layers
Include Footnotes
Include Master Pages

3. **If you're replacing attributes, click the Specify Attributes to Change iconic button to the right of the Change Object Format list.**

   These controls work like the Find Object Format controls.

4. **Limit or expand the search range by choosing an option from the Search pop-up menu: Selection, Document, and All Documents.**

5. **Choose the type of frames to search in the Type pop-up menu: All Frames, Text Frames, Graphic Frames, and Unassigned Frames.**

6. **Determine the scope of your search by selecting or deselecting any of the five buttons at the bottom of the pane.**

   From left to right, the five buttons are Include Locked Layers, Include Locked Stories, Include Hidden Layers, Include Master Pages, and Include Footnotes. Note that the first two buttons apply only to finds; you can't change the formatting of locked objects. (If an icon's background darkens, it's selected.)

7. **Click Find, Change, Change All, or Change/Find as desired to perform your search and/or replace operation.**

8. **Click Done when done.**

Making Fancy Corners

Anytime you're working on an object that has any sharp corners, you have the option to add a little pizzazz to those corners via InDesign's Corner Options feature (Object⇨Corner Options). Figure 8-5 shows a five-sided shape at upper left and a version for each corner option of that shape to the original shape's right. (The figure also shows the Corner Options dialog box.) Note that if the shape contains only smooth points, any corner option you apply won't be noticeable.

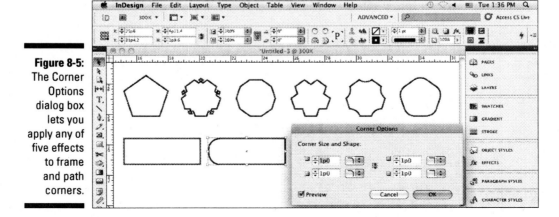

Figure 8-5:
The Corner Options dialog box lets you apply any of five effects to frame and path corners.

To add a corner option:

1. **Select either of the selection tools and click the object to which you want to add a corner effect.**

2. **Choose Object⇨Corner Options to display the Corner Options dialog box.**

   Select the Preview check box to view changes as you make them.

3. **Choose an option from the Shape pop-up menu.**

4. **Enter a distance in the Size field.**

   The Size value determines the length that the effect extends from the corner. You can also use the new nudge buttons to increase or decrease the sizes in increments. (The increments depend on the default measurement unit selected; see Chapter 2.)

   If you deselect the Make All Settings the Same option (the chain iconic button), you can adjust corner options separately for each corner. (If the iconic button in the center of the dialog box is a broken chain, Make All Settings the Same is deselected.)

5. **Click OK to close the dialog box and apply your changes.**

If you can't see a corner effect after applying one, make sure that a color is applied to the stroke or try making the object's stroke thicker. Increasing the Size value in the Corner Options dialog box can also make a corner effect more visible.

You can also edit corners on objects, in two ways.

First, as with any object in InDesign, you can edit its frame, adding, moving, and deleting points on its paths, as Chapter 7 explains.

Second, InDesign CS5 also lets you change corner options on rectangular text and graphics frames using the mouse, saving you a trip to the Corner Options dialog box. To do so, follow these steps:

1. **Make sure that the live corner indicator is turned on by choosing View⇨Extras⇨Show Live Corners.**

   If the menu option is Hide Live Corners, the indicator is already turned on.

2. **Select a rectangular frame with the Selection tool.**

   Note the yellow square that appears on the upper-right side of the frame's edge, as Figure 8-6 shows.

3. **Click the yellow square to enter live corner-editing mode.**

   Yellow diamonds appear at each corner, as Figure 8-6 shows.

4. **Drag any corner to change its corner size.**

   Drag away from the corner to reduce its size and toward the frame's center to increase it. To change just the selected corner's radius, hold Shift while dragging.

5. **Option+click or Alt+click any corner to change its shape.**

   Each Option+click or Alt+click cycles to the next shape. Shift+Option+click or Alt+Shift+click a corner to change just that corner's shape.

6. **Click elsewhere in the document to exit live corner-editing mode.**

Figure 8-6 shows the live corner editing process, from left to right: I clicked the live-corner indicator on the upper-right side of a rectangular frame. Yellow diamonds then appeared at each corner. I dragged a diamond to change the corner size. I then Shift+dragged a diamond to change the corner size of just that corner.

Figure 8-6:
Live corner editing in action (each step is shown, from left to right).

Using Transparency and Lighting Effects

InDesign was a pioneer in the use of transparency effects on objects. These effects let you overlay objects without completely obscuring them, allowing for very interesting visual effects, such as fades and shadows. It provides rich controls over transparency and lighting so that you can create effects such as embossing and beveled edges *and* control the intensity and direction of shadows and light.

Basic transparency

One of InDesign's most sophisticated tools is its set of transparency options, which let you make objects partially transparent. You apply transparency with the Effects panel (Window⇨Effects [Shift+⌘+F10 or Ctrl+Shift+F10]), by choosing Object➪Effects➪Transparency, or by clicking the Effects iconic button (the *fx* icon) in the Control panel and choosing Transparency from its pop-up menu.

The first option displays the Effects panel, which takes the least screen space and is best used for simple operations. The other options open the more complex and larger Effects dialog box. (Be sure that the Transparency pane is visible in the Effects dialog box; if not, click the Transparency option in the option list at left.)

Figure 8-7 shows the Effects panel as well as a text title that uses transparency as it overprints a background photo. The photo has an Opacity setting of 40 percent, making it partially transparent. The text has an Opacity setting of 65 percent but also has a blending mode applied, which changes how the transparency appears.

To set the transparency level, in the Opacity field of the Effects panel or Effects dialog box's Transparency pane, enter a value or choose one from the pop-up menu. A value of 0 is completely invisible, whereas a value of 100 is completely solid.

You can't apply transparency to text selections or to entire layers, but InDesign does let you apply different transparency settings to an object's contents, fill, and stroke, as well as to the object itself. You do so by choosing the desired component in the list in the Effects panel or using the Settings For pop-up menu in the Effects dialog box. (If you see only Object listed in the Effects panel, click the right-facing triangle to its left to display the rest.)

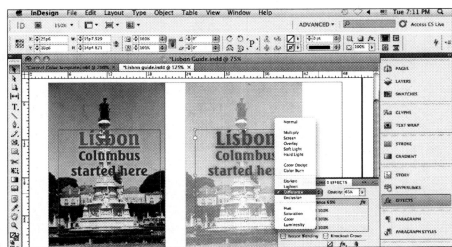

Figure 8-7:
The Effects panel and its flyout menu (right), as well as transparency applied to the image and text (the original objects are at left).

If you want more than basic transparency, you have a lot of other options. Most are for experts, but a few are worth describing. One is the set of 16 transparency types — called *blending modes*. (Photoshop and Illustrator users will recognize these expert options.) You access blending modes in the pop-up menu in the Effects panel or via the Mode pop-up menu on the Effects dialog box's Transparency pane. The differences among them can be subtle or extreme, depending on a variety of issues. Experiment with them to see what effect works best in each case.

The Difference, Exclusion, Hue, Saturation, Color, and Luminosity modes don't blend spot colors — only process colors.

You have two other options in the Effects panel and in the Transparency pane of the Effects dialog box:

- ✔ **Isolate Blending** restricts the blending modes to the objects in a group, instead of also applying them to objects beneath the group. This option can prevent unintended changes to those underlying objects.

- ✔ **Knockout Group** obscures any objects below the selected group. But those objects are still affected by any blend mode settings applied to the group, unless Isolate Blending is also checked.

Drop shadows and inner shadows

The Effects panel and dialog box, as well as the Object➪Effects menu command, give you access to a bunch of other lighting features, including drop shadows.

To get to these other lighting features, choose Effects➪Drop Shadow from the Effects panel's flyout menu or choose Drop Shadow from the *fx* iconic button's pop-up menu. In the Effects dialog box, select Drop Shadow from the option list at left. Or just press Option+⌘+M or Ctrl+Alt+M. No matter how you get there, you see the following options in the Drop Shadow pane of the Effects dialog box:

- ✔ Choose what component of the object to apply the drop shadow to by using the Settings For pop-up menu. (You can apply multiple drop shadows, one to each component of an object.)

- ✔ Enable the Drop Shadow check box option to turn on the drop shadow function for the selected component.

- ✔ Select a lighting type (technically, a *blend mode*) by choosing one of the 16 options in the Mode pop-up menu. (These blending modes are the same ones used for transparencies.)

✔ Specify the opacity by entering a value in the Opacity field — 0% is invisible, whereas 100% is completely solid.

✔ Specify the shadow's position relative to the object by using the X Offset and Y Offset fields. A positive X Offset moves the shadow to the right; a positive Y Offset moves the shadow down. Negative values go in the other direction.

✔ Specify the shadow's size by entering a value in the Distance field — this option blurs a copy of the object used in the drop shadow to make it look like it was created by shining light on the object.

✔ Choose a lighting angle in the Angle field or use the mouse to move the direction within the circle to determine the direction of the shadow. You can also select the Use Global Light option, which then uses whatever settings you define in the Global Light dialog box — a handy way to have consistent settings for all objects. (Choose Object⇨Effects⇨Global Light, or choose Global Light from the Effects panel's flyout menu, to open the Global Light dialog box.)

✔ Choose a color source — Swatches, RGB, CMYK, or Lab — from the Color pop-up menu in the Effect Color dialog box, which you get by clicking the color swatch to the right of the Mode pop-up menu, and then select a color from the sliders or swatches below that menu. You get sliders for RGB, CMYK, and Lab colors, or a set of previously defined color swatches if you selected Swatches in the Color pop-up menu.

✔ Adjust the other settings, if desired, to control other, expert drop shadow characteristics: Size, Spread, Noise, Object Knocks Out Shadow, and Shadow Honors Other Effects.

✔ To see the effects of your various setting adjustments in the actual layout, check the Preview option. (Because the Effects dialog box is so big, you'll likely need a large monitor to have room for both the dialog box and the object you're applying the effects to.)

InDesign has a second shadow option: inner shadows. It works pretty much like drop shadows, with a nearly identical pane in the Effects dialog box. The visual difference is that an inner shadow is contained within the object, as if the frames were cut out from the surface of the paper, whereas a drop shadow occurs outside the frame, as if the frame were casting a shadow outside.

Feathering and other lighting effects

A similar option to drop shadows is *feathering,* which essentially softens the edges of objects. Three types of feathering are available:

✔ **Basic feathering:** This option softens the edges on all sides of an object.

✔ **Directional feathering:** This option lets you control the direction of the feathering as well as separate feather widths for each side, creating a smeared-border effect.

✔ **Gradient feathering:** This option provides a gradient effect to the feathered area.

The other effects are outer glow, inner glow, bevel and emboss, and satin. Figure 8-8 shows examples of each.

You apply them the same ways as you do drop shadows, selecting the object component in the Settings For pop-up menu and modifying the various controls such as opacity, light angle and distance, blending mode, and effect size, as appropriate for the specific effect. Once you get a hang for transparency and drop shadows, it's easy to use the other effects.

Figure 8-8: Various effects applied to a set of objects. Top row: The original object, drop shadow, and inner shadow. Second row: Basic feather, directional feather, and gradient feather. Third row: Outer glow and inner glow. Bottom row: Bevel and emboss, and satin.

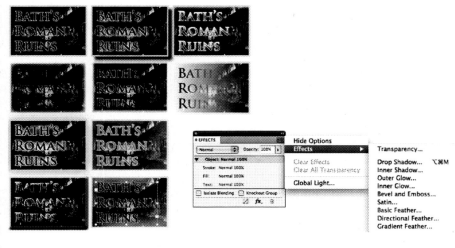

Chapter 9

Organizing Objects

*Y*ou use objects throughout your layout: lines, text frames, graphics frames, shapes, and so on. A big part of working with them involves organizing them — deciding when to group them together, when to lock them in location, how to arrange objects with others, and so on. That's where this chapter comes in.

I also explain a powerful new feature called object styles that lets you save object attributes. Then I show you how to manage objects' relations with their source files, so that you can make sure that you're using the correct version of your graphics and text. Finally, I explain a new feature in InDesign CS5 that lets you create automatic captions for imported graphics.

Combining Objects into a Group

Groups have many uses. For example, you can create a group to

✔ Combine several objects that make up an illustration so that you can move, modify, copy, or scale all objects in a single operation.

✔ Keep a graphics frame and its accompanying caption (text) frame together so that you can reposition both objects at once if you change your mind about their placement.

✔ Combine several vertical lines that are used to separate the columns of a table so that you can quickly change the stroke, color, length, and position of all lines.

InDesign lets you combine several objects into a group. A group of objects behaves like a single object, which means that you can cut, copy, move, or modify all the objects in a group in a single operation.

To create a group, select all the objects (which can include other groups) that you want to include in your group and then choose Object⇨Group (⌘+G or Ctrl+G).

Keep in mind the following when creating groups:

- ✔ If you create a group from objects on different layers, all objects are moved to the top layer and stacked in succession beneath the topmost object.

- ✔ You can't create a group if some of the selected objects are locked and some aren't locked. All selected objects must be locked or unlocked before you can group them. (Locking and unlocking objects are covered in the following section.)

If you want to manipulate a group, choose the Selection tool and then click any object in the group. The group's bounding box appears. Any transformation you perform is applied to all objects in the group.

If you want to manipulate a specific object in a group, use the Direct Selection tool to select that object. If you want to change something that requires the Selection tool to be active, switch to it by selecting the Selection tool or simply by double-clicking the object. (See Chapter 8 for more details on selecting objects.)

If you remove an object applied (via cut and paste or copy and paste) from a group that had transparency, that pasted object will not retain the group's transparency settings.

After creating a group, you may eventually decide that you want to return the objects to their original, ungrouped state. To do so, simply click any object in the group with the Selection tool and then choose Object⇨Ungroup (Shift+⌘+G or Ctrl+Shift+G). If you ungroup a group that contains a group, the contained group isn't affected. To ungroup this group, you must select it and choose Ungroup again.

Locking and Unlocking Objects

If you're certain that you want a particular object to remain exactly where it is, you can select Object⇨Lock (⌘+L or Ctrl+L) to prevent the object from being moved. Generally, you want to lock repeating elements such as headers, footers, folios, and page numbers so that they're not accidentally moved.

(Such repeating elements are usually placed on a master page; you can lock objects on master pages, too.)

A locked object can't be moved whether you click and drag it with the mouse or change the values in the X: and Y: fields in the Control panel or Transform panel. Not only can you *not* move a locked object, but you can't delete it, either. However, you can select a locked object to change other attributes, such as its stroke and fill.

InDesign CS5 lets you make locked objects unselectable: In the General pane of the Preferences dialog box (InDesign➪Preferences [⌘+K] on the Mac or Edit➪Preferences [Ctrl+K] in Windows), select the Prevent Selection of Locked Objects option.

In InDesign CS5, you can no longer unlock a specific locked object. Instead, you have to unlock all locked objects on the current spread by choosing Object➪Unlock All on Spread (Option+⌘+L or Ctrl+Alt+L).

You can also lock entire layers, as described in Chapter 4.

Working with Object Styles

Object styles let you organize your settings so that you can apply them to other objects for consistent, easy formatting.

Object styles are underappreciated and underused, rarely used in real-world documents. That's a pity because the use of styles for object formatting — not just text formatting — makes your work easier by automatically and reliably applying time-consuming settings to multiple objects and ensuring that your object formatting is both consistent and easily managed.

Creating object styles

You create object styles by using the Object Styles panel (Window➪Styles➪ Object Styles [⌘+F7 or Ctrl+F7]) and selecting New Object Style from the flyout menu, shown in Figure 9-1. You can also click the New Object Style iconic button at the bottom of the panel.

The simplest way to create an object style is to select an already-formatted object with any selection tool and then choose New Object Style from the Object Styles panel's flyout menu. InDesign records all the settings from the selected object so that they're in place for the new object style.

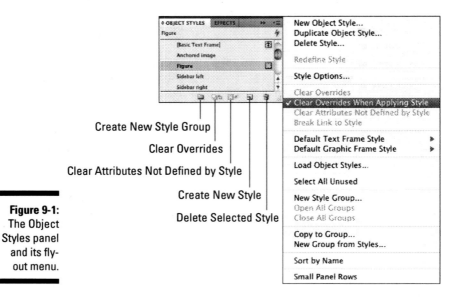

Create New Style Group

Clear Overrides

Clear Attributes Not Defined by Style

Create New Style

Delete Selected Style

Figure 9-1:
The Object
Styles panel
and its fly-
out menu.

Whether you start with an existing object or create a new object style completely from scratch, you use the New Object Style menu option that opens the New Object Style dialog box shown in Figure 9-2.

At the left side of the dialog box is a list of types of attributes that are or can be set. The checked items are in use for this style — you can uncheck an item so that InDesign doesn't apply its settings to objects using the style. For example, if Fill is unchecked, the object style won't apply any Fill settings to objects using that style (and won't change any fill settings that have been applied to that object locally).

To switch from one type of attribute to another, click the item name for the type of attribute that you want to adjust, such as Stroke or Transparency.

Select the Preview option to see the results of object styles on the currently selected object. (Of course, make sure that the object is visible on-screen.)

When you open the New Object Style dialog box, you see the General pane, which lets you create a new style based on an existing object style (by using the Based On pop-up menu), and which lets you assign a keyboard shortcut for fast application of this style (by using the Shortcuts field).

You can use the Based On feature to create families of object styles. For example, you can create a style called *Photo-Standard* for the bulk of your placed photographs and then create variations, such as *Photo-Sidebar* and *Photo-Author*. The Photo-Standard style might specify a hairline black stroke around the photo, while Photo-Sidebar may change that to a white stroke. But if you later decide you want the stroke to be 1 point and change it in Photo-Standard, Photo-Sidebar automatically gets the 1-point stroke while retaining the white color.

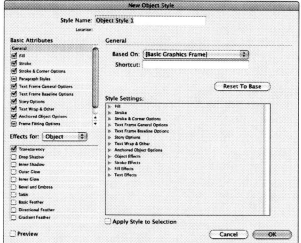

Figure 9-2:
The New Object Style dialog box and its General pane.

The General pane also lets you see the current style settings. Click any of the arrows in the Style Settings section to get more details on how they're set for this object style.

The other panes in the New Object Styles dialog box provide the same capabilities that you find elsewhere in InDesign, brought into one convenient place so that you can use them in styles. Because it has so many panes, the New Object Style dialog box now breaks them into two sections. The first section — Basic Attributes — contains the following panes:

✔ **The Fill pane** lets you set colors for fills using whatever colors are defined in the Swatches panel. You can also set the tint and, if you select a gradient fill, the angle for that gradient. Finally, you can choose to have the fill overprint the contents of the frame by selecting the Overprint Fill option.

✔ **The Stroke pane** is identical to the Fill pane except that options specific to fills are grayed out, and options available to strokes are made available. The color, tint, and gradient angle options are the same as for the Fill pane. You can also choose the type of stroke (solid line, dashed line, or dotted line) by using the Type pop-up menu and adjust the thickness by filling in the Weight field. You can choose to overprint the stroke over underlying content, plus determine — if your stroke is a dotted or dashed line — the color, tint, and overprint for the gap.

✔ **The Stroke & Corner Options pane** lets you set stroke position and how corners and line ends are handled. It also lets you apply fancy corners to frames. The Stroke Options section is where you align the strokes to the frame edges, determine how lines join at corners, and decide what line endings are applied. The Corner Options section is where you select from five fancy corners, such as Bevel and Rounded, by using the Effect pop-up menu, and where you specify the radius, or reach, of the corner by using the Size field. (See Chapter 7 for the low-down on strokes and Chapter 8 for the skinny on corner options.)

✔ **The Paragraph Styles pane** controls what paragraph style, if any, is applied to text in the frame. Chances are you won't use this setting except for frames that contain only consistent, very simple text, such as pull-quotes or bios. (See Chapter 13 for details.)

✔ **The Text Frame General Options pane** controls how text is handled within a frame. This pane essentially replicates the controls in the General pane of the Text Frame Options dialog box (Object⇨Text Frame Options [⌘+B or Ctrl+B]), including number of columns, column width, gutter settings, *inset spacing* (how far from the frame edge text is placed), *vertical justification* (how text is aligned vertically in the frame), and whether text wrap settings are ignored when this frame overlaps other frames. (See Chapter 11 for details on the Text Frame Options dialog box.)

✔ **The Text Frame Baseline Options pane** controls how text is handled within a frame. This pane essentially replicates the controls in the Baseline Options pane of the Text Box Options dialog box (Object⇨Text Frame Options or ⌘+B or Ctrl+B), including how the text baseline is calculated for the frame and whether the text frame gets its own baseline grid. (See Chapter 10 for details.)

✔ **The Story Options pane** enables optical margin alignment — its controls are the same as in the Story panel (Type⇨Story), an expert feature not covered in this book. Optical margin alignment adjusts the placement of text along the left side of a frame so that the text alignment is more visually pleasing.

✔ **The Text Wrap & Other pane** lets you set text wrap, mirroring the features of the Text Wrap panel (Window⇨Text Wrap [Option+⌘+W or Ctrl+Alt+W]), explained in Chapter 11, as well as make an object non-printing (normally handled through the Attributes panel by choosing Window⇨Attributes).

✔ **The Anchored Object Options pane** lets you set the attributes for inline and anchored frames, mirroring the controls in the Anchored Object Options dialog box (Object⇨Anchored Object⇨Options), which I explain in Chapter 10.

✔ **The Frame Fitting Options pane** lets you set the defaults for how frames fit to the graphics and text placed in them, mirroring the controls in the Frame Fitting Options dialog box (Object⇨Fitting⇨Frame Fitting Options), as explained in Chapter 17.

The second set of panes all relate to the features found in the Effects dialog box and panel, as covered in Chapter 8.

Managing object styles

The Object Styles panel's flyout menu (refer to Figure 9-1) has several options for managing object styles:

✔ **Duplicate Object Style:** Click an object style's name and then choose this menu option to create an exact copy. If you want to create an object style that's similar to one you already created, you may want to choose New Object Style rather than Duplicate Object Style and then use the Based On option to create a child of the original. If you choose Duplicate Object Style, the copy is identical to, but not based on, the original; if you modify the original, the copy isn't affected.

✔ **Delete Style:** Choose this option to delete selected object styles. To select multiple styles, press and hold ⌘ or Ctrl as you click their names. To select a range of styles, click the first one and then press and hold Shift and click the last one. You can also delete styles by selecting them in the pane and then clicking the Delete Selected Styles iconic button (the trashcan icon) at the bottom of the panel.

✔ **Redefine Style:** To modify an existing object style, make changes to an object that has an object style defined for it and then select Redefine Style. The newly applied formats are applied to the object style.

✔ **Style Options:** This option lets you modify an existing object style. When a style is highlighted in the Object Styles panel, choosing Style Options displays the Object Style Options dialog box, which is identical to the New Object Style dialog box.

✔ **Load Object Styles:** Choose this option if you want to import object styles from another InDesign document. After selecting the document from which to import the styles, you get a dialog box listing the styles in the chosen document so that you can decide which ones to import. Note the Incoming Style Definitions window at the bottom of the dialog box; it lists the style definitions to help you decide which to import, as well as which to overwrite or rename.

InDesign comes with three predefined object styles — [Basic Text Frame], [Basic Graphics Frame], and [Basic Grid] — that you can modify as desired.

Applying object styles

After you create an object style, it's a simple process to apply it: Just click an object and then click the object style name in the Object Styles panel or press its keyboard shortcut. (Windows users must make sure that Num Lock is on when using shortcuts for styles.)

You can set which object styles are automatically used for new text and graphics frames: In the Object Styles panel's flyout menu, choose Default Text Frame Style and select the desired style from the submenu to set a default text frame; choose Default Graphic Frame Style and select the desired style from the submenu to set a default graphics frame. To no longer have object styles automatically applied to new objects, choose [None] in the Default Text Frame and/or Default Graphic Frame submenus.

When you apply an object style to selected objects, all local formats are retained. All other formats are replaced by those of the applied style — that is, unless you do one of the following:

✔ If you press and hold Option or Alt when clicking a name in the Object Styles panel, any local formatting that has been applied to the objects is removed. You can achieve the same effect by choosing Clear Attributes Not Defined by Style from the Object Styles panel's flyout menu or by clicking the Clear Attributes Not Defined by Style iconic button at the bottom of the Object Styles panel.

✔ If you want to override any local changes with the settings in the object style, choose Clear Overrides in the flyout menu or click the Clear Overrides iconic button at the bottom of the Object Styles panel. The difference is that Clear Attributes Not Defined by Style removes all attributes for which the object style contains no settings, whereas Clear Overrides imposes the object style's settings over conflicting attributes that you set manually.

✔ To have InDesign automatically override local changes when applying a style, be sure the Clear Overrides When Applying Style flyout menu option is checked. Choosing the item toggles between selecting (checking) and deselecting (unchecking) this option.

If a plus sign (+) appears to the right of an object style's name, it means that the object has local formats that differ from those of the applied object style. This formatting difference can occur if you apply an object style to object text to which you've done some manual formatting, or if you modify formatting for an object after applying an object style to it. (For example, you may have changed the fill color, which is a local change to the object style and causes the + to appear.)

Using the Eyedropper to apply formatting

You can apply the formatting of one object onto another using the Eyedropper tool. Select the Eyedropper tool in the Tools panel, then click the object whose formatting you want to copy with the Eyedropper tool.

The Eyedropper tool then becomes the Marker tool. Click the object you want to apply the first object's formatting to. You can continue to click other objects with the Marker tool to apply the same formatting to them.

To switch back to the Eyedropper to sample something else, press and hold Option or Alt,

then click the new source object. You can also select the Eyedropper tool in the Tools panel; in that case, you don't have to hold Option or Alt.

For objects, the following attributes are applied to the objects you click with the Marker tool: strokes, fills, effects such as transparency and drop shadows, corner options, text wraps, and settings from the Attributes panel. Attributes such as rotation, flipping, animation, frame-fitting options, and button states are not applied.

To remove a style from an object, choose Break Link to Style from the Object Styles panel's flyout menu. The object's current formatting won't be affected, but it will no longer be updated when the object style is changed.

Managing object styles

InDesign lets you manage your styles, such as creating groups of styles to make it easier to find relevant ones, and bring in styles from other documents. Because these features work the same for paragraph, character, table, and cell styles as well, I cover these features in one place: Chapter 13.

Managing Links

The Links panel (Window⇨Links [Shift+⌘+D or Ctrl+Shift+D]) is a handy place to manage the links to your graphics and text, particularly when you need to update them. Figure 9-3 shows the Links panel.

Missing-file indicator

Changed-file indicator | Status sort button

Name sort button | Page sort button

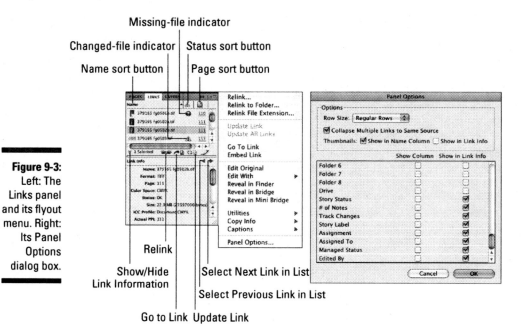

Relink

Show/Hide
Link Information

Select Next Link in List

Select Previous Link in List

Go to Link Update Link

Figure 9-3:
Left: The
Links panel
and its flyout
menu. Right:
Its Panel
Options
dialog box.

InDesign always creates links for graphics files. But it creates links to source text files (including spreadsheets) only when the Create Links When Placing Text and Spreadsheet Files option is checked in the File Handling pane of the Preferences dialog box (InDesign⇨Preferences⇨File Handling [⌘+K] on the Mac, or Edit⇨Preferences⇨File Handling [Ctrl+K] in Windows). This option is *not* checked by default because many designers don't want text files easily updated in their layouts. That's because all the formatting they've done to the file in InDesign is removed when the link to the source file is updated, causing the text to be replaced.

The first four sets of commands in the Links panel's flyout menu let you reestablish links to missing and modified files, display an imported graphic or text file in the document window, open the program used to create a graphic or text file, and work on copies and versions of the source graphics and text:

✔ **Relink:** This command, and the Relink iconic button (at the bottom of the panel), lets you reestablish a missing link or replace the original file you imported with a different file. When you choose Relink or click the button, the Relink dialog box is displayed and shows the original pathname and filename. You can enter a new pathname and filename in the Location field, but clicking Browse is easier, which opens a standard Open a File dialog box. Use the controls to locate and select the original file or a different file, and then click OK. (You can also drag and drop a file icon from the Mac OS Finder or Windows Explorer directly into the Relink dialog box.) If you want to restore broken links to multiple files simultaneously, highlight their filenames in the scroll list and then choose Relink or click the Update Link button.

To relink all instances of a file in your layout, so you only have to do the operation once, be sure to hold Option or Alt when clicking the Relink command or Relink iconic button.

✔ **Relink to Folder:** This command lets you relink multiple files at the same time, and even change the type of graphic files to use at the same time. First, be sure to select all files in the panel you want to relink — only selected files will be updated. Then choose this option and navigate to the folder that has the files. If the filenames in the new folder match the filenames of the selected files in the panel, InDesign updates them. (It leaves alone any it can't find.)

Notice that the Open a File dialog box that appears when you choose this command contains an option called Match This Filename But This Extension. Say that someone gave you JPEG files as placeholders for your layout and then delivered the final TIFF files for high-quality print output. In all previous versions of InDesign, you had to relink every single file manually. Now, you can use this option and enter TIFF (or TIF, depending on the filename extension used) to substitute the high-quality TIFF files for the original low-quality JPEG files. That's a real timesaver! (Note that the new file can be any format supported by InDesign, not just TIFF.)

✔ **Relink File Extension:** This new command lets you relink to a file of the same name and location but with a different filename extension. It's the same capability that the Relink to Folder command offers, but with a simpler dialog box that changes nothing else.

✔ **Update Link:** Choose this option or click the Update Link iconic button (at the bottom of the panel) to update the link to a modified graphic or text file. Highlight multiple filenames and then choose Update Link or click the Update Link button to update all those links at once.

✔ **Update All Links:** Choose this option to update all files marked as modified, without having to select individual files.

✔ **Go to Link:** Choose this option or click the Go to Link iconic button (second from left) in the panel to display the highlighted file in the document window. InDesign will, if necessary, navigate to the correct page and center the frame in the document window.

✔ **Embed Link (for graphics only):** This option lets you embed the complete file of any imported graphics file. (InDesign normally imports only a low-resolution screen preview when you place a graphic that is 48K or larger.) If you want to ensure that the graphics file will forever remain with a document, you can choose to embed it — however, by embedding graphics, you'll be producing larger document files, which means it will take you longer to open and save them. If you do use this option, an alert appears to inform you about the increased document size that will result. Click Yes to embed the file. Note that this menu option changes to Unembed File, so you can re-enable the original link at any time.

- ✓ **Unlink (for text files only):** This option removes the link to the source text file, so it can't be updated. Note that you can't undo this option from the Links panel; you have to choose Edit➪Undo (⌘+Z or Ctrl+Z). And this option is available only if you enabled text linking via the Create Links When Placing Text and Spreadsheet Files option in the File Handling pane of the Preferences dialog box.

- ✓ **Edit Original:** If you want to modify an imported graphic or text file, choose Edit Original from the flyout menu or click the Edit Original button (far right) at the bottom of the panel. InDesign tries to locate and open the program used to create the file, which may or may not be possible, depending on the original program, the file format, and the programs available on your computer.

- ✓ **Edit With:** This menu option lets you choose what program to edit a select object with.

- ✓ **Reveal in Finder (Macintosh) and Reveal in Explorer (Windows):** This menu option opens a window displaying the contents of the folder that contains the source file, so you can perhaps move, copy, or rename it. (The Reveal in Bridge option is a similar feature for the expert Adobe Bridge companion program not covered in this book.)

- ✓ **Reveal in Bridge and Reveal in Mini Bridge:** These menu options open the Bridge and Mini Bridge, respectively, and display the file there, giving you access to their file preview and management capabilities.

When you relink missing and update modified graphics, any transformations — rotation, shear, scale, and so on — that you've applied to the graphics or their frames are maintained, unless you've deselected the new Preserve Image Dimensions When Relinking option in the File Handling pane of the Preferences dialog box (InDesign➪Preferences➪File Handling [⌘+K] on the Mac, or Edit➪ Preferences➪File Handling [Ctrl+K] in Windows).

The Utilities and Copy Info menu options in the Links panel's flyout menu provide access to several expert features not covered in this book.

You can control what appears in the Links panel using the Panel Options option in the flyout menu. In the Panel Options dialog box (refer to Figure 9-3), you can specify what information appears with each filename, including whether icons of the file contents display.

Finally, you can see extensive information about the file in the Link Info section of the Links panel, containing all the attributes that are also available in Adobe's Bridge, such as file dimensions and color profile. To toggle this information off, just click the Show/Hide Item Information iconic button at the bottom left of the Links panel.

Adding Metadata Captions

The Links panel contains a new menu option, Captions, that lets you create captions for your images. These captions use link information — called *metadata* — as their basis. Some of that metadata is added as files are created (such as the filename and the image resolution); other metadata can be added in programs such as Adobe Bridge that use a metadata standard called XMP.

Being based on metadata limits when you can use this feature. You can't, for example, use it to create free-form captions; you would create those by adding a text frame and entering or placing text in it, then positioning that caption next to your image and perhaps grouping it with the graphics frame so it moves with the graphic.

But metadata captions are helpful for captions that are based on metadata vcontained in the image file, such as copyright notices, photographer credits, or creation dates.

The caption setup applies to all linked images in your document — you can't set separate caption-creation rules for different images.

To set up metadata captions, follow these steps:

1. **Choose Captions⇨Caption Setup in the Links panel's flyout menu.**

   The Caption Setup dialog box, shown in Figure 9-4, appears. Here, you build the caption.

2. **Choose the metadata you want the caption to include, using the unnamed pop-up menu.**

3. **Add any text that should precede the metadata in the Text Before field and/or any text that should follow the metadata in the Text After field.**

   Both fields have right-facing arrow buttons that open menus that let you choose special characters to include in your text. You can add additional lines to the caption by clicking the + button to the right of the Text After field; click – to delete a line.

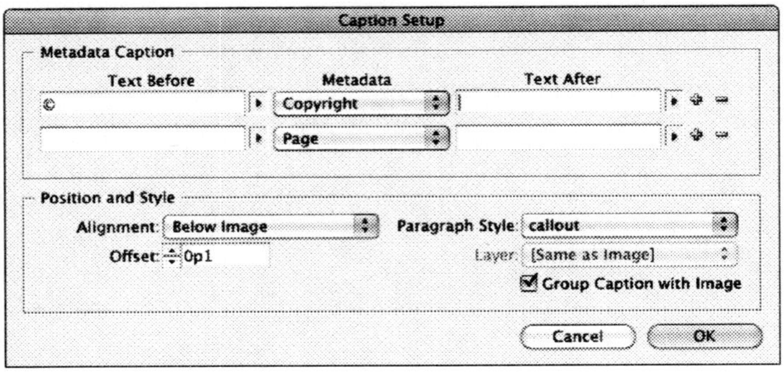

Caption Setup

Metadata Caption

Text Before	Metadata	Text After
©	Copyright	
	Page	

Position and Style

Alignment: Below Image   Paragraph Style: callout

Offset: 0p1   Layer: [Same as Image]

☑ Group Caption with Image

Cancel   OK

Figure 9-4:
The Caption Setup dialog box.

- Use the Position and Style area of the Caption Setup dialog box to control the caption's appearance.

- Use the Alignment pop-up menu to set how the caption's text frame is positioned relevant to the graphics frame: Below Image, Above Image, Right of Image, or Left of Image.

- Use the Offset field to determine how far the caption's text frame is from the graphics frame.

- You can assign a paragraph style to the caption text using the Paragraph Style menu.

- You can choose the layer the caption appears on using the Layer pop-up menu (this option is grayed out if there is only one layer in your document).

- You can have the text captions automatically grouped with their graphics frames by selecting the Group Caption with Image option.

   4. **Click OK when done.**

You can edit these settings at any time by choosing Captions➪Caption Setup in the Links panel's flyout menu.

Once you've set up the caption, you can apply it to all graphics frames containing links. InDesign gives you two choices for generating these captions:

✔ Choose Captions➪Generate Live Captions in the Links panel's flyout menu to create captions whose metadata is automatically updated if the images' metadata changes

✔ Choose Captions➪Generate Static Captions to create captions whose metadata is not updated when the images' metadata changes.

You can convert individual captions from being live to being static by selecting the caption frames and then choosing Captions⇨Convert to Static Caption. Be careful, though: You can't convert them back to being live.

When placing graphics files (see Chapter 17), select the Create Static Captions option to have InDesign create the caption when you place the image. (Note the caption created is a static one, not a live one.) After clicking in your document to place the image, you then click and drag a rectangle to create a text frame containing the metadata caption. (Note that if you haven't set up the caption, InDesign creates a static caption using the filename.)

Chapter 10

Aligning and Arranging Objects

* *

* *

*W*hen you draw objects like frames or lines, they appear where you draw them. That's what you expect, right? But sometimes you want them to appear where you meant to draw them, not where you actually did. Working with the mouse is inexact, but you can overcome that obstacle.

This chapter shows you how to use a variety of InDesign features to precisely control the placement of objects, including the capability to enter actual coordinates for objects, to use grids and guidelines features to ensure that your objects and text line up where you want them to, and to use the Align panel and related commands to make sure that objects line up relative to each other, so that your layouts are all neat and tidy.

The other part of keeping your layouts neat and tidy is managing the arrangements of objects. In addition to the grouping and locking functions covered in Chapter 9, InDesign also lets you control the stacking order of objects that overlap and tie objects to spots in text so they stay close to the text that references them.

Positioning Precisely with Coordinates

The most precise way to position objects is by entering the object's desired coordinates in the X: and Y: fields of the Control panel or the Transform panel. (You can also precisely change the object's size by entering values in the W: and H: fields.) The Control panel is visible by default at the top of the document window. If it's not visible, open the Control panel by choosing Window⇨Control (Option+⌘+6 or Ctrl+Alt+6).

The Control panel is more powerful than the Transform panel, which is a holdover from older versions of InDesign, but if you want to use the Transform panel, choose Window➪Object & Layout➪Transform.

Everyone should use the Control panel's coordinates to make sure that objects are consistently placed from page to page. Many designers place objects by eye, using the mouse, but that approach typically means that small position and size variations that shouldn't be there occur from page to page. Many readers won't notice if the differences are slight, but even small differences make small adjustments to text flow that can add up over pages. And it's all so unnecessary.

You usually want to enter coordinates based on the upper-left corner, so be sure that the upper-left reference point is made into the control point (just click it if it's not). How do you know which reference point is the current control point? The control point is black, while the other reference points are white. (Chapter 1 provides the deeper details.)

Lining Up Objects with Guidelines and Grids

If you've ever seen a carpenter use a chalked string to snap a temporary line as an aid for aligning objects, you understand the concept behind ruler guidelines and grids. They're not structurally necessary, and they don't appear in the final product, yet they still make your work easier.

InDesign provides several types of grids and guidelines:

- ✔ **Ruler guides** are moveable guidelines that are helpful for placing objects precisely and for aligning multiple items.

- ✔ **Margin and column guides** are part of your page setup when you create or modify a document (see Chapter 3), providing the default margin around the sides of the page and the space between the default text frame's columns.

- ✔ **Smart guides** are created on the fly as you work with objects. They use the centerpoints and frame edges of nearby objects and display accordingly so that you can line up your current object to match a nearby object's position or size.

- ✔ A **document grid** is a set of horizontal and vertical lines that help you place and align objects.

✔ A **baseline grid** is a series of horizontal lines that help in aligning lines of text and objects across a multicolumn page. When a document is open and it has a baseline grid showing, the page looks like a sheet of lined paper.

✔ A **frame-based grid** is similar to a baseline grid except that it's just for a specific text frame.

You won't need to display all the grids and guidelines at once. You'll most likely use a combination of guides and grids, but using all four at once is more complicated than necessary.

Using ruler guides

InDesign lets you create individual ruler guides manually. You can also set ruler guides automatically with the Create Guides command (Layout⇨Create Guides).

Manually creating ruler guides

To create ruler guides on an as-needed basis, follow these steps:

1. **Go to the page or spread onto which you want to place ruler guides.**

2. **If the rulers don't appear at the top and left of the document window, choose View⇨Show Rulers (⌘+R or Ctrl+R).**

3. **Drag the pointer (and a guideline along with it) from the horizontal ruler or vertical ruler onto a page or the pasteboard.**

4. **When the guideline is positioned where you want it, release the mouse button.**

   If you release the mouse when the pointer is over a page, the ruler guide extends from one edge of the page to the other (but not across a spread). If you release the mouse button when the pointer is over the pasteboard, the ruler guide extends across both pages of a spread and the pasteboard. If you want a guide to extend across a spread and the pasteboard, you can also hold down the ⌘ or Ctrl key as you drag and release the mouse when the pointer is over a page.

Place both a horizontal and vertical guide at the same time by pressing ⌘ or Ctrl and dragging the *ruler intersection point* (where the two rulers meet, in the upper-left corner of the document window) onto a page. You can also place a guide that extends across the page or spread and pasteboard by double-clicking the vertical or horizontal ruler.

Ruler guides are cyan in color (unless you change the color by choosing Layout➪Ruler Guides) and are associated with the layer onto which they're placed. You can show and hide ruler guides by showing and hiding the layers that contain them. You can even create layers that contain nothing but ruler guides and then show and hide them as you wish. (See Chapter 4 for more information about layers.)

TIP

To create ruler guides for several document pages, create a master page, add the ruler guides to the master page, and then apply the master to the appropriate document pages. (Chapter 5 covers master pages.)

Automatically creating ruler guides

Here's how to create a set of ruler guides automatically:

1. **If the documents contain multiple layers, display the Layers panel (Window➪Layers [F7]) and click the name of the layer to which you want to add guides.**

2. **Choose Layout➪Create Guides to display the Create Guides dialog box, shown in Figure 10-1.**

   To see the guides on the page while you create them, check Preview.

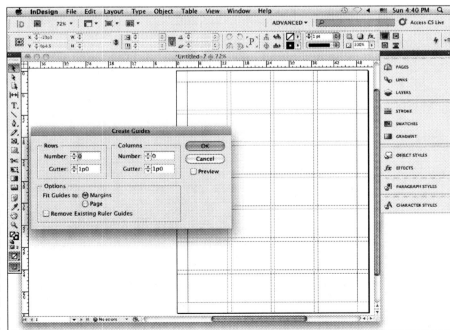

Figure 10-1:
The Create Guides dialog box and the guides it created.

3. **In the Rows and Columns areas, specify the number of guides you want to add in the Number fields and, optionally, specify a Gutter width between horizontal (Rows) and vertical (Columns) guides.**

   Enter **0** (zero) in the Gutter fields if you don't want gutters between guides.

4. **In the Options area, click Margins to fit the guides in the margin boundaries; click Page to fit the guides within the page boundary.**

5. **Remove any previously placed ruler guides by checking Remove Existing Ruler Guides.**

6. **When you finish specifying the attributes of the ruler guides, click OK to close the dialog box.**

Working with ruler guides

You can show and hide, lock and unlock, select and move, copy and paste, and delete ruler guides. Here are a few pointers for working with ruler guides:

- ✔ **Display or hide ruler guides** by choosing View⇨Grids & Guides⇨Show/ Hide Guides (⌘+; or Ctrl+; — note that these are semicolons).

- ✔ **Lock or unlock all ruler guides** by choosing View⇨Grids & Guides⇨ Lock Guides (Option+⌘+; or Ctrl+Alt+;). Ruler guides are locked when Lock Guides is checked.

- ✔ **Select a ruler guide** by clicking it with a selection tool. To select multiple guides, hold down the Shift key and click them. The color of a guide changes from cyan to the color of its layer when it's selected. To select all ruler guides on a page or spread, press Option+⌘+G or Ctrl+Alt+G.

- ✔ **Move a guide** by clicking and dragging it as you would any object. To move multiple guides, select them and then drag them. To move guides to another page, select them, choose Edit⇨Cut (⌘+X or Ctrl+X) — or choose Edit⇨Copy (⌘+C or Ctrl+C) to copy — then display the target page and choose Edit⇨Paste (⌘+V or Ctrl+V). If the target page has the same dimensions as the source page, the guides are placed in their original positions.

- ✔ **Delete ruler guides** by selecting them and then pressing Delete or Backspace.

- ✔ **Change the color of the ruler guides and the view percentage above which they're displayed** by choosing Layout⇨Ruler Guides. The Ruler Guides dialog box appears. Modify the View Threshold value, choose a different color from the Color pop-up menu, and then click OK. If you change the settings in the Ruler Guides dialog box when no documents are open, the new settings become defaults and are applied to all subsequently created documents.

✔ **Display ruler guides behind — instead of in front of — objects** by choosing InDesign⇨Preferences⇨Guides & Pasteboard (⌘+K) on the Mac or Edit⇨Preferences⇨Guides & Pasteboard (Ctrl+K) in Windows. Then select the Guides in Back option in the Guide Options section of the dialog box.

✔ **Make object edges snap (align) to ruler guides when you drag them into the snap zone** by selecting the Snap to Guides option (View⇨Grids & Guides⇨Snap to Guides [Shift+⌘+; or Ctrl+Shift+;]). To specify the snap zone (the distance — in pixels — at which an object will snap to a guide), choose InDesign⇨Preferences⇨Guides & Pasteboard (⌘+K) on the Mac or Edit⇨Preferences⇨Guides & Pasteboard (Ctrl+K) in Windows and enter a value in the Snap to Zone field in the Guide Options section of the dialog box.

Working with column guides

You can adjust column guides if your document has them, though you don't get the same flexibility in adjusting column guides as you do ruler guides. Column guides are created when you create a new document and set it up as having multiple columns (see Chapter 3).

By default, column guides are locked. To unlock them (or relock them) choose View⇨Grids & Guides⇨Lock Column Guides. (If the menu option has a check mark to its left, the column guides are locked.)

To move a column guide, click and drag it. Note that the color of a selected column guide doesn't change as the color of a selected ruler guide does. Also note that you can't select multiple column guides or move them to other pages. The only way to add or delete column guides is to change the number of guides in the Margins and Columns dialog box (choose Layout⇨Margins and Columns); adjusting the number of columns undoes any custom moves applied to column guides.

Working with smart guides

Using the smart guides feature is easy. First, make sure that smart guides are enabled. You do so in the Guides & Pasteboard pane of the Preferences dialog box by enabling the Align to Object Center and/or the Align to Object Edges options. Aligning to object center tells InDesign to look for the center-point of other objects as you move or resize objects and use those as align-ment targets. Aligning to object frame edges has it look for other objects' edges and use those as alignment targets. Turning on both produces more smart guides as you work on objects.

Figure 10-2 shows the smart guide feature in action in three sequences (in each sequence, at left is an existing object):

- ✔ The top sequence shows me adding a second frame. The mouse pointer is near neither the nearby object's centerpoint nor its edge, so no smart guide appears.

- ✔ The middle sequence shows what happens as the mouse pointer moves near the edge of the nearby object: InDesign displays a smart guide to let me know that if I want the bottom edge of the new frame to align with the bottom of the nearby object, all I have to do is let go.

- ✔ The third sequence shows me moving a circular frame from the bottom to the upper-right of the page. You can see the smart guide that indicates the mouse is aligned to the centerpoint of the second object, and if I let go here, the circular frame's centerpoint will align to that other object's centerpoint.

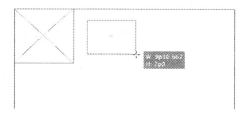

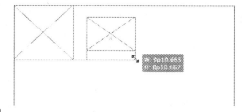

Figure 10-2:
Smart
guides in
action,
shown
in three
sequences.

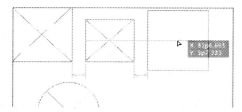

You probably noticed additional visual indicators in the third sequence: the spacing indicators between each set of objects. This visual indication is called *smart spacing,* which you also enable in the Guides & Pasteboard pane of the Preferences dialog box. When smart spacing is on, InDesign looks at the relative spacing of nearby objects as you work with one and highlights when the spacing is the same, or close to being the same (in which case it moves them for you).

A fourth "smart" feature comes with smart guides (it, too, must be enabled in the Guides & Pasteboard pane): smart measurements. In this case, as you resize or rotate objects, InDesign shows a smart guide when the object being transformed matches the specs — such as dimensions or rotation angle — of other nearby angles, under the assumption that maybe you want them to be the same. As with the other smart-guides functions, let go of the mouse when the guides appear so that you can get those matching settings.

Using document grids

A *document grid* is like the grid paper you used in school, a visual crutch to help ensure that the objects you draw and reposition are placed at desired increments. Using a grid can help ensure that objects align and are sized consistently.

If you plan to use a grid, set it up before you start working in the document. Because documents tend to have different grid settings based on individual contents, you probably want to set Grids preferences with a specific document open so that the grid will apply only to that document. Do so in the Grids pane of the Preferences dialog box (InDesign⇔Preferences⇔Grids [⌘+K] on the Mac, or Edit⇔Preferences⇔Grids [Ctrl+K] in Windows).

You have the following options:

- ✔ **Color:** The default color of the document grid is Light Gray. You can choose a different color from the Color pop-up menu or choose Other to create your own.

- ✔ **Gridline Every:** The major gridlines, which are slightly darker, are positioned according to this value. The default value is 6p0; in general, you want to specify a value within the measurement system you're using. For example, if you work in inches, you might enter **1 inch** in the Gridline Every field. You set the horizontal and vertical settings separately.

- ✔ **Subdivisions:** The major gridlines established in the Gridline Every field are subdivided according to the value you enter here. For example, if you enter **1 inch** in the Gridline Every field and **4** in the Subdivisions field, you get a gridline at each quarter-inch. The default number of subdivisions is 8. You set the horizontal and vertical settings separately.

By default, the document grid appears on every spread behind all objects. You can have grids display in front by deselecting the Grids in Back check box.

To make object edges snap (align) to the grid when you drag them into the snap zone, select the Snap to Document Grid option (View➪Grids & Guides➪Snap to Document Grid [Shift+⌘+' or Ctrl+Shift+' — note that these are apostrophes]). To specify the *snap zone* (the distance — in pixels — at which an object will snap to a gridline), InDesign uses whatever settings you specified for guidelines, as explained in the "Using ruler guides" section earlier in this chapter.

To display the document grid, choose View➪Grids & Guides➪Show Document Grid (⌘+' or Ctrl+').

Using baseline grids

You may not already realize that each and every new document you create includes a baseline grid. A baseline grid can be helpful for aligning text baselines across columns and for ensuring that object edges align with text baselines.

But chances are that the default settings for the baseline grid won't match the baselines (leading) for the majority of your text. The default baseline grid begins ½ inch from the top of a document page; the default gridlines are light blue, are spaced 1 pica apart, and appear at view percentages above 75 percent. If you change any of these settings when no documents are open, the changes are applied to all subsequently created documents; if a document is open, changes apply only to that document.

So here's how to modify the baseline grid:

1. **Choose InDesign➪Preferences➪Grids (⌘+K) on the Mac or Edit➪Preferences➪Grids (Ctrl+K) in Windows.**

   The Grids pane appears. (If you used a shortcut, then select the Grids pane from the list at left.)

2. **Pick a color for the baseline from the Color pop-up menu in the Baseline Grid area.**

3. **In the Start field, enter the distance between the top of the page and the first gridline.**

   If you enter **0**, the Increment Every value determines the distance between the top of the page and the first gridline.

4. **In the Increment Every field, enter the distance between gridlines.**

   If you're not sure what value to use, enter the leading value for the publication's body text.

5. **Choose a View Threshold percentage from the pop-up menu or enter a value in the field.**

   You probably don't want to display the baseline grid at reduced view percentages because gridlines become tightly spaced.

6. **Click OK to close the dialog box and return to the document.**

The Show/Hide Baseline Grid command (View⇨Grids & Guides⇨Show/Hide Baseline Grid [Option+⌘+' or Ctrl+Alt+']) lets you display and hide a document's baseline grid.

When you set a baseline grid, it applies to the entire document. Gridlines are displayed behind all objects, layers, and ruler guides. To get text to line up to the baseline grid, you need to ensure that the Align to Grid pop-up menu is set to either First Line Only or All Lines in your paragraph style or that the Align to Baseline Grid check box is selected in the Paragraph panel or Control panel. Chapter 14 covers such paragraph formatting in detail.

A document-wide baseline grid is all fine and dandy, but often it's not enough. The document-wide baseline grid is basically useful for your body text and often your headline text, assuming that the baseline grid's increments match the leading for that text. But what if you have other elements, like sidebars, that have different leading?

The answer is to use text frame–specific baseline grids. You set the grid as part of the text frame options by choosing Object⇨Text Frame Options (⌘+B or Ctrl+B) and then going to the Baseline Options pane. Its options are almost identical to those in the Grids pane of the Preferences dialog box. A baseline grid established for a text frame affects only the text in that frame.

Aligning Objects to Each Other

InDesign lets you align and distribute objects, saving you the hassle of manually moving and placing each element, or figuring out the correct locations in the Control panel or Transform panel to do so.

In the section "Working with smart guides," earlier in this chapter, I explain how the smart guides feature helps you align objects and adjust their spacing (as well as dimensions and even rotation angle) as you work with them. That's great for alignment as you work with individual objects. But what if you want to align multiple objects at the same time? That's where the Align panel comes in.

Using the Align panel

The Align panel (Window⇨Object & Layout⇨Align [Shift+F7]), shown in Figure 10-3, has several iconic buttons that let you manipulate the relative position of multiple objects in two ways. (The buttons show the alignments they provide.) You can

- ✔ **Line up objects along a horizontal or vertical axis.** For example, if you've randomly placed several small graphics frames onto a page, you can use the alignment buttons in the Align panel to align them neatly — either horizontally or vertically.

- ✔ **Distribute space evenly among objects along a horizontal or vertical axis.** Here's a typical problem that's easily solved by using this feature: You've carefully placed five small pictures on a page so that the top edges are aligned across the page and you have equal space between each picture. Then you find out that one of the pictures needs to be cut. After deleting the unneeded picture, you can use the Align panel to redistribute the space among the remaining pictures so that they're again equally spaced.

The Align buttons don't work with objects that have been locked or that are on locked layers. Chapter 9 explains how object locking works; Chapter 4 explains how layers work.

When you click an iconic button in the Align panel, selected objects are repositioned in the most logical manner. For example, if you click the Horizontal Align Left button, the selected objects are moved horizontally (to the left, in this case) so that the left edge of each object is aligned with the left edge of the leftmost object. Along the same lines, if you click the Vertical Distribute Center button, the selected objects are moved vertically so that an equal amount of space appears between the vertical center of each object.

Spacing can appear uneven if you click the Horizontal or Vertical Distribute buttons when objects of various sizes are selected. For objects of different sizes, you'll usually want to use the Distribute Spacing buttons (which make the space between objects even) rather than space objects based on their centers or sides (which is how the Distribute Object buttons work).

If the two Distribute Spacing icons don't appear at the bottom of the panel and you want to distribute objects, choose Show Options from the flyout menu.

Figure 10-3:
The Align panel contains 14 iconic buttons that let you control the alignment and space among selected objects.

Working with live distribution

InDesign CS5 lets you redistribute the spacing between objects as you drag the mouse using its live-distribution capability. Normally when you select multiple objects and begin moving one of the control points for the selected objects' marquee, each object is resized based on the direction and length you move the mouse. But if you press and hold the spacebar shortly after beginning that mouse movement, InDesign instead redistributes the object within the area defined by the marquee. (Release the spacebar and the mouse button to apply the new spacing.) The new marquee shape determines the space within which the objects are equally redistributed.

Figure 10-4 shows the live-distribution capability in action, and compares it to the normal resizing behavior.

Figure 10-4:
Live distribution in action.

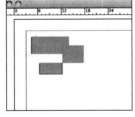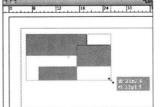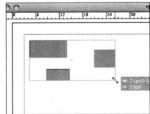

At far left is the original set of objects. The middle image shows the normal operation when you drag a control point in the objects' marquee: All the objects are resized accordingly. At far right is the new live-distribution capability: If you press and hold the spacebar immediately after you begin to drag a control point on the marquee, the objects are distributed within the new marquee dimensions instead of being resized.

Using the Gap tool

When you are working with several objects close together, you often end up adjusting their relative size and margins to fit within a set space on the page. That means adjusting each object one by one. The Gap tool lets you adjust them together, saving effort and making it easier to try out different adjustments. (Note that the Gap tool ignores locked items and master page items.)

When you select the Gap tool and position the mouse between objects, you see a gray highlight for the gap between the objects — that gap might be horizontal or vertical, depending on where the mouse pointer happens to be and what objects are near it. When the desired gap is highlighted, there are four adjustments you can make, as Figure 10-5 shows:

- ✔ If you hold the mouse button and drag the mouse, the objects are resized. The gap between them remains the same size. So, for a vertical gap, as in the upper-left corner of Figure 10-5, moving the gap to the right widens the objects on the left side of the gap and narrows the objects on the right side of the gap.

- ✔ If you hold Shift, only the objects nearest the mouse pointer are adjusted when you drag the mouse, as shown in the upper-right corner of Figure 10-5.

- ✔ If you hold ⌘ or Ctrl, dragging the mouse changes the gap's width. Dragging to the right on a vertical gap widens the gap (and narrows the objects on either side to make room); dragging to the left on a vertical gap narrows the gap (widening the objects on either side to take up the extra space). Dragging up on a horizontal gap widens the gap, and dragging down on horizontal gap narrows the gap. The lower left corner of Figure 10-5 shows the vertical gap being narrowed.

- ✔ If you hold Option or Alt, dragging the mouse moves all the items on either side of the gap in the direction you move the mouse, as the lower-right corner of Figure 10-5 shows.

You can combine the keyboard shortcuts when using the Gap tool. Thus, Shift+⌘+dragging or Shift+Alt+dragging a gap moves just the gap's immediately adjacent objects, not all the objects that border the gap.

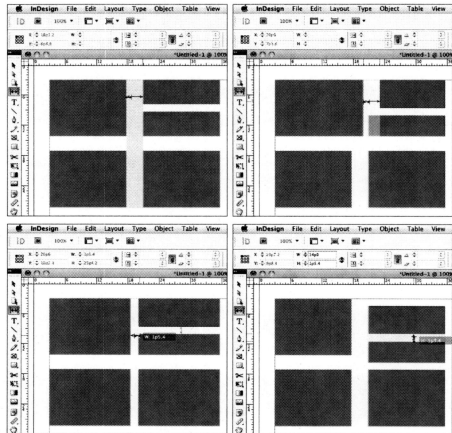

Figure 10-5:
The Gap tool
in action.

Stacking Objects

Arranging your objects is as key to having neat and tidy layouts as using grids and so on to align objects. (For more on this topic, see the section "Lining Up Objects with Guidelines and Grids," earlier in this chapter.)

Each time you begin work on a new page, you start with a clean slate (unless the page is based on a master page, in which case the master objects act as the page's background; see Chapter 5 for more on master pages). Every time you add an object to a page — either by using any of InDesign's object-creation tools or with the Place command (File⇨Place [⌘+D or Ctrl+D]) — the new object occupies a unique place in the page's object hierarchy, or *stacking order*.

The first object you place on a page is automatically positioned at the bottom of the stacking order; the next object is positioned one level higher than the first object (that is, in front of the backmost object); the next object is stacked one level higher; and so on for every object you add to the page. (It's not uncommon for a page to have several dozen, or even several hundred, stacks.)

Although each object occupies its own stack level, if the objects on a page don't overlap, the stacking order isn't an issue. But some of the most interesting graphic effects you can achieve with InDesign involve arranging several overlapping objects, so you need to be aware of the three-dimensional nature of a page's stacking order.

You may change your mind about what you want to achieve in your layout after you've already placed objects in it. To change an object's position in a page's stacking order, use the Arrange command (Object⇨Arrange), which offers four choices (note the use of brackets in the shortcuts):

- **Bring to Front** (Shift+⌘+] or Ctrl+Shift+])
- **Bring Forward** (⌘+] or Ctrl+])
- **Send Backward** (⌘+[or Ctrl+[)
- **Send to Back** (Shift+⌘+[or Ctrl+Shift+[)

To select an object that's hidden behind one or more other objects, press and hold ⌘ or Ctrl and then click anywhere within the area of the hidden object. The first click selects the topmost object; each successive click selects the next lowest object in the stacking order. When the bottom object is selected, the next click selects the top object. If you don't know where a hidden object is, you can simply click the object or objects in front of it and then send the object(s) to the back. (See Chapter 8 for more on selecting stacked objects.)

Creating Inline and Anchored Frames

In most cases, you want the frames you place on your pages to remain precisely where you put them. But sometimes, you want to place frames relative to related text in such a way that the frames move when the text is edited.

The simplest way is to use inline graphics. For example, if you're creating a product catalog that's essentially a continuous list of product descriptions and you want to include a graphic with each description, you can paste graphics within the text to create inline graphics frames.

A close cousin to the inline frame is the *anchored frame,* in which a frame follows a point in the text, but that frame isn't actually in the text. For example, you might have a "For More Information" sidebar that you want to appear to the left of the text that first mentions a term. By using an anchored frame, you can have that sidebar move with the text so that it always appears to its left, perhaps in an adjacent column or in the page margins.

Figure 10-6 shows examples of both an inline frame and an anchored frame.

Note that the process of creating inline and anchored frames — especially anchored frames — can appear overwhelming. It does require thinking through the frame's placement and visualizing that placement so that you pick the right options in the various dialog boxes. But relax: You can experiment until you get the hang of it. That's why InDesign lets you undo your work.

Working with inline frames

An inline frame is treated like a single character (even if it does go deeper than a single line). If you insert or delete text that precedes an inline frame, the frame moves forward or backward along with the rest of the text that follows the inserted or deleted text. Although inline frames usually contain graphics, they can just as easily contain text or nothing at all.

Figure 10-6:
The Anchored Object Options dialog box and the anchored frame it set up (to the dialog box's left), as well an inline frame (immediately above the dialog box).

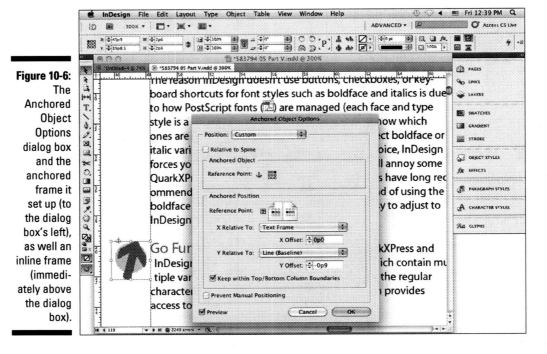

Inline frames may interfere with line spacing in paragraphs that have automatic leading. If the inline frame is larger than the point size in use, the automatic leading value for that line is calculated from the inline frame, which leads to inconsistent line spacing in the paragraph. To work around this issue, you can apply a fixed amount of leading to all characters in the paragraph, adjust the size of inline frames, place inline frames at the beginning of a paragraph, or place inline frames in their own paragraphs.

You can create inline frames in three ways:

- By pasting the frame into text
- By placing the frame into text
- By using the Anchored Object menu option

The first two methods are the simplest, but the third gives you more control over the inline frame when you create it. The third way also lets you create anchored frames, which are covered later in this chapter in the section "Working with anchored frames."

Using the Paste command

If you want to create an inline frame from an object you already created, all you have to do is copy or cut the object and then paste it into text as you would a piece of highlighted text. Here's how:

1. **Use the Selection tool to select the object you want to paste within text.**

   You can use any type of object: a line, an empty shape, a text or picture frame, or even a group of objects.

2. **Choose Edit⇨Copy (⌘+C or Ctrl+C).**

   If you don't need the original item, you can use the Cut command (Edit⇨ Cut [⌘+X or Ctrl+X]) instead of the Copy command.

3. **Select the Type tool and then click within the text where you want to place the copied object.**

   Make sure that the cursor is flashing where you intend to place the inline frame.

4. **Choose Edit⇨Paste (⌘+V or Ctrl+V).**

Inline frames often work best when placed at the beginning of a paragraph. If you place an inline frame within text to which automatic leading has been applied, the resulting line spacing can be inconsistent. To fix this problem, you can resize the inline frame.

Using the Place command

You can also use the Place command to create an inline graphics frame from an external picture file. (You *can't* use this technique for inline text frames because InDesign thinks you're just inserting the new text at the current location, not trying to insert a new text frame there.) Here's how:

1. **Select the Type tool and then click within a text frame to establish the insertion point.**

2. **Choose File⇨Place (⌘+D or Ctrl+D).**

3. **Locate and select the graphics file you want to place within the text; choose Open.**

To delete an inline frame, you can select it and then choose Edit⇨Clear or Edit⇨Cut (⌘+X or Ctrl+X), or you can position the text cursor next to it and press Delete or Backspace — just like any other "character."

Adjusting inline frames

After you create an inline frame, you can adjust its position vertically or horizontally. Again, you have your choice of several methods.

Two quick-and-dirty methods to move an inline frame vertically are as follows:

- ✔ Use the Type tool to highlight the inline frame as you would highlight an individual text character. In the Character panel or Control panel's Character pane (the A icon), type a positive value in the Baseline Shift field to move the inline frame up; type a negative value to move the frame down.

- ✔ Use the Selection tool or Direct Selection tool to select the inline frame; drag the frame up or down.

A quick way to move an inline frame horizontally is to follow these steps:

1. **With the Type tool selected, click between the inline frame and the character that precedes it.**

2. **Use the kerning controls in the Character panel or Control panel to enlarge or reduce the space between the inline frame and the preceding character.**

You can more precisely control the position of inline frames by using the Anchored Object Options dialog box, covered in the next section.

Of course, you can also adjust the inline frame's other attributes as needed, such as strokes, fills, dimensions, rotation, and skew, by using the Tools panel, Control panel, and other panels.

Working with anchored frames

Anchored frames give you a whole new way of organizing objects. Essentially, they follow the relevant text within the parameters you specify, such as staying to the left of the text or staying at the top of the page that contains the text.

Note that an inline frame is a type of anchored frame, one where the frame stays within the text it is linked to. For simplicity, I'm using the term *anchored frame* to mean only those frames that are at least partially outside the text frame but remain linked to a specific point in the text.

In addition to preserving anchored frames in imported Microsoft Word files, InDesign lets you create anchors in your layout. To create anchored frames, do the following:

1. **Select the Type tool and then click within a text frame to establish the insertion point.**

2. **Choose Object⇨Anchored Object⇨Insert.**

   The Insert Anchored Object dialog box appears.

3. **In the Object Options section of the dialog box, specify the anchored frame's settings.**

   You can choose the type of content (text, graphics, or unassigned) with the Content pop-up menu, apply an object style by using the Object Style pop-up menu, apply a paragraph style via the Paragraph Style pop-up menu (if Content is set to Text), and set the anchored frame's dimensions in the Height and Width fields. Note that the paragraph style you choose, if any, applies to the anchored frame, not to the paragraph in which the anchored frame is linked.

4. **In the Position pop-up menu, choose what kind of frame you're creating: Inline or Above Line (both are inline frames) or Custom (an anchored frame).**

   The dialog box displays different options based on that choice, as Figure 10-7 shows.

Anchored frames that you add by choosing Object⇨Anchored Object⇨Insert don't have text automatically wrap around them. Use the Text Wrap panel (Window⇨Text Wrap [Option+⌘+W or Ctrl+Alt+W]) to open this panel and set text wrap. But anchored frames created by pasting a graphic into text *do* automatically have text wrap around them.

Selecting the Prevent Manual Positioning option ensures that the positions of individual anchored frames can't be adjusted by using InDesign's other text and frame controls (such as Baseline Shift). This option forces users to use this dialog box to change the anchored frame's position, reducing the chances of accidental change.

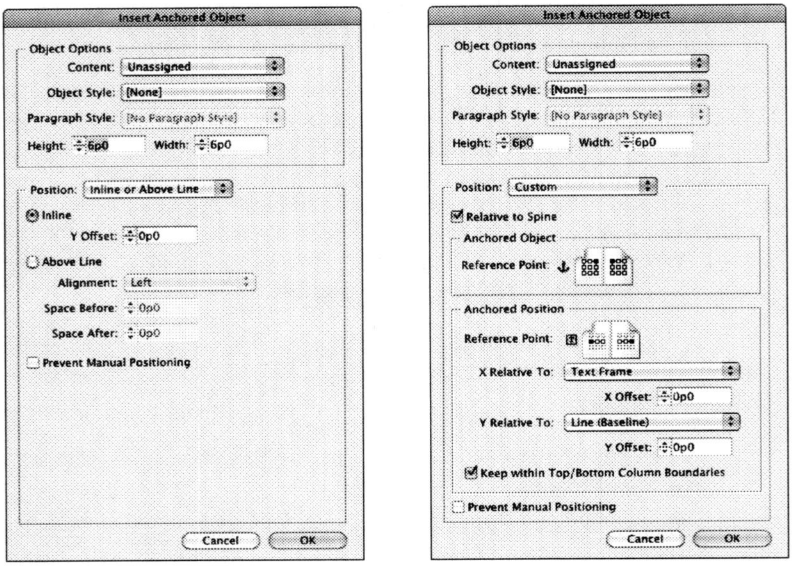

Figure 10-7:
The Insert
Anchored
Object
dialog box
for inline
frames
(left) and
anchored
frames
(right).

5. **Decide whether to select the Relative to Spine option.**

If this option is *not* selected, the anchored frame is placed on the same side of the text frame on all pages, whether those pages are left-facing or right-facing. If the Relative to Spine option is selected, InDesign places the text frame on the outside of both pages or inside of both pages, depending on how the anchored position is set.

6. **In the Anchored Object section of the dialog box, click one of the positioning squares to set up the text frame's relative position.**

Note that you need to think about both the horizontal and vertical positions you desire. For example, if you want the anchored frame to appear to the right of the text reference, click one of the right-hand squares. (Remember that selecting the Relative to Spine option overrides this setting, making the right-hand pages' positions mirror that of the left-hand pages, rather than be identical to them.) If you choose the topmost right-hand square, the anchored frame is placed to the right of the text reference and vertically appears at or below that text reference. But if you choose the bottommost right-hand square, you're telling InDesign you want the anchored frame to appear vertically above the text reference. Experiment with your layout to see what works best in each case.

7. **In the Anchored Position section of the dialog box, click one of the positioning squares to set up the text reference's relative position.**

Although nine squares appear, the only three that matter are those in the middle row. Typically, you place the text reference on the opposite side of the anchored frame — if you want the anchored frame to be to the left, you'd indicate that the text reference is to the right. (If you set the text reference on the same side as the anchored frame, InDesign places the anchored frame over the text.) The reason three squares (left, middle, and right) appear is to accommodate layouts in which you want some anchored frames to appear to the left of the text and some to the right; in that case, choose the middle position here and select the right- or left-hand position in the Anchored Object section as appropriate to that object.

8. **If necessary, use the options in the Anchored Position section to give InDesign more precise instructions on how to place the anchored frames.**

   You have the following options:

   • **The X Relative To pop-up menu** tells InDesign from where the horizontal location is calculated, using the following options: Anchor Marker, Column Edge, Text Frame, Page Margin, and Page Edge. The right option depends both on where you want the anchored frames placed and whether you have multicolumn text boxes (in which case Text Frame and Column Edge result in different placement, while in a single-column text frame they do not). You can also specify a specific amount of space to place between the chosen X Relative To point and the anchored frame by typing a value in the X Offset field.

   • **The Y Relative To pop-up menu** tells InDesign from where the vertical location is calculated, using the following options: Line (Baseline), Line (Cap-height), Line (Top of Leading), Column Edge, Text Frame, Page Margin, and Page Edge. As you expect, you can also indicate a specific amount of space to place between the chosen Y Relative To point and the anchored frame by typing a value in the Y Offset field.

   • The **Keep Within Top/Bottom Column boundaries check box** does exactly what it says.

9. **Click OK to insert the anchored frame.**

You can create inline frames using this same basic process, choosing Inline or Above Line in Step 4 in the preceding steps. You get most of the same controls as for anchored objects, such as the frame size and type, but, of course, you don't see controls for the relative position because an inline frame goes at the text-insertion point. If you want to create an inline frame, use the techniques described in the previous section for copying or placing a frame into text.

Anchoring caveats

Consider these caveats when creating anchored frames:

- ✔ Because an anchored frame follows its text as it flows throughout a document, you need to ensure that your layout retains clear paths for those anchored objects to follow. Otherwise, anchored frames may overlap other frames as they move.

- ✔ Anchored frames should generally be small items and/or used sparingly. The more items you have anchored to text, the greater the chance that they'll interfere with each other's placement. Likewise, you can move large items only so far within a page, so the benefit of keeping them close to their related text disappears.

- ✔ Items such as pull-quotes are obvious candidates for use as anchored frames. But in many layouts, you want the pull-quotes to stay in specific locations on the page for good visual appearance. The InDesign anchored-frame function can accommodate that need for specific positioning on a page, but you need to be careful as you add or delete text. You don't want to end up with some pages that have no pull-quotes at all because you have so much text between the pull-quotes' anchor points. Conversely, you need to make sure that you don't have too many pull-quotes anchored close to each other, which can result in overlapping.

Typically, you use anchored frames for small graphics or icons that you want to keep next to a specific paragraph (such as the Tip and Warning icons used in this book). Another good use is for cross-reference ("For More Information") text frames.

Converting existing frames to anchored frames

After you get the hang of when and how to use anchored frames, you'll likely want to convert some frames in existing documents into anchored frames. InDesign doesn't offer a direct way to do that task, but you can take a somewhat circuitous path. Follow these steps:

1. **Use the Selection or Direct Selection tool to cut the existing frame that you want to make into an anchored frame by choosing Edit⇨Cut (⌘+X or Ctrl+X).**

   You can also copy an existing frame by choosing Edit⇨Copy (⌘+C or Ctrl+C).

2. **Switch to the Type tool and click in a text frame at the desired location to insert the text reference to the anchored frame.**

3. **Paste the cut or copied frame into that insertion point by choosing Edit⇨Paste (⌘+V or Ctrl+V).**

   You now have an inline frame.

4. **Select the frame with the Selection tool and then choose Object⇨ Anchored Object⇨Options to display the Anchored Object Options dialog box.**

   This dialog box looks like the Insert Anchored Options dialog box, shown in Figure 10-7, except that it doesn't include the top Object Options section; you can see that section in Figure 10-6.

5. **Choose Custom from the Position pop-up menu.**

   This step converts the frame from an inline frame to an anchored frame.

6. **Adjust the position for the newly minted anchored frame as described in the preceding section.**

7. **Click OK when you're done.**

Adjusting anchored frames

After you create an anchored frame, you can adjust its position.

A quick-and-dirty method is simply to click and drag anchored frames or use the Control panel to adjust their position. If the text that the frame is anchored to moves, however, InDesign overrides those changes. (You can't manually move an anchored frame if the Prevent Manual Positioning option is selected in the Insert Anchored Object dialog box or Anchored Object Options dialog box. This option is deselected by default.)

For the most control of an anchored frame's position, choose Object⇨ Anchored Object⇨Options. The resulting Anchored Object Options dialog box is nearly identical to the Insert Anchored Object dialog box but lacks the Object Options section.

And, of course, you can adjust the frame's other attributes as needed, such as strokes, fills, dimensions, rotation, and skew.

Releasing and deleting anchored frames

If you no longer want an anchored frame to be anchored to a text location, you can release the anchor. To do so, select the anchored frame with the Selection or Direct Selection tool and then choose Object⇨Anchored Object⇨Release.

It's also easy to delete an anchored frame: Select the frame with the Selection or Direct Selection tool and then choose Edit⇨Clear or press Delete or Backspace. If you want to remove the object but keep it on the Clipboard for pasting elsewhere, choose Edit⇨Cut (⌘+X or Ctrl+X).

Part IV
Text Essentials

The 5th Wave   By Rich Tennant

AIRPORT SECURITY

"They won't let me through security until I remove the bullets from my document."

In this part . . .

Getting words on the page is an important part of what you do with InDesign. After you have the words in place, you'll want to tweak the letters and lines, and the space between them, to make your pages sparkle.

This part shows you how to arrange words on the page, including words made up of exotic characters. You find out how to set text in columns and how to add bullets and numbers to that text. You also discover how to stretch, squeeze, rotate, and add special effects to text. Additionally, you see how to become skilled at using character and paragraph styles to make your life easier and to speed up your publishing workflow.

Chapter 11

Putting Words on the Page

*T*ext is more than words — it's also a layout element that flows through your pages in the locations that you need. Much of the work you do in InDesign involves controlling that flow and working with the text as blocks that need to have the right arrangement to fit your layout's goals.

This chapter helps you manage that flow and arrangement, showing you how to deftly maneuver the text through your layout, just as you would move your way through the dance floor.

After you have the steps nailed down, you can do the dance: bringing in text from your source files.

Working with Text Frames

When you're creating a simple layout, such as a single-page flyer or a magazine advertisement, you'll probably create text frames — the containers for text — as you need them. But if you're working on a book or a magazine, you'll want your text frames placed on master pages so that your text will be consistently framed automatically when it appears on document pages. And you'll still have individual text frames you create for specific elements like sidebars.

Chapter 7 shows you how to create frames (including text frames), whereas Chapter 5 shows you how to create master pages. This chapter brings those two concepts together to show you how to work with text frames, both those in master pages and those you create in your document pages.

Creating master text frames

Master pages — predesigned pages that you can apply to other pages to automate layout and ensure consistency — can contain several types of text frames:

✔ Text frames containing standing text, such as page numbers or page headers.

✔ Text frames containing placeholder text for elements such as figure captions or headlines.

✔ One master text frame (an automatically placed text frame for flowing text throughout pages), which you create in the New Document dialog box (File⇨New⇨Document [⌘+N or Ctrl+N]). You accomplish this by selecting the Master Text Frame check box and then specifying the frame's size and placement by entering values in the Margins area for Top, Bottom, Inside, and Outside (or Left and Right if Facing Pages is unchecked) fields.

You can set the number of columns in the master text frame by entering a value in the Number of Columns field and optionally specifying the space between the columns in the Gutter field.

Think of a master text frame as an empty text frame on the default master page that lets you automatically flow text through a document.

After you create a document with a master text frame, you'll see guides on the first document page that indicate the placement of the frame.

Creating individual text frames

Although the master text frame is helpful for containing body text that flows through a document, you'll probably need additional text frames on both master pages and document pages. Generally, these smaller text frames hold text such as headlines, sidebars, or captions.

To add text frames to a master page for repeating elements such as headers and footers, first display the master page. Choose Window⇨Pages (⌘+F12 or Ctrl+F12) to display the Pages panel. Then double-click the A-Master icon in the upper portion of the panel, as shown in Figure 11-1, which displays the `A-Master` master page. (If you have multiple master pages in your document, you can follow these instructions to add text frames to any of them. Just choose the desired master page.)

Figure 11-1:
To switch to a desired master page, double-click its master page icon in the top of the Pages panel.

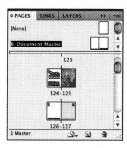

To add text frames to a document page, first go to the page. You can use any of the techniques described in Chapter 4 to move among pages.

Now draw the desired frame using any of the frame or shape tools, or the Type tool, as described in Chapter 7. Modify them with the Control panel (or Transform panel) or by using the mouse, also as described in that chapter.

Text frames you add to a master page will show up on any document pages based on that master page.

If you're working on a document page and want to type inside a text frame placed on the page by a master page, select the Type tool and then Shift+⌘+click or Ctrl+Shift+click the frame.

Setting up automatic page creation

Often when you import a large text file, such as for a book or report, you don't know how many pages you need. Chances are that you have a few pages in your document already set up and then add more pages until the text is all placed.

InDesign has a handy feature called *autoflow* that adds pages to the end of your document until all the text has been placed. For autoflow to work, you must do two things:

1. **Enable autoflow in the Type pane of the Preferences dialog box (choose InDesign➪Preferences➪Type [⌘+K] on the Mac or Edit➪Preferences➪Type [Ctrl+K] in Windows).**

   Be sure that Smart Text Reflow is checked and then choose the appropriate reflow options in the Add Pages To pop-up menu — End of Story, End of Section, and End of Document — to determine where the extra pages are added.

   I recommend that you use this feature with the Limit to Master Text Frames and Preserve Facing-Page Spreads options enabled. The first option assumes that you set up master text frames, as described in the "Creating master text frames" section, earlier in this chapter. If you don't use such master text frames, don't check this option. Instead, be sure that if you set up your own text frames in the master page (see the preceding section) that you have threaded them to each other, as described in the "Threading text frames" section, later in this chapter. The second option means that if you have spreads already set up in your document, they won't get messed up (in other words, be split up) by the added pages.

2. **When you place your text, do so in your master text frame or in a text frame defined on your master page.**

   InDesign uses these (and only these) frames to create the new pages. Remember that you can place text in a frame that already has text (to replace that text or to add more text), as well as place text in an empty frame. No matter which approach you take, InDesign adds the necessary number of pages for the placed text to flow into.

The smart text reflow feature doesn't work if you place text into a document text frame; it must be placed in a master text frame or in a text frame that is defined on a master page.

InDesign offers two other methods to autoflow text into master frames, whether or not the Smart Text Reflow check box is selected in the Type pane of the Preferences dialog box:

✔ If you hold the Shift key when placing text, InDesign flows the text into the master frame and keeps going until it runs out of pages with master frames. Then it creates more master frames until the text is all placed. Unlike with the smart text reflow feature, you can't control where those pages are added.

✔ If you hold Option+Shift or Alt+Shift when placing text, InDesign flows the text into the nearest master frame and automatically flows it into the subsequent "open" master frames in your document. Unlike the Shift-only option, it does *not* add new pages.

The details on placing text are covered in the "Importing Text" section, later in this chapter.

Making changes to text frames

You're not confined to the settings you originally established when you set up a master text frame or an individual text frame; you can change the size, shape, and/or number of columns in the text frame later. Use the Selection tool to click the desired text frame and then modify it with the following options (the first six are covered in detail in Chapter 8):

- ✔ Change the placement of a selected master text frame by using the X: and Y: fields in the Control panel.

- ✔ Change the size of the master text frame by using the W: and H: fields.

- ✔ Change the angle by using the Rotation Angle field.

- ✔ Change the skew by using the Shear X Angle field.

- ✔ Enter values in the Scale fields to increase or decrease, by percentage amounts, the width and height of the text frame.

- ✔ Use the General pane of the Text Frame Options dialog box (Object⇨ Text Frame Options [⌘+B or Ctrl+B]) to make further modifications:

  - • Change the number of columns and the space between them using the Number and Gutter fields.

  - • Specify how far text is inset from each side of the frame using the Inset Spacing fields.

  - • Align text vertically within the frame using the Align pop-up menu. InDesign CS5 allows you to vertically align text in nonrectangular frames.

- ✔ Use the Baseline Options pane of the Text Frame Options dialog box to set a baseline grid, if desired, for the text to align to. Chapter 10 describes this feature in more detail.

  If you don't want the text inside this text frame to wrap around any items in front of it, check Ignore Text Wrap at the bottom of the dialog box.

  If you open the Text Frame Options dialog box with no document open, any changes you make become the default for all new documents.

- ✔ Specify character styles, paragraph styles, object styles, Story panel settings, text-wrap settings, and other text attributes to apply in the text frame to the document text you flow into that frame. (You can always override those attributes by applying other styles or formatting to the text later.) The rest of Part IV covers these other settings.

Additionally, if you select the frame with the Direct Selection tool, you can change its shape by dragging anchor points on the frame to other positions, as described in Chapter 8.

Importing Text

You can import text from a word processor file (Word 97/98 or later, RTF, ASCII [text-only], or InDesign Tagged Text files) into an InDesign text frame using the Place dialog box (File⇨Place [⌘+D or Ctrl+D]). You can also import Microsoft Excel spreadsheets (version 97/98 or later). Many of the text's original styles will remain intact, although you will want to review the imported text carefully to see whether any adjustments need to be made.

Follow these steps to place imported text:

1. **Choose File⇨Place (⌘+D or Ctrl+D) to open the Place dialog box.**

2. **Locate the text files you want to import and select them.**

   To select multiple files, ⌘+click or Ctrl+click each file you want to import. You can also Shift+click a range of files in the Place dialog box.

3. **To specify how to handle current formatting in the file, check the Show Import Options check box.**

   The appropriate Import Options dialog box for the text file's format opens. (Note that no import options exist for ASCII text.) Then click OK to return to the Place dialog box. (I cover this dialog box later in this chapter.)

4. **Click the Open button to import the text.**

   If you selected an empty frame with the Type tool, InDesign will flow the text into that frame. If you selected a text frame with the Type tool, InDesign will flow the text at the text-insertion point in that frame, inserting the new text within the existing text.

   If you hadn't already selected a frame before starting to import the text, specify where to place it by clicking and dragging the loaded-text icon to create a rectangular text frame, clicking in an existing frame, or clicking in any empty frame.

The loaded-text icon shows the number of files to be placed, as well as a mini-preview of each file, as shown at left.

When placing multiple files, you can use the keyboard left- and right-arrow keys to move through the thumbnail previews before clicking to place the one whose thumbnail preview is currently displayed. That way, you can place the files in any order you want. Also, when you place multiple files, InDesign puts each in its own frame; just click once in the layout (or in an existing frame) for each file. If you don't want to place each file individually, you can Shift+⌘+click or Ctrl+Shift+click to have InDesign place all files on the page in separate frames in one fell swoop.

You can't click on a master text frame — a text frame that is placed on the page by the master page in use — and simply start typing. To select a master text frame and add text to it, Shift+⌘+click or Ctrl+Shift+click it. (For more on master pages, see Chapter 5.)

Import options for Microsoft Word and RTF files

InDesign offers a comprehensive set of import options for Word and RTF files. (The Microsoft Word Import Options dialog box is identical to the RTF Import Options dialog box.) With these options, you can control how these files import into InDesign. To save time on future imports, you can save your import preferences as a preset file for repeat use.

The Preset pop-up menu, at the top of the dialog box, lets you select from saved sets of import options. You can save the current settings by clicking the Save Preset button. And you can set a preset as the default import behavior by clicking the Set as Default button; these settings are used for all Word file imports unless you choose a new default or make changes in this dialog box. This default preset capability lets you avoid using the Import Options dialog box for your routine imports.

The Include section of the Import Options dialog box is where you decide whether to strip out specific types of text (Table of Contents Text, Index Text, Footnotes, and Endnotes) from the Word file. If you check items, their corresponding text will be imported. You probably won't want to import table-of-contents or index text because you can create much nicer-looking tables of contents and indexes in InDesign.

The third section, Options, has just one option: Use Typographer's Quotes. If this box is checked, InDesign converts keyboard quotes from your source file (' and ") to "curly" typographic quotes (', ', ", and ").

The fourth section, Formatting, is fairly complex, so take it one step at a time. Start with deciding whether to remove or retain the formatting in your imported text.

To *remove* text formatting during import so that you can do the formatting in InDesign, select the Remove Styles and Formatting from Text and Tables option. You have two additional controls for this option:

  ✔ Preserve Local Overrides, which retains local formatting such as italics and boldface while ignoring the paragraph style attributes. You'd usually want this option checked so that meaning-related formatting is retained.

✔ You also can choose how tables are "unformatted" during import via the Convert Tables To pop-up menu. Unformatted Tables retains the table's cell structure but ignores text and cell formatting, while Unformatted Tabbed Text converts the table to tabbed text (with a tab separating what used to be cells and a paragraph return separating what used to be rows) and strips out any formatting. If you intend to keep tables as tables but format them in InDesign, choose Unformatted Tables.

To *retain* text formatting during import so that the InDesign document at least starts out using the settings used in Word, choose the Preserve Styles and Formatting from Text and Tables option. This option includes several controls and bits of information:

✔ The Manual Page Breaks pop-up menu lets you retain any page breaks entered in Word, convert them to column breaks, or strip them out.

✔ Checking the Import Inline Graphics check box enables the import of any graphics in the Word text.

✔ Checking the Import Unused Styles check box means that all Word style sheets transfer into InDesign, rather than just the ones you actually applied to text in the file. Unless you want all those extra Word styles, keep this box unchecked.

✔ Checking the Track Changes check box preserves the revisions tracking information from Word so that you can see it in InDesign's Story Editor. (Chapter 12 explains how to work with tracked changes.)

✔ Checking Convert Bullets & Numbers to Text removes any automatic bullet and numbering lists in Word, converting the bullets and numbers into the actual characters. If you select this option and insert an item in an imported numbered list, the list doesn't renumber automatically, as it would if you leave this unchecked. (In InDesign CS3 and earlier, bullets and numbers were converted to actual characters, preventing automatic renumbering.)

✔ If InDesign detects that the Word file has a style with the same name as your InDesign document, it notes how many to the right of the Style Name Conflicts label. You have choices in how to handle these conflicts:

• Use InDesign Style Definition preserves the current InDesign style sheets and applies them to any text in Word that uses a style sheet of the same name. Redefine InDesign Style causes the Word style sheet's formatting to permanently replace that of InDesign's style sheet. Auto Rename renames the Word file's style sheet and adds it to the Paragraph Styles or Character Styles panel. This option preserves your existing InDesign style sheets while also preserving those imported from the Word file.

• Customize Style Import lets you decide which specific InDesign styles override same-name Word styles, which Word styles override same-name InDesign styles, and which Word styles are renamed during import to prevent any overriding.

Import options for Microsoft Excel files

When importing Excel spreadsheets, you have several options in the Microsoft Excel Import Options dialog box.

In the Options section, you can control the following settings:

- ✔ The Sheet pop-up menu lets you choose which sheet in an Excel workbook to import. The default is the first sheet, which is usually named `Sheet1` unless you renamed it in Excel. (If you want to import several sheets, you'll need to import the same spreadsheet several times, choosing a different sheet each time.)

- ✔ The View pop-up menu lets you import custom views that are defined in Excel for that spreadsheet. If the spreadsheet has no custom views, this pop-up menu is grayed out. You can also ignore any custom views by choosing [Ignore View] from the pop-up menu.

- ✔ In the Cell Range pop-up menu, you specify a range of cells using standard Excel notation *Sx:Ey,* where *S* is the first row, *x* the first column, *E* the last row, and *y* the last column, such as A1:G35. You can enter a range directly in the pop-up menu, which also acts as a text-entry field, or choose a previously entered range from the pop-up menu.

- ✔ Checking the Import Hidden Cells Not Saved in View check box imports hidden cells. Be careful when doing so, because these cells are usually hidden for a reason. (Typically, they show interim calculations and the like.)

In the Formatting section, you can control the following settings:

- ✔ In the Table pop-up menu, you choose from Formatted Table, which imports the spreadsheet as a table and retains text and cell formatting; Unformatted Table, which imports the spreadsheet as a table but doesn't preserve formatting; and Unformatted Tabbed Text, which imports the spreadsheet as tabbed text (tabs separate cells and paragraph returns separate rows) with no formatting retained.

- ✔ In the Table Style pop-up menu, you choose an InDesign table style to apply to the imported table or leave it alone (by choosing [No Table Style]).

- ✔ In the Cell Alignment pop-up menu, you tell InDesign how to align the text in cells. You can retain the spreadsheet's current alignment settings by choosing Current Spreadsheet or override them by choosing Left, Right, or Center.

- ✔ Checking the Include Inline Graphics check box imports any graphics placed in the Excel cells.

- ✔ The Number of Decimal Places to Include field is where you enter how many decimal places to retain for numbers.

- ✔ Check the Use Typographer's Quotes check box to convert keyboard quotes (' and ") to the "curly" typographic quotes (', ', ", and "). Keeping this box checked is a good idea.

Pasting text into an InDesign document

As you probably know, you can hold text on the Mac or Windows Clipboard by cutting it or copying it from its original location. After you've captured some text on the Clipboard, you can paste it into an InDesign document at the location of the cursor. You can also replace highlighted text with the text that's on the Clipboard. If no text frame is active when you do the pasting, InDesign creates a new text frame to contain the pasted text.

InDesign uses standard menu commands and keyboard commands for cutting/copying text to the Clipboard, and for pasting text. On the Mac, press ⌘+X to cut, ⌘+C to copy, and ⌘+V to paste. In Windows, press Ctrl+X to cut, Ctrl+C to copy, and Ctrl+V to paste.

Keep characters to a minimum

When you're working with text in a professional publishing application, such as InDesign, you need to keep in mind some differences between the professional method and traditional way of typing:

- ✔ Remember that you don't need to type two spaces after a period or colon; books, newspapers, magazines, and other professional documents all use just one space after such punctuation.

- ✔ Don't enter extra paragraph returns for space between paragraphs and don't enter tabs to indent paragraphs — instead, set up this formatting using InDesign's paragraph attributes (Type⇨Paragraph [Option+⌘+T or Ctrl+Alt+T]).

- ✔ To align text in columns, don't enter extra tabs; place the same number of tabs between each column and then align the tabs (Type⇨Tabs, or Shift+⌘+T or Ctrl+Shift+T).

To see where your InDesign document has tabs, paragraph breaks, spaces, and other such invisible characters, choose Type⇨Show Hidden Characters (Option+⌘+I or Ctrl+Alt+I). You can also view them from the application bar's View Options pop-up menu (see Chapter 1).

Text that is cut or copied from InDesign normally retains its formatting, whereas text pasted from other programs loses its formatting. But you can specify whether pasted text from other programs always retains its formatting. Go to the Clipboard Handling pane in the Preferences dialog box (choose InDesign⇨Preferences⇨Clipboard Handling [⌘+K] on the Mac, or choose Edit⇨Preferences⇨Clipboard Handling [Ctrl+K] in Windows) and select the All Information option in the When Pasting Text and Tables from Other Applications section. If you select this option, you can still tell InDesign to *not* preserve the formatting on a case-by-case basis by choosing Edit⇨Paste without Formatting (Shift+⌘+V or Ctrl+Shift+V).

Dragging and dropping text

You can drag highlighted text from other programs — or even text files from the desktop or a folder — into an InDesign document. Text that you drag and drop is inserted at the location of the cursor, replaces highlighted text, or is placed in a new rectangular text frame.

When you drag and drop a text selection, its original formatting is usually retained — unless you hold the Shift key when dragging. If you hold the Shift key, the text takes on the attributes of the text you drag it into.

When you drag and drop a text *file,* the process is more like a text import: The text retains its formatting and styles. Unlike the Place command (File⇨Place [⌘+D or Ctrl+D]) that imports text, drag-and drop-doesn't give you the option to specify how some of the formatting and styles in the imported text file are handled.

Threading Text Frames

The text that flows through a series of frames is what InDesign considers a *story,* and the connections among those frames are called *threads.* When you edit text in a threaded story, the text reflows throughout the text frames. You can also spell-check and do a find/change operation for an entire story, even though you have just one of the story's text frames active on-screen.

When you have threaded text frames, you'll see visual indicators on your text frame, assuming that you choose View⇨Extras⇨Show Text Threads (Option+⌘+Y or Ctrl+Alt+Y) and have selected the frame with one of the selection tools. At the lower right of the text frame is a small square, called the *out port,* which indicates the outflow status:

✔ If the square is empty, that means you have no text flowing to another frame, and not enough text to flow to another frame.

✔ If the square is red and has a plus sign in it, that means you have more text than fits in the selected frame but that it's *not* flowing to another frame. This condition is called *overset text.*

✔ If the square has a triangle icon, the text is flowing to another frame. That doesn't mean that text *is* flowing, just that if you have more text than the current frame can hold, it *will* flow.

Similarly, an *in port* at the upper left of a text frame indicates whether text is flowing from another frame into the current frame:

✔ If the square is empty, no text is flowing from another frame, making this frame the first (and perhaps only) frame in a story.

✔ If the square has a triangle icon, the text is flowing from another frame. That doesn't mean that text *is* flowing, just that if you have more text than the other frame can hold, it *will* flow into this frame.

So how do you thread the frames in the first place? You have four options in InDesign: manual, semi-autoflow, and two types of autoflow. Each of these options has its own icon. The method you choose depends on the amount of text you're dealing with and the size and number of your text frames:

✔ **To link two empty text frames across several pages** (for example, for an article that starts on page 2 and continues on page 24) — for frames where you will later want the text to flow across — you might use the manual method, in which you click the first text frame's out port and then click on the second text frame.

✔ **To link a text frame with text to another text frame,** you might also use the manual method, in which you click the first text frame's out port and then click on the second text frame.

✔ **To link a succession of text frames,** you might want to use the semi-autoflow method, which allows you to click a series of text frames to flow text from one frame to the next. Hold the Option or Alt key when clicking the mouse during text placement. Remember to, as you're threading frames, Option+click or Alt+click each text frame, or you'll revert to manual threading.

✔ **To import text that is intended for long documents** (such as a book chapter, or brochure), you might want to use the autoflow method to add text frames and pages that accommodate the text you're importing. Hold the Shift key when clicking the mouse during text placement to fill all open master frames and create new ones as needed. Be sure to Shift+click near the upper-left corner of the master text frame so that

InDesign uses that frame rather than create a new one. Note that even if you've already placed a text file into a single text frame or a threaded chain of text frames, you can still autoflow text from the last text frame. To do so, click the out port and then Shift+click any page to indicate where to start the autoflow.

✔ **To import text into a long page where you don't want new pages added,** hold Option+Shift or Alt+Shift. The text autoflows into each open page, but no new pages are added.

✔ **To place multiple text frames in an array — such as for bios or other snippet-size text —** hold Shift+⌘ or Ctrl+Shift when dragging the mouse in your document. The files will be placed in an array, each in its own frame within the area defined when dragging the mouse. This method creates as many frames as it can in that array, placing the text files into them. Any files not placed remain in the load-text icon for placement elsewhere.

For a quick glance at your text threads while you're threading text across pages, simply change the document view briefly to 20 percent or so.

Text flows in the order in which you select frames. If you move a frame, its order in the text flow remains unchanged. If you're not careful, you can, for example, accidentally have text flow from a frame at the top of the page to a frame at the bottom of a page and then to one in the middle of a page.

Always switch to a selection tool when you're threading frames. Oddly, you can't thread frames while the Type tool is selected. Oh, well.

Breaking and rerouting threads

After text frames are threaded, you have three options for changing the threads: You can break threads to stop text from flowing, insert a text frame into an existing chain of threaded text frames, and remove text frames from a thread. Here are the techniques in a nutshell:

✔ **Break the link between two text frames by double-clicking either an out port or an in port.** The thread between the two text frames is removed, and all text that had flowed from that point is sucked out of the subsequent text frames and stored as overset text.

✔ **Insert a text frame after a specific text frame in a chain by clicking its out port.** Then, click and drag the loaded-text icon to create a new text frame. That new frame is automatically threaded to both the previous and the next text frames.

✔ **Reroute text threads — for example, to drop the middle text frame from a chain of three — by clicking the text frame with the Selection tool and then pressing Delete or Backspace.** This technique deletes the text frame and reroutes the threads. You can also Shift+click to multiple-select text frames to remove. Note that you can't reroute text threads without removing the text frames.

Working with Columns

Where you place columns on the page — and the amount of space you allow between columns — has a big impact on readability. Used with a little know-how, column width works with type size and leading to make text easier to read. Columns help you keep from getting lost from one line to the next, and from getting a headache as you're trying to read the words on the page.

Generally, as columns get wider, the type size and leading increase. For example, you might see 9-point text and 15-point leading in 2½-inch columns, whereas 15-point text and 13-point leading might work better in 3½-inch columns.

InDesign lets you place columns on the page automatically, create any number of columns within a text frame, and change columns at any time.

Specifying columns in master frames

You can specify the number of columns at the same time you create a *master text frame* — a text frame placed automatically within the margin guides.

In the Columns area in the New Document dialog box, use the Number field to specify how many columns, and the Gutter field to specify how much space to place between the columns. (The *gutter* is the space between columns.) Whether or not you check Master Text Frame (which makes the frame appear on all pages), guides for these columns are still placed on the page and can be used for placing text frames and other objects.

Changing columns in text frames

You can change the number of columns in a text frame (whether an individual text frame or a master text frame), even after you've flown text into the frame — and doing so isn't difficult. First, select the text frame with a selection tool or the Type tool (or Shift+click to select multiple text frames and change all their columns at once). Then choose Object⇨Text Frame Options (⌘+B or Ctrl+B) and set the desired Number and Gutter values in the General pane of the Text Frame Options dialog box.

The Text Frame Options dialog box has a new option, Balance Columns. If it's selected, InDesign CS5 makes the bottom of columns align as evenly as possible, rather than letting the text frame end with one column much shorter than the others.

You can also use the Control panel to quickly change the number of columns, set the gutter, and turn column balancing on or off. Note, however, that these controls don't display on a monitor set below 1152-×-870-pixel resolution unless you customize the Control panel interface (to disable other controls to make room for these ones) using the Customize command in its flyout menu.

Some designers like to draw each column as a separate frame. I strongly recommend against this practice; it's too easy to create columns of slightly different widths and slightly different positions, so text doesn't align properly. Instead, specify columns in your text frames so that you don't have to worry about sloppy layouts.

Note that the options in the Columns area of the Text Frame Options dialog box work differently depending on whether Fixed Column Width is checked or unchecked:

- ✔ **If Fixed Column Width is unchecked,** InDesign subtracts from the text frame the space specified for the gutters and then divides the remaining width by the number of columns to figure out how wide the columns can be. For example, if you specify a 10-inch-wide text frame with three columns and a gutter of ½ inch, you end up with three 3-inch columns and two ½-inch gutters. The math is $(10 - (2 \times 0.5)) \div 3$.

- ✔ **If Fixed Column Width is checked,** InDesign resizes the text frame to fit the number of columns you selected at the indicated size, as well as the gutters between them. For example, suppose that you're using a 10-inch-wide text frame with a column width of 5 inches and a gutter of ½ inch, and you choose three columns: You end up with a 15-inch-wide text frame containing three 5-inch columns and two ½-inch gutters. The math is $(5 \times 3) + (2 \times 2)$.

Check Preview to see the effects of your changes before finalizing them.

Wrapping Text around Objects

In the days before personal computers and page-layout software, wrapping text around a graphic or other object was a time-consuming and expensive task. Text wraps were rare, found only in the most expensively produced publications. Not any more. Not only do all page-layout programs let you create text runarounds, most programs — including InDesign — provide several options for controlling how text relates to graphics and other objects that obstruct its flow.

When a frame is positioned in front of a text frame, InDesign provides the following options. You can

- ✔ Ignore the frame and flow the text behind it.
- ✔ Wrap the text around the frame's rectangular bounding box.
- ✔ Wrap the text around the frame itself.
- ✔ Jump the text around the frame (that is, jump the text from the top of the frame to the bottom).
- ✔ Jump the text to the next column or page when the text reaches the top of frame.
- ✔ Specify the amount of distance between the text and the edge of the obstructing shape.
- ✔ Flow text within the obstructing shape rather than outside it.

InDesign lets you wrap text around frames on hidden layers — as well as remove text wrap for objects on hidden layers. This technique is handy when you want to hide images or other distracting items but preserve the layout. See Chapter 4 for details on using layers.

If you want to wrap text around only a portion of a graphic — perhaps you need to isolate a face in a crowd — the best solution is to open the graphics file in its original program, create a clipping path around that portion, and then resave the file and import it and its clipping path into an InDesign document. (Chapter 17 explains clipping paths.)

The Text Wrap panel

The controls in the Text Wrap panel (see Figure 11-2) let you specify how a selected object will affect the flow of text behind it. Remember, the flow of text around an obstructing object is determined by the text-wrap settings applied to the obstructing object.

You can override the text-wrap settings of objects that are in front of a text frame by telling the text frame to ignore them. To do so, click a text frame and then choose Object➪Text Frame Options (⌘+B or Ctrl+B). In the Text Frame Options dialog box's General pane, select Ignore Text Wrap and then click OK. Text in the frame now flows behind any obstructing items regardless of the text-wrap settings applied to them.

The Text Wrap panel has three options that may not display when you open it: Wrap Options, Contour Options, and Include Inside Edges. You can more easily hide/show these functions by double-clicking the double-arrow symbol to the left of the Text Wrap label in the panel's tab or by choosing Hide Options/Show Options from the flyout menu.

Here's how to apply text-wrap settings to a frame or other object:

1. **If the Text Wrap panel isn't displayed (as shown in Figure 11-2), choose Window➪Text Wrap (Option+⌘+W or Ctrl+Alt+W).**

2. **Click either of the selection tools.**

3. **Click the object to which you want to apply text-wrap settings.**

   The object can be anywhere, but you'll probably want to position it on top of a text frame that contains text so that you can see the results of the settings you apply.

4. **Click one of the five text-wrap iconic buttons at the top of the Text Wrap panel.**

   The iconic buttons show you what each wrap does conceptually.

5. **If you want, adjust the space between the surrounding text and the obstructing shape by typing values in the Top Offset, Bottom Offset, Left Offset, and Right Offset fields.**

   These fields aren't available if you click the No Text Wrap button. If the object is a rectangle, all four fields are available if you click the Wrap around Bounding Box button or Wrap around Object Shape. Only the Top Offset field is available if you click the Wrap around Object Shape button for a free-form shape or the Jump to Next Column button. The Top Offset and Bottom Offset fields are available if you click the Jump Object button.

   If the Make All Settings the Same iconic button displays a chain, then changing any of the offset values will cause the other offset values to match. If the icon shows a broken chain, each offset value is independent of the others. Click the button to switch between these two modes.

6. **Select Invert if you want to flow the text inside the obstructing shape.**

7. **If you choose the Wrap around Object Shape button and a graphic is in the frame, you can also select from the Contour Options's Type pop-up menu.**

   You have six options:

   - Bounding Box is the same as clicking the Wrap around Bounding Box button.

   - Detect Edges tries to determine the graphic's outside boundary by ignoring white space — you'd use this option for bitmapped images that have a transparent or white background.

   - Alpha Channel uses the image's alpha channel, if any, to create a wrapping boundary (see Chapter 17).

   - Photoshop Path uses the image's clipping path, if any, to create a wrapping boundary (see Chapter 17).

   - Graphic Frame uses the frame's boundary rather than the bounding box.

   - Same as Clipping uses the clipping path for the graphic created in InDesign (see Chapter 17).

8. **You can control how text wraps around an object that splits a column by choosing an option from the Wrap To pop-up menu.**

   The options are Right Side, Left Side, Both Right & Left Sides, Side Towards Spine, Side Away from Spine, and Largest Area. You'll rarely choose Both Left & Right Sides, because unless the object is small, readers' eyes will stop at the interposed object and not see the rest of the text on the other side of it. Use either of the spine options to have the text stay on the outside or inside of a page, relative to the object, based on whether the page is right-facing or left-facing. You'll often choose Largest Area because that gives the text the most space next to the interposed object, which tends to be what looks good in many situations.

9. **By selecting the Include Inside Edges option, InDesign lets text appear inside any interior "holes" in the graphic.**

   You'll rarely use this technique, because in most cases, it's hard for the reader to follow text that wraps around an image, flows inside it, and then continues to flow outside it. But if the interior is large enough and not too distant from the text that flows on the outside, this effect may be readable.

If you specify text-wrap settings when no objects are selected, the settings are automatically applied to all new objects.

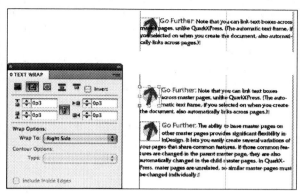

Figure 11-2:
Left: The
Text Wrap
panel.
Upper right:
A graphics
frame with
text wrap
turned off.
Bottom
right: Two
graphics
frames with
text wrap
turned on.

To apply text-wrap settings to a master item on a document page, press and hold Shift+⌘ or Ctrl+Shift to select the item and then use the controls in the Text Wrap panel as described in the preceding steps. If you don't want the text wrap applied to existing document items, only to new ones, choose Apply to Master Page Only in the flyout menu.

Setting text-wrap preferences

Be aware of several global text-wrap options, all of which are accessed via the Composition pane of the Preferences dialog box. (Choose InDesign⇨ Preferences⇨Composition [⌘+K] on the Mac or Edit⇨Preferences⇨ Composition [Ctrl+K] in Windows.) Here are the options:

- **Justify Text Next to an Object:** This option is useful when you have left-aligned text that wraps around an object at the right. (It also works if you have right-aligned text that wraps around an object at the left.) This option can lead to an awkward wrap, however, because InDesign won't try to make the text align precisely to the wrap's contour (because the text isn't justified). Use this option to justify the text just around the wrap and then continue using the text's specified nonjustified alignment.

- **Skip by Leading:** This option makes text wrap below or above an object based on the text's leading so that you have at least a full line space between the text and the object, even if the object's text-wrap settings would allow less space.

✔ **Text Wrap Only Affects Text Beneath:** This option, if selected, prevents text frames placed on top of an object from wrapping, while those behind the graphic frame will still be allowed to wrap. This option allows some text to overlap the graphic and other text to wrap around it. Note that this setting is global, affecting all objects. To override wrap settings of individual text frames, choose Object➪Text Frame Options (⌘+B or Ctrl+B) and enable the Ignore Text Wrap option in the General pane.

Chapter 12

The Ins and Outs of Text Editing

In This Chapter

▶ Editing text in your layout

▶ Working with tracked changes

▶ Searching and replacing words and formats

▶ Checking spelling as you type or all at once

▶ Customizing the spelling and hyphenation dictionaries

*W*hether you import text or type it into text frames directly in InDesign, you'll appreciate the tools that let you edit, search and replace, spell-check, and hyphenate your text, as well as work with tracked changes. You find out all about these capabilities in this chapter.

Editing Text

InDesign offers basic editing capabilities, not unlike those found in a word processor: cutting and pasting, deleting and inserting text, searching and replacing text and text attributes, and spell-checking. (Cutting, pasting, inserting, and deleting text works just like it does for any standard Mac or Windows program, so I don't repeat those details for you here.)

To do anything with text, you need to use the Type tool. When the Type tool is selected, you can click in any empty frame. (If it's not already a text frame, it becomes one automatically when you click it with the Type tool.) Or you can click and drag to create a new text frame. You can even click in an existing block of text. From this point, start typing to enter text.

Chapter 7 gets into more of the nitty-gritty of creating frames. And you can discover all about importing text in Chapter 11.

Controlling text view

In many layout views, the text is too small to work with. Generally, you zoom in around the block of text using the Zoom tool. Select the tool and then click to zoom in. To zoom out, hold the Option or Alt key when clicking.

Another way to zoom in is to use the keyboard shortcut ⌘+= or Ctrl+=. Each time you use it, the magnification increases. (Zoom out via ⌘+– or Ctrl+–.)

In addition to seeing the text larger, zooming in also helps you see the spaces, tabs, and paragraph returns that exist in the text. Choose Type⇨Show Hidden Characters (Option+⌘+I or Ctrl+Alt+I) to have the non-printing indicators for those characters display. You can also use the Show Options iconic pop-up menu in the application bar to access this command, as Chapter 1 explains.

Navigating through text

To work at a different text location in your InDesign document, click in a different text frame or another location in the current text frame. You can also use the four arrow (cursor) keys on the keyboard to move one character to the right, one character to the left, one line up, or one line down. Hold ⌘ or Ctrl when pressing the arrow keys to jump one word to the right or left, or one paragraph up or down. The Home and End keys let you jump to the beginning or end of a line; hold ⌘ or Ctrl when pressing those keys to jump to the beginning or end of a story. (A *story* is text within a text frame or that is linked across several text frames.)

Highlighting text

To highlight (or select) text, you can click and drag. Or you can use some keyboard options. For example, Shift+⌘+→ or Ctrl+Shift+→ highlights the next word to the right. Likewise, Shift+⌘+End or Ctrl+Shift+End highlights all the text to the end of the story.

To highlight a word, double-click (this action doesn't select its punctuation) and triple-click to select the entire paragraph. If you're highlighting a word and also want to include the punctuation that follows the word, double-click, and then press Shift+⌘+→ or Ctrl+Shift+→ to extend the selection.

To select an entire story, choose Edit⇨Select All (⌘+A or Ctrl+A).

To deselect text, choose Edit⇨Deselect All (Shift+⌘+A or Ctrl+Shift+A). An even easier way to deselect text is simply to select another tool or click another area of the page.

Undoing text edits

InDesign makes it easy for you to change your mind about text edits. Choose Edit⇨Undo (⌘+Z or Ctrl+Z) and Edit⇨Redo (Shift+⌘+Z or Ctrl+Shift+Z) any time you change your mind about edits.

Using the Story Editor

The Story Editor is a window that lets you see your text without the distractions of your layout. In it, you see your text without line breaks or other nonessential formatting — you just see attributes like boldface and italics, as well as the names of the paragraph styles applied in a separate pane to the left (see Figure 12-1). After clicking in a text frame, you open the Story Editor by choosing Edit⇨Edit in Story Editor (⌘+Y or Ctrl+Y).

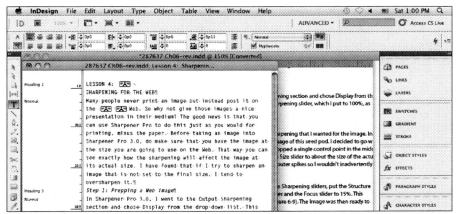

Figure 12-1:
The Story
Editor.

In the Story Editor, you use the same tools for selection, deletion, copying, pasting, and search and replace as you would in your layout. The Story Editor isn't a separate word processor; it's simply a way to look at your text in a less distracting environment for those times when your mental focus is on the meaning and words, not the text appearance.

The Story Editor also shows you the column depth for text, using a ruler along the left side of the text, just to the right of the list of currently applied paragraph styles. *Overset text* (text that goes beyond the text frame or beyond the final text frame in a threaded story) is indicated by the word *Overset* and is furthermore noted with a red line to the right of the text.

You can dock the Story Editor window into the document tabs so that you can more easily switch in and out of it as needed. Just drag the Story Editor window into the tabs, and InDesign converts it for you. Drag it back out to make it a floating window.

Tracking text changes

To track the text changes that different people make in an InDesign layout, you use several new capabilities in InDesign. You can also see the tracked changes in an imported Microsoft Word file. (Note that you can't track layout or graphics changes, such as formatting.)

If you need to know *who* is making each text change, all users should set up unique usernames in their individual copies of InDesign:

1. **Choose File⇨User to open the User dialog box.**

2. **Enter a name for yourself.**

3. **Choose your preferred color from the Color pop-up menu, then click OK.**

Once your username is set up, any document you edit now or in the future in that copy of InDesign will have any tracked changes attributed to that username. If more than one person uses a specific copy of InDesign, each person should set their username in the User dialog box to ensure any tracked changes are attributed to him or her, not to the previous user.

Enabling change tracking

You can enable tracking two ways:

✔ Select a single story.

✔ Simultaneously enable tracking for all *currently open* documents, and all *new* documents you create (until you shut down this session in InDesign).

Enabling tracked changes for your copy of InDesign isn't enough: You also need to enable tracked changes separately for each story in open documents — if you open a document later, you will need to enable tracked changes in its stories. If you close a document and reopen it later, you also need to turn tracked changes back on for each story you want to track.

To enable tracked changes for the *current story,* first select a text frame that contains the story. (Use the Selection, Direct Selection, or Type tool to select the frame.) Next, use one of these options to enable tracking:

✔ In the Track Changes panel (choose Window⇨Editorial⇨Track Changes), either

  • Click the Enable Track Changes in Current Story iconic button.

  • Choose Enable Track Changes in Current Story in the flyout menu.

✔ Choose Type⇨Track Changes⇨Track Changes.

  Figure 12-2 shows the Track Changes panel and its flyout menu.

To turn on tracked changes for all stories in the *currently open documents* and in *any documents you create while the current session of InDesign remains active,* use either of these actions:

✔ Choose Type⇨Track Changes⇨Enable Track Changes in All Stories.

✔ Choose Enable Track Changes in All Stories in the Track Changes panel's flyout menu.

For InDesign to show you revisions from your original Microsoft Word file (if you used its changes-tracking feature), you must have selected the Track Changes option in the Import Options dialog box when you first placed the text file, as explained in Chapter 11.

The Enable Track Changes in All Stories option is in effect only for documents already open and for documents you create in that same session of InDesign. Any documents you open later won't have tracked changes turned on unless you turned tracked changes on for them previously. When you exit and reopen InDesign later, Track Changes is turned off — you must turn it on each time you use InDesign.

Now, any deletions and insertions to text are tracked, as are occurrences of moved text. Formatting changes are *not* tracked.

Viewing changes

To see the changes, make sure a text frame you want to see the changes in is selected with the Selection, Direction Selection, or Type tool, and then open the Story Editor (choose Edit⇨Edit in Story Editor or press ⌘+Y or Ctrl+Y).

You'll see the highlighting for added and deleted text in the Story Editor window, as well as the change bars letting you know which lines have changed text. (You can change how this highlighting displays in the Track Changes pane of the Preferences dialog box. Choose InDesign⇨Preferences or press ⌘+K on the Mac, or choose Edit⇨Preferences or press Ctrl+K in Windows, to open the Preferences dialog box.)

Wherever the text cursor is located or text is selected, the Track Changes panel shows who made the change, when the change was made, and the type of change (addition, deletion, or moved text).

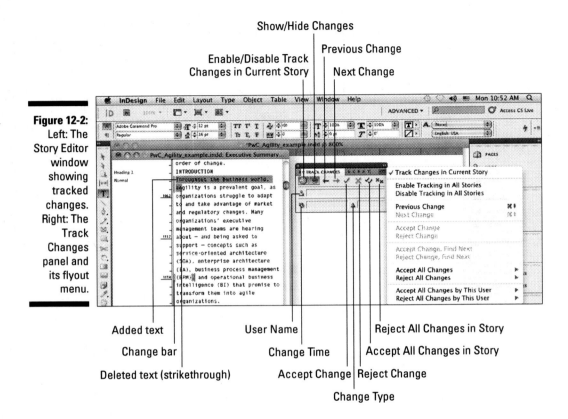

Figure 12-2:
Left: The
Story Editor
window
showing
tracked
changes.
Right: The
Track
Changes
panel and
its flyout
menu.

Working with changed text

You can do more than see changes and who made them in the Story Editor
and Track Changes panel. You can decide whether to *accept* or *reject* the
changes:

- ✔ Accepting a change means to remove the indicators that the text was
  added, deleted, or moved, making it appear as if it was part of the original story.

- ✔ Rejecting a change means to undo the change, as if it never happened.

The Track Changes panel is the best place to accept or reject changes. You
can also use the Type➪Track Changes menu's options (they match the
options in the Track Changes panel's flyout menu).

Most of the time, you'll use the iconic buttons in the Track Changes panel, as
shown in Figure 12-2, to navigate through the changes and accept or reject
them.

While you're deciding whether to accept or reject changes, you can save time by automatically moving to the next change when you make your decision:

- ✔ If you Option+click or Alt+click the Accept iconic button, InDesign moves to the next change for you after accepting the current change.
- ✔ Option+clicking or Alt+clicking the Reject iconic button moves to the next change for you after rejecting the change.

If you want to inspect the changes *without* deciding whether to keep them, use a couple of navigation shortcuts:

- ✔ ⌘+Page Up or Ctrl+PgUp navigates to the preceding change.
- ✔ ⌘+Page Down or Ctrl+PgDn navigates to the next change.

For faster acceptance or rejection of a bunch of changes, you can use the Track Changes panel's flyout menu options (or the Type➪Track Changes menu's options) to accept or reject all changes, or accept or reject all changes by the user who made the current change. Submenu options let you decide whether to accept or reject these changes in the current story only or in all stories in the current document.

There's one other option to note for tracked changes, which is found in the Track Changes pane of the Preferences dialog box: Include Deleted Text When Spellchecking. If selected, this option tells InDesign to check the spelling of deleted text (the idea being that if you restore the deletion, you want to make sure it is correctly spelled); if this option is deselected, InDesign ignores deleted text while spell-checking. (I explain how to spell-check in InDesign later in this chapter.)

Searching and Replacing Text

InDesign has a handy Find/Change feature (Edit➪Find/Change [⌘+F or Ctrl+F]) that is similar to the search-and-replace features with which you may already be familiar if you've used any word processor or page-layout application. With the Find/Change dialog box, you can find and change text, or you can extend the search to include attributes. Before starting a Find/Change operation, first determine the scope of your search:

- ✔ To search within a text selection, highlight the selection.
- ✔ To search from one point in a story to its end, click the cursor at that beginning location.

> ✔ To search an entire story, select any frame or click at any point in a frame containing the story.
>
> ✔ To search an entire document, simply have that document open.
>
> ✔ To search multiple documents, open all of them (and close any that you don't want to search).

Then choose the appropriate search scope — InDesign's term for *range* — using the Search pop-up menu and the scope iconic buttons below it.

Figure 12-3 shows the Find/Change dialog box. It can search for much more than just text, including special characters (glyphs) and object attributes (see Chapter 8), plus it lets you save search/replace queries so you can use them repeatedly. (It also lets you use the Unix grep syntax for conducting criteria-based searches; this feature is for experts familiar with grep searching and so is not covered in this book.)

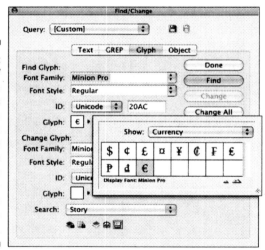

Figure 12-3:
The Find/
Change
dialog box's
Text pane
(left), with
its Special
Characters
for Search
iconic pop-
up menu
active
(right).

Replacing text

To search for text, follow these steps:

1. **Determine the scope of your search, open the appropriate documents, and insert the text cursor at the appropriate location.**

2. **Choose Edit⇨Find/Change (⌘+F or Ctrl+F).**

   Go to the Text pane if it's not already displayed.

3. **Use the Search pop-up menu, as shown in Figure 12-3, to specify the scope of your search by choosing All Documents, Document, Story, To End of Story, or Selection.**

   Note that the Search options that display are based on what you've selected before going to the Find/Change dialog box. For example, if you didn't select text, there'll be no Selection option. Likewise, if no story is selected, the Story and To End of Story options won't appear.

4. **Type or paste the text you want to find in the Find What field.**

   To use special characters, use the Special Characters for Search pop-up list (the icon to the right of the Find What field) to select from a menu of special characters (see Figure 12-3).

5. **Type or paste the replacement text into the Change To field.**

   To use special characters, use the Special Characters for Replace pop-up list (to the right of the Find What field).

6. **Specify any additional parameters for your search by selecting or deselecting the seven iconic buttons at the bottom of the pane: Include Locked Layers, Include Locked Stories, Include Hidden Layers, Include Master Pages, Include Footnotes, Case Sensitive, and Whole Word.**

   If an icon's background darkens, it's selected.

7. **To search for or replace with specific formatting, use the Find Format and Replace Format areas.**

   If the Find Format and Replace Format areas don't display in the dialog box, click the More Options button. (Look for details in the "Replacing formatting" section that comes next.)

8. **Click the Find button to start the search.**

   After the search has begun, click the Find Next button (it changes from the Find button after you start the search) to skip instances of the Find What text, and click the Change, Change All, or Change/Find buttons as appropriate. (Clicking the Change button simply changes the found text, clicking the Change All button changes every instance of that found text in your selection or story, and clicking the Change/Find button changes the current found text and moves on to the next occurrence of it — it basically does in one click the actions of clicking Change and then Find Next.)

   If you use the Change All feature, InDesign reports how many changes were made. If the number looks extraordinarily high and you suspect the Find/Change operation wasn't quite what you wanted, remember that you can use InDesign's undo function (Edit⇨Undo [⌘+Z or Ctrl+Z]) to cancel the search and replace and then try a different replace strategy.

9. **Click the Done button when you're finished finding and replacing.**

Replacing formatting

To find and change formatting or text with specific formatting, use the expanded Find/Change dialog box. For example, you can find all the words in 14-point Futura Extra Bold and change them to 12-point Bodoni.

The expanded dialog box contains two areas where you specify the formatting to search and change: Find Format and Replace Format. If these aren't visible in the Find/Change dialog box, click the More Options button.

To replace text formatting, follow these steps:

1. **Use the Specify Attributes to Find iconic button (the magnifying-glass-over-a-T icon) to open the Find Format Settings dialog box. (It's to the right of the Find Format area.)**

   In the Find Format Settings dialog box, your options are Style Options (paragraph and character styles), Basic Character Formats, Advanced Character Formats, Indents and Spacing, Keep Options, Bullets and Numbering, Character Color, OpenType Features, Underline Options, Strikethrough Options, Conditions, and Drop Caps and Other. You can change multiple attributes at once by making selections from as many panes as needed.

   Go to each pane whose formatting you want to find and select the desired formatting to search. Click OK when done; InDesign will bring you back to the Find/Change dialog box's Text pane.

2. **Use the Specify Attributes to Change iconic button (the magnifying-glass-over-a-T icon) to open the Change Format Settings dialog box. (It's to the right of the Replace Format area.)**

   The options in the Change Format Settings dialog box are the same as in the Find Format settings dialog box. Go to each pane whose formatting you want to change and select the desired formatting to replace. Click OK when done; InDesign returns you to the Find/Change dialog box's Text pane.

3. **Click Find Next and then Change to change the next occurrence or click Change All to change all occurrences.**

4. **Click Done when you're finished with the search and replace.**

To search and replace formatting only — regardless of the text to which it is applied — leave the Find What and Change To fields blank.

Changing special characters

InDesign also lets you replace special characters (glyphs) through a separate Glyph pane in the Find/Change dialog box, shown in Figure 12-4. The Glyphs pane makes it easier to actually enter the desired characters than using the Text pane's Special Characters for Search iconic pop-up menu (the @ icon). The process is mostly straightforward (just ignore the parts of the pane not described in the following steps):

1. **In the Find Glyph section, choose the font of the desired character in the Font Family pop-up menu and its style in the Font Style pop-up menu.**

2. **To choose the character itself, click the unnamed pop-up menu to the right of the Glyph field.**

   You get a dialog box that mimics the Glyphs panel (see Chapter 15); choose the character from the panel by double-clicking it.

3. **Repeat Steps 1 and 2 using the controls in the Change Glyph section to select the replacement glyph.**

4. **Set the scope of your search using the Search pop-up menu and the Include Locked Layers, Include Locked Stories, Include Hidden Layers, Include Master Pages, and Include Footnotes buttons, as described in the "Replacing text" section, earlier in this chapter.**

5. **Execute the search and/or replace using the Find, Change, Change All, and Change/Find buttons as described in the "Replacing text" section.**

6. **Click Done when done.**

If you want to quickly wipe out the selected glyphs, click the Clear Glyphs button.

Figure 12-4:
The Find/
Change
dialog box's
Glyph pane
with its
Glyph
pop-up
menu
active.

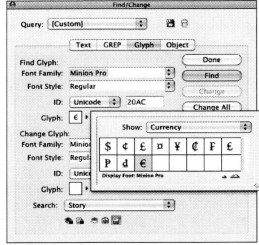

The solution to missing fonts

Sometimes, when you open a document, InDesign tells you that it can't find the fonts used in the documents on your computer. You get the option of finding the missing fonts, which opens the Find Fonts dialog box. (You can also open it after opening a document by choosing Type⇨Find Font.) This dialog box shows the names of all missing fonts; if you select one, you can change all occurrences of that font to one that you do have by selecting a new font family and font style from the menus at the bottom of the dialog box and then clicking Change All. If selected, the Redefine Style When Changing All check box ensures that any font replaced is also replaced in any paragraph and character styles that used the original font.

Of course, another — often preferable — solution is to get the fonts installed on your computer. After all, the design shouldn't change just because you don't happen to have the needed fonts on your computer.

InDesign CS5 has a handy new feature: Rather than require you to install fonts on your computer, all you have to do is have the fonts for a specific document in a folder named Document Fonts. That Document Fonts folder needs to be in the same folder as your InDesign document. These fonts are available only for that document, so using this feature makes sense for temporary use of fonts — ones that you pass around with the document for use with just that project. (Remember: If you plan on using these fonts for other purposes, you should get your own copies and install them in your computer for all your programs to use.)

Working with saved queries

If you plan to do the same search and/or replace operation repeatedly, you can save queries in InDesign. After entering the find and search information, click the Save Query iconic button, enter a name in the Save Query dialog box that appears, and click OK. That query now appears in the Query pop-up menu in the Find/Change dialog box.

To run a saved query, just choose it from the Query pop-up menu. (You'll see those that you saved plus some that came preinstalled with InDesign.) To delete a saved query, choose it from the Query pop-up menu and then click Delete Query iconic button.

That's all there is to it!

Checking Spelling

The spell-check feature helps you eradicate spelling errors and catches repeated words, as well as words with odd capitalization, such as internal capitalization (called *intercaps*) in words such as *InDesign*. InDesign also flags words not found in the spelling dictionary. You can customize the spelling dictionary, and you can purchase additional spelling dictionaries.

Checking spelling as you type

You can have InDesign check your spelling as you type by simply choosing Edit⇨Spelling⇨Dynamic Spelling. If that menu option is checked, your spelling will be checked as you type, as will the spelling of any text already in the document. Suspected errors are highlighted with red squiggle underlining so that you can correct them as needed. If you want InDesign to suggest proper spelling, you need to use the Check Spelling dialog box, covered in the next section.

Correcting mistakes on the fly

If you use a word processor, chances are it's one that corrects mistakes as you type. Microsoft Word, for example, has a feature called AutoCorrect that lets you specify corrections to be made as you type, whether those be common typos you make or the expansion of abbreviations to their full words (such as having Word replace *tq* with *thank you*).

InDesign offers much of the same functionality, which it calls *Autocorrect.* Unlike Word, you can't use this feature to replace symbols, such as having InDesign convert *(R)* to the ® symbol as you type. Note that — like Word — Autocorrect works only for text entered in InDesign after Autocorrect is turned on; it doesn't correct imported or previously typed text.

You enable Autocorrect in the Autocorrect pane of the Preferences dialog box. Choose InDesign⇨Preferences⇨Autocorrect (⌘+K) on the Mac or choose Edit⇨Preferences⇨Autocorrect (Ctrl+K) in Windows. If you want InDesign to automatically fix capitalization errors, check the Autocorrect Capitalization Errors check box. Typically, this feature finds typos involving capitalizing the second letter of a word in addition to the first. For example, InDesign replaces *FOrmat* with *Format.*

To add your own custom corrections, click the Add button. You see the Add to Autocorrect List dialog box, where you can enter the typo text or code that you want InDesign to be alert for in the Misspelled Word field, as well as the corrected or expanded text you want InDesign to substitute in the Correction field.

You can't use special characters in the Autocorrect pane, such as to automatically replace two hyphens (--) with an em dash (—).

Using the Check Spelling dialog box

The Check Spelling dialog box lets you choose what part of the document to spell-check and also provides suggestions on correct spelling. Plus, you can use the dialog box to add correctly spelled words to InDesign's spelling dictionary. Even if you use the new dynamic spell-checking feature, you'll still want to do a final spell-checking pass with the Check Spelling dialog box.

Specifying the text to check is a two-step process: First set up the spell-check's scope in the document (in other words, exactly what text you want to be checked). Second, specify the scope in the Search pop-up menu. Here's how:

1. **To set up the scope for the spell-check, highlight text, click in a story to check from the cursor forward, select a frame containing a story, or open multiple documents.**

2. **Open the Check Spelling dialog box (Edit⇨Spelling⇨Check Spelling [⌘+I or Ctrl+I]) and choose an option from the Search pop-up menu: Document, All Documents, Story, To End of Story, and Selection.**

Figure 12-5 shows the dialog box.

You may not see all the options in the Search pop-up menu; the list of options depends on how you set up the scope. For example, if you didn't highlight text, the Selection option isn't available. However, you can change the scope setup in the document while the Check Spelling dialog box is open — for example, you can open additional documents to check. You can also make the spell-check case-sensitive by checking the Case Sensitive check box.

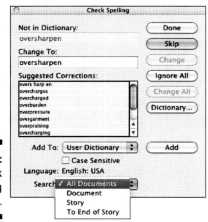

Figure 12-5:
The Check
Spelling
dialog box.

Note that when you first open the Check Spelling dialog box, if text is selected or the text cursor is active, it immediately begins checking the spelling, going to the first suspect word. Otherwise, the dialog box displays Ready to Check Spelling at the top.

3. **To begin checking the text, click Start.**

4. **As InDesign finds suspect words and phrases, it displays that text to you and provide several options to fix them.**

   When the spell-checker encounters a word without a match in the dictionary or a possible capitalization problem, the dialog box displays Not in Dictionary at the top and shows the word. When the spell-checker encounters a duplicate word, such as *of of,* the dialog box displays Duplicate Word and shows which word is duplicated. Use the buttons along the right side of the dialog box to handle flagged words, like:

   • Click the Skip button (it appears only after the spell-check has started) to leave the current instance of a Not in Dictionary word or Duplicate Word unchanged. To leave all instances of the same problem unchanged, click the Ignore All button.

   • To change the spelling of a Not in Dictionary word, click a word in the Suggested Corrections list or edit the spelling or capitalization in the Change To field. To make the change, click the Change button.

   • To correct an instance of a Duplicate Word, edit the text in the Change To field, and then click the Change button.

   • To change all occurrences of a Not in Dictionary word or a Duplicate Word to the information in the Change To field, click the Change All button.

   • To add a word flagged as incorrect — but that you know is correct — to InDesign's spelling dictionary, click the Add button. (If you have multiple dictionaries, first choose the dictionary to add it to using the Add To pop-up menu.)

   • To add a word flagged as incorrect to a specific dictionary, click the Dictionary button. A Dictionary dialog box appears, which lets you choose the dictionary to which you want to add the word, as well as what language to associate it with.

5. **After you finish checking spelling, click the Done button to close the Check Spelling dialog box.**

Changing the spelling and hyphenation dictionaries

The spelling dictionary that comes with InDesign is pretty extensive, but you'll likely need to add words to it. For example, your company may use words that are company-specific terms. Or you may use some product or individuals' names that wouldn't typically be found in the dictionary. Additionally, you may have some words that you prefer not to hyphenate or others that you want to hyphenate in a specific manner. To address these issues, you can customize InDesign's spelling and hyphenation dictionaries. InDesign handles both spelling and hyphenation in one dictionary for each language so that you use the same controls to modify both spelling and hyphenation.

If you're in a workgroup, be sure to share the edited dictionary file so that everyone uses the same spelling and hyphenation settings. (The file is located in the Dictionaries folder inside the Plug-ins folder inside your InDesign folder.) You can copy it for other users, who must then restart InDesign or press Option+⌘+/ or Ctrl+Alt+/ to reflow the text according to the new dictionary's hyphenation.

Customizing the spelling dictionary

When you add a word to the spelling dictionary, this word won't be flagged any more when you check spelling.

When you add words to the dictionary, you can specify their capitalization. For example, InDesign's dictionary prefers *E-mail*. You can add *e-mail* if you prefer a lowercase *e* or *email* if you prefer to skip the hyphen. To add words to the dictionary, follow these steps:

1. **Choose Edit⇨Spelling⇨Dictionary.**

   The Dictionary dialog box, shown in Figure 12-6, appears.

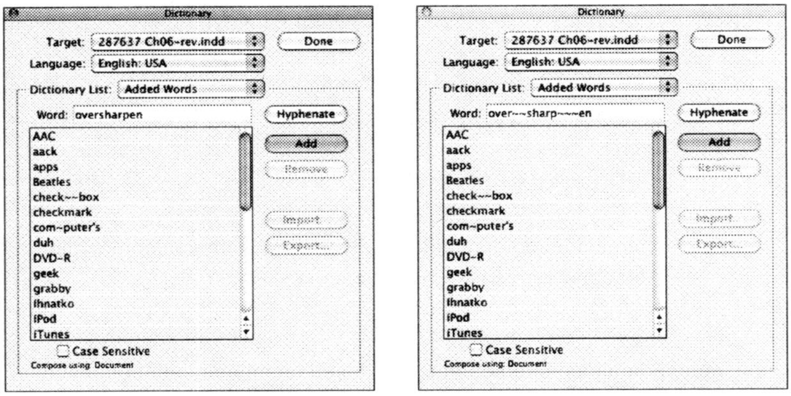

Figure 12-6:
Use the Dictionary dialog box to add words to the dictionary (left) and to add custom hyphenations (right).

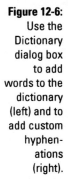

2. **Choose whether the addition to the dictionary affects just this document or all documents.**

   The Target pop-up menu lists the current document name as well as the name of the user dictionary.

3. **Choose the dictionary that you want to edit from the Language pop-up menu.**

4. **Type or paste a word in the Word field.**

   The word can have capital letters if appropriate, and it can include special characters, such as accents and hyphens.

5. **To have the added word accepted as being spelled correctly only with the capitalization specified in the Word field, check the Case Sensitive check box.**

6. **To edit the hyphenation of the word, click the Hyphenate button.**

   I cover hyphenation in the next section.

7. **Click the Add button.**

8. **To import a word list or export one for other users to import into their copies of InDesign, click the Import or Export button.**

   You then navigate to a folder and choose a filename in a dialog box. Note that when you click the Export button, InDesign exports all selected words from the list. If no words are selected, it exports all the words in the list.

9. **When you're finished adding words, click the Done button.**

To delete a word that you added to the dictionary, select it in the list and click the Remove button. To change the spelling of a word you added, delete it and then re-add it with the correct spelling. You can see all deleted words — just those deleted since you opened the dialog box — by selecting Removed Words from the Dictionary List pop-up menu so that you can add back any deleted by error.

Customizing hyphenation points

People can be particular about how to hyphenate words. Fortunately, InDesign lets you modify the hyphenation dictionary by specifying new, hierarchical hyphenation points.

Follow these steps to specify hyphenation points:

1. **Choose Edit⇨Spelling⇨Dictionary.**

2. **In the Language pop-up menu, pick the dictionary that you want to edit.**

3. **Type or paste the word in the Word field.**

   You can also double-click a word in the list.

4. **To see InDesign's suggestions for hyphenating the word, click the Hyphenate button.**

   If you want to change the hyphenation, continue on to Step 5.

5. **Type a tilde (~, obtained by pressing Shift+`, the open single keyboard quote at the upper left of the keyboard) as your first preference for a hyphenation point in the word.**

   If you don't want the word to hyphenate at all, type a tilde in front of it.

6. **To indicate an order of preference, use two tildes for your second choice, three tildes for your third choice, and so on.**

   InDesign first tries to hyphenate your top preferences (single tildes), and then it tries your second choices if the first ones don't work out, and so on.

7. **Click the Add button.**

8. **Continue to add words until you're finished.**

9. **Click the Done button.**

To revert a word to the default hyphenation, select it in the list and click the Remove button. To change the hyphenation, double-click a word in the list to enter it in the Word field, change the tildes, and then click the Add button. When you're adding variations of words, you can double-click a word in the list to place it in the Word field as a starting place.

Chapter 13

The Styles of Text

*I*t's the dirty secret of desktop publishing: Most users avoid using styles, even though they know they should. Instead, they apply formatting locally to text, hoping it's the same as a few pages back. It's a lot like not eating your vegetables: Even though you know that they're good for you (and most of them even taste good), it's easier to get something already made, never mind what's in it.

So, I'm going to tell you about styles before I get to the other ways to format text. Styles really are good for you: They save you lots of work, help you avoid embarrassingly inconsistent formatting, and give you more time to indulge in the guilty pleasure of local formatting.

I cover the particulars of paragraph and character formatting in Chapters 14 and 15, respectively. The formats themselves are the same whether you apply them directly (locally) or through a style (globally). I cover table styles and cell styles in Chapter 18 and object styles in Chapter 9, although the basic creation and management methods are the same for all styles.

Text in your layout may already have styles applied, using styles defined in Microsoft Word, as Chapter 11 explains.

Creating Styles

A *style* is a simple but powerful concept: It's a collection of formatting attributes that you can apply to text all at once, saving you time. Even better, if you change the style, all text that uses it is automatically updated, saving you time *and* ensuring consistency. That's got to be appealing!

InDesign gives you two kinds of styles for text: paragraph and character. Paragraph styles apply formatting to entire paragraphs, while character styles apply formatting to text selections. Unless you're doing a one-page ad, the formatting of which won't be repeated, you should have paragraph styles for all different types of paragraphs in your layout. You also need character styles for places where you consistently want to override your paragraph styles, such as for the lead-in of a bulleted paragraph that may have the first few words in a different font or color.

The easiest way is to format your text using the Paragraph and Character panels, as described in Chapters 14 and 15, and then make sure that you've selected the text you want to use as the model for your new style. Next, create the appropriate type of new style:

- ✔ For paragraph styles, open the Paragraph Styles panel by choosing Type⇨Paragraph Styles (⌘+F11 or Ctrl+F11). Then choose New Paragraph Style from the flyout menu to open the New Paragraph Style dialog box.

- ✔ For character styles, open the Character Styles panel by choosing Type⇨Character Styles (Shift+⌘+F11 or Ctrl+Shift+F11). Then choose New Character Style from the flyout menu to open the New Character Style dialog box.

In both cases, the style picks up the selected text's formatting. Adjust the style further if desired, give the style a name using the Style Name field in the General pane, and then click OK.

Of course, you can specify all the formatting directly in the New Paragraph or New Character Style dialog boxes rather than having InDesign pick it up from existing text. Create the new styles as just described and then go through each pane (selecting each from the list at the left of the dialog box) and choose your settings.

In the General pane of the New Paragraph Style and New Character Style dialog boxes are several controls that make styles work more intelligently:

- ✔ The Based On pop-up menu displays the names of other styles. You use this feature to create families of styles. Thus, if you change a style that other styles are based on, all those styles are updated with the new settings.

- ✔ In the Shortcut field, hold down any combination of ⌘, Option, and Shift (on the Mac) or of Ctrl, Alt, and Shift (in Windows) and press any number on the keypad. (You can't use letters, punctuation, and nonkeypad numbers for keyboard shortcuts, and Windows users need to make sure that Num Lock is on.)

- ✔ If you want to apply a new style to text that is selected, be sure to check the Apply Style to Selection check box before clicking OK to save the new style.

InDesign comes with a predefined default paragraph style called [Basic Paragraph] that text in a new frame automatically has applied to it. You can edit [Basic Paragraph] like any other style. Similarly, InDesign offers a pre-defined character style called [Basic Character]. (Style names that include surrounding brackets mean you can't delete the styles, even though you can modify them.)

You need to keep in mind several things when creating paragraph styles. (Character styles are pretty straightforward, so I'm not presenting a similar list for them.)

✔ To have InDesign automatically apply a different style to the next paragraph when you type text, choose a style name from the Next Style pop-up menu while defining a style. For example, when you define a style named Headline, you can choose Byline as the next style, so after you type in a headline, the next paragraph will be formatted for a byline. Obviously, you need to have the Byline style available.

✔ If you want your paragraph style to use a character style, you must define that character style first. (Drop caps and nested styles use character styles.)

Getting Fancy with Nested Styles

A special function available only in paragraph styles is something called a *nested style*. Basically, a nested style is a way of applying a series of character styles within a paragraph style based on a set of parameters you specify. For example, in a numbered list, you might want one character style applied to the numeral, and another to the first sentence, and then have the paragraph style's text formatting applied to the rest of the paragraph. With nested styles, you build all that into the paragraph style and let InDesign do the heavy lifting. Here's how it works:

1. **Define any character styles that you'll apply to text through a nested style.**

   Even if all you're doing is making text italic, you need to define a character style to do so. The Nested Styles feature can't apply any attributes other than those available in a character style.

2. **Open the Paragraph panel (Type⇨Paragraph Styles [⌘+F11 or Ctrl+F11]), choose Style Options from the flyout menu to open the Paragraph Style Options dialog box, and go to the Drop Caps and Nested Styles pane.**

3. **Click New Nested Style.**

   An entry appears in the Nested Styles section of the dialog box. This entry is what will be applied to text.

4. **Click the style name in the Nested Styles section of the pane to choose from an existing character style.**

   When you click the style name, a list of other styles appears, including [None], which uses the paragraph style's default formatting.

   You also have the [Repeat] option, which, if selected, lets you repeat a sequence of previous styles. (You choose the number of repetitions in the third column.)

5. **Click in the second column to determine the scope end point.**

   Your choices are Through and Up To. For example, if you choose Through for a nested style that is set for four words, all four words will get the nested style. If you choose Up To, the first three words will get the style, and the fourth will not.

6. **In the third column, specify how many items you want InDesign to count in determining the scope's end point.**

   For example, if you want the first seven characters to have the style applied, choose 7. If you want the style applied up to the first tab, choose 1.

7. **Click the item in the fourth column to specify the scope of text to which you're applying the nested styles.**

   Figure 13-1 shows the options. They break into three groups: a number of items (characters, words, and so on), a specific character (tab, em space, and so on), and a specific marker character (inline graphic marker, auto page number, and section marker). Whatever you choose needs to be consistent in all your text because InDesign will follow these rules slavishly.

Figure 13-1: A nested style that applies a character style to the first two words in a paragraph.

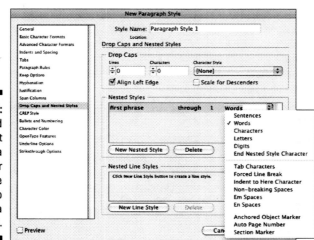

8. **Create multiple nested styles in one paragraph with different rules for each.**

   Obviously, you may not need to do this step, but the option exists. InDesign applies the styles in the order in which they appear in the dialog box, and each starts where the other ends. Use the up and down arrow buttons to change the order of nested styles.

9. **Select the Preview option to preview the formatting if you selected sample text before opening the dialog box.**

10. **Click OK when you're done.**

At the bottom of the Nested Styles dialog box is a useful feature: nested line styles. A nested line style works just like other nested styles except that it lets you apply a character style to a certain number of lines in a paragraph — a popular design approach, such as having the first line in small caps. You specify the desired character style and how many lines you want it applied to, and InDesign does the rest.

Managing Styles

InDesign provides lots of ways to manage your styles. In this section, I cover the common ones.

The options described here also apply to object styles, table styles, and cell styles — so, for example, the Load Paragraph Styles menu option will have a counterpart in the Character Styles, Object Styles, Table Styles, and Cell Styles panels' flyout menus. If I'm referring to features found in these five panels, I use the phrase "styles panel" rather than a specific panel's name.

Updating styles

If you've already created a style and want to change it, just go to the appropriate styles panel and choose Style Options from its flyout menu. If you've selected text that has the formatting you want the style to use in place of its current formatting, choose Redefine Style from the flyout menu. Remember that all text using the style is automatically updated when the style changes.

Sharing styles with others

The Load Paragraph Styles or Load Character Styles menu option (based on which styles panel is open) and the Load All Text Styles menu option let you import styles from another InDesign document. (Load All Text Styles imports both paragraph and character styles at the same time.) The other styles panels have similar menu options for sharing their styles.

You get a dialog box listing the styles in the chosen document so that you can decide which ones to import.

If you import styles whose names match those in the current document, InDesign gives you a chance to let the imported style overwrite the current style or to leave the current style as is and give the imported style a new name. If an entry appears in the Conflict with Existing Style, you can click that entry for a pop-up menu that provides two choices: Auto-Rename and Use Incoming Style Definition.

Note that at the bottom of the dialog box is the Incoming Style Definitions window, which lists the style definitions to help you decide which to import, as well as which to overwrite or rename.

Using style groups

To help you find the desired style in documents that have dozens of them, InDesign lets you create style groups, which create a folder in the styles panel's style list that you can open and close as desired. To create a group, choose New Style Group from the panel's flyout menu or click the Create New Style Group iconic button (folder icon) on the bottom of the panel. Enter a name in the dialog box that appears and click OK.

When working with style groups (which have a folder icon to the left of their names in the panel list), you have three options to add styles:

✔ You can drag any desired styles into the group.

✔ You can copy a selected style to the group by choosing Copy to Group and then selecting the target group in the dialog box that appears.

✔ If multiple styles are selected, you can create a group and move those styles into it in one fell swoop by choosing New Group from Styles in the flyout menu. (Note that this option is grayed out if any of the predefined styles — [None] and either [Basic Paragraph] or [Basic Character] — are selected.)

To quickly open all groups, choose Open All Groups in the panel's flyout menu. To quickly close them all, choose Close All Groups.

Other management options

The styles panels' flyout menus have four other options to manage your styles:

- ✔ **Duplicate Style** copies the currently selected style so that you can work on the copy.

- ✔ **Delete Style** — no surprise! — deletes selected styles.

- ✔ **Select All Unused** selects all styles not used in the document so that you can delete them all at once with the Delete Style menu option — part of keeping your document neat and tidy.

- ✔ **Sort by Name** alphabetizes the list of style names. (You can change the order of style names by dragging them within the list.)

What's that Quick Apply panel?

Another way to apply paragraph and character styles (and object styles, scripts, menu commands, and other elements) is by using the Quick Apply feature. Quick Apply is a consolidated list of styles that you access by choosing Edit➪Quick Apply, by clicking the Quick Apply iconic button (the lightning-bolt icon) in many panels, or by pressing ⌘+Return or Ctrl+Enter.

If you have selected text or have the text-insertion point active, the Quick Apply panel presents all stored formatting attributes available. You can scroll down to the one you want, or you can type the first few letters of the style name in the text field at the top to jump to styles beginning with those letters and then navigate to the one you want. Then press Return or Enter, which brings you back to where you were working with your text. Pressing ⌘+Return or Ctrl+Enter again closes the Quick Apply panel.

For users who are working on layouts from their keyboards — perhaps a layout artist who's working on a notebook while commuting — Quick Apply can be handy because you can switch to it, apply the style, and return to your text without touching the mouse.

InDesign has tons of attributes in the Quick Apply panel, so it can quickly get overwhelming. To remove attributes you likely will never use in this panel — such as scripts and menu customizations — choose the unnamed pop-up menu at the top of the panel and deselect unwanted attributes. (The check marks indicate attributes that *will* display.) You can also choose what attributes display in the Quick Apply panel by choosing Customize from its flyout menu.

Applying Styles to Text

Applying paragraph styles and applying character styles have some subtle differences, and I cover those particulars in the following sections. But two techniques work the same for both types of style:

- ✔ If your text selection uses more than one paragraph style or more than one character style, the styles panel displays the text (Mixed) at the upper left to let you know.

- ✔ InDesign has a neat capability that lets you apply multiple styles at once to selected text:

  - • Define the various styles and be sure that each style has a different style selected in the Next Style pop-up menu in the Paragraph Style Options or New Paragraph Style dialog boxes. For example, if you have Headline, Byline, and Body Copy styles, make sure that Headline has Byline selected in Next Style and that Byline has Body Copy selected in Next Style.

  - • Highlight *all* the text that uses this sequence of styles. Now Control+click or right-click Headline and select Apply "Headline" Then Next Style from the contextual menu. InDesign applies Headline to the first paragraph, Byline to the second paragraph, and Body Copy to the rest.

    Remember that Headline is just the example style used here; the actual contextual menu option will replace *Headline* with the actual style name you select inside the quote marks.

Paragraph particulars

To apply a paragraph style, click within a paragraph or highlight text in a range of paragraphs, and then click the style name in the Paragraph Styles panel or press its keyboard shortcut. (Windows users must make sure that Num Lock is on when using shortcuts for styles.)

When you apply a style to selected paragraphs, all local formats and applied character styles are retained. All other formats are replaced by those of the applied style. If you want to override those attributes, choose Clear Overrides from the Paragraph Styles panel's flyout menu or hold the Option or Alt key when clicking the style name in the panel.

If you want to remove a style from a paragraph so that it's not changed if the style is later updated, choose Break Link to Style from the flyout menu. The upper left of the panel displays the text (No Style).

The default font in the [Basic Paragraph] paragraph style has changed in InDesign CS5: It is now Minion Pro Regular, which InDesign installs for you. Previously, [Basic Paragraph] used Times on the Mac and Times New Roman in Windows as its default font.

Character characteristics

To apply a character style, highlight text and then click the style name in the Character Styles panel or press its keyboard shortcut. (Windows users must make sure that Num Lock is on when using shortcuts for styles.)

If you want to remove a style from a text selection so that it's not changed if the character style is later updated, choose Break Link to Style from the flyout menu or simply apply the [None] style. Note that if you later apply a paragraph style to text with the [None] character style, the text takes on the paragraph style's formatting rather than retaining its local formatting.

Chapter 14

Fine-Tuning Paragraph Details

*P*aragraphs are more than lines of text; they're chunks of information that themselves help convey meaning by organizing that information into related bits. Various types of paragraph formatting let you both make those chunks clearly distinguishable from each other and highlight certain chunks, such as lists or long quotes, from others.

This chapter explains what you need to know about formatting paragraphs, from setting indents and alignment — the two most commonly used paragraph attributes — to more sophisticated tasks like adding bullets and ruling lines.

Applying Paragraph Formats

InDesign provides three ways to apply paragraph formats:

- ✔ Use the controls in the Paragraph panel, shown in Figure 14-1, or their keyboard shortcuts. This method is great for working on individual paragraphs, although it's not the best method when working with lots of paragraphs you want to have the same formatting. You can open the Paragraph panel in three ways: Choose Type⇨Paragraph, choose Window⇨Type & Tables⇨Paragraph, or press Option+⌘+T or Ctrl+Alt+T.

- ✔ Use the controls in the Control panel. (Be sure that the Type tool is active and that the ¶ iconic button is selected in the panel to display paragraph-oriented functions.) These controls mirror those in the Paragraph panel, and using them instead of the Paragraph panel can reduce screen clutter. If the Control panel isn't visible (it almost always is), display it by choosing Window⇨Control (Option+⌘+6 or Ctrl+Alt+6).

- ✔ Create and apply paragraph styles, as covered in Chapter 13. Paragraph styles let you apply consistent formatting — and easily change it to all affected paragraphs — throughout your document.

Whichever method you use — and you'll use them all — the types of formatting available to you are the same.

The Paragraph panel and Control panel provide access to most of InDesign's paragraph-formatting options. Also, several of the options have keyboard shortcuts, as shown in the menus. But to set tabs, you must open the Tabs panel, as Chapter 18 covers.

Figure 14-1 shows the Paragraph panel and the Control panel's Paragraph (¶) pane. If you choose Hide Options from the flyout menu, the Space Before, Space After, Drop Cap Number of Lines, Drop Cap Number of Characters, Hyphenate, and Align/Do Not Align to Baseline Grid controls aren't displayed. You can use the double-arrow iconic button to the left of the panel name to toggle among showing the panel title, the basic options, and all options.

First Line Left Indent

Left Indent

Paragraph Options

Last line Right Indent

Right Indent

Justify buttons

Align to/from Spine buttons

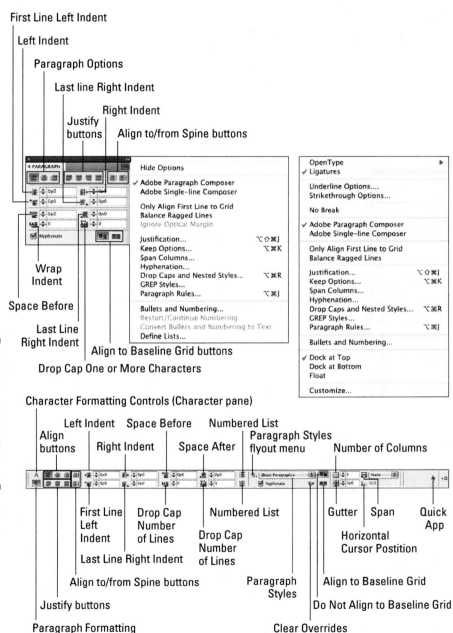

Wrap Indent

Space Before

Last Line Right Indent

Align to Baseline Grid buttons

Drop Cap One or More Characters

Figure 14-1:
Top: The full Paragraph panel. Bottom: The Control panel's Paragraph (¶) pane.

Character Formatting Controls (Character pane)

Align buttons

Left Indent

Right Indent

Space Before

Space After

Numbered List

Paragraph Styles flyout menu

Number of Columns

First Line Left Indent

Drop Cap Number of Lines

Numbered List

Drop Cap Number of Lines

Gutter

Span

Quick App

Horizontal Cursor Postition

Last Line Right Indent

Align to/from Spine buttons

Paragraph Styles

Align to Baseline Grid

Do Not Align to Baseline Grid

Justify buttons

Paragraph Formatting

Clear Overrides

Specifying Alignment and Indents

Alignment and indents give paragraphs their fundamental appearance. Indentation helps readers visually separate paragraphs — the indent acts as the separator, like the blank lines used to separate paragraphs in typewritten documents — while alignment provides visual texture.

The alignment buttons at the top of the Paragraph panel control how a selected paragraph begins and ends relative to the left and right margins. To apply a paragraph alignment to selected paragraphs, click one of the buttons. You can also use the keyboard shortcuts described in the following list. Here's a description of each alignment option (the icons themselves illustrate what they do):

- **Align Left** (Shift+⌘+L or Ctrl+Shift+L): This alignment places the left edge of every line at the left margin (the margin can be the frame edge, frame inset, left indent, or column edge) and fits as many words (or syllables, if the hyphenation is turned on) on the line as possible. In left-aligned paragraphs, the right margin is said to be *ragged* because the leftover space at the right end of each line differs from line to line and produces a ragged edge.

- **Align Center** (Shift+⌘+C or Ctrl+Shift+C): This alignment makes both the left and right edges of the paragraphs equally ragged.

- **Align Right** (Shift+⌘+R or Ctrl+Shift+R): This alignment is a mirror opposite of Align Left. The right edge is straight; the left edge is ragged.

- **Justify, Last Line Aligned Left** (Shift+⌘+J or Ctrl+Shift+J): In justified text, the left and right ends of each line are flush with the margins. (You can find out more about justification in the section "Controlling Hyphenation and Justification," later in this chapter.) Justified text is nearly always hyphenated — if you don't hyphenate justified text, spacing between letters and words is very inconsistent. Aligning the last line flush left is the traditional way of ending a paragraph.

- **Justify, Last Line Aligned Center:** This alignment produces justified text with the last line centered.

- **Justify, Last Line Aligned Right:** This alignment produces justified text with the last line aligned to the right.

- **Justify All Lines** (Shift+⌘+F or Ctrl+Shift+F): This alignment produces justified text with the last line forcibly justified. This option can produce last lines that are very widely spaced. The fewer the number of characters on the last line, the greater the spacing.

The preceding three alignment options are rarely used, and for good reason. People expect justified text to have the last line aligned left; the space at the end of the line marks the end of the paragraph. By changing the position of that last line, you can confuse your reader.

✔ **Align Toward Spine:** Essentially, this option automatically creates right-aligned text on left-hand pages and left-aligned text on right-hand pages. InDesign chooses a left or right alignment based on the location of the spine in a facing-pages document.

✔ **Align Away from Spine:** This option is the same as Align Toward Spine except that the alignment is reversed: Text aligns to the left on left-hand pages and to the right on right-hand pages.

When creating paragraph styles, all the preceding controls are available in the Indents and Spacing pane of the New Paragraph Styles dialog box.

Adjusting indent controls

The indent controls in the Paragraph panel let you both move the edges of paragraphs away from the left and/or right margins and indent the first line.

Here are your options:

✔ **Left Indent:** Moves the left edge of selected paragraphs away from the left margin by the amount you specify in the field. You can also click the up and down arrows. Each click increases the value by 1 point; holding down the Shift key while clicking increases the increment to 1 pica.

✔ **Right Indent:** Moves the right edge of selected paragraphs away from the right margin by the amount you specify in the field. You can also use the up and down arrows.

✔ **First-Line Left Indent:** Moves the left edge of the first line of selected paragraphs away from the left margin by the amount you specify in the field. You can also click the up and down arrows to adjust the indentation. The value in the First-Line Left Indent field is added to any Left Indent value. Using a tab or spaces to indent the first line of a paragraph, which is what was done in the age of typewriters, is usually *not* a good idea. You're better off specifying a First-Line Left Indent.

✔ **Last-Line Right Indent:** Moves the right edge of the last line of selected paragraphs away from the right margin by the amount you specify in the field. You can also click the up and down arrows.

When creating paragraph styles, all the preceding controls are available in the Indents and Spacing pane of the New Paragraph Styles dialog box.

Inserting space between paragraphs

To format a lengthy chunk of text with multiple paragraphs, you can indicate a new paragraph by indenting the paragraph's first line (by specifying a First-Line Left Indent value, as covered in the preceding section, "Adjusting indent controls"). Or you can insert some extra space between the new paragraph and the preceding one. Although no rule states that you can't use both of these spacing methods, it's a good idea to use one or the other — not both:

✔ To insert space before selected paragraphs, enter a value in the Space Before field in the Paragraph panel or Control panel. You can also use the up and down arrow buttons; each click increases the value by 1 point and holding down Shift key increases the increment to 1 pica.

✔ The Space After field works the same as the Space Before field but inserts space below selected paragraphs. If you use Space Before to space paragraphs, you won't need to use Space After, and vice versa; combining both can be confusing.

Don't insert extra paragraph returns between paragraphs. Doing so makes it harder to ensure that columns begin with text (as opposed to blank lines).

Controlling space between lines

Leading (pronounced "ledding") is the space between lines of text *within* a paragraph. Even though leading is traditionally an attribute of the paragraph, InDesign treats it as a character format, which you specify by using the Leading control in the Character panel or Control panel.

To change this character-oriented approach to affect entire paragraphs, select the Apply Leading to Entire Paragraphs option in the Type pane of the Preferences dialog box. (Choose InDesign➪Preferences➪Type [⌘+K] on the Mac or Edit➪Preferences➪Type [Ctrl+K] in Windows.)

Another way to control space between lines of text is to use baseline grids, as described in Chapter 10. Essentially, a baseline grid overrides the leading specified for paragraphs — you choose whether it overrides the spacing of every line in the paragraph or just the first line. To align to baseline grids, you must click the Align to Baseline iconic button in the Paragraph panel (the rightmost iconic button on the bottom of the panel) for the selected paragraphs. To prevent such locking to the baseline, click the Do Not Align to Baseline iconic button to its immediate left. These same buttons also exist on the right side of the Control panel.

Controlling where paragraphs break

InDesign's Keep Options feature lets you prevent widows and orphans; it also lets you keep paragraphs together when they would otherwise be broken at the bottom of a column. A *widow* is the last line of a paragraph that falls at the top of a column. (The poor thing has been cut off from the rest of the family, the last survivor.) An *orphan* is the first line of a paragraph that falls at the bottom of a column. (It, too, has become separated from its family, the only survivor.)

When you choose Keep Options from the Paragraph panel's flyout menu, the Keep Options dialog box appears.

The Keep Options dialog box holds several options for how paragraphs are managed as text breaks across columns and pages:

- ✔ **Keep with Next Lines:** This option applies to two consecutive paragraphs and controls the number of lines of the second paragraph that must stay with the first paragraph if a column or page break occurs within the second paragraph.

- ✔ **Keep Lines Together:** If you click this check box, it prevents paragraphs from breaking. When this box is checked, the two radio buttons below it become available. The radio buttons present an either/or choice. One must be selected; At Start/End of Paragraph is selected by default.

- ✔ **All Lines in Paragraph:** This option prevents a paragraph from being broken at the end of a column or page. When a column or page break occurs within a paragraph to which this setting has been applied, the entire paragraph moves to the next column or page.

- ✔ **At Start/End of Paragraph:** Select this check box to control widows and orphans. When this button is selected, the two fields below it become available:

  - **Start *x* Lines:** This field controls orphans. The value you enter is the minimum number of lines at the beginning of a paragraph that must be placed at the bottom of a column when a paragraph is split by a column ending.

  - **End *x* Lines:** This field controls widows. The value you enter is the minimum number of lines at the end of a paragraph that must be placed at the top of a column when a paragraph is split by a column ending.

- ✔ **Start Paragraph:** From this pop-up menu, choose Anywhere to let the paragraph begin where it would fall naturally in the sequence of text (no forced break). Choose In Next Column to force a paragraph to begin in the next column; choose In Next Frame to make it begin in the next frame in the story chain; choose On Next Page to force a paragraph to begin on the next page (such as for chapter headings). Your other choices are similar: On Next Odd Page and On Next Even Page.

When creating paragraph styles, all the preceding controls are available in the Keep Options pane of the New Paragraph Styles dialog box.

Spanning paragraphs across text columns

InDesign CS5 lets you override the number of columns set in a text frame (see Chapter 11) at a paragraph level. That means you can have a headline and its body text in the same text frame, with the text flowing into, say, two columns within the frame but the headline going across the full frame width, as Figure 14-2 shows. This type of layout is extremely common in newsletters, newspapers, and magazines.

The Span Columns control isn't all-or-nothing. Instead, it lets you specify how many columns the paragraph spans: all columns, two columns, three columns, or four columns. For example, if you have a four-column text frame and set Span Columns to Span 2 for the headline, the headline will stretch across the first two columns of the frame, with the text in those columns appearing below the headline, but the text in the other two columns will not be affected, as Figure 14-2 shows.

The Span Columns control also lets you split text within its column. For example, if you choose a split of 2, the text will be split into two columns within its text column. Figure 14-2 shows an example. At top, I've set a headline to span the entire text frame. In the middle, I've set a headline to span two columns in a four-column text frame. At bottom, I've set a headline to split into two columns in a two-column text frame.

Adding Drop Caps

Drop caps are enlarged capital letters that are often used to embellish paragraphs (usually the first paragraph of a chapter or story) and draw attention to paragraphs. In the Paragraph panel or Control panel, InDesign lets you specify the number of letters you want to include in a drop cap and the number of lines you want to drop them down into.

To add one or more drop caps to selected paragraphs, enter a number in the Drop Cap Number of Characters field in the Paragraph panel or Control panel. The number you enter determines how many characters in a selected paragraph will be made into drop caps. To specify the number of lines a drop cap will extend into a paragraph (and therefore the height of the drop cap), enter a number in the Drop Cap Number of Lines field.

Figure 14-2:
The new
Span
Columns
control and
three exam-
ples of what
it can do.

After you create a drop cap, you can modify it by highlighting it and changing any of its character formats — font, size, color, and so on — by using the
Character panel or Control panel, as well as other panes such as Stroke and
Swatches. Even better: Apply a character style to it that has all the desired
attributes stored in one place. Figure 14-3 shows two examples of drop caps:
At top, I've set a one-character drop cap three lines deep, and at bottom I've
set a two-line, four-character drop cap with the first word set in small caps.

When creating paragraph styles, the preceding controls are available in the
Drop Caps and Nested Styles pane of the New Paragraph Styles dialog box.
(See Chapter 13 for details on nested styles.)

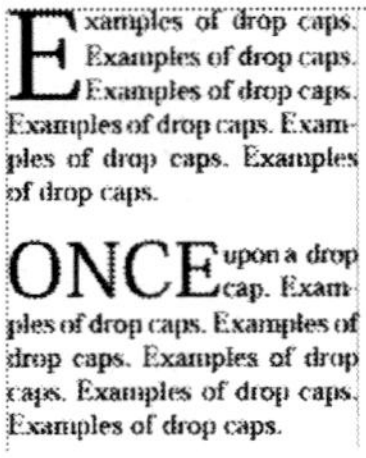

Figure 14-3:
Two examples of drop caps.

Examples of drop caps. Examples of drop caps. Examples of drop caps. Examples of drop caps. Examples of drop caps. Examples of drop caps.

ONCE upon a drop cap. Examples of drop caps. Examples of drop caps. Examples of drop caps. Examples of drop caps. Examples of drop caps.

Controlling Hyphenation and Justification

Hyphenation is the placement of hyphens between syllables in words that won't fit at the end of a line of text. A hyphen is a signal to the reader that the word continues on the next line. InDesign gives you the option to turn paragraph hyphenation on or off. If you choose to hyphenate, you can customize the settings that determine when and where hyphens are inserted.

Justification is the addition or removal of space between words and/or letters that produces the flush-left/flush-right appearance of justified paragraphs. InDesign's justification controls let you specify how space is added or removed when paragraphs are justified. If you justify paragraphs, you almost certainly want to hyphenate them, too. If you opt for left-aligned paragraphs, whether to hyphenate is a personal choice.

InDesign offers both manual and automatic hyphenation.

Manual hyphenation

To break a particular word in a specific place, you can place a *discretionary hyphen* in the word. If the word doesn't entirely fit at the end of a line in a hyphenated paragraph, InDesign uses the discretionary hyphen to split the word if the part of the word before the hyphen fits on the line. To insert a discretionary hyphen, use the shortcut Shift+⌘+– or Ctrl+Shift+– (note the hyphen in the shortcuts) in the text where you want the hyphen to appear.

If a word has a discretionary hyphen, and hyphenation is necessary, InDesign breaks the word *only* at that point. But you can place multiple discretionary hyphens within a single word. If a word needs to be hyphenated, InDesign uses the hyphenation point that produces the best results.

You can prevent a particular word from being hyphenated either by placing a discretionary hyphen in front of the first letter or by highlighting the word and choosing No Break from the flyout menu of the Control panel or Character panel. (You need to select the A iconic button in the Control panel to get this option in its flyout menu.) But be careful: If you select more than a line's width of text and apply No Break, InDesign doesn't know what to do, and so it doesn't display the rest of the story.

To prevent hyphenation for an entire paragraph, click anywhere inside of it and uncheck Hyphenate from the Paragraph panel or Control panel. (Be sure the ¶ button is selected in the Control panel.)

Automatic hyphenation

To have InDesign automatically hyphenate selected paragraphs, all you have to do is check the Hyphenate check box in the Paragraph panel or Control panel. (Remember that in the Paragraph panel, the Hyphenate check box appears only if you choose Show Options from the flyout menu.)

You can control how InDesign actually performs the hyphenation via the Hyphenation option in the flyout menu. When you choose Hyphenation, the Hyphenation Settings dialog box appears.

The options in the Hyphenation Settings dialog box include

- ✔ **Hyphenate:** This option is a duplicate of the Hyphenate check box in the Paragraph panel and Control panel. If you didn't check it before opening the Hyphenation Settings dialog box, you can check it here.

- ✔ **Words with at Least *x* Letters:** This spot is where you specify the number of letters in the shortest word you want to hyphenate.

- ✔ **After First *x* Letters:** In this field, enter the minimum number of characters that can precede a hyphen.

- ✔ **Before Last *x* Letters:** The number entered in this field determines the minimum number of characters that can follow a hyphen.

- ✔ **Hyphen Limit: *x* Hyphens:** In this field, you specify the number of consecutive lines that can be hyphenated. Several consecutive hyphens produce an awkward, ladder-like look, so consider entering a small number, such as **2** or **3**, in this field.

- ✔ **Hyphenation Zone:** The entry in this field applies only to nonjustified text and only when the Adobe Single-Line Composer option is selected (in the Paragraph panel's flyout menu). A hyphenation point must fall within the distance specified in this field in relation to the right margin in order to be used. Acceptable hyphenation points that don't fall within the specified hyphenation zone are ignored. You can also use the Better Spacing/Fewer Hyphens slider below the field to pick a value rather than entering a value in the Hyphenation Zone field.

✔ **Hyphenate Capitalized Words:** If you check this box, InDesign hyphenates, when necessary, capitalized words. If you don't check this box, a capitalized word that would otherwise be hyphenated gets bumped to the next line, which may cause excessive spacing in the preceding line.

✔ **Hyphenate Last Word:** Check this box to allow InDesign to break the last word in a paragraph. Otherwise, InDesign moves the entire word to the last line and spaces the preceding text as necessary. Many typographers believe hyphenating the last word in a paragraph looks bad, so it's rare to enable this option.

✔ **Hyphenate Across Column:** Check this box to let text hyphenate at the end of a column. Many typographers believe hyphenating the word at the end of a column looks bad, so it's also rare to enable this option.

When creating paragraph styles, all the preceding controls are available in the Hyphenation pane of the New Paragraph Styles dialog box — except for the composer setting, covered in the next sections.

Controlling justification

To control how justification is achieved, you can

✔ Condense or expand the width of spaces between words.

✔ Add or remove space between letters.

✔ Condense or expand the width of characters.

The options in the Justification dialog box let you specify the degree to which InDesign adjusts normal word spaces, character spacing, and character width to achieve justification. Access this dialog box by choosing Justification in the flyout menu in the Control panel or in the Paragraph panel, or by pressing Option+Shift+⌘+J or Ctrl+Alt+Shift+J. When specifying values in the Justification dialog box, Minimum values must be smaller than Desired values, which in turn must be smaller than Maximum values.

The Justification dialog box lets you specify three options:

✔ **Word Spacing:** Enter the percentage of a character that you want to use whenever possible in the Desired field. (The default value is 100%, which uses a font's built-in width.) Enter the minimum acceptable percentage in the Minimum field; enter the maximum acceptable percentage in the Maximum field. The smallest value you can enter is **0%**; the largest is **1000%**.

✔ **Letter Spacing:** The default value of 0% in this field uses a font's built-in letter spacing. In the Desired field, enter a positive value to add space (in increments of 1% of an en space) between all letter pairs; enter a negative value to remove space. Enter the minimum acceptable percentage in the Minimum field; enter the maximum acceptable percentage in the Maximum field.

✔ **Glyph Scaling:** The default value of 100% uses a character's normal width. In the Desired field, enter a positive value to expand all character widths; enter a negative value to condense character widths. Enter the minimum acceptable percentage in the Minimum field and the maximum acceptable percentage in the Maximum field. If you apply glyph scaling, keep it to a range of 97 to 103 percent at most.

If you use the Adobe Paragraph Composer option (see the next section) for justified paragraphs, specifying a narrow range between minimum and maximum Word Spacing, Letter Spacing, and Glyph Scaling generally produces good-looking results. However, if you choose the Adobe Single-Line Composer option, a broader range between Minimum and Maximum gives the composer more leeway in spacing words, letters, and hyphenating words, and can produce better-looking results. The best way to find out what values work best is to experiment with several settings. Print hard copies and let your eyes decide which values produce the best results.

When creating paragraph styles, all the preceding controls are available in the Justification pane of the New Paragraph Styles dialog box.

Composing text

The Paragraph panel's flyout menu offers two options for implementing the hyphenation and justification settings you establish:

✔ **Adobe Single-Line Composer:** In single-line composition, hyphenation and justification settings are applied to each line in a paragraph, one line at a time. The effect of modifying the spacing of one line on the lines above and below it isn't considered in single-line composition, so it can cause poor spacing.

✔ **Adobe Paragraph Composer:** InDesign's Adobe Paragraph Composer is selected by default. It takes a broader approach to composition than the Adobe Single-Line Composer by looking at the entire paragraph at once. If a poorly spaced line can be fixed by adjusting the spacing of a previous line, the Adobe Paragraph Composer reflows the previous line.

The Adobe Paragraph Composer is more sophisticated than the Single-Line Composer, offering better overall spacing because it sacrifices optimal spacing a bit on one line to prevent really bad spacing on another, something the single-line method doesn't do. But it can result in longer text than the Adobe Single-Line Composer does.

These options are also available in the Justification dialog box, covered in the preceding section.

Ruling Your Paragraphs

If you want to place a horizontal line within text so that the line moves with the text when editing causes the text to reflow — an often effective highlighting device — you need to create a paragraph rule. A paragraph rule looks much like a line created with the line tool but behaves like a text character. Here's how to create paragraph rules:

1. **Select the paragraphs to which you want to apply a rule above and/ or a rule below and then choose Paragraph Rules from the Paragraph panel's or Control panel's flyout menu.**

   Alternatively, you can use the shortcut Option+⌘+J or Ctrl+Alt+J.

   You can also specify rules as part of a paragraph style. The Paragraph Rules dialog box, shown in Figure 14-4, is displayed.

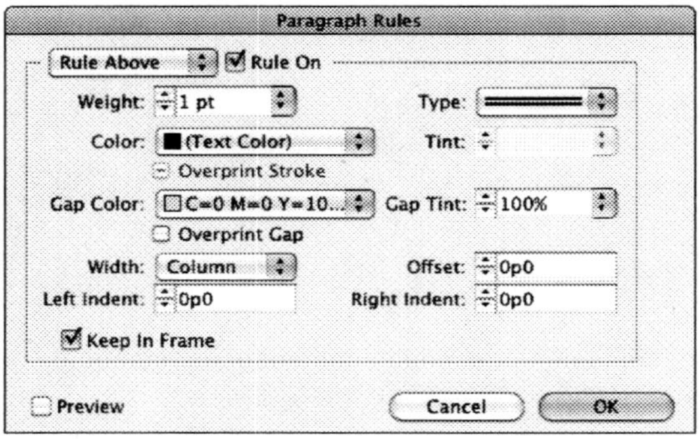

Figure 14-4:
The
Paragraph
Rules dialog
box.

2. **Choose Rule Above or Rule Below and then click Rule On.**

   To add rules both above and below, click Rule On for both options and specify their settings separately. To see the rule while you create it, select the Preview option.

3. **Choose a predefined thickness from the Weight pop-up menu or enter a value in the Weight field.**

4. **Choose a rule type from the Type pop-up menu.**

   You can choose from 17 types, including dashed, striped, dotted, and wavy lines.

5. **Choose a color for the rule from the Color pop-up menu.**

   This menu lists the colors displayed in the Swatches panel (Window➪Color➪Swatches [F5]).

6. From the Width pop-up menu, choose Column to have the rule extend from the left edge of the column to the right edge of the column; choose Text to have the rule extend from the left edge of the frame or column to the right.

7. To indent the rule from the left and/or right edges, enter values in the Left Indent and/or Right Indent fields.

8. Control the vertical position of the rule by entering a value in the Offset field.

   For a rule above, the offset value is measured upward from the baseline of the first line in a paragraph to the bottom of the rule; for a rule below, the offset is measured downward from the baseline of the last line in a paragraph to the top of the rule.

9. Check the Overprint Stroke box if you want to print a rule on top of any underlying colors.

   This option ensures that any misregistration during printing won't result in white areas around the rule where the paper shows through. A similar Overprint Gap check box is available for lines that have a gap color.

10. To ensure that a rule over a paragraph at the top of a frame displays within the frame, check the Keep in Frame option.

11. Click OK to close the dialog box, implement your changes, and return to the document.

To remove a paragraph rule, click in the paragraph to which the rule is applied, choose Paragraph Rules from the Paragraph panel's flyout menu, uncheck the Rule On box, and then click OK.

When creating paragraph styles, all the preceding controls are available in the Paragraph Rules pane of the New Paragraph Styles dialog box.

Chapter 15

Finessing Character Details

*W*hen you create documents, you have lots of opportunities to make decisions about how the text appears. With its comprehensive set of character-formatting tools, InDesign lets you change the look of type so that it can precisely match the communication needs of your publications. You can control the font and size of type, and many other variations.

Decisions about type matter. A document relies on good typography to allow others to easily read and understand it. The appearance of type supports the message you're conveying, and doing a good job of character formatting is worth your time.

Specifying Character Formats

InDesign lets you modify the appearance of highlighted characters or selected paragraphs with the following options:

✔ **Character panel:** Highlight the text and open the Character panel (Type➪Character [⌘+T or Ctrl+T]), which is shown in Figure 15-1. (You can also choose Window➪Type & Tools➪Character.) Be sure Show Options is visible in the flyout menu in order to see all the possible options. You can also use the double-arrow iconic button to the left of the panel name to toggle among showing the panel title, the basic options, and all options.

The Character panel provides access to most of InDesign's character formatting options. Three options — Font Family, Font Style, and Font Size — are also available via the Type menu, and several options have keyboard shortcuts.

✔ **Paragraph panel:** Select a paragraph and open the Paragraph panel (Type⇨Paragraph [Option+⌘+T or Ctrl+Alt+T]). Chapter 14 covers these settings in detail.

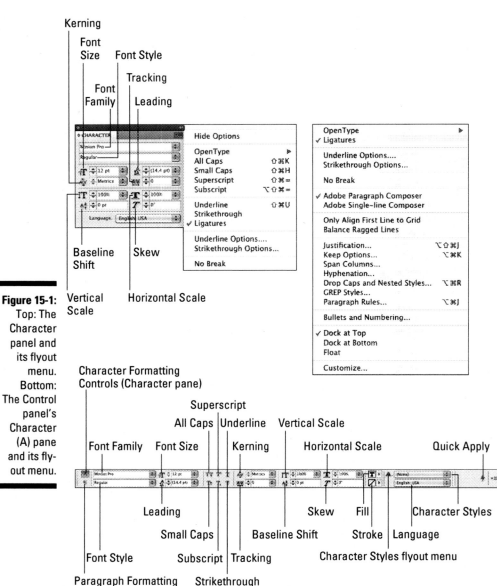

Figure 15-1: Top: The Character panel and its flyout menu. Bottom: The Control panel's Character (A) pane and its flyout menu.

- ✔ **Control panel:** The Control panel offers all the formatting options of the Character panel plus others. If the Control panel doesn't show all the character formatting options, select the text and then click the A iconic button on the panel. If the Control panel isn't visible (it almost always is), display it by choosing Window➪Control (Option+⌘+6 or Ctrl+Alt+6).

To change the default character formats — the settings that InDesign uses when you type text into an empty frame — make changes in the Character panel or Control panel when no text is selected or when the text-insertion cursor isn't flashing. That step saves you the hassle of having to reformat new text.

You can choose to apply character formats to highlighted text in three ways:

- ✔ **Create and apply character styles.** Character styles offer an important advantage: A character style's settings are stored, so you can apply the exact same settings easily to other text. When you change a character style's settings, any text based on that style is automatically changed to reflect the new settings. (Chapter 13 covers styles in detail.)

- ✔ **Use the local controls** in the Character panel, the Control panel, the Type menu, or their keyboard shortcuts, which I cover in the upcoming sections. Even when you do use character styles, you'll probably also do some local formatting from time to time. For example, you'd probably use the Character panel to format the type on the opening spread of a feature magazine article and then use character styles to quickly format the remainder of the article.

- ✔ **Use the Eyedropper tool** to "sample" the formatting of text and then apply it to other text using the Marker tool. After you click the Eyedropper tool on the text you want to sample, the tool turns into the Marker tool. Click and drag the Marker tool over the text you want to apply the formatting to.

  To switch back to the Eyedropper tool to select different formatting, press Option or Alt, or click the Eyedropper tool again.

If you have a smallish monitor, set at 1024 by 768 pixels — the norm for a 17-inch display — the Character and Character Styles panels may be shoved to the bottom of the panel dock. When they're selected, the only things you see are their panel tab and flyout menu icon. You have a few choices: Shorten other panel groups in the dock to make room for them, remove other panel groups to make room for them, or drag them out of the dock and make them floating.

Modifying Font, Type Style, and Size

Many people use typographic terms — *font, face, typeface, font family,* and *type style* — inconsistently. Which terms you use doesn't matter as long as you make yourself understood, but I recommend becoming familiar with the font-related terms in InDesign's menus and panels:

- **Font or typeface:** A collection of characters — including letters, numbers, and special characters — that share the same overall appearance, including stroke width, weight, angle, and style.

  For example, Helvetica Regular and Adobe Garamond Semibold Italic are well-known fonts.

- **Font family:** A collection of several fonts that share the same general appearance but differ in stroke width, weight, and/or stroke angle.

  For example, Helvetica and Adobe Garamond are font families.

- **Font style:** Each of the fonts that make up a font family. When you choose a font family from the Character panel's Font Family menu, InDesign displays the family's font style variations — what most of the design world calls *type styles* — in the accompanying Font Style pop-up menu.

  For example, Regular and Semibold Italic are examples of font styles.

Changing font family and font style

When you change from one font to another in InDesign, you can choose a new font family and font style independently in the Character panel. For example, changing from Arial Bold to Times Bold or from Arial Regular to Berthold Baskerville Regular is a simple change of font family (Arial to Berthold Baskerville). However, if you switch from, say, Bookman Light to Century Schoolbook Bold Italic, you're changing both family and style (Bookman to Century and then Light to Bold Italic).

InDesign can display previews of fonts when you select fonts via the Control panel, various text-oriented panels, and the Type menu. You turn on this capability in the Type pane of the Preferences dialog box by choosing InDesign⇨Preferences⇨Type (⌘+K) on the Mac or Edit⇨Preferences⇨Type (Ctrl+K) in Windows. But doing so makes your menus huge, often so much that they're unwieldy to use. Although it can help you get familiar with your fonts, its unwieldy nature may not be worth that benefit. Only you can decide, but if you do use the preview feature, I recommend keeping the preview size small to limit its size.

Whether you use the Control panel or Character panel, you can choose between two methods for changing the font family:

- ✔ Choose the Font Family menu and then select a name from the list of available font families.

- ✔ Place the cursor in front of or highlight the font name displayed in the Font Family field, type the first few letters of the font family you want to apply, and then press Return or Enter. For example, entering **Cas** might select Caslon (if it's available on your computer).

If you choose only a font family when font styles are available in an accompanying submenu, no changes are applied to the selected text. So be sure to select a font style from the submenu.

When creating character styles, the preceding controls are available in the Basic Character Formats pane of the New Character Styles and New Paragraph Styles dialog boxes.

Changing type size

You can be very precise with type sizes (what InDesign calls *font size*). InDesign supports sizes from 0.1 point to 1,296 points (108 inches) in increments as fine as 0.001 point. Of course, you want to use good judgment when choosing type sizes. For example, headlines should be larger than subheads, which in turn are larger than body text, which is larger than photo credits, and so on.

Change the type size of highlighted text with the following methods:

- ✔ Choose Type⇨Size and then choose one of the predefined sizes listed in the Size submenu. If you choose Other from the submenu, the Font Size field is highlighted in the Character panel. Enter a custom size and then press Return or Enter.

- ✔ Use the Character panel or Control panel:

  1. Choose one of the predefined sizes from the Font Size menu.

  2. Highlight the currently applied type size displayed in the accompanying editable field, enter a new size, and then press Return or Enter.

  3. Make sure that the Font Size field is selected and then use the up and down arrow keys to increase or decrease the size in 1-point increments. Pressing Shift multiplies the increment to 10.

- ✔ Control+click or right-click a text selection and then choose a size from the Size submenu. If you choose Other from the submenu, the Font Size field is highlighted in the Character panel. Enter a custom size and then press Return or Enter.

If text is highlighted and the Font Size field is empty, more than one type size is used in the selected text.

When creating character styles, the Font Size control is available in the Basic Character Formats pane of the New Character Styles dialog box.

Using Other Character Formats

In the Control panel, you can adjust other character formats, including all caps, small caps, superscript, subscript, underline, strikethrough, kerning, tracking, horizontal and vertical scale, baseline shift, skew, font style, and language. Through the flyout menu, you can also set ligatures, modify underline and strikethrough settings, control whether text may break (be hyphenated), select its case (such as all caps and small caps), and select OpenType features. (The next several sections explain each of these terms, except for OpenType features, which let you apply a variety of controls to OpenType fonts — an expert topic that this book doesn't get into detail on.)

In the Character panel, you can adjust kerning, tracking, horizontal and vertical scale, baseline shift, skew, and language. Through its flyout menu (refer to Figure 15-1), you can also set all caps, small caps, superscript, subscript, underline, strikethrough, ligatures, and underline and strikethrough settings, as well as control whether text may break (be hyphenated) and select OpenType features. (InDesign also lets you create custom underlines and strikethroughs, an expert feature not covered in this book.)

When creating character styles, the kerning, tracking, subscript, superscript, case, ligature, underlining, break, and strikethrough controls are available in the Basic Character Formats pane of the New Character Styles and New Paragraph Styles dialog boxes. The scale, baseline shift, skew, and language controls are in the Advanced Character Formats pane. OpenType controls are in the OpenType Features pane.

You must choose Show Options from the Character panel's flyout menu to display the Vertical Scale, Horizontal Scale, Baseline Shift, Skew, and Language options in the panel.

The Control panel has the same functions as the Character panel, except the all caps, small caps, superscript, subscript, underline, and strikethrough options are in the panel itself rather than in its flyout menu.

Figure 15-2 shows the various effects in action. In its top row, the word *InDesign* has a different font style applied, *incredible* has been scaled horizontally, and *control* is in all caps, while *over* has had each letter's baseline shifted by a different amount. In the middle row, the word *text* has been skewed, the word *with* is in small caps, a gradient and underline are applied to *typographic,* a custom underline has been applied to *capabilities,* and the word *formatting* has been vertically scaled. In the bottom row, compare the baseline shifts in the top row to the true superscript and subscript following the words *most* and *people.* The word *never* has a custom strikethrough applied, while *even* uses a standard one. The word *heard* has a colored stroke applied and a fill of white.

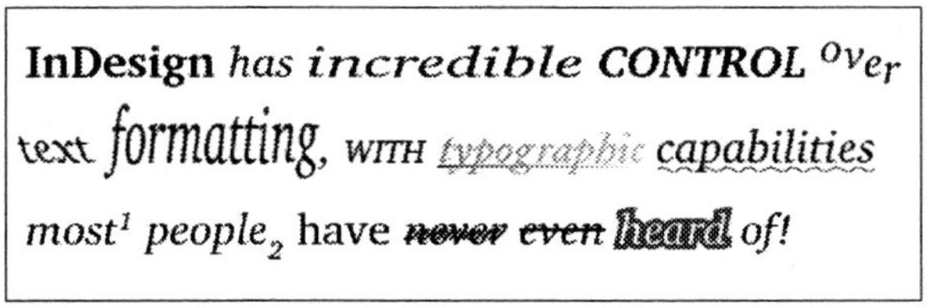

Figure 15-2:
Various
character
formatting
options
applied to
text.

InDesign *has incredible* **CONTROL** ^{o}v$_{e}$r text *formatting,* ᴡɪᴛʜ *typographic* capabilities *most*[1] *people*[2] have never even heard *of!*

Horizontal Scale and Vertical Scale options

InDesign's Horizontal Scale option lets you condense and expand type by squeezing or stretching characters. Similarly, the Vertical Scale option lets you shrink or stretch type vertically.

Typographers tend to agree that you should avoid excessive scaling. If you need to make text bigger or smaller, your best bet is to adjust font size; if you need to squeeze or stretch a range of text a bit, use InDesign's kerning and tracking controls because the letter forms aren't modified — only the space between letters changes when you kern or track text. (For more on this topic, see the upcoming section "Controlling Space between Characters and Lines.")

Unscaled text has a horizontal and vertical scale value of 100 percent. You can apply scaling values between 1 percent and 1,000 percent. If you apply equal horizontal and vertical scale values, you're making the original text proportionally larger or smaller. In this case, changing font size is a simpler solution.

To change the scale of highlighted text, enter new values in the Horizontal and/or Vertical Scale fields in the Character panel or Control panel. If a value is highlighted in the Horizontal Scale or Vertical Scale field, you can also use the up and down arrow keys to increase and decrease the scaling in 1-percent increments; press Shift to increase or decrease in 10-percent increments.

Baseline shift

The *baseline* is an invisible horizontal line on which a line of characters rests. The bottom of each letter sits on the baseline (except descenders, such as in y, p, q, j, and g). When you perform a *baseline shift,* you move highlighted text above or below its baseline. This feature is useful for carefully placing such characters as trademark and copyright symbols and for creating custom fractions.

To baseline-shift highlighted text, enter new values in the Baseline Shift field in the Character panel or Control panel. You can also use the up and down arrow keys to increase the baseline shift in 1-point increments or press Shift with the arrow keys to increase or decrease it in 10-point increments.

Skew (false italic)

For fonts that don't have an italic type style, InDesign provides the option to skew, or slant, text to create an artificial italic variation of any font. Like horizontal and vertical text scaling, skewing is a clunky way of creating italic-looking text. Use this feature to create special typographic effects, as shown in Figure 15-3, or in situations where a true italic style isn't available.

Skewing works better for sans-serif typefaces than for serif typefaces because the characters are simpler and have fewer embellishments that can get oddly distorted when skewed.

To skew highlighted text, you have three options:

- ✔ Enter an angle value between –85 and 85 in the Skew field in the Character panel or Control panel. Positive values slant text to the left; negative values slant text to the right.

- ✔ Press the accompanying up/down arrow keys when the cursor is in the Skew field to skew text in 1-degree increments. Pressing the Shift key with an arrow key changes the increment 4 degrees.

- ✔ Skew all the text in a text frame using the Shear tool or by changing the value in the Shear X Angle field in the Control panel after selecting the frame. Slanting text by shearing a text frame doesn't affect the skew angle of the text. You can specify a skew angle for highlighted text independently from the frame's shear angle.

Figure 15-3:
Characters
in skewed
text can
slant for-
ward, like
italics, or
backward.

Capitalization options

When you choose All Caps, the uppercase version of all highlighted characters is used: Lowercase letters are converted to uppercase, and uppercase
letters remain unchanged.

Similarly, the Small Caps option affects just lowercase letters. When you
choose Small Caps, InDesign automatically uses the Small Caps font style if one
is available for the font family. (Few font families include this style.) If a Small
Caps type style isn't available, InDesign generates small caps from uppercase
letters using the scale percentage specified in the Advanced Type pane of
the Preferences dialog box. (Choose InDesign⇨Preferences⇨Advanced Type
[⌘+K] on the Mac or Edit⇨Preferences⇨Advanced Type [Ctrl+K] in Windows).
The default scale value used to generate small caps text is 70% (of uppercase
letters).

Another handy way to change the case of text is to highlight the text, choose
Type⇨Change Case, and then select from the appropriate submenu option:
Uppercase, Lowercase, Title Case, and Sentence Case. Title Case capitalizes
the first letter in each word, whereas Sentence Case capitalizes the first letter
in the beginning of each sentence.

Superscript and Subscript

When you apply the Superscript and Subscript character formats to highlighted text, InDesign applies a baseline shift to the characters, lifting them
above (for *superscript*) or lowering them below (for *subscript*) their baseline,
and reduces their size.

The amount of baseline shift and scaling that's used for the Superscript
and Subscript formats is determined by the Position and Size fields
in the Advanced Type pane of the Preferences dialog box. (Choose

InDesign⇨Preferences⇨Advanced Type [⌘+K] on the Mac or choose Edit⇨Preferences⇨Advanced Type [Ctrl+K] in Windows.) The default Position value for both formats is 33.3%, which means that characters are moved up or down by one-third of the applied leading value. The default Superscript and Subscript Size value is 58.3%, which means that super-scripted and subscripted characters are reduced to 58.3% of the applied font size. The Advanced Type pane lets you specify separate default settings for Superscript and Subscript.

To apply the Superscript or Subscript format to highlighted text, choose the appropriate option from the Character panel's flyout menu.

Underline and Strikethrough

Underline and Strikethrough formats are typographically considered to be unacceptable for indicating emphasis in text, which is better accomplished by using bold and/or italic font styles.

Underlines can be useful in kickers and other text above a headline, as well as in documents formatted to look as if they're typewritten. Strikethrough can be used in cases where you want to indicate incorrect answers, elimi-nated choices, or deleted text.

If you use underlines and strikethrough, InDesign lets you specify exactly how they look through the Underline Options and Strikethrough Options dialog boxes available in the flyout menus of the Character panel and Control panel.

Ligatures

A *ligature* is a special character that combines two letters. Most fonts include just two ligatures — fi and fl. When you choose the Ligature option, InDesign automatically displays and prints a font's built-in ligatures — instead of the two component letters — if the font includes ligatures.

One nice thing about the Ligature option is that even though a ligature looks like a single character on-screen, it's still fully editable. That is, you can click between the two-letter shapes and insert text, if necessary. Also, a ligature created with the Ligature option doesn't cause InDesign's spell-checker to flag the word that contains it.

To use ligatures within highlighted text, choose Ligatures from the Character panel's or Control panel's flyout menu. (Ligatures is set to On by default.) Figure 15-4 shows an example of text with a ligature.

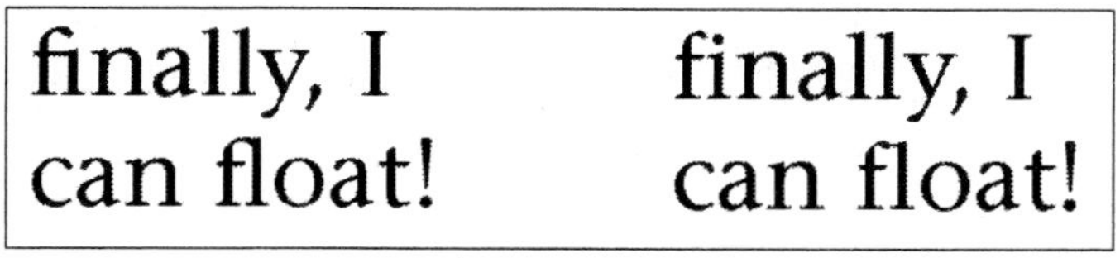

Figure 15-4:
The fi*fi* and
fl*fl* ligatures
are used in
the words
finally and
float at left
but not
at right.

finally, I
can float!

finally, I
can float!

You can also insert ligatures manually:

✔ On the Mac, press Option+Shift+5 to insert the fi ligature and Option+
Shift+6 to insert the fi ligature. You can also use Mac OS X 10.5
Leopard's Character Palette utility, Mac OS X 10.6 Snow Leopard's
Character Viewer utility, or InDesign's Glyphs panel (Type➪Glyphs
[Option+Shift+F11 or Alt+Shift+F11]) to choose them visually.

✔ In Windows, you have to use a program such as the Character Map utility
that comes with Windows. Choose Start➪All Programs➪Accessories➪
System Tools➪Character Map; if you have the Classic Start menu interface
enabled, choose Start➪Programs➪Accessories➪System Tools➪
Character Map.

However, if you do enter ligatures yourself, InDesign's spell-checker flags any
words that contain them. For this reason, you'll typically want InDesign to
handle the task of inserting ligatures automatically.

Turning off hyphenation and other breaks

You can prevent individual words from being hyphenated or a string of
words from being broken at the end of a line. For example, you may decide
that you don't want to hyphenate certain product names, such as InDesign.
The No Break option was created for situations such as these.

To prevent a word or a text string from being broken, highlight it and then
choose No Break from the Character panel's flyout menu or the Control
panel's flyout menu. You can also prevent a word from being hyphenated by
placing a discretionary hyphen (Shift+⌘+– or Ctrl+Shift+–) in front of the first
letter. (See Chapter 14 for more on hyphenation controls.)

Controlling Space between Characters and Lines

The legibility of a block of text depends as much on the space around it — called *white space* — as it does on the readability of the font. InDesign offers two ways to adjust the space between characters:

- ✔ *Kerning* is the adjustment of space between a pair of characters. Most fonts include built-in kerning tables that control the space between character pairs, such as *LA, Yo,* and *WA,* that otherwise may appear to have a space between them even when there isn't one. For large font sizes — for example, a magazine headline — you may want to manually adjust the space between certain character pairs to achieve consistent spacing.

- ✔ *Tracking* is the process of adding or removing space among all letters in a range of text.

You can apply kerning and/or tracking to highlighted text in ⅟‚000-em increments, called units. An *em* is as wide as the height of the current font size (that is, an em for 12-point text is 12 points wide), which means that kerning and tracking increments are relative to the applied font size.

Leading (rhymes with sledding) controls the vertical space between lines of type. It's traditionally an attribute of paragraphs, but InDesign lets you apply leading on a character-by-character basis. To override the character-oriented approach, ensuring that leading changes affect entire paragraphs, check the Apply Leading to Entire Paragraphs option in the Type pane of the Preferences dialog box. (Choose InDesign⇨Preferences⇨Type [⌘+K] on the Mac or Edit⇨Preferences⇨Type [Ctrl+K] in Windows.)

Kerning

The Kerning controls in the Character panel and Control panel provide three options for kerning letter pairs:

- ✔ **Metrics:** Controls the space between character pairs in the highlighted text using a font's built-in kerning pairs.

- ✔ **Optical:** Evaluates each letter pair in highlighted text and adds or removes space between the letters based on the shapes of the characters.

- ✔ **Manual:** Adds or removes space between a specific letter pair in user-specified amounts.

When the flashing text cursor is between a pair of characters, the Kerning field displays the pair's kerning value. If Metrics or Optical kerning is applied, the kerning value is displayed in parentheses.

To apply Metrics or Optical kerning to highlighted text, choose the appropriate option from the Kerning pop-up menu. To apply manual kerning, click between a pair of letters and then enter a value in the Kerning field or choose one of the predefined values. Negative values tighten; positive values loosen.

When letter shapes start to collide, you've tightened too far.

Tracking

Tracking is uniform kerning applied to a range of text. (For more on kerning, see the preceding section.) You can use tracking to tighten character spacing for a font that you think is too spacey or loosen spacing for a font that's too tight. Or you can track a paragraph tighter or looser to eliminate a short last line or a *widow* (the last line of a paragraph that falls at the top of a page or column).

To apply tracking to highlighted text, enter a value in the Character panel's or Control panel's Tracking field or choose one of the predefined values. Negative values tighten; positive values loosen (in 0.001-em increments).

You may wonder how tracking is different than kerning. They're essentially the same thing, with this difference: Tracking applies to a selection of three or more characters, whereas kerning is meant to adjust the spacing between just two characters. You use tracking to change the overall tightness of character spacing; you use kerning to improve the spacing between letters that just don't quite look right compared to the rest of the text.

Leading

Leading (rhymes with *sledding*, not *heeding*) refers to the vertical space between lines of type as measured from baseline to baseline. Leading in InDesign is a character-level format, which means that you can apply different leading values within a single paragraph. InDesign looks at each line of text in a paragraph and uses the largest applied leading value within a line to determine the leading for that line.

By default, InDesign applies Auto Leading to text, which is equal to 120 percent of the type size. As long as you don't change fonts or type sizes in a paragraph, Auto Leading works pretty well. But if you do change fonts or sizes, Auto Leading can result in inconsistent spacing between lines. For this reason, specifying an actual leading value is safer.

In most cases, using a leading value that is slightly larger than the type size is a good idea. When the leading value equals the type size, text is said to be set *solid*. That's about as tight as you ever want to set leading, unless you're trying to achieve a special typographic effect or working with very large text sizes in ad-copy headlines. As is the case with kerning and tracking, when tight leading causes letters to collide — ascenders and descenders are the first to overlap — you've gone too far.

You can change InDesign's preset Auto Leading value of 120%. To do so, choose Type⇨Paragraph (Option+⌘+T or Ctrl+Alt+T) to display the Paragraph panel. Choose Justification in the flyout menu, enter a new value in the Auto Leading field, and then click OK. (Why a character format setting is accessed via the Paragraph panel and what Auto Leading has to do with Justification are both mysteries.)

To modify the leading value applied to selected text, choose one of the pre-defined options from the Leading pop-up menu in the Character panel or Control panel or enter a leading value in the field. You can enter values from 0 to 5,000 points in 0.001-point increments. You can also use the up and down arrow keys to change leading in 1-point increments.

Part V
Graphics Essentials

The 5th Wave   By Rich Tennant

"I customized my cookbook in InDesign. The
other programs just don't look fresh."

In this part . . .

They say a picture is worth a thousand words, and, well, a lot of them are. Graphics make layouts come alive, providing a visceral connection that text by itself just can't. So it should be no surprise that InDesign has tons of features that let you work and even create graphics. This part shows you how to work with imported graphics files, cropping them and making them fit your layout's canvas.

You may wonder why this part is so short, given how many graphical effects InDesign offers. If you haven't read Part III, that confusion is understandable: InDesign lets you apply most of its special effects and controls to *any* object, not just those containing graphics, so Part III covers that common razzle-dazzle in one place.

Chapter 16

Importing Graphics

● ●

In This Chapter

▶ Getting graphics ready for InDesign

▶ Bringing graphics into your layout

▶ Working with layered images

● ●

*W*hat is a layout without graphics? Boring, that's what. And that's why InDesign lets you import a wide variety of graphics types so that you have a lot of choices and flexibility in the images you use.

And through the Mac and Windows Clipboards (via copy and paste), you can import file formats — to a limited degree — that aren't directly supported by InDesign.

The terms *graphic* and *picture* are interchangeable, referring to any type of graphic — though InDesign consistently uses the word *graphic* in its user interface and documentation. An *image* is a bitmapped graphic, such as that produced by an image editor, digital camera, or scanner, while an *illustration* or *drawing* is a vector file produced by an illustration program.

Preparing Graphics Files

InDesign offers support for many major formats of graphics files. Some formats are more appropriate than others for certain kinds of tasks. The basic rules for creating your graphics files are as follows:

✔ Save line art (drawings) in a format such as EPS, PDF, Adobe Illustrator, Windows Metafile (WMF), Enhanced Metafile (EMF), or PICT. (These object-oriented formats are called *vector* formats. Vector files are composed of instructions on how to draw various shapes.) InDesign works best with EPS, PDF, and Illustrator files.

✔ Save bitmaps (photos and scans) in a format such as TIFF, Adobe Photoshop, PNG, JPEG, PCX, Windows Bitmap (BMP), GIF, Scitex Continuous Tone (SCT), or PICT. (These pixel-oriented formats are also called *raster* formats. Raster files are composed of a series of dots, or pixels, that make up the image.) InDesign works best with TIFF and Photoshop files.

InDesign can also import InDesign files as if they were graphics — in a multipage document, you choose the page you want to import and which layers you want to display — you can do the same with PDF files. (Be sure to select Show Import Options in the Place dialog box to get these controls.)

Note that you can't edit InDesign files imported as graphics in your InDesign layout. (You must update the original file instead.) But you can quickly open the InDesign file for editing by selecting it and then choosing Edit➪Edit Original. (The Edit Original command works with any graphics file, not just InDesign files.)

New to InDesign CS5, you can select multiple files simultaneously and use the Edit Original command to open them all in the appropriate software for editing. You can also use the new Edit With command to choose a specific program to open the imported files with, rather than what your computer chooses to use.

Make EPS and TIFF formats your standards because these formats have become the standard in publishing. If you and your service bureau are working almost exclusively with Adobe software, you can add the PDF, Illustrator, and Photoshop formats to this mix. (The Illustrator and PDF formats are variants of EPS.) If you use transparency in your graphics, it's best to save them in Photoshop, Illustrator, or PDF formats, because other formats (particularly EPS and TIFF) remove much of the transparency layering data that will help an imagesetter optimally reproduce those transparent files.

The graphics file formats that InDesign imports include (the text in monofont is the filename extension for the format):

- ✔ **BMP:** The native Windows bitmap format (`.bmp`, `.dib`).
- ✔ **EPS:** The Encapsulated PostScript file format favored by professional publishers (`.eps`).
- ✔ **GIF:** The Graphics Interchange Format common in Web documents (`.gif`).
- ✔ **JPEG:** The Joint Photographers Expert Group compressed bitmap format often used on the Web (`.jpg`).
- ✔ **Illustrator:** The native format in Adobe Illustrator 5.5 through CS5. This file format is similar to EPS (`.ai`).
- ✔ **PCX:** The PC Paintbrush format that was very popular in DOS programs and early version of Windows; it's now been largely supplanted by other formats (`.pcx`, `.rle`).

- ✔ **PDF:** The Portable Document Format that is a variant of EPS and is used for Web-, network-, and CD-based documents. InDesign CS5 supports PDF Versions 1.3 through 1.8 (the formats used in Acrobat 4 through 9) (.pdf).

- ✔ **Photoshop:** The native format in Adobe Photoshop 5.0 through CS5 (.psd). (Note that InDesign can't import the Photoshop Raw format.)

- ✔ **PICT:** Short for *Picture,* the Mac's native graphics format until Mac OS X (it can be bitmap or vector) that is little used in professional documents and has become rare even for inexpensive clip art (.pct).

- ✔ **PNG:** The Portable Network Graphics format introduced more than a decade ago as a more capable alternative to GIF (.png).

- ✔ **QuickTime movie:** For use in interactive documents, InDesign supports this Apple-created, cross-platform format (.mov).

- ✔ **Scitex CT:** The continuous-tone bitmap format used on Scitex prepress systems (.ct).

- ✔ **TIFF:** The Tagged Image File Format that is the bitmap standard for professional image editors and publishers (.tif, .tiff).

- ✔ **Windows Metafile:** The format native to Windows but little used in professional documents. Since Office 2000, Microsoft applications create a new version called Enhanced Metafile, also supported by InDesign (.wmf, .emf).

Spot colors (called spot inks in Photoshop) are imported into InDesign when you place Photoshop, Illustrator, and PDF images into InDesign, as well as for InDesign documents imported as graphics. They appear in the Swatches panel, which is covered in Chapter 6.

Importing and Placing Graphics

There are several ways to import graphics into InDesign:

- ✔ Drag and drop graphics file icons from your computer's desktop into InDesign documents.

- ✔ Drag graphics files from Adobe Bridge or the new Mini Bridge panel.

- ✔ For Illustrator files, you can drag or copy and paste objects directly from Illustrator into InDesign.

- ✔ Use your computer's Copy (choose File➪Copy or press ⌘+C or Ctrl+C) and Paste (choose File➪Paste or press ⌘+V or Ctrl+V) commands to move a graphics file between two InDesign documents or from a document created with another program into an InDesign document.

The Place command is the method you typically use to bring graphics into your InDesign layout, because it gives you the most control and establishes a link between the graphics file and the document file and then sends the original graphics file to the printer when the document is output. (For more details on managing linked files, see Chapter 9.)

InDesign links to graphics because a graphics file, particularly a high-resolution scanned graphic, can be very large. If the entire graphics file is included in an InDesign document when you import it, InDesign documents would quickly become prohibitively large. Instead, InDesign saves a low-resolution preview of an imported graphics file with the document, and it's this file that you see displayed on-screen. InDesign remembers the location of the original file and uses this information when printing.

Here's how to use the Place command to import a graphic:

1. **Choose File⇨Place (⌘+D or Ctrl+D).**

   If you want to import a graphic into an *existing frame,* select the target frame using either of the selection tools (either before or after you choose File⇨Place). If you want InDesign to create a *new frame* when you import the graphic, make sure that no object is selected when you choose Place. Either way, the Place dialog box appears.

   You can import a graphic into any kind of frame or shape (including a curved line created with the Pen tool) except a straight line. Be careful: If the Type tool is selected when you use the Place command to import a graphic into a selected text frame, you'll create an inline graphic at the text cursor's location.

2. **Use the controls in the Place dialog box to locate and select the graphics files you want to import.**

   You can select multiple files — graphics and/or text — by Shift+clicking a range or ⌘+clicking or Ctrl+clicking multiple files one by one. InDesign lets you place each file in a separate frame. Just click once for each file imported or Shift+⌘+click or Ctrl+Shift+click to have InDesign place all files on the page in separate frames. The loaded-graphic icon shows the number of files to be placed, as well as a mini-preview of each file, as Figure 16-1 shows. You can also navigate through these previews using the keyboard's left and right arrow keys so that you can control more easily which file is placed when.

Figure 16-1:
At left: The
standard
loaded-
graphic
icon. At
right: The
two icon
variants for
PDF and
InDesign
files.

3. **Specify the desired import options, if any are applicable.**

   If you want to display import options that let you control how the selected graphics file is imported, either select the Show Import Options check box and then click the Open button or hold down the Shift key and double-click the filenames or Shift+click the Open button.

   If you had selected a frame and want whatever you've selected to replace the contents of that frame, select Replace Selected Items.

4. **Click Open, whether or not you selected any import options, to bring the graphics into the layout.**

   Note that if you choose Show Import Options, the dialog box that appears — EPS Import Options, Place PDF, Place InDesign Document, or Image Import Options — depends on what kind of graphic you're importing. If you select multiple graphics, you'll get the appropriate dialog box for each in turn. (These options are covered in the "Specifying Import Options" section, later in this chapter.) After selecting the desired options, click OK to place the graphic.

5. **Based on whether a frame was selected when you initiated the Place command, you may need to tell InDesign where to put the imported graphics:**

   • If an empty frame is selected, the graphic is automatically placed in the frame. The upper-left corner of the graphic is placed in the upper-left corner of the frame, and the frame acts as the cropping shape for the graphic.

   • If a frame already holding a graphic is selected, InDesign replaces the existing graphic with the new one if you've selected the Replace Selected Item check box in the Place dialog box. Otherwise, InDesign assumes that you want to put the new graphic in a new frame.

- To place the graphic into a new frame, click the loaded-graphic icon on an empty portion of a page or on the pasteboard. The point where you click establishes the upper-left corner of the resulting graphics frame, which is the same size as the imported graphic and which acts as the graphic's cropping shape.

- To place the graphic in an existing, unselected frame, click in the frame with the loaded-graphic icon. The upper-left corner of the graphic is placed in the upper-left corner of the frame, and the frame acts as a cropping shape.

After you place a graphic, it's displayed in the frame that contains it, and the frame is selected. If the Selection tool is selected, the eight handles of its bounding box are displayed; if the Direct Selection tool is selected, handles appear only in the corners. At this point, you can modify either the frame or the graphic within, or you can move on to another task.

The loaded-graphic icon is made up of an image preview, as well as an icon in the preview's upper-left corner that indicates the type of file being imported: bitmap, Illustrator, and EPS files all have a paintbrush icon, while PDF and InDesign files show special icons, as Figure 16-1 shows. Also, if you're importing multiple files simultaneously, the number of files loaded and ready to be placed also displays in the upper-right corner of the loaded-graphic icon's preview image.

As you place each graphic, the preview image for the next file displays. You can move through the files by pressing ← or →, which lets you choose which specific file to place when you click mouse.

If you select multiple graphics files for placement, you can hold Shift+⌘ or Ctrl+Shift when dragging the mouse in your document to place an array of the files, each in its own frame within the area defined when dragging the mouse. This feature lets you place multiple images in a contact-sheet arrangement. InDesign creates as many frames as can fit that array, placing a file into each frame. Any files not placed remain in the loaded-graphic icon for placement elsewhere.

When importing JPEG files, InDesign automatically scales the image to fit in the page. This feature helps deal with digital-camera graphics that tend to be very large in dimension and, when imported, end up taking much more than the width of a page. Although you'll likely still need to scale the image to fit your layout, you can at least see the whole image before doing so.

Specifying Import Options

If you've ever used a graphics application — for example, an image-editing program like Adobe Photoshop or an illustration program like Adobe Illustrator or CorelDraw — you're probably aware that when you save a graphics file, you have several options that control such things as file format, image size, color depth, preview quality, and so on. When you save a graphics file, the settings you specify are determined by the way in which the image will be used. For example, you can use Photoshop to save a high-resolution TIFF version of a scanned graphic for use in a slick, four-color annual report or a low-resolution GIF version of the same graphic for use on the company's Web page. Or you can use Illustrator or CorelDraw to create a corporate logo that you'll use in various sizes in many of your printed publications.

If you choose to specify custom import settings when you import a graphics file, the choices you make depend on the nature of the publication. For example, if it's bound for the Web, you don't need to work with or save graphics using resolutions that exceed a computer monitor's 72-dpi resolution. Along the same lines, if the publication will be printed, the image import settings you specify for a newspaper that will be printed on newsprint on a SWOP (Specifications for Web Offset Publications) press are different than those you specify for a four-color magazine printed on coated paper using a sheet-fed press.

If you select Show Import Options when you place a graphic, the options displayed in the resulting dialog boxes depend on the file format of the selected graphic. When you set options for a particular file, the options you specify remain in effect for that file format until you change them. If you don't select the Show Import Options check box when you place a graphic, the most recent settings for the file format of the selected graphic are used.

Import options for bitmap graphics

InDesign gives you two sets of import options for the following types of bitmap images: TIFF, GIF, JPEG, Scitex CT, BMP, and PCX. You get three options for PNG files, and a different set of three for Photoshop files. No import options are available for PICT or QuickTime movie files.

Figure 16-2 shows the four possible panes for bitmap images: The Image and Color panes are for most bitmap formats; PNG files have a third pane, PNG Settings; and Photoshop files also have a third pane, Layers, covered later in this chapter.

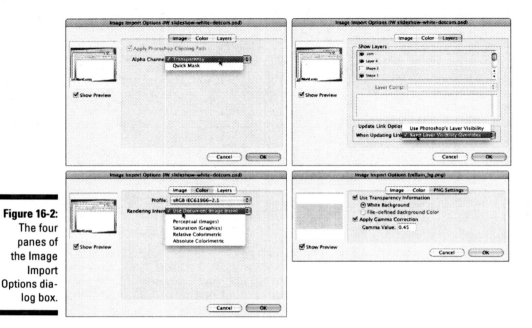

Figure 16-2:
The four
panes of
the Image
Import
Options dia-
log box.

If you import a Photoshop, TIFF, or EPS file that contains an embedded clipping path, the Image pane lets you apply any embedded clipping path and/
or alpha channel to the image in order to *mask,* or cut out, part of the image.
(Otherwise, these options are grayed out.) Check the Apply Photoshop
Clipping Path option to import the clipping path along with the image; select
an alpha channel from the Alpha Channel pop-up menu to import the alpha
channel along with the image. (Chapter 17 covers clipping paths in more
detail.)

In the Color pane, you can turn on color management for the image and control how the image is displayed. Select the Enable Color Management check
box to enable color management. This option is an expert feature, so ask
your production manager or service bureau whether you should make any
adjustments here.

Use the PNG Settings pane — available only if you place a PNG file — to use
the transparency information in a PNG file, assuming that it has a transparent
background. You have two choices for controlling transparency handling:
White Background and File-Defined Background. The former forces the transparent portion to display as white in InDesign; the latter uses whatever background color is specified in the PNG file itself.

This pane also lets you adjust the gamma value during import — an expert
color-management feature you should leave alone unless told otherwise by a
production manager or service bureau.

Import options for vector file formats

If you're importing vector files, enabling the Import Options check box results in one of two dialog boxes appearing, depending on what the vector file type is. If you import older-version Illustrator or EPS files, you get the EPS Import Options dialog box; if you import PDF and newer-version Illustrator files, you get the Place PDF dialog box, which has two panes. (Both dialog boxes are shown in Figure 16-3.) No import options are available for Windows Metafile or Enhanced Metafile graphics.

Illustrator CS through CS5 uses PDF as its native file format, even though the filename extension is `.ai`. InDesign detects these files as PDF files and provides the PDF options during import. In earlier versions of Illustrator, the native format was actually a variant of EPS.

Figure 16-3:
The Place
PDF and
EPS Import
Options dia-
log boxes.

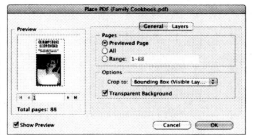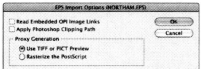

EPS Import Options dialog box

Use this dialog box to import any clipping paths embedded in images that are in the EPS file. Check the Apply Photoshop Clipping Path option to enable this option.

Also, use this pane to control how the EPS file appears on-screen in InDesign. If you select the Use TIFF or PICT Preview option, InDesign uses the low-resolution proxy image embedded in the EPS file for display on-screen and prints the graphic using the embedded high-resolution PostScript instructions. If you select the Rasterize the PostScript option, InDesign converts the PostScript file into a bitmap image during import. You rarely have a reason to rasterize an imported EPS file — it just takes up some of your valuable time.

Place PDF dialog box

When you use the Place command to import a PDF file and you select the Show Import Options check box, the Place PDF file dialog box (refer to Figure 16-3) is displayed. It provides several controls for specifying how the file is imported. The General pane provides the following options:

✔ In the Pages section, select Previewed Page, All, or Range to determine which page(s) you want to import. You can change the previewed page by using the arrow buttons under the preview image at left or entering a specific page number in the field below the preview image. If you want to import a range, use commas to separate pages and a hyphen to indicate range; for example, typing in **3, 5-9, 13** imports pages 3, 5 through 9, and 13.

When you place the PDF in InDesign, you get a separate loaded-graphic icon for each page. As you place each page, a new loaded-graphic icon appears for the next page, until no more pages are left to place. You can tell you're placing multiple pages because the loaded-graphic icon has a plus sign in it.

✔ In the Options section, select one of the cropping options from the Crop To pop-up menu. If you choose Content, the page's bounding box or a rectangle that encloses all items, including page marks, is used to build the graphics frame. Choosing Art places the area defined by the file's creator, if any, as placeable artwork. For example, the person who created the file may have designated a particular graphic as placeable artwork. Choosing Crop places the area displayed and printed by Adobe Acrobat. Choosing Trim places the graphic in an area equal to the final, trimmed piece. Choosing Bleed places the page area plus any specified bleed area. Choosing Media places an area defined by the paper size specified for the PDF document, including page marks.

✔ Also in the Options section, select the Transparent Background check box if you want the white areas of the PDF page to be transparent. Uncheck this option if you want to preserve the page's opaque white background.

Import options for placed InDesign files

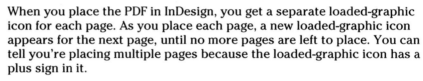

When you import InDesign files to use as a graphic, you can use exactly the same options as for PDF files. The Place InDesign Document dialog box is identical to the Place PDF dialog box covered in the preceding section, except of course, for the dialog box's name.

Working with Image Layers

InDesign lets you work with individual layers in some imported graphics. What that means is that you have more control over what displays because you can turn on or off individual layers. Of course, to use this capability, the source graphic must be constructed with multiple layers.

You can work with layers while you're importing graphics, using the Image Import Options dialog box described in the preceding section, or after you've placed graphics, using the Object Layer Options dialog box covered in the "Working with layers after import" section, later in this chapter.

Working with layers during import

Use the Layers pane in the Image Import Options dialog box, the Place PDF, or Place InDesign Document dialog box to select which layers you want visible in InDesign. (The Layers pane is available only if you place an Illustrator, PDF, or Photoshop graphic or InDesign file.)

In the Layers pane, you see a list of image layers. Any that have the eye icon will display in InDesign, and you can select or deselect layers by clicking the box to the right of the layer name to make the eye icon appear or disappear. (You can't change their order — you'd need to go back to Photoshop or Illustrator and change the layer order there.) Figure 16-3 shows the Layers pane for the Place PDF dialog box, but it looks the same in Place InDesign, and Import Options dialog boxes.

Although you can save an image file in the TIFF format and preserve any layers, InDesign doesn't give you the capability to manage which layers you import from a TIFF file into InDesign.

The When Updating Link pop-up menu also has an option to control how changes to the file are handled in terms of layer management: If you choose Use Photoshop's Layer Visibility or Use Illustrator's Layer Visibility, InDesign makes all layers that are visible in Photoshop, InDesign, or Illustrator visible when you update the link to the graphic from InDesign. If you choose Keep Layer Visibility Overrides in the When Updating Link pop-up menu, InDesign imports only the layers chosen in this dialog box if you later update the graphic in Photoshop, InDesign, or Illustrator.

Working with layers after import

You may not know what layers you want visible when you import a graphic that has several layers. That's okay. Just select the graphic in your layout and choose Object⇨Object Layer Options. The Object Layer Options dialog box appears, with the same options as in the Layers pane described in the preceding section.

Using the Object Layer Options dialog box, you can also change any layer visibility settings you made during import in the Layers pane of the Image Import Options dialog box.

Chapter 17

Fitting Graphics and Setting Paths

*A*fter you import a graphic into an InDesign document, you can modify either the graphic or the frame that contains it. The most common actions you'll take are cropping, repositioning, and resizing. And if you want to get really fancy, you might work with clipping paths to create "masks" around picture portions or even cut the graphic into pieces.

Transformations such as resizing, flipping, rotating, and skewing that you're likely to apply to graphics use the same tools for graphics as for any InDesign objects. So I cover all these transformations in one place, in Chapter 8.

In almost every case, you select graphics with the Direct Selection tool to work with the graphic itself, rather than the frame. If you use the Selection tool, the work you do will apply to the frame, as Chapter 8 explains.

Cropping Graphics

Remember, when you import a graphic using the Place command (File➪Place [⌘+D or Ctrl+D]) or by dragging a graphics file into a document window (see Chapter 16), the graphic is contained in a graphics frame — either the frame that was selected when you placed the graphic or the frame that was automatically created if a frame wasn't selected. The upper-left corner of an imported graphic is automatically placed in the upper-left corner of its frame.

Cropping is a fancy term for deciding what part of the picture to show by altering the dimensions of the frame holding the graphic. The easiest way to crop a graphic is to resize the frame that contains it using the Selection or Position tool. To discover how to resize the frame, go to Chapter 8. Note that resizing the frame does *not* resize the graphic.

The other way to crop a graphic is to leave its frame alone and instead move the graphic within the frame. (The advantage of moving the image within the frame is that you don't have to move the frame from its desired position in the layout.) To do so, you have two options:

✔ Click on a graphic with the Direct Selection tool and then drag the graphic within its frame to reveal and conceal different parts of the graphic. For example, you can crop the top and left edges of a graphic by dragging the graphic above and to the left of its original position (in the upper-left corner of the frame).

✔ Use the X+ and Y+ fields in the Control panel and Transform panel, which let you determine precisely how much to move the graphic horizontally and vertically within its frame by entering specific values. Positive values move the graphic to the right or down relative to the frame, while negative values move it to the left or up relative to the frame. This method is more precise than using the mouse.

If you want to *mask out* (hide) portions of an imported graphic, you have the option of using an irregular shape as the frame, a graphic's built-in clipping path (if it has one), or a clipping path you generated in InDesign, as covered in the last section of this chapter.

Figuring out the Fitting Commands

If you've placed a graphic in a frame that's either larger or smaller than the graphic, you can use the Fitting options (available by choosing Object⇨ Fitting or by using the appropriate iconic buttons in the Control panel) to scale the graphic to fit the frame proportionately or disproportionately or to scale the frame to fit the graphic. Another option lets you center the graphic in the frame. These options are very handy, and a *lot* easier than trying to resize a graphic or frame to fit using the mouse or the Control panel.

Keep in mind that the fitting commands for graphics are available only if you've used the Selection or Position tool to select a graphic's frame. Here are descriptions of the seven options:

✔ **Fit Content to Frame:** To scale a graphic to fill the selected frame, choose Object⇨Fitting⇨Fit Content to Frame (Option+⌘+E or Ctrl+ Alt+E). If the frame is larger than the graphic, the graphic is enlarged; if the frame is smaller, the graphic is reduced. If the graphic and the frame have different proportions, the graphic's proportions are changed so that the image completely fills the frame — this Fit Content to Frame option can distort the graphic's appearance.

✔ **Fit Frame to Content:** To resize a frame so that it wraps snugly around a graphic, choose Fit Frame to Content (Option+⌘+C or Ctrl+Alt+C). The frame is enlarged or reduced depending on the size of the graphic, and the frame's proportions are changed to match the proportions of the graphic.

✔ **Center Content:** To center a graphic in its frame, choose Center Content (Shift+⌘+E or Ctrl+Shift+E). Neither the frame nor the graphic is scaled when you center a graphic.

✔ **Fit Content Proportionally:** To scale a graphic to fit in the selected frame while maintaining the graphic's current proportions, choose Object⇨Fitting⇨Fit Content Proportionally (Option+Shift+⌘+E or Ctrl+Alt+Shift+E). If the frame is larger than the graphic, the graphic is enlarged; if the frame is smaller, the graphic is reduced. If the graphic and the frame have different proportions, a portion of the frame background shows above and below or to the left and right of the graphic. If you want, you can drag frame edges to make the frame shorter or narrower and eliminate any portions of the background that are visible.

✔ **Fill Frame Proportionally:** To resize a graphic so that it fills its frame on all sides, choose Object⇨Fitting⇨Fill Frame Proportionally (Option+Shift+⌘+C or Ctrl+Alt+Shift+C). Note that this option may crop out part of the image, so no gap appears between any part of the image and the frame. (By contrast, the Fit Frame to Content Proportionally option can result in extra space at the bottom and/or right sides of a graphic so that the entire graphic is visible.)

✔ **Clear Frame Fitting Options:** To undo any frame-fitting options applied to a selected frame, choose Object⇨Fitting⇨Clear Frame Fitting Options.

✔ **Frame Fitting Options:** To control the default fitting for newly placed graphics, use the Frame Fitting Options dialog box, shown in Figure 17-1. Here, you can set the amount of crop, choose the control point for the imported graphic (see Chapter 1), and automatically apply your choice of the Fit Content to Frame, Fit Content Proportionally, and Fill Frame Proportionally options.

For frames with strokes, the Fitting options align the outer edge of a graphic with the center of the stroke. A stroke obscures a strip along the graphic's edge that's half the width of the stroke. The wider the stroke, the more of the graphic that gets covered up.

Figure 17-1:
The Frame
Fitting
Options dia-
log box.

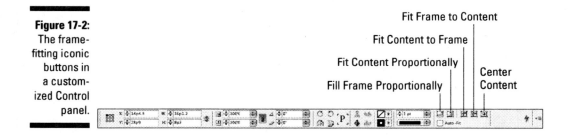

You can also use the frame-fitting iconic buttons in the Control panel, shown in
Figure 17-2. But note that these buttons may not display in your Control panel;
by default, InDesign shows them only if your monitor is set to a resolution width
of 1,280 or more pixels. You can make room for them at smaller resolutions by
customizing the Control panel display: Choose Customize from the panel's
flyout menu and then deselect some of the Object controls to make room.

Figure 17-2:
The frame-
fitting iconic
buttons in
a custom-
ized Control
panel.

You can set a frame to autofit a graphic to it, which means it automatically
resizes the graphic to fit the frame proportionally as the frame is resized —
not just when the graphic is placed in the frame. To enable autofit, select the
Auto-Fit option in the Control panel or in the Frame Fitting Options dialog box.

Working with Graphics in Irregular Shapes

Although most graphics you use will be placed in rectangular frames,
InDesign does give you other choices:

✔ You can select any type of frame — oval or polygonal, not just rectangular — to place or copy your graphic into.

✔ You can draw your own shape using the Pencil or Pen tool and then place or copy your graphic into it. When you create the free-form shape, make sure that the default color for the Pen tool is set to None so that the shape you create is transparent. Otherwise, the colored area in the shape will obscure the graphic behind it.

The Pen tool lets you create one shape at a time. The Compound Paths command lets you combine multiple shapes to create more complex objects. For example, you can place a small circle on top of a larger circle and then use the Compound Paths command to create a doughnut-shaped object. (This expert feature isn't covered in this book.)

If you copy the graphic into a frame or shape, you must use the Paste Into command (Edit⇨Paste Into [Option+⌘+V or Ctrl+Alt+V]) to place the copied graphic inside the selected shape, rather than on top of it.

✔ You can use a clipping path that was defined in the graphic itself when it was created or a clipping path that was created in InDesign.

So what is a clipping path, anyway? A *clipping path* is used to mask certain parts of a graphic and reveal other parts; it's basically an invisible outline placed in the graphic that InDesign can then work with. For example, if you want to create a silhouette around a single person in a crowd, open the file in an image-editing program, such as Photoshop, and then create and save a clipping path that isolates the shape of the person. (You can also erase everything except the person you want to silhouette; this approach can be time-consuming, and if you want to reveal other parts of the graphic later, you're out of luck.) TIFF, Photoshop EPS, and Photoshop-native (.psd) files can have embedded clipping paths.

Regardless of the method you use to clip an imported graphic, you can modify a clipping path by moving, adding, deleting, and changing the direction of anchor points and by moving direction lines.

You can convert a clipping path — whether imported or created in InDesign — to a frame by choosing Convert Clipping Path to Frame for a selected object using the contextual menu (Control+click or right-click the object).

See the *Photoshop For Dummies* series (Wiley Publishing) for more on creating clipping paths in Photoshop.

Using a graphic's own clipping path

In an ideal world, any graphics that you want to have fit in an irregular shape will come with their own clipping paths. But many don't, so you need to create your own in InDesign, as described in the next section.

But for those graphics that do have their own clipping paths, you would first import the clipping path when you place the graphic and then use InDesign's Text Wrap panel to access that clipping path.

The steps are easy:

1. **Select the Show Import Options check box in the Place dialog box (File⇨Place [⌘+D or Ctrl+D]) when you import the graphic and select the Apply Photoshop Clipping Path option in the Image Import Options dialog box.**

2. **Open the Text Wrap panel (Window⇨Text Wrap [Option+⌘+W or Ctrl+Alt+W]).**

3. **Select the graphic.**

4. **Click the Wrap Around Object Shape iconic button (the third one from the left) at the top of the Text Wrap panel.**

5. **(Optional) Adjust the space between the surrounding text and the obstructing shape by typing values in the Top Offset field.**

6. **Select the clipping source from the Type pop-up menu in the Contour Options section of the Text Wrap panel.**

   Choose from two relevant options:

   • Alpha Channel uses the image's alpha channel, if any, to create a wrapping boundary. (An *alpha channel* is another type of clipping path and is also created in the source program such as Photoshop.)

   • Photoshop Path uses the image's clipping path, if any, to create a wrapping boundary. Use the Path pop-up menu to select which path to use, if your image has more than one embedded clipping path.

See Chapter 11 for the basics of text wraps.

Creating a clipping path in InDesign

If you import a graphic that doesn't have a clipping path, you have two sets of options for creating one.

The easiest is to use the Text Wrap panel as described in the preceding section but to instead choose one of the following options from the Type pop-up menu:

✔ Detect Edges tries to determine the graphic's outside boundary by ignoring white space. You'd use this option for bitmapped images that have a transparent or white background.

✔ Same as Clipping uses the clipping path for the graphic created in InDesign. You'd use this approach when the desired clipping path can't be created through the Detect Edges option. (I cover this method of clipping-path creation shortly.)

You can further modify the clipping path by selecting the graphic with the Direct Selection tool. The text-wrap boundary appears as a blue line. You can make the boundary easier to select by setting offsets in the Text Wrap pane, which moves the boundary away from the frame edge.

A slightly more difficult way to create a clipping path — but one that gives you more control — is to use the Clipping Path command to generate one automatically. Follow these steps:

1. **Select the graphic to which you want to add a clipping path.**

   Use the Direct Selection tool so that you can see the clipping path within the frame as you work.

2. **Choose Object⇨Clipping Path⇨Options (Option+Shift+⌘+K or Ctrl+Alt+Shift+K).**

   The Clipping Path dialog box appears, as shown in Figure 17-3.

3. **To have InDesign detect the likely boundary of the image, as opposed to a white or other light background, choose Detect Edges from the Type pop-up menu.**

   You can use the other options to select Alpha Channel or Photoshop Path as the clipping path for graphics that have one or more of these. (InDesign can use only one alpha channel or Photoshop path as the clipping path, so use the Path pop-up menu to choose the one you want.)

4. **Type a value in the Threshold field or click and drag the field's slider to specify the value below which pixels will be placed outside the clipping path shape (that is, pixels that will become transparent).**

   Pixels darker than the Threshold value remain visible and thus are inside the clipping path shape. The lowest possible Threshold value (0) makes only white pixels transparent. As the value gets higher, less of the graphic remains visible. The lightest areas are removed first, then mid-tones, and so on. (Select the Preview option to see the results of your changes without closing the dialog box.)

5. **Type a value in the Tolerance field.**

   This value determines how closely InDesign looks at variations in adjacent pixels when building a clipping path. Higher values produce a simpler, smoother path than lower values. Lower values create a more complicated, more exact path with more anchor points.

6. **If you want to enlarge or reduce the size of the clipping path produced by the Threshold and Tolerance values, type a value in the Inset Frame field.**

   Negative values enlarge the path; positive values shrink it. (The Inset Frame value is also applied to the path's bounding box.)

7. **Select the Invert option to switch the transparent and visible areas of the clipping path produced by the Threshold and Tolerance values.**

8. **If you want to include light areas in the perimeter shape InDesign generates based on the Threshold and Tolerance values, select the Include Inside Edges option.**

   For example, if you have a graphic of a doughnut and you want to make the hole transparent (as well as the area around the outside of the doughnut), click Include Inside Edges. If you don't click Include Inside Edges, InDesign builds a single shape (in the case of a doughnut, just the outside circle). The portion of the graphic in the shape remains visible; the rest of the graphic becomes transparent.

9. **Select the Restrict to Frame option if you want InDesign to generate a clipping path from just the portion of the graphic visible in the graphic frame, as opposed to the entire graphic (such as if you cropped the graphic).**

10. **Select the Use High Resolution Image option if you want InDesign to use the high-resolution information in the original file instead of using the low-resolution proxy image.**

    Even though using the high-resolution image takes longer, the resulting clipping path is more precise than it would be if you didn't check Use High Resolution Image.

11. **When you've finished specifying clipping path settings, click OK to close the dialog box and apply the settings to the selected graphic.**

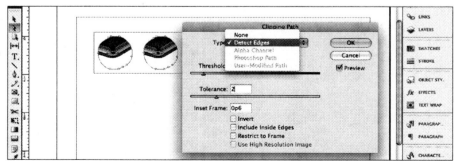

Figure 17-3:
The Clipping Path dialog box and its effect on a graphic.

If you use the Clipping Path command to generate a clipping path for a graphic that has a built-in clipping path, the one that InDesign generates replaces the built-in path.

Figure 17-4 shows a graphic before and after a clipping path was applied to it using the Clipping Path command. At left is a graphic of coastal France with a graphic of a glider superimposed. At right is the same set of graphics, but with a clipping path applied to the glider so that the outside area is masked out, making it transparent.

Figure 17-4:
A super-
imposed
image
before (left)
and after
applying
a clipping
path (right).

The Clipping Path command works very well for images that have a white or light background but no clipping path. It's less useful for graphics with back-grounds that contain a broad range of intermingling values.

You can remove a clipping path by choosing None as the Type in the Clipping Path dialog box. You can also select a different path — Detect Edges, Alpha Channel, Photoshop Path, or User-Modified Path — that was selected previously if you decide to change the current clipping path.

InDesign lets you convert a clipping path into a frame so that you get the exact shape as your clipping path to use as a container or silhouette in your layout. Select the clipping path with the Direct Selection tool and choose Object⇨Clipping Path⇨Convert Clipping Path to Frame. It's as easy as that!

Part VI

Getting Down to Business

The 5th Wave   By Rich Tennant

"We should cast a circle, invoke the elements, and direct the energy. If that doesn't work, we'll read the manual."

In this part . . .

Microsoft Word, move over. It used to be that a word processor did all the business-y stuff like footnotes, tables, tables of contents, indexes, and mail-merges. Not anymore. Over the years, like a slow-moving movie monster nonetheless catching up with the terrorized teens, more and more of these business functions have found their way into InDesign. This version, InDesign CS5, has even *more* such features, such as tracked changes.

This part shows you how to suit up your documents. But relax — you'll still be a designer at heart!

Chapter 18

Working with Tabs and Tables

In This Chapter

▶ Working with tabs

▶ Setting up and adjusting tables

▶ Formatting tables directly and with styles

▶ Turning tabbed text to tables, and vice versa

*P*erhaps the most common business-oriented formatting done in InDesign involves tabular material, whether financial tables or simple comparative feature lists. InDesign provides two methods for creating tabular material: old-fashioned tabs and more sophisticated tables. Although you can create tables with tabs, you have less control over the formatting and thus can create just basic tables when you use tabs. On the other hand, for simple tables, using tabs is often the faster method. So don't feel you should never use tabs — but do be sure that when you mix methods that you don't let visual consistency suffer as a result.

Tabs and tables in InDesign work somewhat like the same functions in Microsoft Word, so if you're familiar with Word's tabs and tables, you'll have a quick adjustment to InDesign's, at least for the basic capabilities.

Setting Tabs

To set tabs in InDesign, you use the Tabs panel, which floats above your text so that you can keep it open until you're finished experimenting with tabs. To open the Tabs panel, choose Type⇨Tabs (Shift+⌘+T or Ctrl+Shift+T). Figure 18-1 shows the Tabs panel along with a simple table created using one tab stop.

You can also set up tabs in the Tabs pane of the New Paragraph Styles and Paragraph Style Options dialog boxes, so tabs are consistently applied to all paragraphs. Chapter 13 covers styles in more detail.

Four buttons — Left, Center, Right, and Align On — on the Tabs panel let you control how the text aligns with the tab you're creating. The Align On option is usually used for decimal tabs, which means that a period in the text aligns on the tab stop. But you can align on any character, not just periods — simply specify the align-on character in the Align On field. (If you enter nothing in the Align On field, InDesign assumes that you want to align to periods.) If the Align On field isn't visible in the Tabs panel, just widen the panel by dragging one of its sides so that the field displays.

The X: field of the Tabs panel lets you specify a position for a new tab stop. You can type a value in this field in 0.01-point increments and then press Shift+Enter or Shift+Return to create a tab. InDesign positions tabs relative to the left edge of the text frame or column.

Rather than typing values in the X: field, you can position tabs by clicking at the desired location on the ruler at the bottom of the Tabs panel. You can also drag tab stops within the ruler to change their position. And you can reposition left and right indents and indent hangs using the arrow sliders on the tab ruler. (The arrow sliders have the same effects as changing indents using the Paragraph panel or Paragraph Styles panel, as explained in Chapter 14.)

To have the Tabs panel "snap" to your text frame so that you can see exactly where the tab stops will be, click the Position Panel Above Text Frame iconic button (the magnet icon).

If you need a tab flush with the right margin — for example, to position a dingbat at the end of the story — press Shift+Tab. You don't need to use the Tabs panel.

Figure 18-1:
The Tabs panel, its flyout menu, and a table created using tab settings.

	2001	2002	2003	2004	2005
Airports	85	152	292	378	423
Hotels	569	2,274	11,687	22,021	23,663
Retail Outlets	474	11,109	50,287	82,149	85,567
Enterprise Guesting Areas	64	624	1,762	3,708	5,413
Stations and Ports	—	88	623	2,143	3,887
Community Hot Spots	2	266	5,637	20,561	30,659
Others	—	240	780	1,526	2,156
Total Market	1,274	14,752	71,079	132,486	151,768

SOURCE: GARTNER

Clear All
Delete Tab
Repeat Tab
Reset Indents

InDesign lets you specify up to eight characters, including special characters, that will repeat to fill any white space. These repeating characters are called *leaders*. When you set a leader for a tab stop, the leaders actually fill any space prior to that tab stop (between the preceding text and the tab location). To spread out the leader characters, type spaces between the characters you enter. Don't enter spaces before and after a single character (unless that's the look you're going for), though, as that will result in two spaces between the characters when the pattern repeats.

In addition to setting tabs in the Tabs panel, InDesign provides four additional options through its flyout menu: Clear All, Delete Tab, Repeat Tab, and Reset Indents.

- ✔ The **Clear All command** deletes any tabs you've created, and any text positioned with tabs reverts to the position of the default tab stops. (You can delete an individual tab stop by dragging its icon off the ruler.)

- ✔ The **Delete Tab command** deletes the currently selected tab. (Just click it in the tab ruler.)

  You can also delete tabs by dragging them off the tab ruler using the mouse.

- ✔ The **Repeat Tab command** lets you create a string of tabs across the ruler that are all the same distance apart. When you select a tab on the ruler and choose this command, InDesign measures the distance between the selected tab and the preceding tab (or, if it's the first tab on the ruler, the distance between the selected tab and the left indent/text inset). The program then uses this distance to place new tabs, with the same alignment, all the way across the ruler. InDesign repeats tabs only to the right of the selected tab, but it inserts tabs between other tab stops.

- ✔ The **Reset Indents command** removes any changes to the left indent, right indent, or indent hang settings made in the Tabs panel using the arrow sliders, and reverts to the indents defined in the paragraph style currently applied to the text.

Setting Up Tables

You can create tables using tabs, but the more complex the table, the more work that requires. So make your life easier and use InDesign's table editor, which lets you specify almost any attribute imaginable in a table through the Table panel and the Table menu.

InDesign lets you import tables from Microsoft Word, RTF, and Microsoft Excel files, including some of their cell formatting. Likewise, you can convert their tables to tabbed text by using the options in the Import Options dialog box that is accessible when you place a file through the Place dialog box (File⇨Place [⌘+D or Ctrl+D]), as covered in Chapter 11.

You can edit tables' contents in the Story Editor view (see Chapter 12).

To create a table in InDesign, follow these steps:

1. **Create or select a text frame with the Type tool and then choose Table⇨Insert Table (Option+Shift+⌘+T or Ctrl+Alt+Shift+T).**

   If you select an existing text frame, the table is inserted at the cursor's location in the existing text.

   The Insert Table dialog box appears.

2. **Type the number of body rows and columns and the number of header and footer rows.**

   Header and footer rows repeat on each page for tables that go across multiple pages

3. **Click OK to have InDesign create the basic table.**

   The table is set as wide as the text frame. The depth is based on the number of rows, with each row defaulting to the height that will hold 12-point text.

You can also apply a table style to the new table by selecting one from the Table Style pop-up menu. I cover how to create these styles in the "Using table and cell styles" section, later in this chapter.

With the basic table in place, you now format it using the Table panel and the Table menu. In both, you can increase or decrease the number of rows and columns, set the row and column height, set the text's vertical alignment within selected cells (top, middle, bottom, and justified), choose one of four text-rotation angles, and set the text margin within a cell separately for the top, bottom, left, and right. Note that all the Table panel's options affect only the currently selected cells, except for the Number of Rows and Number of Columns fields. Figure 18-2 shows the Table panel and its flyout menu, as well as an example table created using these tools.

If you have a smallish monitor, set at 1024 by 768 pixels — the norm for a 17-inch display — the Table, Table Styles, and Cell Styles panels may be shoved to the bottom of the panel dock, and, when they're selected, the only things you see are their panel tab and flyout menu icon. You have a few choices:

Shorten other panel groups in the dock to make room for them, remove other panel groups to make room for them, or drag them out of the dock and make them floating.

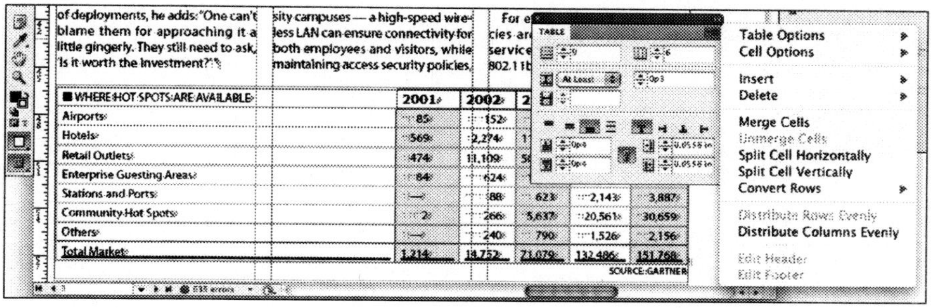

Figure 18-2:
The Table panel and its flyout menu, with an example table.

You set cell text's horizontal alignment using the paragraph formatting controls (see Chapter 14). You can apply character formatting to cell text (see Chapter 15). You can also apply tabs within cells using the Tabs panel covered in the "Setting Tabs" section, earlier in this chapter.

To add items to a table, you can type text in any cell, paste text or graphics into a cell, or place text or graphics into a cell by choosing File⇨Place (⌘+D or Ctrl+D). Note that any tabbed text pasted into a cell retains the tabs, with all the text pasted into the same cell — InDesign doesn't look at those tabs and assume that you wanted the tabbed text converted into multiple cells.

To insert a tab character into a table cell, don't press Tab — that just advances you to the next cell. Instead, choose Type⇨Insert Special Character⇨Other⇨Tab.

Adjusting tables

InDesign lets you add and delete rows and columns, as well as split and join cells using the Insert, Delete, Merge, and Split commands in the Table menu and in the Table panel's flyout menu. You can also select rows, columns, and entire tables using the Table menu. Several shortcuts, shown in Table 18-1, speed things along if you're a keyboard-oriented person.

These commands work intuitively, so I won't bore you with detailed explanations here. For example, to delete a row, select it or a cell within it using the Type tool and then choose Table⇨Delete⇨Row. To split a cell vertically, select the cell and choose Table⇨Split Cell Vertically. You get the idea.

Table 18-1	Table-Editing Shortcuts	
Command	*Macintosh Shortcut*	*Windows Shortcut*
Select cell	⌘+/	Ctrl+/
Select row	⌘+3	Ctrl+3
Select column	Option+⌘+3	Ctrl+Alt+3
Select table	Option+⌘+A	Ctrl+Alt+A
Insert column	Option+⌘+9	Ctrl+Alt+9
Insert row	⌘+9	Ctrl+9
Delete column	Shift+Delete	Shift+Backspace
Delete row	⌘+Delete	Ctrl+Backspace

Formatting tables

For more sophisticated table attributes, use the Table Options dialog box and its five panes. (Choose Table⇨Table Options and then the desired pane from the submenu. To go straight to the Table Setup pane, you can also just press Option+Shift+⌘+B or Ctrl+Alt+Shift+B.) You see the Table Setup pane, shown in Figure 18-3. If you want to go straight to one of the four other panes, you can do so by choosing the desired pane in the submenu after choosing Table⇨Table Options.

When formatting tables, take advantage of the Preview option in most dialog boxes to see the effects of your changes before committing to them.

If you select more than one cell — meaning the entire cell, not just some of its contents — the Control panel's options change to display many of the controls available in the Table panel, as well as some cell-oriented controls, such as setting cell boundary line weights and line types.

Here are some of the basics to keep in mind:

✔ The Table Setup pane lets you change the number of rows and columns, as well as footer rows and columns. You also can specify the table border, color, line type, and even tint. Use the Table Spacing options to have space automatically added before and after a table that is in the same text frame as other text.

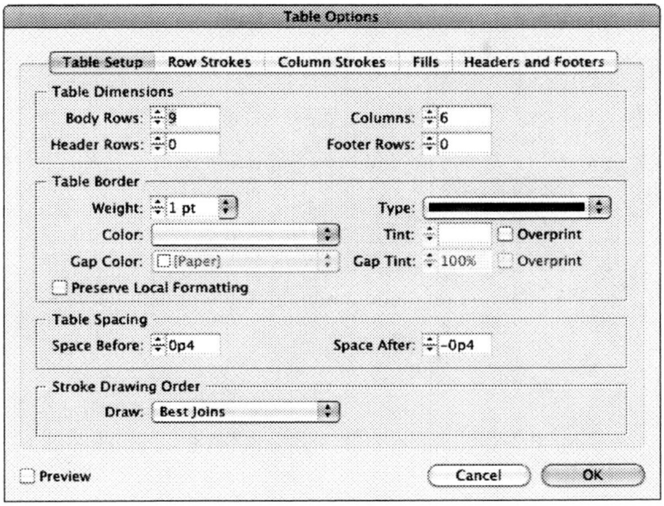

Figure 18-3:
The Table
Setup pane
of the Table
Options
dialog box.

✔ The Row Strokes pane lets you decide how often rows have an alternating pattern of strokes applied to them. For example, you may want every third row to have a thicker stroke than the first and second rows, because each set of three rows is related to each other and the third row marks the end of that set. You choose how many rows you want the special stroke to skip before being applied in the Alternating Pattern pop-up menu and then use the rest of the controls to choose the stroke weight, color, type, and so on.

✔ The Column Strokes pane works just like the Row Strokes pane, except it lets you alternate the strokes across columns rather than rows.

✔ The Fills pane (shown in Figure 18-4) works like the Row Strokes pane and Column Strokes pane, except that it applies a fill to the cells in the specified series of rows or columns. The reason that there is just one pane for fills but two for strokes is that you can't have both row fills and column fills automatically applied to the same table — that would usually make for a hard-to-read checkerboard. Of course, you can use horizontal fills to accentuate rows and use strokes on columns to help keep them visually separate.

✔ The Headers and Footers pane lets you change the number of header and footer rows — just like the Table Setup pane — but it also lets you control how often the header and/or footer rows repeat: Every Text Column, Once Per Frame, or Once Per Page.

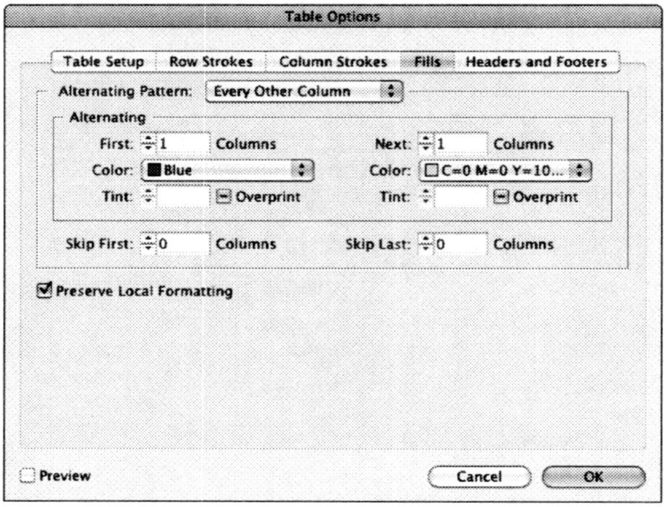

Figure 18-4:
The Fills
pane of
the Table
Options
dialog box.

InDesign also provides formatting controls over cells, using the Cell Options dialog box. (Choose Table⇨Cell Options and then one of the four desired panes: Text, Strokes and Fills, Rows and Columns, and Diagonal Lines. You can go straight to the Text pane by pressing Option+⌘+B or Ctrl+Alt+B.) After you selected the cells you want to format, use the various panes as desired:

✔ The Text pane works very much like the General pane of the Text Frame Options dialog box (see Chapter 11). Here, you set how far text is inset from the cell boundaries, how text is vertically aligned within the cell, and where the text baseline begins within the cell. Unique to cells, you can also specify whether the cell grows to fit the text automatically (by unchecking Clip Contents to Cell) and the degree of text rotation (0, 90, 180, and 270 degrees).

✔ The Strokes and Fills pane, shown in Figure 18-5, lets you set the stroke and fill for selected cells. You can select which cell boundaries to apply a stroke to, by selecting the sides from the preview image at the top of the pane and then choosing the desired options. You can also set the desired fill color and tint.

✔ The Rows and Columns pane lets you set the row height, including its maximum for rows that are allowed to expand automatically as specified in the Text pane, as well as the column width. You also can specify which rows must be kept together and if certain rows should start at a new page, frame, or column.

You can also adjust column and row heights by dragging on the row and column boundaries with the mouse.

✔ The Diagonal Lines pane lets you place three types of diagonal lines within cells — upper left to lower right, lower right to upper left, or both — and then specify the stroke weight, type, color, and tint. You can also choose whether the diagonal lines overprint the cell contents or vice versa. To remove a diagonal line, just click the No Diagonal Lines iconic button.

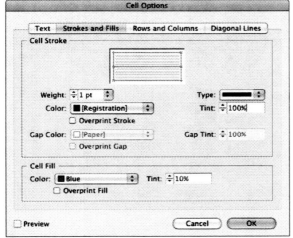

Figure 18-5: The Strokes and Fills pane of the Cell Options dialog box.

Using table and cell styles

To make it easy to apply and update table formatting across a document, InDesign lets you create and apply table and cell styles. They work like paragraph, character, and object styles, taking the table formatting features covered in the preceding section and bringing them together into the New Table Style and New Cell Style dialog boxes.

To work with table styles, open the Table Styles panel by choosing Window⇨Styles⇨Table Styles. To work with cell styles, open the Cell Styles panel by choosing Window⇨Styles⇨Cell Styles. Choose New Table Style or New Cell Style from the appropriate panel's flyout menu and then use the various panes to specify the desired formatting. The panes, and their options, are the same as described in the preceding section, "Formatting tables." Figure 18-6 shows the New Table Style dialog box's General pane.

TIP

Whether creating a new table style or a new cell style, the easiest method is to format an existing table or cell the way you want it, select it, and then create a new table or cell style — InDesign picks up the existing formatting for the new style. Otherwise, you have to specify everything in the New Table Style or New Cell Style dialog box, where it's harder to see the effects of your settings. (Even if you enable the Preview option, the dialog boxes are fairly large and tend to obscure most of your document.)

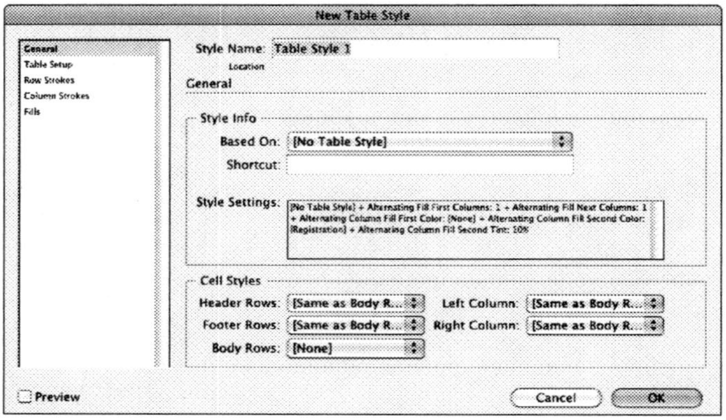

Figure 18-6:
The General pane of the New Table Styles dialog box.

Keep in mind a few notes about creating table and cell styles — in the General pane of the New Table Style and New Cell Style dialog boxes — that you should know before getting too far into them:

- ✔ You give each style its own name. Choose names that will make sense a week or a month later so that you know what they're meant to be used for!

- ✔ You can base a new table style on an existing one, so changes to the parent style are automatically reflected in the children styles based on it.

- ✔ You can assign a keyboard shortcut to styles you use frequently.

When creating table styles, you can also have the table style automatically apply the cell styles of your choosing to the following table elements: header rows, footer rows, body rows, the leftmost column, and the rightmost column.

When creating cell styles, you can choose a paragraph style to be automatically applied to text in cells using the style.

To apply styles to selected tables or cells, just choose the desired style from the Table Style or Cell Style panel. To override existing formatting, use the options indicated for paragraph and character styles described in Chapter 13.

Modifying and managing table and cell styles

To modify styles, double-click the style name in the Table Styles or Cell Styles panel to open the Table Style Options or Cell Style Options dialog box, which is identical to the New Table Styles or New Cell Styles dialog box explained in the preceding section. Make your changes, click OK, and your styles and all tables and cells using them are instantly updated!

InDesign also lets you manage your styles, such as creating groups of styles to keep them better organized, and bringing in styles from other documents. Because these features work the same for paragraph and character styles as well, I cover them in Chapter 13.

Converting Tabs to Tables (and Back)

Often, you'll have a table done using tabs — whether imported from a word processor or originally created in InDesign with tabs — that you want to convert to a real InDesign table. All you have to do is select the tabbed text you want to convert using the Type tool and choose Table⇨Convert Text to Table.

In the Convert Text to Table dialog box, you can choose a Column Separator (Tab, Comma, Paragraph, or a text string you type in the field) or a Row Separator (same options). Although most textual data uses tabs to separate columns and paragraphs to separate rows, you may encounter other data that uses something else. For example, spreadsheets and databases often save data so that commas, rather than tabs, separate columns. That's why InDesign lets you choose the separator characters before conversion.

During the conversion, InDesign formats the table using the standard settings, using the current text formatting and the default cell insets and stroke types. You can then adjust the table using the tools covered in the "Formatting tables" section, earlier in this chapter. Note that the conversion treats all rows as body rows.

You can also convert a table to text by selecting multiple cells or an entire table and choosing Table⇨Convert Table to Text. InDesign presents the same options as it does in the Convert Text to Table dialog box so that you can determine how the converted data appears.

Chapter 19

Working with Footnotes, Indexes, and TOCs

Many business documents — books, reports, white papers, and so on — use features traditionally associated with academic book publishing: footnotes to cite sources, indexes to provide a map to specific content's location in the document, and tables of contents (TOCs) to provide an overview of the document's structure and contents.

When you're working on any type of document — a report, a magazine, a textbook — you can easily spend more time manually creating tables of contents, keeping footnotes updates, and laboriously managing indexes than you spend designing the publication. InDesign helps reduce this labor while also ensuring that your footnotes, indexes, and tables of contents stay automatically updated as your document is revised.

You can extend the power of these tools to book-length projects composed of multiple InDesign documents (see Chapter 21), creating consistent indexing and tables of contents in one fell swoop.

Adding Footnotes

Many documents, including academic and technical documents, use footnotes. InDesign lets you add footnotes to your document with very little fuss.

You can import footnotes from Microsoft Word files (see Chapter 11), or you can add footnotes directly in InDesign. With the text-insertion cursor in your text where you want the footnote marker to appear, choose Type⇨Insert Footnote to add a footnote to the bottom of the column that contains the footnote marker, as shown in Figure 19-1. You need to manually enter the text that will go with each numbered footnote, but InDesign updates the footnote numbering as you add and delete footnotes.

You can't insert footnotes into tables. But you can simulate footnotes by adding a superscripted footnote character in the table text and typing your footnote text below the table — note this "footnote" isn't linked to the text, doesn't renumber automatically as a real footnote would, and can't be formatted with InDesign's footnote formatting controls.

Figure 19-1:
Inserting
a footnote
(shown
below the
first
column).

You can control much of the appearance of footnotes by choosing Type⇨ Document Footnote Options to open the Footnote Options dialog box, shown in Figure 19-2.

The Numbering and Formatting pane controls the formatting of the footnote text and footnote character in the current InDesign document. The Layout pane controls the placement of the footnote relative to the rest of the document.

Among the features you should note in the Numbering and Formatting pane are

- ✔ Choose the numbering style — such as 1, 2, 3, 4 ... or I, ii, iii, iv ... — via the Style pop-up menu.
- ✔ Control whether the footnote numbers start anew (such as at the beginning of a section) or continue from the preceding number via the Start At field.
- ✔ Control whether numbering automatically resets every page, spread, or section via the Restart Numbering Every pop-up menu.
- ✔ Add a prefix and/or suffix to your footnote numbers via the Prefix and Suffix fields. Note the unnamed pop-up menus that let you add special characters such as a thin space or bracket.

✔ Use the Position and Character Style options in the Footnote Reference Number in Text subsection to determine how the footnote characters appear in text.

✔ Similarly, use the Paragraph Style and Separator options in the Footnote Formatting subsection to determine how the footnote text appears. (Note that any Separator options will display after any Suffix options chosen.)

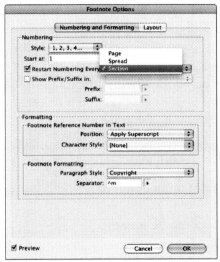
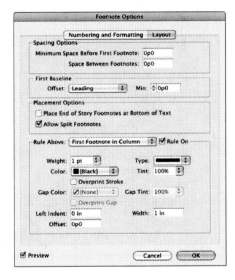

Figure 19-2:
The
Footnote
Options
dialog box's
two panes.

Among the features to note in the Layout pane are

✔ Set the preferred spacing for the footnote text in the Spacing Options section.

✔ Convert Word's endnotes (which appear at the end of a story) to InDesign footnotes (which appear in the column or page that the footnote reference occurs in) by checking the Place End of Story Footnotes at Bottom of Text option.

✔ Control whether footnotes can break across columns via the Allow Split Footnotes option. Enabling this option can improve the layout when you have long footnotes that otherwise eat up a column of text.

✔ Control the ruling line above footnotes using the Rule Above options. They work like the paragraph rules (see Chapter 14).

To change these settings for future documents, open the dialog box while no document is open and set your new defaults.

Creating Indexes

When trying to locate information in a book, nothing is as wonderful as a good index. Once upon a time, book indexing was a labor-intensive process involving piles of index cards. InDesign makes indexing much easier, while still allowing you to make key decisions about how the index is formatted.

But be warned: Indexing is complicated business and is, by and large, an expert feature. I cover just the basics here.

Choosing an indexing style

Before you begin indexing your document, ask yourself the following questions:

- Do you want to initial-cap all levels of all entries, or do you just want sentence case?
- Should index headings appear in boldface?
- What type of punctuation will you use in your index?
- Will you capitalize secondary entries in the index?
- Should the index be nested or run-in style? (A *nested index* is an indented list, with each entry on its own line. A *run-in index* puts all related entries in one paragraph, separated by semicolons.)

After you make these decisions, making a small dummy index is a good idea. From the dummy, create a master page for index pages, paragraph styles for index headings (the letters *A, B, C,* and so on), paragraph styles for each level of the index (including indents as appropriate), and character styles for any special formatting you want on page numbers or cross-reference text. InDesign doesn't do any of these tasks for you.

Inside the Index panel

When you want to index a chapter or document, open the Index panel by choosing Window➪Type & Tables➪Index (Shift+F8). Use this panel to add words to the index in up to four indent levels, edit or delete index entries, or create cross-references. The Index panel is shown in Figure 19-3.

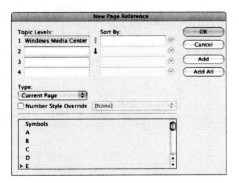

Figure 19-3:
Left: The Index panel and its flyout menu. Right: The New Page Reference dialog box.

Two radio buttons appear at the top of the Index panel: Reference and Topic. You use Reference mode to add and edit entries from selected text. (Although it's a well-intentioned feature meant to help standardize index entries, the Topic mode's use isn't intuitive, and most indexers simply ignore it and add entries manually from selected text or type phrases into the Index panel in Reference mode. You should ignore it, too.)

Select the Book check box if you're creating an index for multiple chapters in a book (see Chapter 21). You must have a book open for this option to be available. If you have a book open and don't select the Book check box, the index is saved with the current document and not opened when you open other chapters of the book.

Adding index items via the Index panel

To add entries to the index, be sure the Type tool is active and then choose New Page Reference from the Index panel's flyout menu (⌘+7 or Ctrl+7) to get the dialog box shown in Figure 19-3.

If the Type tool isn't active when you open the dialog box, the flyout menu option is called New Cross-Reference instead, letting you add a cross-reference entry to the index. The resulting New Cross-Reference dialog box is identical to the New Page Reference dialog box, except the various options default to ones appropriate for a cross-reference.

Here's how the controls work:

✔ If you selected text first in your document, the text is entered automatically into Topic Level 1. Otherwise, type the text that you want to add to the index. In Figure 19-3, you can see that I typed **Windows Media Center**. The text is added to the Topic list and to the list of index entries.

✔ You can enter text that controls how the entry is sorted in the Sort By column. For example, if the selected text you're indexing is *The X-Files,* but you want it sorted as if it were *X-Files, The* (so it appears with the X entries in the index), enter **X-Files, The** in the Sorted By column. This technique is also handy for names, such as indexing *Barack Obama* as *Obama, Barack* by entering **Obama, Barack** in the Sorted By column.

✔ If you want a more complex index, you may want to use some or all of the four possible entry levels. You may want an index entry to appear under a higher-level topic. For example, you may want *Border Collies* to appear in the index under *Herding Dogs,* in which case you'd enter **Herding Dogs** in the Topic Level 1 field and **Border Collies** in the Topic Level 2 field. Or you may want *Collies* in the Topic Level 1 field and then *Border* in the Topic Level 2 field, because you plan on listing the different varieties of collies under one Level 1 index entry, with the varieties listed within that entry as Level 2 subentries.

✔ Use the Type pop-up menu to determine the page entries for the index entry. For example, if you select To End of Section, the page numbers for the selected text in the index cover the range from the index entry to the end of the section it's in.

✔ To add just the selected text as an index entry, click Add. (If no text is selected, the text is added to the Topic list, but no index entry appears for it.) To add all occurrences of the text in the book, click Add All.

✔ To change previously defined index entries, select an entry and then choose Page Reference Options in the Index panel's flyout menu.

✔ At the bottom of the New Page Reference dialog box is a list of letters as well as the entry Symbols (where entries that begin with numbers and other nonletter characters will be grouped in the index). You can scroll through this list of headings to see what is already in the index under each letter. Although you may think clicking a letter would force the current index entry to appear in that letter's section of the index, it doesn't.

To quickly add a word or text selection to an index, highlight the text and press ⌘+7 or Ctrl+7 to add the text to the New Page Reference dialog box. To index a word without opening that dialog box, just press Option+Shift+⌘+[or Ctrl+Alt+Shift+[. This shortcut adds the text to the index using the index's default settings. (You can always edit them later.) And to enter an index entry such as Barack Obama as a proper name (last name, first name, or *Obama, Barack* in this example), use the shortcut Option+Shift+⌘+] or Ctrl+Alt+Shift+].

Polishing and generating the index

The Index panel's flyout menu has several options useful for generating and fine-tuning an index:

- **Duplicate Topic** lets you duplicate a topic entry so that you can use the settings from one entry without having to re-enter those settings in a new entry.

- **Delete Topic** removes a topic (and any associated entries) from the index.

- **Import Topics** lets you import topic lists from other InDesign documents.

- **Go to Selected Marker** causes InDesign to jump to the text that contains the selected index entry in the Index panel.

- **Topic Options** lets you edit the Level and Sort By settings for topic entries; these settings affect all index entries that use them.

- **Capitalize** lets you standardize the capitalization of topic entries — you can choose Selected Topic, Selected Topic and All Subtopics, All Level 1 Topics, and All Topics.

- **Update Preview** updates the index entries in the Index panel to reflect page-number changes, new occurrences of index text occurrences, and deleted occurrences of indexed text.

- **Generate Index** creates the index via the dialog box shown in Figure 19-4. In this dialog box, you specify the following: a title for the index, the paragraph style for that title, whether a selected index is replaced with the new one, whether an entire book is indexed, whether text on hidden layers is indexed, whether the index is nested or run-in, whether empty index headings and sections are included, what paragraph styles are applied to each level of index entry, what character styles are applied to different portions of index entries, and which characters will be used as separators within index entries.

  Click the More Options button to see the nested/run-in and later options, as shown in Figure 19-4. Note that the button changes to Fewer Options, which if clicked hides those extra options and becomes More Options again.

  After you generate an index, you get the standard InDesign loaded-text icon (the paragraph icon); click an existing text frame into which you want to flow the index, or click anywhere else in a document to have InDesign create the text frame for you and flow the index text into it.

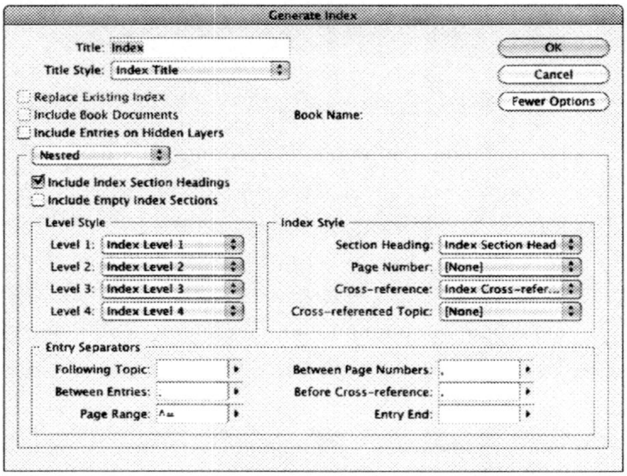

Figure 19-4:
The
Generate
Index dialog
box, with
all options
displayed.

Creating Tables of Contents

A table of contents (TOC) is useful in a long document because it helps read-ers locate information quickly. A *TOC* is simply a list of paragraphs that are formatted with the same styles. This dependence on styles means that if you want to use the table of contents feature, you have to use paragraph styles. Not only do styles guarantee consistent formatting, but they also tell InDesign what text you want to include in your TOC.

After you create a book (or even a single document), InDesign can build a table of contents by scanning pages for the paragraph styles you specify. For example, if you create a book, you might use paragraph styles named *Chapter Title, Section,* and *Subsection.* Using its table of contents feature, InDesign can generate a table of contents that includes all three levels.

TOC styles manage the text that you want in a table of contents, the order in which it appears, how page numbers are added, and how the various TOC elements are formatted. To create a TOC style, choose Layout⇨Table of Contents Styles.

In the Table of Contents Styles dialog box, click New to create a new TOC style. You can also edit an existing TOC style via the Edit button, delete one via the Delete button, and import one from another InDesign document via the Load button.

Here's how to create a TOC style after clicking the New button:

1. **Enter a name for the TOC style in the TOC Style field (shown in Figure 19-5).**

   The default is TOC Style 1.

2. **In the Title field, enter a heading for the TOC.**

   This text appears in your table of contents.

   If you don't want a title, leave the Title field blank, but note that you still get an empty paragraph at the top of your TOC for this title. You can always delete that paragraph.

3. **Use the Style pop-up menu to choose the paragraph style that this title will have.**

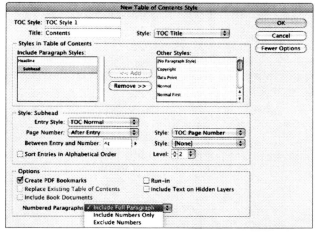

Figure 19-5:
The New
Table of
Contents
Style
dialog box.

4. **In the Styles in Table of Contents section, click a paragraph style that you want to appear in your TOC from the Other Styles list at right.**

   For example, you might click Chapter Title.

5. **Click Add to add it to the Include Paragraph Styles list at left.**

   Select a style from the Include Paragraph Styles section and click Remove to remove any paragraph styles you don't want in the TOC.

6. **Repeat Steps 4 and 5 until you have added all the paragraph styles that you want to include in the TOC.**

7. **Use the Entry Style pop-up menu to select a TOC level, and then choose the paragraph formatting for that style.**

   If the Entry Style, Page Number, and other options don't display, click the More Options button to see them.

   • Use the Page Number pop-up menu to determine how page numbers are handled: After Entry, Before Entry, and No Page Number. If you want the page numbers to have a character style applied, choose that style from the Style pop-up menu to the right of the Page Number pop-up menu.

- Use the Between Entry and Number field and pop-up menu to choose what appears between the TOC text and the page number. You can enter any characters you want; use the pop-up menu to select special characters such as bullets and tabs. In most cases, you should select a tab; the paragraph style selected earlier for the TOC entry includes leader information, such as having a string of periods between the text and the number. You can also apply a character style to the characters between the text and the page numbers via the Style pop-up menu at right.

- To sort entries at this level alphabetically, such as for a list of products in a brochure, select the Sort Entries in Alphabetical Order check box.

- To change the level of the current TOC entry, use the Level pop-up menu. If you change the level of entries, InDesign correctly sorts them when it creates the TOC, even if the levels seem out of order in the Include Paragraph Styles list.

- In the Options section of the dialog box, choose the appropriate options. Check Create PDF Bookmarks if you're exporting the document to PDF format and want the PDF TOC file to have *bookmarks* (a clickable set of TOC links). Check Run-in if you want all entries at the same level to be in one paragraph. (This option isn't common for TOCs, but it's used in indexes and lists of figures.) Check Replace Existing Table of Contents if you want InDesign to automatically replace an existing TOC if the TOC style is changed. Check Include Text on Hidden Layers if you want to include text on hidden layers in the TOC. Check Include Book Documents if you have a book open and want InDesign to generate a TOC based on all chapters in that book. (InDesign shows the current open book's name.) Finally, control whether numbers are included in the table of contents for numbered paragraphs using the Numbered Paragraphs pop-up menu.

 8. Continue this process for each paragraph style whose text should be in the TOC.

   Note that the order in which you add these styles determines the initial levels: The first paragraph style added is level 1; the second is level 2, and so on. But you can change the order by changing the Level setting, as described in Step 7.

   You can also reorder the paragraph styles by dragging them up and down in the list — but this doesn't change their levels and thus won't change the order in which they are sorted in the TOC. All it does is change the order you see them in the dialog box.

To make changes to a TOC style, go to the Edit Table of Contents Style dialog box. Choose Layout⇨Table of Contents Styles, select the TOC style to edit, and click Edit.

With a TOC style in place and your document properly formatted with the paragraph styles that the TOC style will look for when generating a TOC, you're ready to have InDesign create the actual TOC for you.

To generate a TOC, choose Layout⇨Table of Contents. You get the Table of Contents dialog box, which is identical to the New Table of Contents Style dialog box shown in Figure 19-5. In this dialog box, you can make changes to the TOC style settings. (If you want to save those TOC style changes, be sure to click the Save Style button.) Then click OK to have InDesign generate the TOC. You might also get a dialog box asking whether you want to include items in *overset text* (text that didn't fit in your document after you placed it) in your TOC. It may take a minute or two for the program to generate the TOC. (See Chapter 12 for more details on overset text.)

Be sure you allow enough space (a single text frame, a series of linked text frames, or one or more empty pages) for the TOC before generating a final TOC because if you end up adding or deleting pages based on the TOC length, the TOC will display the old page numbers.

If you select a text frame before generating a TOC, InDesign places the TOC text in it when you generate the TOC. If you don't select a text frame, you see the familiar loaded-text icon (the paragraph pointer) that you see when you place a text file. Click a text frame to insert the TOC text in that frame, or click in an empty part of your document to create a text frame in which the TOC text will flow.

To update page numbering after flowing a TOC, simply rebuild the TOC by selecting one or more text frames holding the TOC and then choosing Layout⇨Update Table of Contents.

The feature that creates a TOC is actually a list generator, and you can use it to create other kinds of lists. Basically, you can create a list from anything that is tagged with a paragraph style. For example, if your figure captions all use their own paragraph style (called Caption Title in this example), you can generate a list of figures by creating a TOC style that includes just the Caption Title paragraph style. An InDesign document can have more than one TOC so that you can include multiple lists in your document.

Chapter 20

Working with Automatic Text

A key area of improvement over the years in InDesign is the increased use of automated text. From the very beginning, InDesign offered automatic page numbers so that your folios and cross-references would reflect the current pages as your layout changed. Later versions enhanced this capability with section markers, which let you create variable names in folios for your section titles. Still later came the capability to use data files and merge their contents into a layout to customize your output, similar to how word processors let you customize labels with their mail-merge feature. More recently, InDesign added to this mix a capability called *variable text,* which gives you more flexibility in where and how you can have InDesign update text automatically throughout a document based on your specifications.

Altogether, these features have helped InDesign stake significant ground in reducing the labor and time of manual processes, such as searching and replacing for text that changes predictably throughout the document.

Another type of text variable is the cross-reference, which can insert the page number or other text for you (such as *See page 227* or *Learn how color works in the "All about Color" chapter*). InDesign supports such automated cross-references. It also retains those cross-references imported from Word files. I cover this type of automated text later in this chapter.

Automating Page Numbers

You'll often want page references in text — the current page number in a folio, for example, or the target page number for a "continued on" reference.

You can type a page number manually on each page of a multipage document, but that can get old fast. If you're working on a multipage document, you should use master pages (see Chapters 4 and 5). And if you use master pages, you should handle page numbers on document pages by placing page-number characters on their master pages.

If you want to add the current page number to a page, you can choose Type⇨Insert Special Character⇨Markers⇨Current Page Number (Option+Shift+⌘+N or Ctrl+Shift+Alt+N) whenever the Type tool is active and the text-insertion cursor is flashing. If you move the page or the text frame, the page-number character is automatically updated to reflect the new page number.

To create "continued on" and "continued from" lines, choose Type⇨Insert Special Character⇨Markers⇨Next Page Number to have the next page's number inserted in your text, or choose Type⇨Insert Special Character⇨ Markers⇨Previous Page Number to have the preceding page's number inserted. (There are no shortcuts for these complex menu sequences.) That next or preceding page will be the next or preceding page in the *story,* not the next page in the document.

One flaw in InDesign's continued-line approach is that the text frames must be linked for InDesign to know what the next and preceding pages are. Thus, you're likely to place your continued lines in the middle of your text. But if the text reflows, so do the continued lines. Here's a way to avoid that problem: Create separate text frames for your continued-on and continued-from text frames. Now link just those two frames, not the story text. This way, the story text can reflow as needed without affecting your continued lines.

Using Section Markers

InDesign offers another marker called the *section marker,* which lets you insert specific text into your document and update it by just changing the marker text.

The section marker is defined as part of a section start (see Chapter 4), and it's meant to be used in folios to put in the section name or chapter name. But you can use it anywhere you want — and for anything you want, not just for section or chapter labels.

To define a section marker (you can have only one per section, of course), open the Pages panel (Window⇨Pages, [⌘+F12 or Ctrl+F12]) and choose Numbering & Section Options from the panel's flyout menu. In the resulting dialog box, type a text string in the Section Marker field. Then click OK.

To use the marker, have the text insertion point active in whatever text frame you want to insert it and then choose Type⇨Insert Special Character⇨Markers⇨Section Marker. That's it!

Using Cross-References

InDesign uses the Hyperlinks panel (see Chapter 23) to provide a related capability: cross-references. Automated cross-references are used just for text, such as to automatically keep page numbers and chapter titles updated in text such as *see page 227* and *Learn more about color in the chapter "All about Color."*

To work with cross-references, you have two choices for their "to" locations.

- ✔ Specify locations by adding text anchors in your documents using the hyperlinks destination feature described in Chapter 23. Then you select that text anchor in the New Cross-Reference dialog box.
- ✔ Choose from a list of paragraphs and make the cross-reference link to that selected paragraph in the New Cross-Reference dialog box.

You open the New Cross-Reference dialog box, shown in Figure 20-1, by choosing Insert Cross-Reference from the Hyperlinks panel's flyout menu or by clicking its Create New Cross-Reference iconic button. (Open the Hyperlinks panel by choosing Window⇨Type & Tables⇨Cross-References.)

In the Linked To pop-up menu, choose Text Anchor if your "to" destination is a text anchor. If you want to select a specific paragraph instead, choose Paragraph; InDesign shows all the first words of each paragraph in the document so that you can scroll through the list and choose the desired one. You can also filter that list by choosing from the styles at left; only paragraphs with the selected style appear (so, for example, you can see just headings by choosing the paragraph style for your headings).

Use the Cross-Reference Format section of the New Cross-Reference dialog box to control what text displays for that cross-reference. You can be as basic as the page number (note that the word *page* appears with it automatically) or as complex as, for example, showing the full paragraph text (such as a heading) and the page number.

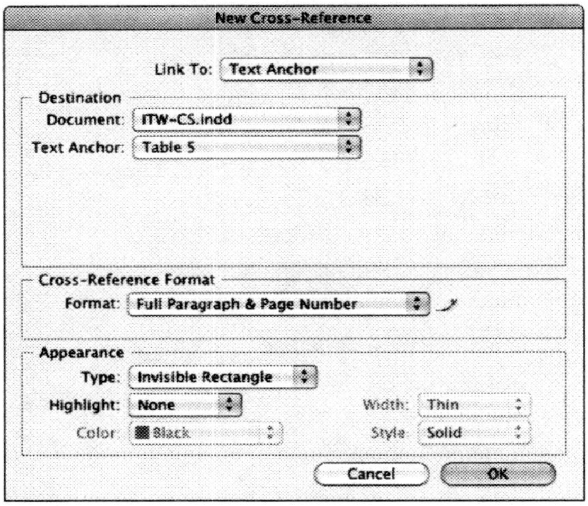

Figure 20-1:
The New
Cross-
Reference
dialog box.

You can create your own cross-reference formats and modify the existing ones by using the Cross-Reference Formats dialog box shown in Figure 20-2. This is an expert feature, so I don't cover it in detail, but feel free to experiment.

To open that dialog box, click the button to the right of the Format pop-up menu in the New Cross-Reference dialog box (handy when you want to create a new format as you are adding a cross-reference) or choose Define Cross-Reference Formats from the Hyperlinks panel's flyout menu. You can also edit an existing format this way.

The basic procedure for a cross-reference format is to add the text you want to display for any cross-references using the format combined with the codes for the text that is added and updated automatically. Use the iconic pop-up menu (the + icon) to the right of the Definition shown in Figure 20-2 to select those codes. The iconic pop-up menu below it (the @ icon) lets you choose special characters, such as em spaces. You can also have a character style applied to the cross-reference text as part of that format using the Character Style for Cross-Reference option.

You can control how the cross-reference appears using the Appearance section's controls. They work just like the Appearance controls in the New Hyperlinks dialog box, covered in the preceding section.

To edit an existing cross-reference, choose Cross-Reference Options from the Hyperlinks panel's flyout menu; it's identical to the New Cross-References dialog box.

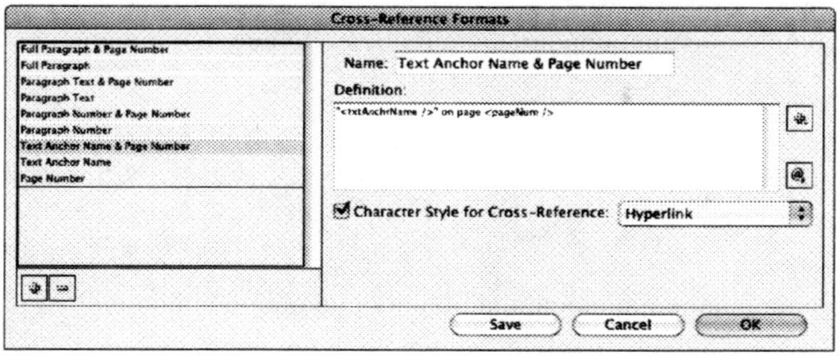

Figure 20-2:
The Cross-
Reference
Formats
dialog box.

Using Text Variables

With InDesign text variables, you can define an unlimited number of text variables that InDesign will happily update across your documents whenever you change them or your layout changes them.

To create a text variable, choose Type⇨Text Variables⇨Define. You see get the Text Variables dialog box, shown in Figure 20-3. It lists existing text variables — including the eight predefined ones in InDesign: Chapter Number, Creation Date, File Name, Last Page Number, Modification Date, Output Date, and the two types of Running Header. Any of them that you create are added to this list.

The source of the number used in the Chapter Number text variable is something you define as part of a book. Chapter 21 explains books and how to set the chapter number.

To create a new text variable, click New. The New Text Variable dialog box appears, as shown in Figure 20-3. Give the variable a name in the Name field, and choose the type of variable you want from the Type pop-up menu. Your choices are the seven predefined types plus Custom Text, which lets you put in any text of your choosing. (This means you can create more than one variable for, say, File Name or Modification Date. You might do this because you want them formatted differently in different usage scenarios.)

The options for formatting the chosen type of variable varies based on the type of variable it is. Three options are available for more than one type of text variable:

✔ **Text Before and Text After:** These two fields — available for all Type pop-up menu options except Custom Text — let you add any text you want before or after the variable. For example, you might enter the word **Chapter** in the Text Before field for a Chapter Number variable. Note that both fields have an unnamed pop-up menu to their right from which you can select a variety of common symbols and spaces.

✔ **Style:** This pop-up menu lets you select the style to apply in the Chapter Number, Running Header (Character Style), and Running Header (Paragraph Style) text variables.

✔ **Date Format:** This field and its associated pop-up menu let you choose the desired date and time formats for the Creation Date, Modification Date, and Output Date text variables. Examples include *MM/dd/yy* to get a date like 05/08/62 and *MMMM d, yyyy* to get a date like August 15, 1962. Don't worry about memorizing codes — just pick the desired options from the pop-up menu instead.

Several other variables have unique options:

✔ **Custom Text:** This variable has the fewest options. Just enter the desired text, including choosing special characters, such as spaces and dashes, from the unnamed pop-up menu to the right of the Text field. That's the only field to adjust for this text variable.

✔ **Last Page Number:** In addition to the Text Before, Text After, and Style formatting controls, this type includes one unique control: the Scope pop-up menu. Here, you choose between Section and Document to tell InDesign what you mean by last page number: the section's last page or the document's.

✔ **File Name:** In addition to Text Before and Text After formatting controls, this type has two unique check boxes — Include Entire Folder Path and Include File Extension — to tell InDesign exactly how much of the filename to include. If both are unchecked, InDesign includes just the core filename, such as Jun 10 TOC. Checking the Include Entire Folder Path adds the file location before the core filename, such as MacintoshHD:Projects:Jun 10 TOC or C:\Projects\Jun 10 TOC. Checking the Include File Extension appends the filename extension, such as June 10 TOC.indd.

✔ **Metadata Caption:** In addition to Text Before and Text After formatting controls, this type has the Metadata pop-up menu, where you choose the image metadata attribute to include in the captions. (The metadata caption feature is covered in Chapter 9.)

✔ **Running Header:** The formatting options for these two types — Paragraph Style and Character Style — are the most complex, as shown in Figure 20-3. The two Running Header menu options have two options not available to other Type pop-up menu options:

• **Use:** This option determines which text to use. First on Page uses the first text on the page that has the specific style applied, while Last on Page uses the last text on the page that has the specific style applied.

• **Options:** Here, you can control whether the punctuation of the source text is retained in the running header (check Delete End Punctuation to remove it) and whether the running header overrides the text of the source text's capitalization (check Change Case and then choose the appropriate capitalization option: Upper Case, Lower Case, Title Case, or Sentence Case).

Title case means that the first letter of each word is capitalized, while *Sentence Case* means that only the first letter of the first word in each sentence is capitalized.

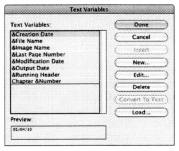

Figure 20-3:
Left: The
Text
Variables
dialog box.
Right: The
New Text
Variable
dialog box.

Editing and managing text variables

Editing text variables is very much like creating them: In the Text Variables dialog box, just select the variable to change and click Edit. You get the Edit Text Variable dialog box, which is identical (except for its name) to the New Text Variable dialog box covered in the preceding section.

You can also import text variables from other documents by clicking Load in the Text Variables dialog box and then choosing the document to import the variables from. After choosing a document, you get the Load Text Variables dialog box, where you can select which variables are imported and handle name conflicts.

To get rid of a text variable, select it from the list in the Text Variables dialog box and click Delete.

To convert a text variable in your document to the actual text, highlight it and either choose Type⇨Text Variables⇨Convert Variable to Text or, if you happen to be in the Text Variables dialog box, click Convert to Text.

Inserting text variables

Inserting text variables in your document uses the same essential process as inserting a special character such as a section marker, except you use the Text Variables menu option: Choose Type⇨Text Variables⇨Insert Variable, and then choose the desired variable from the submenu. If you happen to be in the Text Variables dialog box, click Insert.

Using Conditional Text

Have you ever worked on a document that has variations, forcing you to create separate copies that you must then ensure have any changes applied to all copies? Perhaps you used the layers feature (see Chapter 4) to restrict the unique content to its own layer so that you could make visible each version's layer when you wanted to print that specific version. But you realized this technique doesn't work well for text inside paragraphs, because changes to the text mean whatever you placed in layers won't be at the right location if your text changes move the text's locations in the "main" layer.

That's where the *conditional text* feature comes in. It's sort of a layer that works within text, so if the text moves, the conditional "layers" do, too.

For example, say you have a publication that is distributed in Canada, Ireland, and the U.K., where pricing is different (dollars, euros, and pounds, respectively). You can't really duplicate the main "dollars" layer and duplicate all the text in it for the "euros" and "pounds" layers. Why? The reason is that if you changed the text in the main layer that includes the dollar prices, the pounds and euros layers would have the old text and need to be changed also (a management nightmare). You may think that you can avoid this problem by having a main layer for the text, and then separate layers for the dollar, euro, and pound pricing. Unless your pricing wouldn't move ever (such as if it's in an independent table), if the main text is edited and reflows, those text frames would get out of place — an even worse situation.

With conditional text, you instead have just one layer for your text, and where the text may need to change (such as for pricing), you insert conditional text. Then, if you want to display the price in dollars, you enable the dollars condition, and the right text appears, no matter how the text is flowing. When you want to display the price in euros, you enable the euros condition. Ditto for pounds.

Here's how it works:

1. **In your text, enter each of the text variations you want.**

   For example, as you can see above the Conditional Text panel in Figure 20-4, if you have three prices, enter all three in sequence as if they were one piece of text. Apply any formatting desired. Don't worry for the moment that you don't want them all to display or print at the same time.

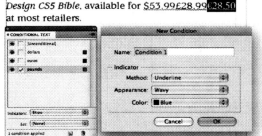
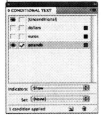

2. **Open the Conditional Text panel (Window⇨Type & Tables⇨ Conditional Text) and choose New Condition from the flyout menu.**

3. **In the New Conditions dialog box, give the condition a name and determine how you want it to be highlighted (using the Method, Appearance, and Color pop-up menus) in the layout, as shown in Figure 20-4.**

   Your highlighting options are Underline and Highlight (which puts a colored background behind conditional text), either of which you can apply a color to. If you choose Underline, you can select a line type in the Appearance pop-up menu. (It's unavailable if you choose Highlight.) This highlighting doesn't print; it just lets you know in InDesign where and what conditions are applied to text.

   You can modify conditions later by choosing Condition Options from the Conditional Text panel's flyout menu. The dialog box is identical to the New Conditions dialog box.

4. **In the text, highlight a piece of text (such as the euro price), and then click the related condition to apply that condition to the selected text.**

A check mark appears to the immediate left of the active condition for whatever text is selected or in which your text cursor is active. In your layout, the text also has whatever line type in whatever color you specified in the New Conditions dialog box so that you have a visual guide as to what conditions are applied to what text.

Add as many conditions using Steps 3 and 4 as you need. The figure's example has three: one for each price. (Note that the [Unconditional] condition is just your regular text, which always displays and prints.)

 5. **Now, click the squares in the Conditional Text panels to the far left of the various conditions.**

If the square shows an eye, any text tagged with that condition is visible. If the square is empty, any text tagged with that condition isn't displayed. By controlling which conditions are active (eye icons), you determine what displays and prints in your document. The text will also reflow automatically based on what you show and hide. (This process is exactly how you make layers visible and invisible in the Layers panel, as Chapter 4 explains.)

Pretty easy, isn't it? Just turn off and on the text you want to display, and print by hiding and showing the appropriate conditions.

Chapter 21

Publishing Books

In This Chapter

▶ Creating books

▶ Tackling chapters

▶ Printing your masterpieces

▶ Numbering pages and sections

*N*ot only is InDesign useful for short documents like ads and newsletters, but it also can comfortably handle longer, multichapter documents, such as books and manuals. The most common and easiest way to build longer documents, especially those created by more than one author or contributor, is to create multiple InDesign documents and then assemble them into a larger book.

InDesign's book feature lets you

✔ See who is working on each chapter (that is, on each document in the book) and when.

✔ Update styles and swatches across documents for consistency.

✔ Update page numbers across multiple documents.

✔ Create a unified table of contents and a unified index for multiple documents, using the techniques in Chapter 19.

✔ Easily print or create a PDF file from all the chapters of a book.

Creating a Book

In InDesign, a *book* is a specific type of file that you create to track chapters or multiple documents that make up the book. Using InDesign's book panel, you can add, open and edit, rearrange, and print chapters of the book. The book panel is nice for workgroups because multiple users can open the same book and access different chapters; it also works well if you are a single user working on a multichapter book.

To create a new book, choose File➪New➪Book. The New Book dialog box lets you specify a location for the book and give it a name. Click Save to create and open the book. The book panel will displays the book's filename in its header; if you have multiple books open as panes within a book pane, each pane's tab will show its book's filename.

You can open an existing book by using the File➪Open command (⌘+O or Ctrl+O). When viewing folder and disk contents via the Mac's Finder or Windows's Explorer, you can also double-click a book's icon or filename to open it.

If multiple books are open, they each appear in a separate tabbed pane in a floating panel. If you want them to appear in individual panels, you can just drag their respective tabs out of the panel, and InDesign will create a new panel for each dragged-out pane. To always have InDesign open or create books in separate panels, disable the Open Documents as Tabs option in the Interface pane of the Preferences dialog box (choose InDesign➪Preferences➪Interface [⌘+K] on the Mac or Edit➪Preferences➪ Interface [Ctrl+K] in Windows). Note that changing this option also means that any documents created or opened also appear in separate windows.

To close a book's pane and any book documents that are in it, click the book's tab to select it and choose Close Book from the flyout menu. If a book displays alone in a panel, simply click its Close box. And if you click the Close box in a panel with multiple book panes, all the panes are closed along with the panel.

Working with Book Chapters

A new book pane (or panel) is empty — you need to add chapter documents to fill it up. To do so, click the Add Document iconic button — the + icon on the bottom right of the book panel (see Figure 21-1) — or use the Add Document option in the book panel's flyout menu. Use the Add Chapter dialog box to locate and select the first chapter you want to add. Click the Add button to make this the first chapter in the book. Repeat this process to add to the book all the chapters you have ready. (You can also add more chapters later.)

Chapters are listed in the book pane in the order in which you add them. You may want to rearrange them to match the actual order of the book project — especially if you're numbering the book automatically from start to finish, since InDesign will number them based on their order in the book pane. To rearrange the relative position of chapters, just click and drag chapter names up or down within the pane to put them in the desired order.

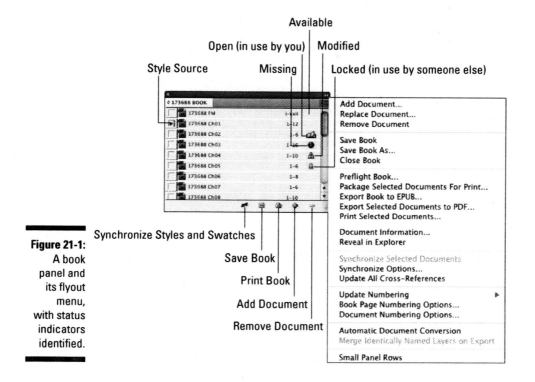

To work on a chapter in a book, first open the book and then double-click the chapter name in the book's pane. The chapter opens in InDesign just like any other InDesign document. For a chapter to be opened, it must be marked as Available, as explained in the next section. When you finish editing a chapter, save and close it as usual.

You can replace and delete chapters using the controls in the book panel's flyout menu for whatever book pane is selected:

- ✔ Replace an existing chapter with another document by selecting the chapter in the book panel and choosing Replace Document from the flyout menu. Navigate to a new document, select it, and click the Open button. InDesign replaces the selected chapter with the new document.

- ✔ Delete chapters from a book by choosing Remove Document from the flyout menu or by clicking the Remove Document iconic button (the – icon) at the bottom of the panel.

InDesign CS5 adds the Reveal in Finder (Mac) and Reveal in Explorer (Windows) options to the Book panel's flyout menu. Choosing this option opens a Finder window on the Mac or an Explorer window in Windows with the folder that contains the open book file.

InDesign offers three other menu options in the flyout menu that come in handy for managing a book: You can save a book by choosing Save Book, save it to a new name by choosing Save Book As, and close a book by choosing Close Book. (With the last option, any changes to the book are not saved, although a warning box gives you the chance to save any unsaved changes.)

Finding out about chapter status

When you use the book panel in a workgroup, it provides helpful status reports about each chapter. (Figure 21-1 shows the icons used to indicate a chapter's status.) The statuses are

- ✔ **Available:** You can open, edit, or print the chapter. Only one user at a time can open a chapter.

- ✔ **Open:** You have the chapter open and can edit it or print it. Nobody else can open the chapter at this time.

- ✔ **In Use:** Another user has the chapter open. In this case, you can't edit or open the chapter.

- ✔ **Modified:** The chapter has been changed since the last time you opened the book panel. Simply click the chapter name to update it.

- ✔ **Missing:** The chapter's file has been moved since it was added to the book. Double-click the chapter name to open the Find File dialog box and locate the file.

The Document Information menu option in the book panel's flyout menu provides useful information. When you select a chapter and choose this option, you can see the file's modification date, location, and page range, and you can replace the chapter with a different document.

Taking advantage of style sources

The first chapter you add to the book is, by default, the style source. You can tell which chapter is the style source by the icon to the left of the chapter name. In most cases, you want the styles, swatches, and so on to remain the same from chapter to chapter. The style source in an InDesign book defines the styles and swatches that are common to all the chapters in the book.

If you decide to make a different chapter the style source, all you need to do is (in the book pane) click in the column to the left of that chapter's filename. The icon indicating the style source moves to that chapter. But note that indicating a style source isn't the end of the story; to ensure formatting consistency, you need to synchronize all the book's chapters to that source, as explained in the next section.

Synchronizing formatting

When you use the Synchronize feature, InDesign makes sure that the paragraph styles, character styles, table styles, cell styles, object styles, trap presets, TOC styles, master pages, and color swatches in each chapter in the book match those in the style source. This synchronization enforces consistency, but also means you have to make sure that you choose the correct chapter as the standard, because its settings will override the other chapters' settings.

The book panel includes a Synchronize iconic button (the two facing arrows), as well as a Synchronize Selected Documents or Synchronize Book menu item in the flyout menu. Before you synchronize, make sure that you're happy with the styles, master pages, and other settings you've established in the style source and then follow these steps to synchronize:

1. **Be sure that all chapters are available for editing.**

2. **Choose the style source by clicking the box to the left of the source chapter so that the style-source icon appears.**

3. **Choose Synchronize Options from the book panel's flyout menu, which opens the — wait for it now! — Synchronize Options dialog box.**

   Make sure that every type of item you want to synchronize — Object Styles, TOC Style, Character Styles, Paragraph Styles, Table Styles, Cell Styles, Master Pages, Numbered Lists, Text Variables, Conditional Text Settings, Cross-Reference Formats, Trap Presets, and Swatches — is checked.

4. **Select the chapters you want to synchronize, and either click the Synchronize button or choose Synchronize Selected Documents from the flyout menu.**

   If no chapters are selected, InDesign assumes that you want to synchronize *all* chapters; the menu option Synchronize Book appears in the flyout menu rather than Synchronize Selected Documents in that case.

5. **Compare the styles (character, paragraph, object, table, cell, and TOC), swatches (color, tint, and gradient), text variables, numbered lists, master pages, and trap presets in the style source to those in each chapter.**

   If anything is different, the information in each chapter is updated to match the style source. If someone changed the typeface in a style sheet in a chapter, it reverts to the typeface specified in the style source. If anything is missing from a chapter — for example, if you just added a swatch to the style source but not to other chapters — that information is added to each chapter. If a chapter uses its own style or swatch not defined in the source style, that unique style or swatch is *not* changed or removed — these local additions are retained.

By using the synchronize feature, you give each chapter the same basic set of styles and swatches as the style source, although you can still add more of these specifications to individual chapters. Keep in mind that synchronizing doesn't repair the formatting fiascos that can happen when multiple users work on the same book. Be sure everyone who needs to know the standards for the design has access, ahead of time, to that information.

Printing Chapters and Books

Using the book panel, you can print any chapters with the status of Available or Open. Here's how:

1. **To print the entire book, make sure that no chapters are selected.**

   To print a contiguous range of chapters, Shift+click the first and last chapters that you want to print. To print noncontiguous chapters, ⌘+click or Ctrl+click the chapters to select them.

2. **Click the Print Book iconic button or choose Print Book or Print Selected Documents in the book panel's flyout menu.**

   The option you see depends on whether chapters are selected in the book panel. Either way, the standard InDesign Print dialog box opens. Note that the option to choose all pages or a range of pages is grayed out — you must print all chapters in the selected chapters.

3. **Make any adjustments in the Print dialog box.**

4. **Click Print to print the chapters.**

You can also output a book to PDF by using the Export Book to PDF or Export Selected Documents to PDF menu items in the flyout menu. Similar EPUB options let you export to the EPUB e-book format. These menu items work like their equivalent Print versions. (Chapter 22 covers PDF and e-book options.) And you can collect all the chapters, images, and fonts into one place using the Package Book for Print or Package Selected Documents for Print options (see Chapter 22).

Working with Sections in Chapters

Section-based page numbering is fairly common in book-length documents because it lets you, for example, restart page numbering in each new section, such as 4.1, 4.2, and so on. Creating a section start is also the only way to start a document on a left-facing page. InDesign gives you two choices for numbering book pages: You can let the book panel number pages consecutively from one chapter to the next, or you can add sections of page numbers, which carry through the book until you start a new section.

Numbering pages consecutively

If your book chapters don't have sections, use consecutive page numbering, in which the first page number of a chapter follows the last page number of the preceding chapter (for example, one chapter ends on page 224, and the next chapter starts on page 225).

Consecutive page numbering is applied by default in InDesign. If, for some reason, a document resets its numbering, go to that document, open the Section dialog box (choose Numbering & Section Options in the Pages panel's flyout menu), and select Automatic Page Numbering.

Here's how consecutive page numbering works:

- ✔ Whenever you add a chapter that contains no sections or that has section numbering set to Automatic Page Numbering, InDesign numbers pages consecutively throughout the book.

- ✔ As you add and delete pages from chapters, InDesign updates all the page numbers in the chapters that follow.

- ✔ You can force InDesign to renumber all the pages by choosing Repaginate from the book panel's flyout menu — handy if you changed section options in some chapters and want the book to see those changes.

Numbering pages with sections

When chapters you add to books already contain sections of page numbers (implemented through the Section dialog box, which you access via the Numbering & Section Options menu option in the Pages panel's flyout menu), section page numbering overrides the book's consecutive page numbering. The section page numbering carries through chapters of the book until InDesign encounters a new section start. So if one chapter ends on page *iv,* the next chapter starts on page *v* unless you start a new section for that chapter.

For more in-depth information about section numbering, see Chapter 4.

Setting chapter numbers

You can also see and modify any chapter's page numbering settings by selecting the chapter in the book panel and then choosing Document Numbering Options from the flyout menu. Figure 21-2 shows the Document Numbering Options dialog box. The top half of the dialog box is the same as the Pages panel's Section dialog box, whereas the bottom half — the Document Chapter Numbering area — lets you control the chapter numbering style and the chapter number itself.

You can force a chapter to have a specific number by selecting the Chapter Number option, have the chapter use the same chapter number as the previous document (such as when you break a chapter into two documents), and have InDesign automatically number the current document by incrementing from the previous document's chapter number.

The chapter number defined here — whether manually overridden or automatically adjusted — is what is used by the Chapter Number text variable, explained in Chapter 20.

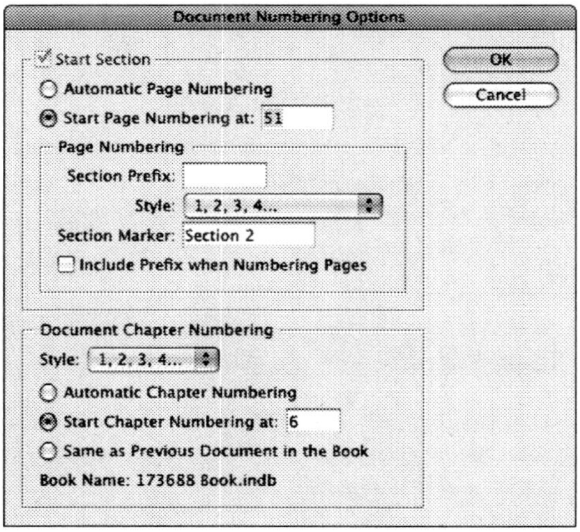

Figure 21-2:
The
Document
Numbering
Options
dialog box.

Document Numbering Options

☑ Start Section
   ○ Automatic Page Numbering
   ◉ Start Page Numbering at: 51
   Page Numbering
     Section Prefix: [　　　]
     Style: [1, 2, 3, 4...]
   Section Marker: [Section 2]
   ☐ Include Prefix when Numbering Pages

OK
Cancel

Document Chapter Numbering
   Style: [1, 2, 3, 4...]
   ○ Automatic Chapter Numbering
   ◉ Start Chapter Numbering at: 6
   ○ Same as Previous Document in the Book
   Book Name: 173688 Book.indb

Part VII
Printing, Presentation, and Web Essentials

The 5th Wave   By Rich Tennant

"Well, here's your problem. You only have half the ram you need."

In this part . . .

Finally, your layout is done. It's beautiful, it's well-written, and you're eager to share it with your readers. This part shows you how to take the final step to print or create an electronic version of your layout. InDesign gives you a lot of control over output, so you can optimize the results based on what you're printing it to, such as ensuring color fidelity and the best possible image resolution. Then you can start the whole creation, refinement, and output process over again with your next layout!

Plus, this part explains how to go beyond print into the brave new world of Web and interactive media by exporting files in the Web's HTML format, creating interactive PDF files with effects such as pushbutton actions and embedded movies, and even creating Flash animation files from your InDesign layout. Can 3-D be far behind?

Chapter 22

Printing and PDF'ing Your Work

*Y*ou've finished your document, and you want to share it with the whole world, or at least your audience. So you reach for your mouse and choose File➪Print or quickly press ⌘+P or Ctrl+P so that you can print.

Stop. Cancel. If this print job is your first with InDesign, you need to make sure that you've properly set up your printer to get the results you need. The process for doing so varies based on your operating system, and you can find instructions at the author's Web site at www.InDesignCentral.com.

Printing is more complex than just choosing File➪Print (⌘+P or Ctrl+P). At least it can be, depending on what you're printing and on what printing device you're using. For example, printing a full-color brochure involves more settings and steps than printing a proof copy to your laser printer or inkjet printer. So as you go through this chapter, keep in mind that many steps aren't relevant every time you print — but understanding the basics of printing ensures that you follow the right steps for each type of project. When you know the steps for printing one document, the process for printing every other document takes little effort.

Likewise, maybe you don't want to kill any trees to share your document. Instead, you want to distribute it electronically as a PDF file or as an e-book. Here, too, you need to take a step back before choosing File➪Export or pressing ⌘+E or Ctrl+E.

Checking Your Document before Printing

Before you print, you should do a visual proof of your layout. It's amazing what you don't notice when you're focused on specific elements as you lay out a page. Change your view setting so that the entire page or spread fits in the window (choose View➪Fit Page in Window [⌘+0 or Ctrl+0 — note the use of the numeral zero in the shortcut] or View➪Fit Spread in Window [Option+⌘+0 or Ctrl+Alt+0], as desired) and then review your pages.

This visual check is a critical step before printing, but you should also use InDesign's preflight tool to examine your document. The *preflighting* capability examines your document for any issues of concern and gives you a report on what you may need to fix.

You may wonder why you need a preflighting capability to check for things such as missing fonts and images: After all, InDesign lists any missing fonts and graphics when you open a document. The answer is that sometimes fonts and graphics files are moved *after* you open a file, in which case you won't get the alerts from InDesign. This mistake is more likely to happen if you work with files and fonts on a network drive, rather than with local fonts and graphics. Preflighting also checks for other problematic issues, such as the use of RGB files and TrueType fonts.

Identifying and fixing errors

InDesign preflights your document as you're working on it so that you can deal with surprises before the end of the project when you're likely on a tight deadline. At the bottom of the document window, InDesign reveals whether it has found any errors and lets you access the Preflight panel and other options to both specify what the preflighting should be checking for and show you the issues it has found. Figure 22-1 shows this alert and its options.

If you're working with the InDesign book feature (see Chapter 21), you can pre-flight the book's chapters from an open book's panel by using the Preflight Book option in its flyout menu. (If one or more documents in the book are selected in the panel, the menu option changes to Preflight Selected Documents.) The options are the same as for preflighting individual documents.

Figure 22-1:
The preflight
alert and
its menu
options.

Preflight Panel　　　⌥⇧⌘F
Define Profiles...

✓ Preflight Document
✓ Enable Preflight for All Documents

653 errors

You can turn preflighting on or off using either of these methods:

- ✔ In the Preflight pop-up menu at the bottom of the document window, choose Preflight Document to toggle between off and on. If the menu option is checked, preflighting is turned on. You can also toggle off and on Enable Preflight for All Documents, which sets the default action for all documents.

- ✔ In the Preflight panel (File➪Preflight [Shift+Option+⌘+F or Ctrl+Alt+Shift+F]), enable the On option to turn preflighting on; disable it to turn preflighting off. The flyout menu has the Enable Preflight for All Documents option.

The Preflight panel shows all errors that InDesign has found in the Error pane, as Figure 22-2 shows. The errors are grouped by type; to see the individual errors, click the right-facing triangle to expand the group's information. In the list of issues that appears, you'll get a brief description and a hyperlink to the page that has the error. Each list may have several occurrences, in which case you'll see another right-facing triangle that if clicked expands the list to show them all. And to get even more detail on a selected item, expand the Info pane by clicking its right-facing triangle (unless it's already expanded, of course).

To "collapse" any lists (such as to get them out of the way as you look at other items), click the down-pointing triangles.

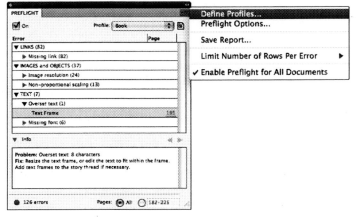

Figure 22-2:
The Preflight panel, the expanded Info pane, and the fly-out menu.

To get rid of the error notices, go to each page that has an issue and correct it. InDesign updates the preflight errors status as you do.

Telling InDesign what to check for

InDesign has its default set of issues to look for when preflighting. But you can set up your own options based on your specific needs. Although the process is simple, you'll likely need to consult with your production manager or service bureau to determine what settings you want to enable in your profile — these settings are typically expert decisions.

Even if the choices require expertise to make, the process for setting up your preflight options is easy:

1. **In the Preflight pop-up menu at the bottom of the document window or in the Preflight panel's flyout menu, choose Define Profiles.**

2. **In the Preflight Profiles dialog box, shown in Figure 22-3, click the + iconic button to add a new profile.**

   Use the – iconic button to delete a selected profile.

3. **Give your profile a name. Go through the options, and select the ones you want InDesign to preflight for as you work.**

   A triangle to the left of an option means that you can select from suboptions; click the triangle (it then points down) to get those suboptions. (Click it again to "collapse" the suboptions so that they're not in view.)

4. **Click Save when done.**

5. **Use the + and – iconic buttons at left to add more profiles or remove existing profiles.**

6. **Click OK when done to exit the Preflight Profiles dialog box.**

7. **In the Preflight panel, choose the desired profile for the current document from the Profile pop-up menu.**

   If the Preflight panel isn't open, choose File⇨Preflight (Shift+Option+⌘+F or Ctrl+Alt+Shift+F) to open it.

Figure 22-3: Left: The Preflight Profiles dialog box. Right: The Preflight Options dialog box.

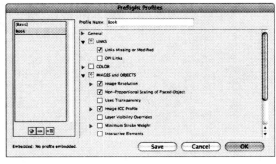

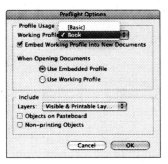

Setting Up Booklets

One of the trickiest types of documents to print is a folded booklet: You can't simply print the pages in sequence and have them end up on the right location on the final sheets of paper — when you fold them, you'll find the page order is rearranged because of the folding, especially in two-sided documents.

The tried-and-true approach is to use a booklet template that essentially provides a map of where pages should be so that when they're printed and folded, they end up in the right place — and then arrange your pages in that order via the Pages panel. Figure 22-4 shows the natural order (1–8) that you typically think a booklet has, as well as the actual page order (8,1; 2,7; 4,5; and 6,3) in which it must be printed to appear as a sequence of 1 through 8.

Figure 22-4:
Left: The layout order of pages for a folded booklet. Right: The printing order.

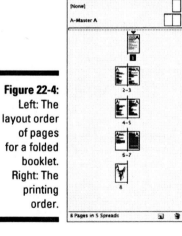
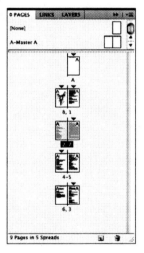

To simplify this approach, use the Print Booklet dialog box (File➪Print Booklet). Here, you arrange your pages in the Pages panel in sequential order (1–8, in this case) and let the InDesign software figure out how to rearrange them for printing. Much easier!

Here are the key controls in the Print Booklet dialog box's Setup pane:

✔ **Booklet Type:** This pop-up menu is the key control. Here, you choose the type of booklet, which tells InDesign how to arrange the pages when printing so that they're in the right sequence after folding. Your options are

• **2-up Saddle Stitch:** A folded sheet that contains two pages on each side, with the staples in the centerfold, between the pages.

Newsletters, smaller magazines, and many office documents use this option.

- **2-up Perfect Bound:** A folded sheet that contains two pages on each side, where the pages are stacked and folded and then cut and held together with a glued backing or spine-based binding. This option is typically used in books, larger magazines, and catalogs (because the square binding holds more pages than saddle stitching does).

- **2-up Consecutive:** A sheet that contains two pages on one side, with each page then cut and bound. This setup is essentially normal printing except that it uses a two-page sheet to print two pages at a time rather than a separate sheet for each page.

- **3-up Consecutive:** Like 2-up Consecutive, except three pages are on a sheet.

- **4-up Consecutive:** Like 2-up Consecutive, except four pages appear on a sheet.

✔ **Space Between Pages** (not available for 2-up Saddle Stitch) and **Bleed Between Pages** (available for 2-up Perfect Bound only): These options let you adjust the relative spacing among pages and objects, typically to provide additional white space around the folds.

✔ **Creep** (not available for the Consecutive options): This option shifts pages' contents away from the spine in increasing amounts as pages fall from the center of the booklet to the outside of the booklet. Because outside pages have to fold over many inside pages, their content can end up obscured in the inside margins because their gutter is eaten up by folding over those other pages. The Creep option corrects this problem.

✔ **Signature Size** (available only for 2-up Perfect Bound): This option specifies how many pages are printed on each side of a sheet: 4, 8, 16, or 32.

✔ **Automatically Adjust to Fit Marks and Bleeds:** This option ensures that crop marks, bleeds, and other content that appears outside the page boundary are properly handled for the chosen booklet type. If not checked, you can manually adjust these settings using the Top, Bottom, Left, and Right fields.

When using these features, consult with your professional printer or service bureau for the appropriate settings. If you're printing the documents yourself, do a test run, then fold, cut, and/or staple the sample document to make sure that it works as expected before printing lots of copies. The Preview pane shows the results of your choices, but doing a dry run is always the safest option.

When you're happy with your settings, choose Print to get the standard Print dialog box (covered in the "Choosing Print Options" section, later in this chapter). You can also choose Print Settings to set up printer-specific controls (also covered in that section).

Calibrating Color

If you're producing color documents for printing on a printing press, you may want to use InDesign's built-in color calibration tools. In a sense, you have to, because InDesign's color calibration is always on. But color calibration is something you don't do in a vacuum — you have to do it in your graphics programs as well so that every piece of software that handles your graphics is working from the same color assumptions.

If you use Adobe Creative Suite 5, you can use a consistent color management system (CMS) in all print-oriented CS5 programs, ensuring consistent color. For scanned images, digital camera photos, and the like, you can also tell InDesign the source device so that InDesign knows the color assumptions that the device makes and can use that information to adjust the colors during printing accordingly.

You can set the CMS settings in InDesign by choosing Edit⇨Color Settings to get the Color Settings dialog box shown in Figure 22-5.

Many of Adobe's Creative Suite 5 applications have the same dialog box, although sometimes you access it in different ways:

- ✔ **Bridge CS5:** Choose Edit⇨Creative Suite Color Settings (Shift+⌘+K or Ctrl+Shift+K). This action sets the defaults for all CS5 applications (see Figure 22-5), although you can modify individual applications, as described in the next three bullets. Note that if individual applications' color settings differ from the CS5-wide settings, you see a note to that effect at the top of the affected applications' Color Settings dialog boxes.

- ✔ **Acrobat Professional 9:** Choose Acrobat⇨Preferences (⌘+K) on the Mac or choose Edit⇨Preferences (Ctrl+K) in Windows. Then go to the Color Management pane. Note that this pane's appearance differs from the appearance of the Color Settings dialog boxes in the other Creative Suite 5 applications.

- ✔ **Illustrator CS5:** Choose Edit⇨Color Settings (Shift+⌘+K or Ctrl+Shift+K).

- ✔ **Photoshop CS5:** Choose Edit⇨Color Settings (Shift+⌘+K or Ctrl+Shift+K).

Note that the Web- and video-oriented CS5 applications — such as Adobe Device Manager, Dreamweaver, Flash Professional, Sound Booth, and Premiere — have no CMS controls.

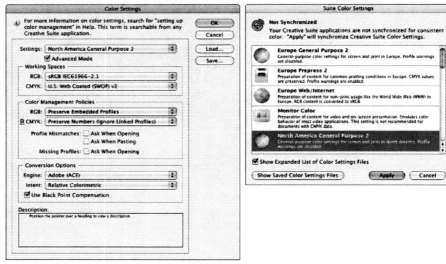

Figure 22-5:
Left: The
Color
Settings
dialog box
in InDesign.
Right: The
Suite Color
Settings
dialog box
in Adobe
Bridge.

When you place a bitmapped image into InDesign, the CMS applies the default settings defined in the Color Settings dialog box. (Choose Edit↪Color Settings.) If the document has no embedded color profile, a dialog box appears with a list of color profiles, as well as options to apply the default you've set up in InDesign or to apply no profile. (If you choose not to apply a profile, the color won't be adjusted during printing.)

Whether or not the document has embedded profiles, you can change the color settings for specific images, like this:

✔ As you import each file, select Show Import Options in the Place dialog box (choose File↪Place [⌘+D or Ctrl+D]) when you place a graphic into InDesign. In the resulting Image Import Options dialog box, go to the Color pane and select the appropriate profile from the Profile menu.

✔ Any time after you place an image, select it and choose Object↪Image Color Settings to apply a different profile. (You can also choose Graphics↪Image Color Settings from the contextual menu that appears when you Control+click or right-click a graphic in InDesign.)

You can save and use color management settings in other documents. The process is simple: Click Save in the Color Settings dialog box to save the current dialog box's settings to a file. If you want to use the saved color-settings information in another document, open that document, click Load in the Color Settings dialog box, and then browse for and select the color settings file. That's it! This technique is a handy way to ensure consistency in a workgroup.

If you put together a document with specific color settings, but then decide you want to apply a new profile across your pictures or replace a specific profile globally in your document, you have a couple of options:

✔ Choose Edit➪Assign Profiles to replace the color management settings globally for the document, setting the target color settings for output.

✔ Choose Edit➪Convert to Profile to change the document's *working* color workspace. It also lets you change the CMS engine, rendering intent, and black-point compensation settings. This does not change your output color settings but instead changes the source profiles assigned to the images so you can test different color settings in on-screen preview mode (View➪Proof Colors).

Be sure to consult with a production manager or service bureau manager if you change these expert settings.

When you're ready to output your document to a printer or other device, set the profile and rendering intent for that destination device in the Color Management pane of the Print dialog box (choose File➪Print [⌘+P or Ctrl+P]), which has an Options section with the Color Handling and Printer Profile pop-up menus. Here, you select the appropriate option for your output device. (If you don't know, ask an expert.)

Choosing Print Options

When your document is ready to print, go to the Print dialog box. (Choose File➪Print [⌘+P or Ctrl+P].) The Print dialog box has eight panes as well as several options common to all the panes. (I cover just the essential ones here.) Change any options and click Print, and InDesign sends your document to the printer. Figure 22-6 shows the dialog box.

 If you're working with the InDesign book feature (see Chapter 21), you can print the book's chapters from an open book's panel by using the Print Book option in its flyout menu. (If one or more documents in the book are selected in the panel, the menu option changes to Print Selected Documents.) The setup options are the same as for printing individual documents.

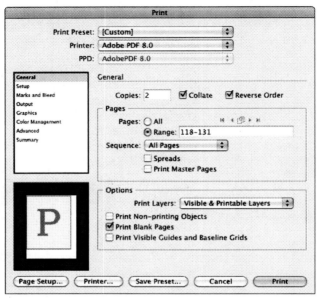

Figure 22-6:
The default
view for
the Print
dialog box's
General
pane.

Here are the common options available in the dialog box, no matter what pane is selected:

✔ **Print Preset pop-up menu:** This pop-up menu lets you choose a previously defined set of printer settings, which makes it easy to switch between, say, a proofing printer and a final output device.

✔ **Printer pop-up menu:** This pop-up menu lets you select the printer to use.

✔ **PPD pop-up menu:** This pop-up menu lets you select PostScript Printer Descriptions, which are files that contain configuration and feature information specific to a brand and model of printer. You usually install these files into your operating system by using software that comes from your printer manufacturer. If InDesign finds no compatible PPDs, it uses generic options. If InDesign finds just one compatible PPD, it uses that automatically; otherwise, it lets you select a PPD.

✔ **Save Preset button:** Clicking this button saves any settings that you change in the Print dialog box and lets you choose a name for those saved settings for reuse. If you change the dialog box's settings but don't save these changes as a print preset, InDesign changes the name of the current settings in the Print Preset pop-up menu to [Custom] to remind you that the settings are changed and unsaved.

You can also create print presets by choosing File⇨Print Presets⇨Define or edit an existing preset by choosing File⇨Print Presets⇨*preset name*. When you click New or Edit in the resulting dialog box, a dialog box identical to the Print dialog box appears, except that the Print button becomes the OK button.

✔ **Setup button (Windows); Page Setup and Printer buttons (Mac):** These buttons give you access to printer-specific controls. You use these dialog boxes to specify options such as printing to file, paper sources, and printer resolution. Note that if you add a printer, you may need to quit InDesign and restart it for it to see the new printer.

✔ **Cancel button:** Clicking this button closes the Print dialog box without printing. Use this button if you've clicked Save Preset but don't want to print, as well when you have any reason not to print.

✔ **Print button:** Clicking this button prints the document based on the current settings.

✔ **Page preview subpane:** This subpane at the lower left shows the current settings graphically. The page is indicated by the blue rectangle, and the direction of the large *P* indicates the printing orientation; in Figure 22-6 the *P* is unrotated. The figure's subpane shows that the paper itself is the same size as the page (the page is shown in white, and if the paper were larger than the page, you'd see a light gray area around the page indicating the excess paper). This preview changes as you adjust settings in the dialog box.

The General pane

The General pane contains the basic settings for your print job. Most are self-explanatory, but note these points:

✔ When specifying a range of pages in the Pages Range option, you can type nonconsecutive ranges, such as **1–4, 7, 10–13, 15, 18, 20**. If you want to print from a specific page to the end of the document, just type the hyphen after the initial page number, such as **4–**. InDesign figures out what the last page is. Similarly, to start from the first page and end on a specified page, just start with the hyphen, as in **–11**. InDesign lets you type absolute page numbers in the Range field. For example, typing **+6–+12** would print the document's 6th through 12th pages, no matter what their page numbers are.

✔ To the right of the All radio button are five new iconic buttons. These let you select pages of the same size as the first page in the current page range. If your document has multiple page sizes (as described in Chapter 4), you should use these buttons to print all pages of each size on the appropriate paper. (You change the paper tray for your printer using the Page Setup button on the Mac and the Setup button in Windows.) The buttons are, from left to right, Select First Range of Same-Size Pages, Select Previous Range of Same-Size Pages, Select All Pages Matching Size of Current Page, Select Next Range of Same-Size Pages, and Select Last Range of Same-Size Pages. (If all your pages are the same size, these buttons are grayed out.)

✔ Selecting the Spreads option prints facing pages on the same sheet of paper, such as putting two letter-size pages on one 11-×-17-inch sheet. This option is handy when showing clients proposed designs, but make sure that you have a printer that can handle a large paper size or that you scale the output down to fit (through the Setup pane, which I cover in the following section).

✔ The Options section lets you print various layout components that you typically don't want in final output but may be useful when sharing comps and other in-progress printouts with others, such as baseline grids, and nonprinting objects, such as formatting notes.

✔ A handy control in the Options section is the Print Layers pop-up menu, which gives you additional control over how layers are marked as non-printing print. The default option, Visible & Printable Layers, honors your layers' printing status. Visible Layers prints all visible layers, including those marked as nonprinting. All Layers prints both visible and hidden layers, including those marked as nonprinting. (See Chapter 4 for more on layers.)

The Setup pane

The Setup pane is where you tell InDesign how to work with the paper (or other media, such as film negatives) to which you're printing. The options are straightforward, so I just highlight a few notes and tips:

✔ **Custom paper size:** Choosing some printer models will in turn let you choose a Custom option in the Paper Size pop-up menu, in which case you type the dimensions in the Width and Height fields, as well as position the output through the Offset and Gap fields. These latter two options are usually used when printing to a roll, such as in an imagesetter using photo paper (called *RC paper,* a resin-coated paper that keeps details extremely sharp), so that you can make sure that a space appears between the left edge of the roll and the page boundary (the *offset*), as well as between pages (the *gap*). Most printers can't print to the edge, thus the Offset setting. You also want a gap between pages for crop and registration marks, as well as to have room to physically cut the pages.

✔ **Transverse option:** Don't use the Transverse option, which rotates the output 90 degrees, unless your service bureau or production department tells you to. Otherwise, you may have your pages cut off on the final negatives.

✔ **Tile options:** Use the Tile options to print oversized documents. InDesign breaks the document into separate pages — called *tiles* — that you later can assemble together. To enable tiling, select the Tile check box and then choose the appropriate option from the adjoining pop-up menu:

- **Manual:** This option lets you specify the tiles yourself. To specify a tile, you change the origin point on the document ruler, and the new origin point becomes the upper-left corner of the current tile. (To change the origin point, just drag the upper-left corner of the rulers to a new position in your document.) To print multiple tiles this way, you need to adjust the origin point and print, adjust the origin point to the next location and print, and so on, until you're done.

- **Auto:** This option lets InDesign figure out where to divide the pages into tiles. You can change the default amount of overlap between tiles of 1.5 inches by using the Overlap field. The overlap lets you easily align tiles by having enough overlap for you to see where each should be placed relative to the others.

- **Auto Justified:** This option is similar to Auto except that it makes each tile the same size, adjusting the overlap if needed to do that. (The Auto option, by contrast, simply starts at the origin point and then does as much of the page as will fit in the tile, which means the last tile may be a different width than the others.) You can see the difference between the two by watching how the page preview window at left changes as you select each option.

The Marks and Bleed pane

The Bleed and Slug area of the Marks and Bleed pane controls how materials print past the page boundary. A *bleed* is used when you want a picture, color, or text to go right to the edge of the paper. Because there is slight variation on positioning when you print because the paper moves mechanically through rollers and might move slightly during transit, publishers have any to-the-edge materials actually print beyond the edge so that gaps never appear. It's essentially a safety margin. A normal bleed margin is 0p9 (⅛ inch), although you can make it larger if you want.

A *slug* is an area beyond the bleed area in which you want printer's marks to appear. The reader never sees this area, but the workers at the commercial printer do, and it helps them make sure that they have the right pages, colors, and so on. Like the bleed, the slug area is trimmed off when the pages are bound into a magazine, newspaper, or whatever. (The word *slug* is an old newspaper term for this identifying information, based on the lead slug once used for this purpose on old printing presses.) The purpose of the slug is to ensure that you have enough room for all the printer's marks to appear between the bleed area and the edges of the page. Otherwise, InDesign does the best it can.

It's best to define your bleed and slug areas in your document itself when you create the document in the New Document dialog box (choose File⇨New⇨Document [⌘+N or Ctrl+N]), as covered in Chapter 3. You can also use the Document Setup dialog box. (Choose File⇨Document Setup [Option+⌘+P or Ctrl+Alt+P].) The two dialog boxes have the same options; if they don't show the Bleed and Slug section, click More Options to see it.

But if you didn't define your bleeds previously, you can do so in the Print dialog box's Marks and Bleed pane. You can also override those New Document or Document Setup document settings here. To use the document settings, select the Use Document Bleed Settings option. Otherwise, type in a bleed area by using the Top, Bottom, Left, and Right fields. If you want the four fields to be the same, click the broken-chain iconic button to the right of the Top field; it becomes a solid chain, indicating that all four fields will have the same value if any are modified. Any bleed area is indicated in red in the preview pane at the bottom left.

If you want to set the slug area, select the Include Slug Area option. InDesign then reserves any slug area defined in the New Document or Document Setup dialog box. You can't set up the slug area in the Print dialog box.

The Output pane

The next pane is the Output pane, which controls the processing of colors and inks on imagesetters, platesetters, and commercial printing equipment. For proof printing, such as to a laser printer or an inkjet printer, the only option that you need to worry about is on the Color pop-up menu, which controls whether the colors print as color or as grayscale.

The options in the Output pane are for experts and should be specified in coordination with your service bureau and commercial printer — these options can really mess up your printing if set incorrectly.

One area that you should set is in the Ink Manager dialog box. Accessed by clicking Ink Manager, the Ink Manager dialog box, shown in Figure 22-7, gives you finer controls over how color negatives output. If any colors should have been converted to process colors but weren't, you have three choices:

- ✔ **Click the spot color iconic button.** You can override the spot color in the Ink Manager dialog box by clicking this button (a circle icon) to the left of the color's name. That action converts the spot color to a process color. (Clicking the process color button, a four-color box icon, converts a color back to a spot color.) This is the way to go for a quick fix.

- ✔ **Make the spot color a process color instead.** Do so by closing the Ink Manager and Print dialog boxes and editing the color that was incorrectly set as a spot color in the Swatches panel (choose Window➪Swatches [F5]), as I cover in Chapter 6. Using the Swatches panel instead of fixing this color setting at output time in the Print dialog box ensures that the color is permanently changed to a process color for future print jobs.

- ✔ **Convert all spot colors to CMYK process equivalents.** Do so by selecting the All Spots to Process option. This method is the easiest way to make sure that you don't accidentally print spot-color plates for a CMYK-only document.

The other Ink Manager options are for experts and should be changed only in consultation with your service bureau, production department, and/or commercial printer.

Figure 22-7:
Left: The Print dialog box's Output pane. Right: The Ink Manager dialog box.

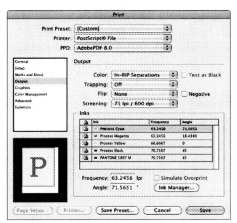
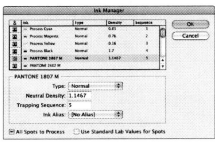

The Graphics pane

By using the Graphics pane, you control how graphics are printed and how fonts are downloaded. The options here are meant for professional printing, such as to imagesetters, in situations where you're working with a service bureau or in-house printing department. This pane is also an expert area, so change these settings only after consulting with an experienced pro.

The Color Management pane

The Color Management pane is where you manage color output (apply color calibration). Most options should be changed only in consultation with your service bureau or production department.

One option you should be able to change on your own is Printer Profile. Use this pop-up menu to select the device to which the document will ultimately be printed. This printer is by default the same as the profile selected in the Edit Color Settings dialog box, which I cover earlier in this chapter, in the section "Calibrating Color."

The Advanced pane

The options in the Advanced pane let you control graphics file substitutions in an Open Prepress Interface (OPI) workflow and also set transparency flattening, which controls how transparent and semitransparent objects are handled during output. Again, you should change these expert options only in consultation with your service bureau or production department.

The Summary pane

The final Print dialog box pane is the Summary pane. It simply lists your settings all in one place for easy review. The only option — Save Summary — saves the settings to a file so that you can include it with your files when delivering them to a service bureau or for distribution to other staff members so that they know the preferred settings.

Exporting PDF Files

Sometimes you want to create a PDF file for distribution on the Web, on a CD, on a corporate intranet, or even by e-mail. PDF creation is a simple task in InDesign. First choose File➪Export (⌘+E or Ctrl+E), and then choose Adobe

PDF (Print) in the Format pop-up menu (Mac) or Save as Type pop-up menu (Windows).

If you're working with the InDesign book feature (see Chapter 21), you can export all the book's chapters to a single PDF file from an open book's panel by using the Export Book to PDF option in its flyout menu. (If one or more documents in the book are selected in the panel, the menu option changes to Export Selected Documents to PDF.) The setup options are the same as for exporting individual documents.

After you choose Adobe PDF (Print) in the Export dialog box's Format pop-up menu (Mac) or Save as Type pop-up menu (Windows) and give the file a name and location in the File Name and Save in areas, click Save to get the Export Adobe PDF dialog box, shown in Figure 22-8. The dialog box has six panes; the General pane is displayed when you open the dialog box. Several options are accessible from all six panes.

InDesign CS5 has split its PDF export option into two menu commands: Adobe PDF (Print) and Adobe PDF (Interactive). Chapter 24 covers the creation and exporting of interactive PDF files, which support page actions, buttons, video, audio, and Flash animations. The Adobe PDF (Print) option covered here is meant for static PDF pages where interactivity is limited to hyperlinks.

If you know how to use Acrobat Professional, you know how to set up your PDF export. If not, consult with a local expert because PDF export options are as complex and job-specific as the print options I cover earlier in this chapter.

Some basic options are available in all the panes, and you should feel comfortable setting them on your own:

- ✔ **Adobe PDF Preset pop-up menu:** This pop-up menu lets you select from both predefined sets of PDF-export settings (similar to the printer presets covered earlier in this chapter), as well as any presets you or someone else may have created.

- ✔ **Compatibility pop-up menu:** This pop-up menu lets you choose which PDF file version to save the file as. Your options are Acrobat 4 (PDF 1.3), Acrobat 5 (PDF 1.4), Acrobat 6 (PDF 1.5), Acrobat 7 (PDF 1.6), Acrobat 8 (PDF 1.7), and Acrobat 9 (PDF 1.8).

  Choosing Acrobat 4 (PDF 1.3) is the best option for plain documents that you want to distribute on CD or over the Web because it ensures the broadest number of people will be able to view the file. But it also limits the capability to use some features, particularly those that protect the document from unauthorized usage such as copying its contents.

  Choose a later version if you need specific features. For example, choose Acrobat 6 (PDF 1.5) or later if your document uses transparency or high-level security settings. Use Acrobat 7 (PDF 1.6) or later for files with video, audio, and other multimedia features.

✔ **Save Preset button:** Click this option to save any settings made in the Export Adobe PDF dialog box as a new preset. (You can also define new PDF presets by choosing File⇨PDF Export Presets⇨Define.)

✔ **Export button:** Click this option to create the PDF file based on the settings that you selected in the various panes.

The General pane

Use the General pane, shown in Figure 22-8, to determine what is exported. The Pages option gives you the same flexibility as the Print dialog box's Pages option, which I cover earlier in this chapter. Similarly, the Spread option works like the same-name option in the Print dialog box, also covered earlier in this chapter.

In the Options section, you can select the following options:

✔ **Embed Page Thumbnails:** Select this option if you're creating a PDF file to be viewed on-screen. Thumbnails help people to more easily navigate your document in the Adobe Reader program. However, if you're sending the PDF files to a service bureau or commercial printer for printing, you don't need to generate the thumbnails.

✔ **Optimize for Fast Web View:** Always select this option. It minimizes file size without compromising the output.

✔ **Create Tagged PDF:** Select this option to embed XML tag information into the PDF file. It's useful for XML-based workflows and Adobe eBooks. If you don't know what XML or eBooks are, you don't need to select this option.

✔ **View PDF after Exporting:** Select this option if you want to see the results of the PDF export as soon as the export is complete. Typically, however, you shouldn't select this option because you'll likely have other things you want to do before launching Adobe Reader (or the full Acrobat program, if you own it) to proof your files.

✔ **Create Acrobat Layers:** If you selected Acrobat 6 (PDF 1.5) or later in the Compatibility pop-up menu, you can select this option, which outputs any InDesign layers to separate layers in Acrobat. (Acrobat 6 was the first version of Acrobat to support layers.) If you choose an earlier version in the Compatibility option, Create Acrobat Layers is grayed out.

✔ **Export Layers:** This pop-up menu gives you additional control over how layers marked as nonprinting are exported to the PDF file. It used to be that if you marked a layer as nonprinting, you'd have to leave the Export Adobe PDF dialog box to open the Layers panel to make it exportable. Now, you can skip that step and override layers' nonprinting status using this pop-up menu. The default option, Visible & Printable Layers, honors your layers' printing status. Visible Layers exports all visible layers, including those marked as nonprinting. All Layers exports both visible and hidden layers, including those marked as nonprinting. (See Chapter 4 for more on layers.)

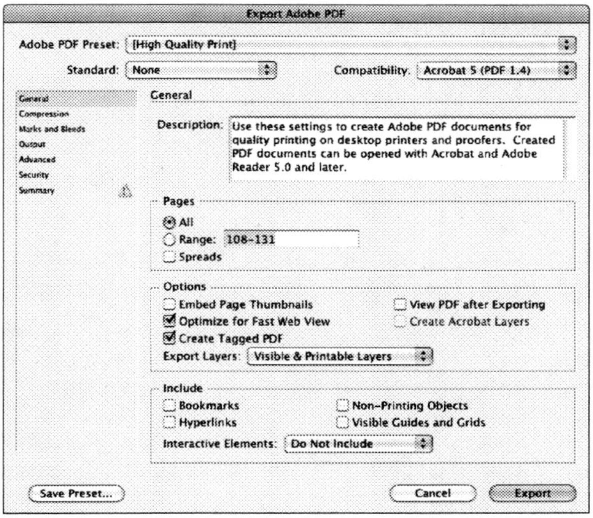

Figure 22-8:
The General pane of the Export Adobe PDF dialog box.

In the Include section, you set what elements of the document are included in the PDF file. You can select five options:

✔ **Bookmarks:** This option takes InDesign table-of-contents (TOC) information and preserves it as bookmarks in the exported PDF file. (See Chapter 19 for details on TOCs.)

✔ **Hyperlinks:** This choice preserves any hyperlinks added in InDesign. Otherwise, the hyperlinks are converted to standard text in the PDF file. (Chapter 23 explains how to create hyperlinks in InDesign.)

✔ **Visible Guides and Grids:** This setting includes the on-screen guides and grids in the output version — an option you'd use only when creating PDF files meant to be used as designer examples, not for readers or for prepress.

✔ **Non-Printing Objects:** This option includes any objects marked as Nonprinting through the Attributes pane. (Choose Window➪Output➪Attributes.)

✔ **Interactive Elements:** This pop-up menu has two options — Include Appearance and Do Not Include — to control what happens to interactive objects such as buttons and movie files. The Include Appearance option places a static image of the object in the file, while the Do Not Include option removes the object from the PDF file (blank space appears where the objects had been in the layout).

The Security pane

The Security pane is used to protect your documents from unauthorized usage or copying.

You should strongly protect PDF files distributed on the Web or in other electronic media.

To enable such protections, be sure the Require a Password to Open the Document and the Use a Password to Restrict Printing, Editing, and Other Tasks options are enabled. Here's how their settings work:

✔ **Encryption Level:** This section's options depend on the option set in the Compatibility pop-up menu; Acrobat 5 (PDF 1.4) and higher use High (128-bit RC4) encryption, while earlier versions use 40-bit RC4.

✔ **Document Open Password:** In this section of the Security pane, you can require a password to open the exported PDF file by selecting this option and typing a password in the associated text field. If you don't type a password here, you're forced to type one in a dialog box that appears later. To access protected content, recipients must use the Security pane in Acrobat. (Choose File⇨Document Properties [⌘+D or Ctrl+D] in Acrobat.)

✔ **Permissions:** Here, you determine what restrictions to place on the PDF file. Note that the following options vary based on what version of the PDF format you selected in the General pane.

  • **Use a Password to Restrict Printing, Editing, and Other Tasks:** You can restrict recipients' actions by selecting this option and then specifying permissible actions by using the Printing Allowed and Changes Allowed pop-up menus, as well as selecting from among the options that follow. (The number of options displayed varies based on the preset chosen.) You can also require a password to allow editing of the file in another application.

  • **Printing Allowed:** You can select None, Low-Resolution (150 dpi), or High Resolution. You would disable printing to ensure that the material can be read only on-screen.

  • **Changes Allowed:** You can select None; Inserting, Deleting and Rotating Pages; Filling in Form Fields and Signing; Commenting, Filling in Form Fields, and Signing; or Any Except Extracting Pages. (*Signing* means using digital signatures to verify sender and recipient identities.)

  • **Enable Copying of Text, Images, and Other Content:** If it's okay for recipients to use the PDF file's objects, select this option.

  • **Enable Text Access of Screen Reader Devices for the Visually Impaired:** If you want the file to be accessible to visually impaired recipients who use text-reader applications, select this option.

This option is available only if you're exporting to Acrobat 5 (PDF 1.4) or later.

- **Enable Plaintext Metadata:** For documents with *metadata* (authoring information associated with XML documents and Web pages), you can make that metadata visible to Web-based search engines and similar applications by selecting this option.

This option is available only if you're exporting to Acrobat 6 (PDF 1.5) or later.

Exporting to E-Book Format

Adobe has created a hybrid document format called EPUB that combines some PDF and some Web capabilities. It's meant to be a way to deliver books in a rich-media way for electronic readers and via Adobe's own Digital Editions software. Not many people use this e-book format (though the new Apple iPad's support for it may change that fact), so I don't dwell on it.

The EPUB format for e-books had been called Digital Editions in previous editions of InDesign.

To export a layout to EPUB format as an .epub file, simply choose File➪ Export For➪EPUB. You get the Save As dialog box, where you choose the disk and folder to store the exported Web page, as well as the page's filename. After you click Save, you get the Digital Editions Export Options dialog box, in which you specify how InDesign converts the layout to the eBook format. Unless you're EPUB-savvy, ask your boss what settings to use. Here are the basics:

- ✔ In the General pane, you choose how to handle bulleted and numbered lists (see the next section on exporting to the Web), as well as how to convert styles to the Web's CSS format (also in the next section).

- ✔ In the Images pane, you choose how your images are converted to the Web's GIF and JPEG formats, selecting options such as image quality and color palette.

- ✔ In the Advanced pane, you choose

  - Which flavor of the EPUB format is used (XHTML or DTBook)

  - Whether the InDesign layout's table of contents is exported

    It's likely you would export the TOC because .epub files are typically used for electronic books. Books typically have TOCs.

Click Export when done with your settings.

Creating a Document Package

Have you ever given a page-layout document to a service bureau only to be called several hours later because some of the files necessary to output your document are missing? If so, you'll love the Package feature in InDesign.

This command, which you access by choosing File➪Package (Option+ Shift+⌘+P or Ctrl+Alt+Shift+P), copies into a folder all the font, color-output, and graphics files necessary to output your document. It also generates a report that contains all the information about your document that a service bureau is ever likely to need, including the document's fonts, dimensions, and trapping information. You can also create an instructions file that has your contact information and any particulars you want to say about the document.

When you run the Package command, InDesign preflights your document automatically and gives you the option of viewing any problems it encounters. If you elect to view that information, the Preflight dialog box appears. You can continue to package your document from that dialog box by clicking Package after you assure yourself that none of the problems will affect the document's output. If it finds no problems during the automatic preflighting, InDesign doesn't display the Preflight dialog box.

Although InDesign preflights your document automatically by default, as the "Checking Your Document before Printing" section, earlier in this chapter explains, the Package command still does its own preflighting, using a core set of issues that Adobe has decided need to be handled even if you let them slide in your own preflighting. You can of course ignore them, but don't expect great output results if you do.

Before you can actually package the document, InDesign asks you to save the current document and then fill in the Printing Instructions form. You can change the default filename from `Instructions.txt` to something more suitable, such as the name of your print job. Often, you'll leave the printing instructions blank — use the form only if you have *special* instructions.

If you *don't* want to create an instructions form when packaging a document, don't click Cancel — it cancels the entire package operation. Just click Continue, leaving the form blank. Similarly, you must click Save at the request to save the document; clicking Cancel stops the package operation as well.

The next step is to create the package folder. You do so in the dialog box that follows the Printing Instructions form, which on the Mac is called Create Package Folder and in Windows is called Package Publication.

In the dialog box, you can select what is copied: Select Copy Fonts (Except CJK) to copy the fonts and Copy Linked Graphics to copy placed graphics (graphics pasted into an InDesign document rather than imported are automatically included).

If the Copy Fonts (Except CJK) option is selected, Chinese, Japanese, and Korean (CJK) fonts are not collected with the file. They are very costly and Adobe is trying to discourage their nonpaid distribution.

Via the Update Linked Graphics check box, you can also tell InDesign to update the graphics links for those that were modified or moved; if this Update Graphic Links in Package option isn't selected, any missing or modified graphics files won't be copied with the document.

Via the Include Fonts and Link from Hidden and Nonprinting Content check box, you can tell InDesign to include fonts and links from hidden layers (which you'd do only if you want the service bureau to print those hidden layers or if you were giving the document's files to a colleague to do further work).

When you open a layout file, InDesign CS5 looks in the `Document Fonts` folder inside the package folder containing the InDesign layout file and uses any fonts there for displaying that document — other documents can't use those fonts. If your document uses fonts not in that folder, InDesign then looks to the fonts installed on your computer and uses those, if available. This capability to use fonts packaged with a document makes it much easier to work with layouts produced by others. (Of course, you can create your own `Document Fonts` folder and place fonts in it; the Package feature simply makes the process a no-brainer via the Copy Fonts [Except CJK] option.)

Via the Use Document Hyphenation Exceptions Only check box, you also can specify whether the document should use only the hyphenation exceptions defined within it. This option often makes sense because it ensures that the printer's hyphenation dictionary — which may differ from yours — doesn't cause text to flow differently.

Finally, you can choose to view the report after the package is created by selecting the View Options check box. If it's selected, InDesign launches TextEdit and displays the report file, and on Windows it launches Notepad and displays the report file after the package operation is complete.

Click Save (on the Mac) or Package (in Windows) when everything is ready to go. Your document is placed in the folder you specify, as is the instructions file (the report). Inside that folder, InDesign also creates a folder called `Document Fonts` that includes the fonts and a folder called `Links` that has the graphics files.

Don't panic when you see a dialog box appear that warns you that sharing fonts could be illegal. If you're working with a reputable service bureau, they'll use the packaged fonts only for your job and then delete them. A font license typically allows you to share fonts for such temporary usage, but of course not to give away fonts to others for other uses. Anyone who needs the fonts on an ongoing basis should buy them.

I strongly recommend using the Package feature. It ensures that your service bureau has all the necessary files and information to output your document correctly.

Chapter 23

Web Project Basics

In This Chapter

▶ Setting up documents for the Web

▶ Taking advantage of hyperlinks

▶ Getting your work to the Web

Make no mistake: InDesign is not a Web design tool. You can't create a layout in InDesign and produce a Web page that looks just like your layout. (If you want to do that, export to the PDF or Flash SWF format, as Chapter 24 explains, and make them available for people on their computers or through their browsers.)

So why does InDesign have a Web intent for new documents? And why does it support Web features such as hyperlinks — and then let you export InDesign layouts to the Web's HTML format?

Is this some cruel trick? No. InDesign lets you create the foundations for Web pages, not the final Web pages. Why? Because the visual richness and placement flexibility of a print, PDF, or Flash document isn't available in the Web's HTML format. The fact is, a Web page is a simpler package than other forms of presentation — a reflection of early browsers' capabilities and the until-recently small size of computer screens and low throughput rates of Internet connections — and so the HTML format has simpler capabilities.

Yes, Adobe could have used HTML options such as tables and DIVs to simulate a page's layout, but that would result in an unsatisfying result — trust me on this.

You'll notice use of the acronym XHTML in InDesign dialog boxes and other controls. The *X* stands for "structured," indicating a strict version of the HTML format meant to reduce display variability in various browsers. But don't worry too much about it; when you see "XHTML," you can just think "HTML."

Instead, what InDesign lets you do is create a layout — or more likely convert one originally designed for print or PDF output — that contains all the elements you want in your Web page for refinement and completion in an HTML editor such as Adobe Dreamweaver or BareBones BBEdit. Thus, when you export a layout from InDesign to HTML, all your columns and text wraps and exacting kerning go away; your objects appear in one long column, and the typography is kept to basic formatting. Figure 23-1 shows what I mean.

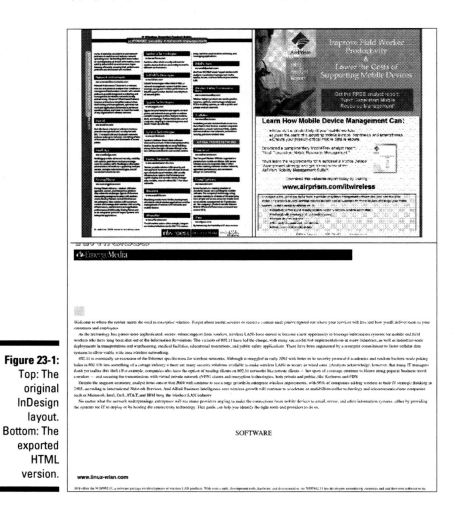

Figure 23-1:
Top: The original InDesign layout. Bottom: The exported HTML version.

Understanding InDesign's Web Intent

When you create a document (File➪New➪Document [⌘+N or Ctrl+N]), you can set the document's intent in the New Document dialog box (covered in Chapter 3). In the Intent pop-up menu, you can choose Print or Web. Doing so is a convenience — either way you have access to all the same capabilities in InDesign.

Choosing the Web option in the Intent pop-up menu simply favors Web-oriented settings such as using pixels as the default measurement unit, deselecting the Facing Pages option, and selecting the landscape page orientation. You can, of course, change these options in the New Document dialog box before you create the actual document — they are not forced on you, just suggested.

So if you're creating a document to be viewed in a Web browser as a Web document (or as a PDF or Flash file to be viewed within a browser), it's handy to choose Web as the document intent, and then modify the specific New Document dialog box settings as needed.

However, you're more likely to have created a document for print use and later want to use the same elements — those that can be displayed on the Web, anyhow — on a Web page. You don't change the document intent from Print to Web (in fact, you can't change the intent once set); you simply export the document to the HTML format and do the real design and layout work in your Web editor. InDesign does let you control how many layout elements export, as I describe later in this chapter, but the basic fact remains that InDesign is just a starting point for Web documents.

Using Hyperlinks

One big feature in InDesign applies directly to the Web: the use of *hyperlinks,* the clickable hot spots that direct a browser to open a new file or page. It's one thing that makes Web pages so dynamic and the Web experience so rich, because you can move among mounds of information easily.

InDesign lets you add hyperlinks to your documents, so if they're exported to the Web's HTML format, those links are clickable. And guess what? The hyperlinks also work in interactive PDF files and in Flash SWF files (but not in Flash FLA files or e-book files).

InDesign uses its Hyperlinks panel (Window➪Interactive➪Hyperlinks) to add, edit, and delete hyperlinks. In a sense, a hyperlink is a character attribute — it's applied to selected text. Figure 23-2 shows the Hyperlinks panel and its flyout menu.

Creating hyperlinks

Although the process is straightforward, InDesign's terminology can make it a very confusing on how to start. You first create a hyperlink destination — the place a hyperlink goes to, or its *target* — by choosing New Hyperlink Destination from the Hyperlinks panel's flyout menu. You give the destination a name in the Name field, and then choose from one of the three options in the Type menu:

- ✔ **URL:** This option is a Web page address (the official name is Uniform Resource Locator). If you select this option, InDesign displays the URL field in which you type the Web address.

- ✔ **Page:** This option lets you specify a specific page in a selected document. If you select this option, InDesign provides a Page field in which you specify the page number to open in the selected document, as well as the Zoom Setting pop-up menu, which lets you select how the page is displayed. (Options are Fixed, meaning at the default size in Adobe Reader; Fit View; Fit in Window; Fit Width; Fit Height; Fit Visible; and Inherit Zoom, which uses the current zoom setting in Adobe Reader.)

- ✔ **Text Anchor:** This option lets you specify a specific piece of text (the selected text) in the selected document, turning that text selection into the destination.

Text anchor hyperlink

URL, e-mail, file or Hyperlink

Page Hyperlink | Hyperlink to missing destination

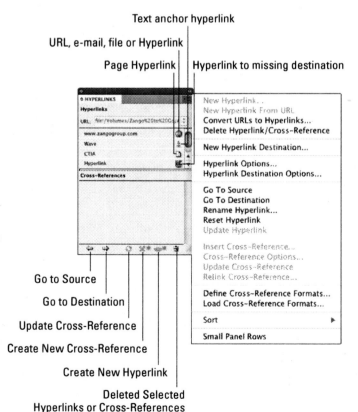

Figure 23-2:
The
Hyperlinks
panel and
its flyout
menu.

Go to Source

Go to Destination

Update Cross-Reference

Create New Cross-Reference

Create New Hyperlink

Deleted Selected
Hyperlinks or Cross-References

With the destinations defined, you can now create the hyperlinks to them (the hyperlink *sources*).

To create a hyperlink source, follow these steps:

1. **Select the text or frame you want to be a hyperlink's source (what the reader clicks to go to the link), and then choose New Hyperlink from the Hyperlinks panel's flyout menu.**

   The New Hyperlink dialog box, shown in Figure 23-3, appears.

2. **Use the Link To pop-up menu to determine what you're hyperlinking to.**

   You have the same three options as in the New Hyperlink Destination dialog box's Type menu — Page, Text Anchor, and URL — as well as three new ones: Email, File, and Shared Destination.

   Email lets you enter an e-mail address, as well as a default subject for that e-mail, if you like. File lets you point to any file and make that into a link; of course, any file you link to this way needs to be something your reader has the software to open. Shared Destination lets you select an InDesign document, including the current one, and then select from any destinations of any type defined in it.

   With the URL, Email, and File options, you can enable the Shared Destination check box, which makes the new hyperlink visible to other users through the Shared Destination option in the Linked To pop-up menu.

3. **In the Character Style section, you can tell InDesign to apply a specific character style to the hyperlinked text.**

   Select the Style check box, and then choose a character style from the adjacent pop-up menu. Note that the character style must already exist; there is no option to create a new character style from this pop-up menu.

4. **In the Appearance section, you can control how the hyperlink appears on-screen:**

   • Use the Type pop-up menu to choose Invisible Rectangle or Visible Rectangle. The Invisible Rectangle option gives no visual indication that the text contains a hyperlink, except that the mouse pointer becomes a hand icon when the reader maneuvers through the document. (You'd typically pick this option when you've used blue underline as a character attribute for the hyperlink text to mirror the standard Web way of indicating a hyperlink.) The Visible Rectangle option puts a box around the text using the following four settings. (They're grayed out if Invisible Rectangle is selected.)

   • The Highlight pop-up menu lets you choose how the source text or frame is highlighted: None, Invert (reverses the foreground and background colors), Outline (places a line around the source), and

Inset (places a line around the source, but inside any frame stroke; for text, it's the same as Outline).

- The Color pop-up menu displays Web-safe colors, as well as any colors you defined in the document.

- The Width pop-up menu lets you choose the thickness of the line used in the Outline and Inset options from the Highlight pop-up menu. The choices are Thin, Medium, and Thick.

- You can choose the type of line in the Style pop-up menu: Solid or Dashed.

5. When you're done defining the hyperlink source, click OK.

A quick way to add a URL-based hyperlink source is simply to enter that URL in the URL field of the Hyperlinks panel and then press Return or Enter. And if your text includes a valid hyperlink, such as www.InDesignCentral.com, you can select it and create a URL hyperlink automatically by choosing New Hyperlink from URL in the Hyperlinks panel's flyout menu.

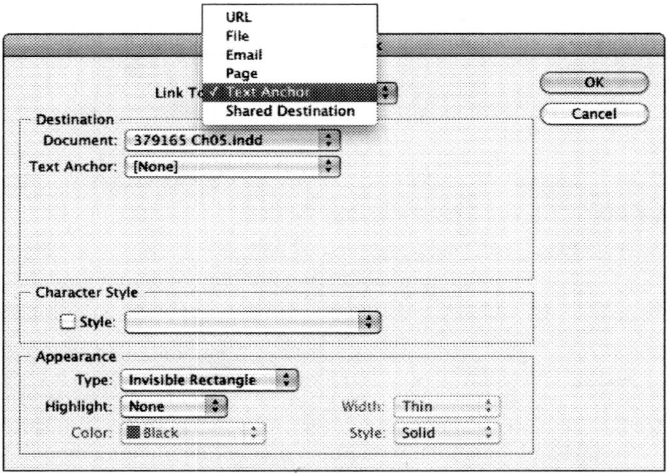

Figure 23-3:
The New
Hyperlink
dialog box.

Remember that I said that InDesign's hyperlinks feature is confusing? Well, you may have noticed that when creating hyperlink sources, you see a section in the dialog box where you indicate what kind of hyperlink you're creating. Hmmm. That means that when you're creating hyperlink sources, you're also creating hyperlink destinations — which you are. So what's the point of the New Hyperlink Destinations dialog box? It's to create destinations before you have a place to link them from, at least for the three types of links supported by the New Hyperlink Destination dialog box: URLs, text anchors, and pages in the current document. So, when you want to add hyperlinks to existing text and objects, use New Hyperlink. When you want to create hyperlinks to be applied later, use New Hyperlink Destination.

While we're at it, also keep in mind one more intricacy of using InDesign's hyperlink destinations: The Shared Destination option in the Link To pop-up menu in the New Hyperlink dialog box lets you choose any previously created hyperlink destinations in the document selected in the Document pop-up menu — both those created via the New Hyperlink Destination dialog box and those created via the New Hyperlinks dialog box.

Adding bookmarks

PDF files use something called *bookmarks* to help readers find information in the file. In a PDF file, a bookmark list acts like a table-of-contents list in a printed book, except that if you click a bookmark item, Adobe Reader or Acrobat brings you to the page the bookmark refers to (see figure).

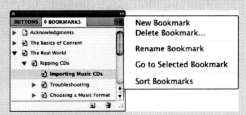

When you export to PDF, as explained in the "Exporting PDF Files" section later in this chapter, you can tell InDesign to take any table of contents set for the document and create PDF bookmarks from it. (Chapter 19 explains how to set up tables of contents.)

But you can add your own independent bookmarks in addition to whatever is in the table of contents. Open the Bookmarks panel (Window⇨Interactive⇨Bookmarks) and then choose what you want to bookmark. To do so, simply select some text or an object (frame or line); if nothing is selected, the bookmark is to the current page. Then choose New Bookmark from the Bookmarks panel's flyout menu or click the Add Bookmarks iconic button — the page icon — at the bottom of the panel. After you create the bookmark, choose the Rename Bookmark option in the flyout menu to give it a meaningful name (see figure); this name appears in the Bookmarks pane in Adobe Reader or Acrobat.

If you want a bookmark to be a subentry of another bookmark — the equivalent to a second-level or third-level headline in a table of contents — make sure that, before you create the bookmark, you select a bookmark in the Bookmarks panel. Any new bookmark is made a child of the selected bookmark.

The other Bookmarks panel flyout menu options are straightforward:

✔ Choose Delete Bookmark to delete any bookmarks selected in the panel. (You can also click the Delete Bookmarks iconic button — the trashcan icon — at the bottom of the panel.)

✔ Choose Go to Selected Bookmark to jump to that page in your InDesign document. An easier way is to simply double-click the bookmark entry in the pane.

✔ Choose Sort Benchmarks to sort benchmark subentries. This alphabetizes second-level, third-level, and other page-based subentries, and it sorts in order of appearance on the page any text- and/or object-based entries. It does not sort the top-level bookmarks, which appear in sequential order from the beginning of the document.

Converting hyperlinks in text automatically

InDesign can search through your text and convert URLs into hyperlink sources for you. The process is easy. Follow these steps:

1. **In the Hyperlinks panel, choose Convert URLs to Hyperlinks.**

2. **In the Convert URLs to Hyperlinks dialog box that appears, choose Document or Story in the Search pop-up menu.**

   This determines where InDesign looks for URLs to convert: in the entire document or just in the currently selected story.

3. **If you want InDesign to apply a character style to the text that is converted into a hyperlink, select the Character Style check box and choose the desired character style from the adjacent pop-up menu.**

   Note that the desired character style must already exist; there is no option to create a new character style in this pop-up menu.

4. **You can have InDesign convert all URLs it finds by clicking Convert All. Or you can search for each URL one by one by clicking Find and, for those URLs you want to convert to hyperlinks, then clicking Convert.**

5. **When done converting URLs to hyperlinks, click Done to close the dialog box.**

The automatic hyperlink conversion tool is smart: It finds URLs written out in several forms. For example, it recognizes `indesigncentral.com`, `www.indesigncentral.com`, and `http://www.indesigncentral.com` as URLs. It also recognizes domain extensions other than `.com`, such as `.net`, `.org`, and the country-specific domain extensions such as `.us`, `.fr`, `.uk`, and `.jp`.

Importing hyperlinks

When you place text that includes embedded hyperlinks (such as in RTF and Microsoft Word files), InDesign imports its hyperlinks as well. In the Hyperlinks panel, these imported hyperlinks appear in the list of hyperlink sources. They are named Hyperlink 1, Hyperlink 2, and so on, or they are named based on the actual embedded URL (such as `www.indesign central.com` or `http://www.wiley.com`) — it depends on how InDesign reads the links during import. Their destinations (the URLs) are available as hyperlink destinations in the InDesign document.

Applying hyperlinks

After your hyperlink sources are defined, you can easily apply them by selecting text and clicking an existing hyperlink source from the Hyperlinks panel. You can also jump to the source or destination by selecting the desired hyperlink in the Hyperlinks panel and choosing either Go to Source or Go to Destination from the flyout menu, or click the Go to Hyperlink Source or Go to Hyperlink Destination iconic buttons at the bottom of the panel. These "go to" options make a handy way to verify the links are correct.

Modifying and deleting hyperlinks

Modify hyperlink sources by choosing Hyperlink Options from the Hyperlinks panel's flyout menu to open the Hyperlink Options dialog box, which has the same options as the New Hyperlink dialog box (refer to Figure 23-3), to modify the source. Similarly, to modify hyperlink destinations, choose Hyperlink Destination Options from the palette menu to open the Hyperlink Destination Options dialog box, and then select the target from the Name pop-up menu. The Hyperlink Destination Options dialog box's options are the same as the New Hyperlink Destination dialog box.

You can change the source text or frame by selecting it, clicking the hyperlink name in the Hyperlinks panel, and choosing Reset Hyperlink from the panel's flyout menu. To change the target for a hyperlink to an InDesign document, choose Update Hyperlink from the flyout menu (press and hold Option or Alt to select a file that is not open).

To delete a hyperlink target, choose it in the Hyperlink Destination Options dialog box and then click Delete. (Click Delete All to delete all targets defined in the document.)

To delete a hypertext source, select it in the Hyperlinks panel and then choose Delete Hyperlink from the flyout menu, or click the Delete Selected Hyperlinks iconic button at the bottom of the panel.

Preserving hyperlinks in PDF files

Your exported files can preserve the hyperlinks you set in InDesign. Here's how:

For print PDF files (see Chapter 22), choose File➪Export (⌘+E or Ctrl+E), and choose Adobe PDF (Print) from the Format pop-up menu (Mac) or Save as Type pop-up menu (Windows), and then click Save. In the Export PDF dialog box

that appears, select the Hyperlinks option in the Include section of the General pane. When done with your settings, click OK.

For interactive PDF files (see Chapter 24), you don't have to worry about preserving hyperlinks: Hyperlinks are always retained when exporting to interactive PDF files.

Exporting to the Web

InDesign lets you export your layouts to the HTML format that Web editors such as Adobe's Dreamweaver can open for further work. (Note that you'll usually want to do further work in a Web editor both to take advantage of Web-specific formatting options and to rework the layout to better fit the horizontal "page" size of a Web browser.)

Tables in exported HTML documents now are assigned a Spry identifier so your Web developer can use the Spry widgets capability in Dreamweaver and other Web-editing programs to create sophisticated tables more akin to what InDesign can create than what standard HTML supports. What's a Spry widget? Don't worry — just let your Web designer know about this new feature so he or she can take advantage of it.

To export a layout to HTML format, choose File⇨Export For⇨Dreamweaver. (And despite the name, your files aren't limited to use by Adobe's Dreamweaver software; any Web editor should be able to open the files.) If you want to export just specific items on a page, select them with one of the selection tools before choosing this menu option.

You get the Save As dialog box, where you choose the drive and folder to store the exported Web page, as well as the page's filename. After you click Save, you get the XHTML Export Options dialog box, in which you specify how InDesign converts the layout to the Web format. Unless you're Web-savvy, ask your Webmaster what settings to use.

In the General pane, you choose whether to export the currently selected objects or the entire document, as well as how to handle bulleted and numbered lists. The default mappings — Map to Unordered Lists for bullets and Map to Ordered Lists for numbers — work for most sites. But you can also have InDesign convert either or both such lists into plain text rather than using the Web's list functions.

In the Images pane, you choose how your images are converted to the Web's GIF and JPEG formats, selecting options such as image quality and color palette.

In the Advanced pane, you set how text formatting is converted to the Web's version of styles, called *cascading style sheets,* or *CSS*. InDesign has three options, and the one you use is very much based on your Web designer's preferences, so be sure to ask.

   ✔ **Embedded CSS:** This option lets you control how text formatting such as paragraph styles and character styles are handled in the CSS style list that a Web document uses to apply text formatting. You have two additional options if you select Embedded CSS:

- **Include Style Definitions:** If selected, this check box creates CSS style definitions in the exported files that include the specific fonts and sizes used in the InDesign layout. This can be dangerous if you use many fonts that aren't available in Web browsers, because unless the CSS style is changed to use Web-standard fonts, browsers will substitute fonts of their choosing for these print-oriented fonts. Of course, by including these fonts in the CSS, the Web designer can easily and consistently replace print-oriented fonts with Web-oriented ones in a Web-editing program.

   Fonts that are generally safe to use for Web pages, due to widespread support for them by popular browsers, are the following TrueType and OpenType fonts: Arial, Courier New, Georgia, Monaco, Tahoma, Times New Roman, and Verdana.

- **Preserve Local Overrides:** If selected, this check box preserves local formatting, such as the use of character styles and font styles such as italics, in the exported HTML file. The Web designer should look out for the `<span class>` tags that result to ensure they don't cause issues for the final Web page's display.

✔ **No CSS:** This ignores style information in the InDesign file. Essentially, you get unformatted text.

✔ **External CSS:** This option adds a link to an external CSS file that your designer should provide you the name of and that you enter in the field below the External CSS radio button. (Don't forge the `.css` filename extension!) This means that after someone creates the specified CSS style file, the document will know what formatting to apply to the text. But of course you have to use the same style names in InDesign that the CSS file has defined in it.

Also in the Advanced pane, you can specify an external JavaScript file to link to — again, something your Web designer or programmer will have created separately.

Click Export when done with your settings.

The export process is simple, so it's easy to forget that converting print layouts to the Web's format is rarely a "point-and-shoot" activity. Expect your Web designer to do major work on those exported pages in his Web editing program, to optimize them for the Web environment. That's no reflection on you or InDesign — just the reality of working in different media.

Chapter 24

Presentation Project Basics

* *

* *

*I*t's 2010, the year we should have bustling moon bases and routine Mars missions happening. We don't, but we can create more than print or even Web documents in InDesign. In fact, InDesign CS5 drags us even further into the 21st century with its enhanced capability to work with video and audio files and its brand-spanking-new capability to create animations in layouts for export to the Flash Player SWF (pronounced "swiff") format used by the Flash Player on people's PCs and in Web browsers. If you're not careful, your documents will end up looking like a racing scene in the *Love Bug,* with objects dashing to and fro!

Well, hopefully not. But you can do some amazing things in InDesign CS5 that let you go way beyond the static world of print documents, and even more than the click-to-play or click-to-link worlds of the Web and PDF. With the new animation features, you can create whiz-bang documents in which objects appear either automatically or in response to readers clicking a button or moving a mouse over a specific object, in addition to simply fun documents that combine video, audio, and animation.

I'll stick with the basics here. When you're ready to go the next step, check out the author's *Adobe InDesign CS5 Bible* for a lot more detail on these inter-active capabilities — particularly the multistate object feature that lets you create quizzes, flow charts, and presentations that take place within a page's frame (rather than turn to a different page).

Working with Video and Sound

As far as InDesign is concerned, video, audio, and animation files are no different than text or graphics files: They're just object to be placed in your layout using the standard Place tool you use for graphics and text. Of course, chances are you would place these files so readers can see or hear them, and you want more than just a speaker graphic or the first still in the video to be what readers get. If you export your InDesign layout to interactive PDF or Flash Player SWF files (as I explain in this chapter), all the glory of these files comes through: Sounds will play and videos will run in video windows.

But before you start placing these media files willy-nilly, you need to understand the ones that InDesign supports:

- ✔ **Video:** InDesign can place Flash video (`.flv` and `.f4v` files), QuickTime (`.mov` files) video files, and Microsoft AVI video files into layouts. The QuickTime and AVI files can be played only in exported interactive PDF files; the other formats can be used in both exported Flash and interactive PDF files.

- ✔ **Animation:** InDesign can place Adobe Flash Player presentations (SWF files), which it can export to interactive PDF files, e-book files, Flash files, and Web (HTML) pages.

- ✔ **Audio:** InDesign supports the MP3, Apple AIFF, and Microsoft WAV formats. It can export all three formats to interactive PDF files, but only MP3 to Flash files.

The Media panel is where you control the playback options for video, animation, and audio files. Open the panel by choosing Window⇔Interactive⇔ Media. Figure 24-1 shows the Media panel for the three kinds of media files.

The Media panel in InDesign CS5 replaces the Movie Options and Sound Options dialog boxes in previous versions of InDesign.

Note the following three options in the Media panel:

- ✔ The Place a Video from a URL iconic button, if clicked, opens the Place Video from URL dialog box in which you enter a Web address for a Flash-compatible video file that you want to place in the InDesign document. Note that for the user to play back the video from the exported file, he or she will have to have an active Internet connection. (The Video from URL flyout menu option also opens Place Video from URL dialog box.)

- ✔ The Place a Video or Audio File iconic button, if clicked, opens the Place Media dialog box, in which you select the audio of video files you want to place in your layout. Unlike the regular Place dialog box, there are no import options.

✔ The Set Interactive PDF Export Options iconic button, if clicked, opens the PDF Options dialog box. In that dialog box, you can add a textual description to describe the file (it appears if you hover the mouse over the media object in an exported interactive PDF file) and can specify that the video plays in a floating window, rather than in the window defined by the object frame in the InDesign layout. You also can set the size and position of that window. Note the capability to specify a floating video window is not available if you have selected an audio file. (The PDF Options flyout menu option also opens the PDF Options dialog box.)

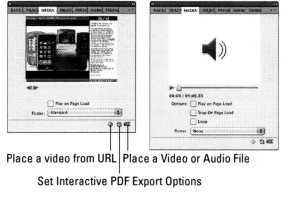

Figure 24-1:
The Media panel for, from left to right, animation, audio, and video files.

Place a video from URL | Place a Video or Audio File

Set Interactive PDF Export Options

Settings for animations

For SWF animations, the Media panel's options are straightforward:

✔ Using the Back and Forward iconic buttons, you can move through each state (such as a slide).

✔ If selected, the Play on Page Load check box ensures that the animation plays when the page containing it is opened in the exported interactive PDF or Flash file.

✔ The Poster pop-up menu lets you choose the preview image for the Flash file that appears in the exported interactive PDF or Flash file. The options are None, Standard, From Current Frame, and Choose Image. The Standard option uses a curved-F icon as the poster image.

Settings for audio

For audio files, the Media panel's options are also straightforward:

✔ Use the Play iconic button to listen to the file. It turns into the Pause iconic button, which you can click to stop the playback. You can also use the slider bar to move within the audio file to choose what to play back; the time indicator below shows the current time position for the audio and the total time.

✔ If selected, the Play on Page Load check box ensures that the audio plays when the page containing it is opened in the exported interactive PDF or Flash file.

✔ The Stop on Page Load check box, if selected, stops the audio playback when the page containing it is opened. You might use this option if you started playback on a different page, such as through a button action, as described earlier in this chapter.

✔ If selected, the Loop check box ensures that the audio file continues to play, returning to the beginning each time it ends. If not selected, the audio file plays just once.

✔ The Poster pop-up menu lets you choose the preview image for the audio file that appears in the exported interactive PDF or Flash file. The options are None, Standard, and Choose Image. The Standard option uses the speaker icon as the poster image.

Settings for video

For video files, the Media panel's options are more complex:

✔ Use the Play iconic button to view the file. It turns into the Pause iconic button, which you can click to stop the playback. You can also use the slider bar to move within the video file to choose what to play back; the time indicator below shows the current time position for the video and the total time.

✔ Use the Audio iconic button to turn audio on or off; if the icon is a speaker with three curves to its right, the audio is on; if only the speaker is visible, the audio is off.

✔ If selected, the Play on Page Load check box ensures that the video plays when the page containing it is opened in the exported interactive PDF or Flash file.

✔ If selected, the Loop check box ensures that the video file continues to play, returning to the beginning each time it ends. If not selected, the video file plays just once. Note that video looping works only if the document is exported to a Flash file.

✔ The Poster pop-up menu lets you choose the preview image for the video file that appears in the exported interactive PDF or Flash file. The options are None, Standard, From Current Frame, and Choose Image. The Standard option uses a filmstrip icon as the poster image.

✔ The Controller pop-up menu lets you change the skin, or frame for the video, that appears in the playback window in the exported document and contains the playback controls. The 17 options control what controls appear. For example, SkinAllOverNoFullscreen displays the skin around the full playback window but removes the full-screen control. And SkinPlaySeekCaption displays the skin below the video window, with the play, seek, and caption controls enabled.

✔ If you've chosen a Controller pop-up menu option other than None, you can select the Show Controller on Rollover check box to have the playback controls display when you move the mouse over the video in the exported document. If unselected, the playback controls display only when the video is playing.

✔ Use the Navigation Points control to set up playback points for the video. First, use the playback slider bar to move to a specific location in the video, or play the video and click Pause when you reach the desired location. Then click the + iconic button to add that location as a navigation point. (You can rename the navigation points by double-clicking their names and entering a new name. Select a navigation point and click the – iconic button to delete it.) Once you have set up navigation points, you can set button actions to play the video from that point in the Buttons panel. (Choose From Navigation Point in the Options pop-up menu in that panel and the desired navigation point from the Point pop-up menu then appears.)

Giving Readers Pushbutton Control

Interactivity means the user gets some control over what happens, and if InDesign's interactivity were limited to including hyperlinks (see Chapter 23) and playing media files, that wouldn't be all that interactive, would it? That's why InDesign lets you create buttons that users can click in exported interactive PDF and Flash files — and you get to set up the actions that occur when the user clicks a particular button, too!

Creating buttons

In InDesign, you use the Buttons panel (Window➪Interactive➪Buttons) to create buttons and other objects that have actions associated with them. After all, InDesign considers any object that launches an action to be a button, even if it doesn't actually look like a button.

The first thing you do is draw your button using any InDesign frame, shape, line, or path tool. Even a text frame can be a button, though a text selection cannot. Select the object and choose Object⇨Interactive⇨Convert to Button to turn the object into a button. The Buttons panel will then appear. Or select the object and click the Convert to Button iconic button at the bottom of the Buttons panel.

You can convert a button to a regular object the same way, removing all associated states and actions: Select the button and then either choose Object⇨Interactive⇨Convert to Object, or click the Convert to Object iconic button at the bottom of the Buttons panel.

Be sure to add a name for the button in the Name field of the Buttons panel; InDesign will put in a default name such as Button 1, but that kind of generic name is hardly going to help you remember what that button is if you need to work on it later.

InDesign comes with a library of buttons you can use rather than having to create your own. Just choose Sample Buttons from the Buttons panel's flyout menu to open the Sample Buttons library file. Then just drag the desired buttons from that library to your layout. Close the library when done. (Chapter 5 covers libraries.)

Figure 24-2 shows the Buttons panel and its flyout menu, as well as a button created from a graphic. Note the button icon at the lower-right of the graphic frame; InDesign places this nonprinting indicator automatically so that you know what objects are buttons.

Figure 24-2:
A sample
button (left),
the Buttons
panel, and its
flyout menu.
Lower right:
The bottom
of the
Buttons
panel when
you select a
non-button
object.

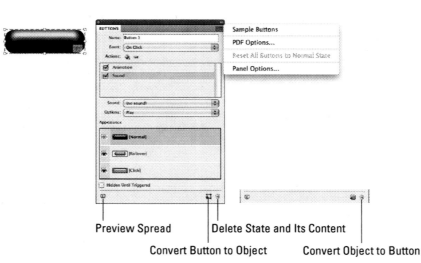

Preview Spread   Delete State and Its Content

Convert Button to Object   Convert Object to Button

Creating button states

The secret sauce for buttons is called *states*. Buttons work by invoking different states, or appearances, based on what the user is doing with them. Each button has three possible states: [Normal], [Rollover], and [Click]:

- The [Normal] state is added automatically when you create a button — it's how the button appears when the user's mouse is not over it or hasn't clicked it. In other words, it's what shows when the user has done nothing other than display the page.

- The [Rollover] state determines what happens when a user passes the mouse over the button. Typically, you want a visual change to occur so that the user realizes that the object is in fact a button.

- The [Click] state determines what happens when a user clicks the button. Here, you would typically have a visual indication that the button was in fact clicked.

To determine the button appearance for any state, select the button and then the desired state in the Buttons panel, then make your modifications using InDesign's standard tools. For example, for the [Rollover] state in Figure 24-2, I used the Swatches panel to change the button's color. You could do more than that, such as change a frame's contents, shape, and other attributes. You can also use InDesign's standard methods to place content into the buttons (such as choosing File⇨Place [⌘+D or Ctrl+D] or choosing Edit⇨Paste Into [Option+⌘+V or Ctrl+Alt+V]).

InDesign CS5 has two new options in the Buttons panel.

- The Preview Spread iconic button opens the Preview panel. The Preview panel shows you a preview of the current spread to test buttons and other interactive functions before exporting your interactive PDF or Flash file. (The Preview panel is covered later in this chapter.)

- The Hidden Until Triggered check box prevents the button from appearing until it is triggered, such as if it is clicked or rolled over.

Setting button actions

There are six types of mouse-related conditions you can use as triggers for button actions. Even though at first they may seem related, these actions have nothing directly to do with states; you can have only one state yet have all six triggers invoke actions in any state.

You associate actions to these triggers in the Event pop-up menu. (If no action is associated to a trigger, that trigger is inactive.) Here are the six triggers in the Event pop-up menu:

- ✔ **On Release:** Here, you can set what actions occur when a user releases the mouse after clicking the button. Typically, you want the button to do nothing in this case; if so, you simply set no action.

- ✔ **On Click:** Here, you can set what actions occur when a user clicks the button.

- ✔ **On Roll Over:** Here, you can set what actions occur when a user's mouse moves within the button's boundaries.

- ✔ **On Roll Off:** Here, you can set what actions occur when a user's mouse moves past the button's boundaries. Typically, you want the button to do nothing in this case; if so, you simply set no action.

- ✔ **On Blur (PDF):** Here, you can set what actions occur when a user clicks another button or form element. This trigger works only in interactive PDF documents.

- ✔ **On Focus (PDF):** Here, you can set what actions occur when a user clicks this button after having clicked another button or form element. This trigger works only in interactive PDF documents.

Each event trigger can have one or more actions assigned to it. Click the + iconic button below the Event pop-up menu to add an action, and add as many actions as you want to be triggered by the mouse event shown in the Event pop-up menu. (Use the – iconic button to remove a selected action.) You can reorder actions by dragging them within the list.

When you click the + button, the Buttons panel displays the Actions pop-up menu. Choose the desired action for the current event, and then specify any related settings (such as page number or movie file to play) appropriate for the selected action in the pop-up menus and fields that appear below the actions list. As an example, Figure 24-2's Buttons panel shows an Animation action and a Sound action applied to an On Click event, as well as the specific controls related to that action.

For both interactive PDF and Flash files, the options in the Actions pop-up menu are Go to Destination, Go to First Page, Go to Last Page, Go to Next Page, Go to Previous Page, Go to URL, Show/Hide Buttons, Sound, and Video. For interactive PDF files only, options include Go to Next View, Go to Previous View, Open File, and View Zoom. For Flash files only, options include Animation, Go to Page, Go to State, Go to Next State, and Go to Previous State.

By combining states, events, and actions in the Buttons panel, you can create a truly interactive document for export to interactive PDF or Flash formats.

Previewing interactive documents

InDesign CS5 has a new panel called Preview that lets you test your interactive features before exporting your layout to interactive PDF or Flash formats. You access the panel by choosing Window⇨Interactive⇨Preview (Shift+⌘+Return or Ctrl+Shift+Enter).

As the figure shows here, the panel is simple, with iconic buttons that let you "play" the current preview mode and reset the preview to the initial state. You control what is played using the Set Preview Selection Mode (for selected objects), Set Preview Spread Mode (for the current spread), and Set Preview Document Mode (for the entire document) iconic buttons. The Preview panel's flyout menu has the same preview mode options, as well as the Test in Browser option, to let you preview the document in a Web browser.

A quick way to preview the entire document is to press Shift+Option+⌘+Return or Ctrl+Alt+Shift+Enter. You can also replay a preview by Option+clicking or Alt+clicking the Play iconic button.

The flyout menu's Edit Preview Settings option opens the Preview Settings dialog box, where you can change preview options; the controls here are similar to the ones in the Interactive PDF Export dialog box covered later in this chapter.

Applying Page Transition Effects

You remember how cool it was the first time you saw someone give a PowerPoint presentation with those transition effects, like the horizontal wipe or the swirl? You probably don't remember what the presentation was about, but you do remember those visual effects. Well, InDesign supports these page transitions, too!

These page transitions display only in interactive PDF and Flash Player SWF files. And one page transition — Page Turn — works only in Flash Player SWF files. Furthermore, to see the page transitions, you need to run Adobe Reader or Adobe Acrobat in full-screen mode (for PDF files) or use Flash Player 10 (for SWF files).

You add such transitions in one of four ways:

- ✔ Choose Page Transitions⇨Choose from the Pages panel's flyout menu (Window⇨Pages [⌘+F12 or Ctrl+F12]).
- ✔ Choose Layout⇨Page Transitions⇨Choose.
- ✔ Choose Choose from the Page Transitions panel's flyout menu (Window⇨Interactive⇨Page Transitions).
- ✔ Choose an option from the Page Transitions panel's Transitions pop-up menu.

For the first three methods, you get the Page Transitions dialog box shown in Figure 24-3. If you use the Transitions pop-up menu, you don't get that visual selection when choosing an option. But after you choose a page transition, a thumbnail preview appears in the Page Transitions dialog box; if you hover your mouse on that thumbnail, InDesign animates it so that you can see the effect in action.

Select the transition you want to apply. Unless you select the Apply to All Spreads check box, these page transitions are applied to just the selected pages. The Pages panel shows a double-page icon to the lower-right of the spreads that have transitions applied, as you can see in Figure 24-3. You can edit these effects in the Page Transitions panel, such as by setting the transitions speed and direction, as also shown in the figure. In addition to editing the Page Transitions panel directly, you can also get to it by choosing Layout⇨Page Transitions⇨Edit or by choosing Page Transitions⇨Edit from the Pages panel's flyout menu.

Figure 24-3:
Left: The
Page
Transitions
dialog box.
Center:
The Page
Transitions
panel.
Right: The
Pages panel
showing
page-tran-
sition
indicators.

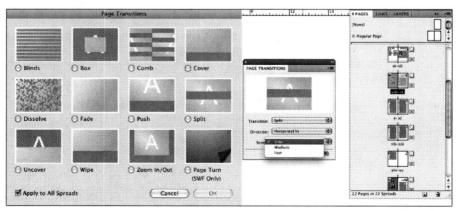

If you applied a page transition to just selected pages but then decide you want to apply a page transition to all spreads, just go to one of the pages that has the page transition applied, or select that page in the Pages panel and then choose Apply to All Spreads in the Page Transitions panel's flyout menu, or click the Apply to All Spreads iconic button at the bottom of the panel. To change selected pages' transitions, choose a new one using the Choose menus described earlier or choose a new transition from the Page Transitions panel.

You have three ways to remove all page transitions:

- ✔ Choose Page Transitions⇨Clear All from the Pages panel's flyout menu.
- ✔ Choose Layout⇨Page Transitions⇨Clear All.
- ✔ Choose Clear All from the Page Transitions dialog box's flyout menu.

Animating Objects

An animation is, at its heart, a moving object in InDesign. That is, you are applying motion and visibility effects to the various kinds of objects InDesign creates for any type of document: frames, shapes, lines, and so on. So, before animating your objects, you create them using the standard methods described throughout this book. You edit them and their contents using the standard techniques as well, even after you apply animation effects to them.

The animation effects applied in InDesign can be viewed only in Flash Player SWF files viewed in Adobe Flash Player 10 or later; they are ignored if you export to HTML, interactive PDF, e-book, or Flash Pro FLA project files.

What do I mean by animation effects? InDesign supports 47 predefined animation effects, or *motion presets,* that fall into the following types: appear/disappear (including fade in and out), move into the desired location from elsewhere, change size, rotate, and move in place (such as bounce up and down or dance).

Some predefined animation effects combine several effects, such as move and scale, but you cannot create your own combinations, such as having an object fly in from the top, then bounce up and down, and finally disappear in a puff of smoke. But you can import more sophisticated animation effects (called *motion presets*) created in Adobe Flash Pro by choosing Manage Presets from the Animation panel's flyout menu and then clicking the Load button in the Manage Presets dialog box.

To apply an animation effect to an object, select that object and choose the desired effect from the new Animation panel's Preset pop-up menu. (To open the Animation panel, choose Window➪Interactive➪Animation.) Note that an indicator icon composed of three circles appears in the object to let you know the object has an animation effect applied. (This indicator does not print or display in the exported Flash Player SWF file.)

To remove an animation effect from an object, choose None from the Preset pop-up menu.

For animations that involve moving the object along a path, you can see the *motion path* that the object will move through by clicking the Show Animation Proxy iconic button at the bottom of the Animation panel. (If the iconic button is selected, it shows as a dark button.) In your layout, you'll see a green line, called the *animation proxy;* it indicates the motion path, as Figure 24-4 shows. The animation proxy has an arrowhead at one end to indicate the direction of motion.

Setting animation effects

Use the other controls in the Animation panel to configure how the animation works for this object; note if the panel doesn't display any options after the Properties label, clicking the disclosure triangle icon to its left reveals the other available options:

- ✔ **Name:** Give the object its own name (a default name such as rectangle appears when you first select the object) so it can be referred to in Adobe Flash Pro CS5's ActionScript scripting language, such as to apply other effects to that specific object.

- ✔ **Event(s):** Choose in the Event(s) pop-up menu the conditions that will cause the animation to run (you can select multiple conditions; selected ones have a check mark next to their names):

  - • **On Page Load:** This option causes the animation to run when the page containing it is displayed.

  - • **On Page Click:** This option causes the animation to run when the user clicks anywhere on the page containing the animation.

  - • **On Click (Self):** This option causes the animation to run when the user clicks the animated object.

  - • **On Roll Over (Self):** This option causes the animation to run when the user moves the mouse over the animated object.

  - • **On Button Event:** This option causes the animation to run when the use clicks a button in the document that has the Animation action associated to it and specifies this specific animation effect. Because a button action must refer to the animation to be able to run it, you should create the animated object first, then create or modify the button to cause the specific animation to run. For example, you might name an animated object `Flyin Intro` in the Animation panel, then in the Button panel, specify that the button invokes the Animate action and choose `Flyin Intro` as the specific animation to run. (I explain how to create buttons and use actions earlier in this chapter.)

The Create Button Trigger iconic button to the right of the Event(s) pop-up menu provides a quick way to make an object into a button to run the current animation. Click the Create Button trigger iconic button to start the process, then click the object you want to be used as a button to make the current animation run. That's it! (The button's appearance will change so it looks as if it is pressed; click it again to clear the button assignment.)

- ✔ **Duration:** Enter a value in this field to set the time interval over which the effect takes place, in seconds.

- ✔ **Play:** Enter a value in this field to indicate how many times the animation should occur when triggered. To have it continually play, select the Loop check box.

- ✔ **Speed:** This pop-up menu lets you adjust the acceleration and deceleration of the animation to appear more natural. The Ease In option gives the initial motion a slight acceleration, while the Ease Out option gives the final motion a slight deceleration. The Ease In and Out option adjusts both the initial and final motions, while None plays the entire motion at a consistent speed. The From Preset option uses the default setting for the selected preset; you use this to reset the speed you later modified from the preset's default. Note that these adjustments are rarely noticeable on animations that occur in a few seconds or over short distances.

- ✔ **Animate:** This pop-up menu is where you tell InDesign if the object's location on the page is where you want the animation to start from (the From Current Appearance option) or finish at. There are two options for specifying that the object's current location is the end point: To Current Appearance and To Current Location. They have the same effect for animations that don't involve moving the object, but they cause different motion directions for animation effects that do move the object: Fly In, Move, and Spring. For example, if you use the Fly In from Left animation effect, choosing To Current Location will have the object move from outside the page's left margin to the location in your layout, but choosing To Current Appearance will have the object move to the left, ending up in its current location but starting roughly a half-screen's width to the right of that location.

✔ **Rotate:** Enter a value in this field to specify the object's rotation as it animates. For example, if you set a Fly In from Left animation to 120 degrees, the object will rotate 120 degrees as it moves to its final location. You set the object's rotation point by clicking one of the control points in the grid to the right of the Rotate field.

✔ **Scale:** Enter values in the W and H fields (for width and height) to indicate how much the object should grow or shrink in size during its animation sequence. (To set the W and H values separately, be sure to click the Constrain the Scale Value iconic button so the appearance changes to a broken-chain icon.) How the object scales depends on your selection in the Animate pop-up menu: If you choose From Current Appearance, the object's *final* size will be the percentage indicated in the Scale fields, but if you choose either To Current Appearance or To Current Location, the object's *initial* size will be the percentage indicated in the Scale fields.

✔ **Opacity:** Use this pop-up menu to have the object fade in or out during the animation by choosing Fade In or Fade Out. (Choose None to have the object not fade in or out.)

✔ **Visibility:** Use the two check boxes here to control when the object is visible. If selected, the Hide Until Animated check box keeps the object from appearing until the animation begins. If selected, the Hide After Animated check box makes the object disappear after the animation has completed. You can select both check boxes so that the object appears only while its animation is running.

Figure 24-4 shows the Animation panel and a sequence of Preview panel views that show the animation in action.

Sharing and managing animation effects

You can save the animation settings applied to a specific object as a motion preset by choosing Save from the Animation panel's flyout menu. In the Save Preset dialog box that appears, enter a name for the preset and click OK. You can then choose this new preset in the Animation panel's Preset pop-up menu for other objects. (To change the preset's settings, change the settings in the Animation panel, choose Save in the flyout menu, enter the same preset name in the Save Preset dialog box, click OK, and then click OK in the warning dialog box that appears.)

You can also delete, import, and export animation presets in the Manage Presets dialog box, which you access by choosing Manage Presets from the Animation panel's flyout menu. Because the motion presets in InDesign CS5 are the same as in Flash Pro CS4 and CS5, you can exchange presets between InDesign and Flash Pro using the Manage Presets dialog box.

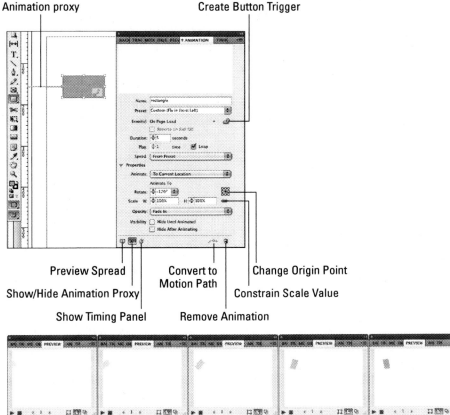

Figure 24-4:
Top: The Animation panel, with the settings for the object to its left. Bottom: A sequence of Preview panel views showing the animation's progress.

Animation proxy

Create Button Trigger

Preview Spread

Show/Hide Animation Proxy

Show Timing Panel

Convert to Motion Path

Remove Animation

Change Origin Point

Constrain Scale Value

Creating and adjusting motion paths

By default, a motion path is either the distance from outside the page to the object, or roughly half the width of the page, depending on the Animate menu option chosen (as described in the preceding section). But you can change the length of animation proxy — thus the motion path it represents — simply by selecting it, then dragging its end point as you would any line. You can also reverse the animation's direction by selecting its animation proxy and choosing Object➪Paths➪Reverse Path.

Also by default, the motion paths for animation effects are straight lines. But they don't have to be.

You can change the shape of the default motion path, such as to make it curve. To do so, select the animation proxy using the Direct Selection tool, then use the Pen tool and related techniques described in Chapter 17 to manipulate the path's shape. For example, you could select its midpoint and choose Object⇨Convert Point⇨Symmetrical to create a simple wave-shaped motion path.

Or you can create a motion path from scratch. To do so, create a path or shape as described in Chapter 17 or use one of the line or frame tools described in Chapter 7. Also create your animated object using the Animation panel, as explained in the preceding section. Select both the animated object and the object you want to be used as the motion path. Then click the Convert to Motion Path iconic button in the Animation panel. The object is converted into a motion path, with its end point placed inside the animated object.

Each time you select an animated object and another object, then click Convert to Motion Path, any previously applied motion path is removed in favor of the one you just applied. Also, the object you convert to the motion path is deleted from the layout and any contents removed. So be sure only to use objects you intended to use only as the motion path before clicking Convert to Motion Path.

Timing animation sequences

The Animation panel covered in the earlier "Setting animation effects" section lets you specify when animations begin based on specific trigger events: when a page loads, when a user clicks in the page, when a user clicks the animated object, when a user moves the mouse over the animated object, and when a specific button is clicked. If you have multiple animations set to begin when a page loads or when a user clicks in the page, the result could be disconcerting, as several animations go off at once. Likewise, even if you have just one animation that occurs when a page loads or is clicked, you may not want the animation to start immediately, before the user has had a chance to take in what's on the page.

That's where the new Timing panel (Window⇨Interactive⇨Timing) comes in. It lets you specify a delay for animations whose trigger is a page load or a page click. Figure 24-5 shows the panel.

In the panel, use the Event pop-up menu to choose which animations to apply timing delays to: On Page Load or On Page Click. A list of animated objects using the chosen trigger appears in the panel. Click an animated object in that list, then enter a delay time in the Delay field. The times can be specified to the thousandth of a second, such as 10.348 seconds. You can also select multiple animated objects and give them the same Delay value all at once.

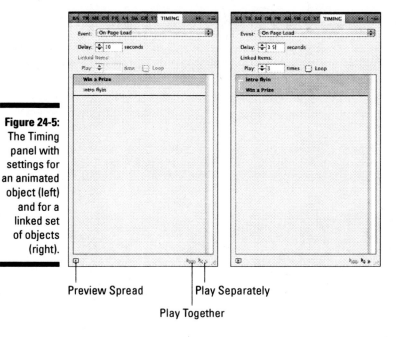

Figure 24-5:
The Timing panel with settings for an animated object (left) and for a linked set of objects (right).

Preview Spread   Play Separately

Play Together

The Timing panel lets you create groups of animations to which you control how often they play as a group. This lets you combine animated objects into sequences. Select all the animated objects you want to treat as a sequence, then link them by clicking the Play Together iconic button. When the group is selected (click the connecting-line icon to their left to select them all), the Timing panel makes the Linked Items options available. Enter a value for how many times you want the group to play in the Play field, or select the Loop check box to make the group play continuously.

Note that you can set a separate delay for each animated object in the group (select each object separately and adjust the Delay settings). Doing so lets you coordinate the sequence of playback timings for each item in the group.

To see the effects of your Timing panel settings for selected animated objects, click the Preview Spread iconic button, choose Window⇪Interactive⇪Preview, or press Shift+⌘+Return or Ctrl+Shift+Enter.

To ungroup linked objects, select the ones to remove from the group and click the Play Separately iconic button.

The Timing panel's flyout menu gives you three additional controls over animated objects:

- ✔ **Reassign to On Page Load:** Choose this option to change the trigger for the selected objects to On Page Load (the change is also reflected in the Animation panel).

- ✔ **Reassign to On Page Click:** Choose this option to change the trigger for the selected objects to On Page Click (the change is also reflected in the Animation panel).

- ✔ **Remove Item:** Choose this option to remove the object from the Timing panel. This also removes any On Page Load or On Page Click triggers from the object, a change that is also reflected in the Animation panel.

Exporting to Interactive PDFs and Flash Files

All the whiz-bang interactivity you can create in InDesign doesn't do a thing until you export the InDesign file to an interactive PDF or Flash file that the reader then opens on his or her computer or Web browser. After you're done creating your interactive documents, you need to export them.

The animations you create in InDesign work only in exported Flash Player SWF files — not in PDF or Flash FLA files, and not in the Web's HTML files. Buttons and actions work in interactive PDF, Flash Player SWF, and Flash FLA files (but not Web pages) — but some specific actions, as noted earlier in this chapter, work only in Flash Player SWF files or only in interactive PDF files. Likewise, not all audio and video files will play back in interactive PDF files, so you should use MP3 audio and Flash video files exclusively to ensure maximum compatibility across export file formats. Finally, page transitions work only in interactive files that are displayed in full-screen mode and in Flash files.

Exporting interactive PDFs

InDesign CS5 has split its export options for PDFs into print PDF and interactive PDF options; use the interactive PDF option to retain button actions, media playback, and page transitions. The interactive-PDF export options in InDesign CS5 have also added more controls than in CS4.

Most of what you need to do to export interactive PDF files is the same as for regular print documents (see Chapter 22). The biggest difference is that there are several options in the Export Adobe PDF dialog box specific to interactive documents that you should use.

To start your export, choose File⇨Export (⌘+E or Ctrl+E) and then choose Adobe PDF (Interactive) in the Format pop-up menu (Mac) or Save as Type pop-up menu (Windows). The Export to Interactive PDF dialog box then appears. The key options are:

- ✔ **Pages:** The options in this section control which pages are exported and how pages are handled. Select the All radio button to export the entire document; enter a range of pages, such as **2–5, 8**, to select specific pages.

- ✔ **View:** This pop-up menu lets you set the zoom level for the exported PDF file when a user opens it. The options are Default, Actual Size, Fit Page, Fit Width, Fit Height, Fit Visible, 25%, 50%, 75%, and 100%. The Default option uses whatever default the user has set in his or her copy of Adobe Acrobat or Adobe Reader.

- ✔ **Presentation:** In this section, if the Open in Full Screen Mode check box is selected, the PDF file opens in full-screen mode, with no Acrobat or Reader controls visible. If the Flip Pages Every check box is selected, you can enter a time in the adjacent text field to have Acrobat or Reader automatically play each page as if it were a slideshow, with each page displaying for the number of seconds specified.

- ✔ **Page Transitions:** This pop-up menu lets you specify which page transitions are used in the exported PDF if displayed in full-screen mode in Acrobat or Reader. If you select From Document, whatever page transitions specified in the InDesign document are used; otherwise, the selected page transition is used, overriding any set in InDesign.

- ✔ **Buttons and Media:** This section lets you control how buttons, button actions, and media files are exported. By default, the Include All radio button is selected, which enables all these interactive features in the exported PDF file. You can turn off these interactive features by selecting Appearance Only instead; this displays the buttons as static graphics and the media files as static poster images.

Click OK when done setting the options to create the interactive PDF file.

Exporting Flash files

When you choose File⇨Export (⌘+E or Ctrl+E), you can also choose to export to either Flash Player SWF or Flash FLA files from the Format pop-up menu (Mac) or Save as Type pop-up menu (Windows):

✔ A **SWF file** is a ready-to-play presentation file that can contain animations, button actions, hyperlinks, and page transitions. Note that you can't edit a SWF file in Adobe Flash Pro, so whatever you create in InDesign CS5 is the limit of what the SWF file can present. SWF files are playable by the Adobe Flash Player, either on a computer or via a Web browser.

✔ An **FLA file** is the default file format that Adobe Flash Professional CS5 uses for its projects. It can contain button actions, hyperlinks, and object states created in InDesign, but not animations. In the exported FLA file, all the supported InDesign layout objects are maintained as individual Flash objects, so you can work with each one. Likewise, all the text is editable. That makes it easy, for example, to apply ActionScript commands in Flash Pro to objects created in an InDesign layout.

After you've selected the desired output format, click Save to open a dialog box where you can specify the export options. (If you're not a Flash expert, consult with your Flash project manager on what settings are appropriate for your files' intended usage.)

The SWF export options

The key export options for SWF files are:

✔ **Export options:** These options let you choose exactly what to export. Use the Selection, All Pages, or Range radio buttons to determine what is exported. If Selection is selected, only selected objects are exported. Note that if you enter page numbers in the Range field, such as **1-4, 7**, the Range radio button is automatically selected.

✔ **Size (pixels):** The three radio button options here let you determine how to size the exported Flash Player SWF file. You have three choices: Scale, which lets you then set a percentage of reduction or enlargement; Fit To, whose pop-up menu lets you select from eight standard Web screen sizes; and Width Height, where you enter the specific width and height in pixels. The last option keeps the dimensions proportional; if you change one of these settings, the other is recalculated automatically.

✔ **Interactivity and Media:** Select the Include All radio button (the default) to include all interactive features used in the layout, such as hyperlinks, page transitions, media files, button actions, and animations. Select the Appearance Only radio button to disable all interactive features and simply show the interactive objects as static graphics.

✔ **Page Transitions:** In this pop-up menu, choose From Document (the default) to have the SWF file use whatever page transitions are specified in the InDesign document, or choose a specific page transition effect to apply instead on all pages. Select the Interactive Page Curl check box to add an animated graphic of a curled page corner at the bottom-right of all pages; this graphic is a page-transition button that, if clicked, moves the user to the next page in the SWF file.

When done choosing your export settings, click OK to create the SWF file.

The FLA export options

The export options for FLA files are similar to those for SWF, so refer to the preceding section for the key SWF export options — they're key for FLA export as well. But you should also be aware of two new options specific to FLA:

✔ **Text:** This pop-up menu controls how text in the InDesign document is handled during export: converted to Flash-format text (the Flash Classic Text and the Flash TLF Text options), converted to vector illustrations (the Convert to Outlines option), or converted to bitmaps (the Convert to Pixels option). The Flash Classic Text option makes each line of text a separate object in Flash Pro; the Flash TLF Text option retains InDesign text frames as text-frame objects in Flash Pro (a new capability in Flash Pro CS5). Note that if you use a text format not supported by Flash Pro, such as outlines, in InDesign, the Flash Classic Text option converts the text to bitmapped images, while the Flash TLF Text option simply removes the formatting and styles the text as normal text.

✔ **Insert Discretionary Hyphenation Points:** If this check box is selected, discretionary hyphens used in InDesign (see Chapter 12) are retained in the Flash FLA file, so they can be used for text flow in Flash Pro.

When done choosing your export settings, click OK to create the FLA file.

Part VIII
The Part of Tens

The 5th Wave   By Rich Tennant

In this part . . .

This part of the book was what inspired David Letterman's Top 10 lists. (Well, it could have!) Forget about slogging through the details. Here, you get the quick hits on everything from the coolest new features to the best resources to augment your InDesign. Think of it as popcorn from a book!

Chapter 25

Top Ten New Features in InDesign CS5

In This Chapter

▶ Looking at finishing touches

▶ Getting the scoop on fancy features

*A*dmit it — you came here before looking at the rest of the book. I can't blame you — everyone loves to know what's new. Well, InDesign CS5 has some really cool new stuff. Much of it falls into the category of nice little touches that make something that much easier to use.

But InDesign also added a bunch of "Hey, let's see what the users can do with this" kind of new thing just to keep everyone's brain sharp. Most of these fall into two areas: changes on how you select and manipulate objects, and all those fancy multimedia features.

You'll have your favorite new features, of course, but because I'm writing the book, I get to tell you mine!

Easier Selection and Manipulation

The many changes Adobe has made in how you select objects will take a little getting used to, but boy do they make things easier once you do. For example, you no longer have to use the Rotate tool to rotate an object — you can do so with the Selection tool instead. And if you want to rotate, shear, scale, or otherwise transform multiple objects, you no longer have to group them to use the transformation tools; just select and transform!

The new content grabber — that doughnut icon (explained in Chapter 8) — is the most visible fruit of these easier-manipulation labors. As you hover your mouse over an object, the content grabber appears. Click the doughnut with the Selection tool to select the object, even if it's buried under other objects.

Click it with the Direct Selection tool to edit the contents. Drag the doughnut to move the object within its frame. You can even rotate the contents using the content indicator's doughnut!

Chapter 8 covers most of the selection- and manipulation-oriented enhancements, while Chapter 10 covers many of the placement-oriented ones.

Column Spanning

It's annoyed me that even though Ventura Publisher in 1986 could let a headline run across multiple columns of text in the same frame, no other leading program has been able to do this common layout need — and Ventura Publisher pretty much went away by 1990. But finally, my prayer is answered: InDesign CS5's Span Column feature lets you put your heads and text (or any text) in the same frame and specify how many columns the heads (in this example) go across. The rest of the text wraps around the spanning text, of course, as Chapter 14 shows.

The Gap Tool

InDesign's designers are on a roll when it comes to making object placement smarter. In version CS4, it was by adding smart guides, spacing, and dimensions. In InDesign CS5, it's the new Gap tool. As Chapter 10 explains, the Gap tool lets you select the gap between objects and then change the size and location of the gap, resizing the object's boundaries for you. A variety of keyboard shortcuts give this tool lots of options.

Gridified Frame Creation

You know what a pain it is to create a matrix of objects that are the same size and properly aligned? Sure, you can create one and use the Step and Repeat feature to duplicate first the objects in a row, and then to duplicate the entire row for as many rows deep as you need. You then can import each object's contents one by one. InDesign CS5 fixes that. Its new gridified frame-creation capability (see Chapter 7) lets you create all the objects, perfectly aligned and sized, in one fell swoop. And the Step and Repeat feature has been enhanced to let you do the same thing when you've got the first object already created.

Tracked Changes

InDesign CS5 lets you see text changes made within InDesign (using the Story Editor, as Chapter 12 explains) and even decide whether to accept or reject them. Tracked changes from imported Word files are also shown. Although InDesign CS4 began tracking text changes made in layouts, only InCopy users could see and act on them — no more, thanks to InDesign CS5.

Animation

I admit that not many layout artists are about to go into the Flash SWF presentation business just because InDesign lets them. It'll take a long time before print-focused designers get media-dextrous and use a single tool to create multiple forms of electronic documents in addition to print documents. But InDesign CS5's capability to create animations from layout objects (explained in Chapter 24) — especially when coupled with the expert multi-state objects feature (not covered in this book) — brings some of the power of Flash to regular Joe and Jane designers.

Interactivity Preview

One problem with working with interactive capabilities such as button actions in a tool originally designed for print usage is that you can't see how your interactivity actually works until you've exported a PDF or Flash SWF file. InDesign CS5 fixes that fairly obvious omission. The new Preview panel, shown in Chapter 24, lets you see how your various interactivity features are actually working *before* you export.

Local Document Fonts

InDesign's Package utility (see Chapter 22) has always collected the fonts used in a layout, so other designers and prepress staff can install them if needed. But now, InDesign CS5 loads any fonts in the package along with the layout file, so I don't have to actually install them in my operating system or font manager. (These package fonts are accessible only by the layout file in that package.) Plus, since I don't have to install them to use them, I don't have to worry about uninstalling fonts I never bought and shouldn't keep once the project is over.

Autofit

InDesign already had a frame-fitting feature for graphics frames in previous versions. But autofit goes one step better. The frame-fitting feature works only when you place an image in a frame that has frame-fitting enabled. As Chapter 17 explains, autofit (if enabled in a frame or in a frame's object style) has InDesign resize the graphic automatically as you resize the frame.

Live Object Redistribution

A new capability inspired by the same need as the Gap tool is live object redistribution. In InDesign, when you've selected multiple objects and begin moving one of the marquee's control points, normally all the objects are resized to fit within the new marquee's size and shape. But in InDesign CS5, if you hold the spacebar shortly after moving one of the marquee's handles, InDesign doesn't resize the objects. It does, however, reposition them within the new marquee size and shape, adjusting the space among all objects appropriately. Chapter 10 explains more.

Two Annoying Bugs No More

Okay, so this is one extra item in my list of top ten new features in InDesign CS5. But since they are not new features, I can get away with it. InDesign CS5 fixes two long-annoying bugs:

- ✔ When you have bulleted or numbered text in a column that wraps to the right of another object, InDesign CS5 properly aligns the bullets or numerals and the text, as Chapter 14 explains. In previous versions, InDesign freaked out and misaligned the text after the bullets or numerals. No longer!

- ✔ When you have a nonrectangular text frame, InDesign CS5 can vertically align the text within the frame, using the Text Frame Options dialog box, as Chapter 11 notes. No more manually spacing text in nonrectangular frames to get them to align to the middle or bottom!

Chapter 26

Top Ten Resources for InDesign Users

In This Chapter

▶ Discovering useful Web sites

▶ Using Adobe Web resources

▶ Finding books to read

*W*hen you're ready to expand your horizons beyond what I can squeeze into the pages of this book, check out the resources listed in this chapter. No matter what type of information you're looking for, you can find it among this handy list of InDesign resources.

Yes, if you count carefully, there are more than ten. Consider them bonus resources!

Web Sites

Web sites are a great ongoing resource because they let you keep up with news, techniques, and product versions. Here are four sites that belong in your bookmarks.

InDesignCentral

www.indesigncentral.com

To help you keep up with the dynamic field of publishing, I've created an independent Web site that helps InDesign users stay current on tools and techniques. InDesignCentral provides the following resources:

- ✔ **Tools:** Links to plug-ins, scripts, utilities, and Adobe downloads.
- ✔ **Tips:** My favorite tips, as well as reader tips.
- ✔ **Resources:** Print publishing links, Web publishing links, Mac OS X links, and Windows links.
- ✔ *Adobe InDesign Bible* **series and** *QuarkXPress to InDesign: Face to Face:* Excerpts from the books, including updates from after the books' releases and color versions of the screen images from the chapters that cover color.

The Adobe Web site

`www.adobe.com`

The friendly people at Adobe, who gave the world InDesign, recognize the value in providing useful information for users of their software solutions. The Adobe Web site offers InDesign tips and tricks, guides, interactive tutorials, and lists of user groups. It's worth your while to visit the site now and then to see what's new. Be sure to check out the InDesign community area for pro tips and help from users just like you.

The Adobe Web site has a special area full of tips and user-to-user discussions as well: `www.adobe.com/designcenter`.

InDesign User Group

`www.indesignusergroup.com`

Seeking to help InDesign users share skills and tips, Adobe is supporting local user groups in many cities. Here's your chance to extend your InDesign knowledge and enlarge your personal network of graphics and layout experts.

You can also find links to several how-to guides from Adobe.

Creativepro

www.creativepro.com

Looking for the latest product and industry news? Go to Creativepro.com, an online magazine that also functions as a how-to resource and reviews center.

Magazine Resources

The Web has revolutionized content delivery, but a good old-fashioned magazine is hard to beat for the richness of its information and the capability to take advantage of its knowledge almost anywhere you happen to be.

InDesign Magazine

www.indesignmag.com

This PDF-delivered bimonthly magazine takes the expertise of a whole bunch of InDesign power users and puts it into one place, giving you a regular flow of great ideas, tips, and tricks. While it's not as convenient as a print magazine, the PDF format does have the advantage of being easy to store and keep with you wherever your computer happens to be. Plus, you can always print an article and take it with you if you want.

Layers magazine

www.layersmagazine.com

A great resource for tips and tricks specific to the Adobe universe of products is *Layers* magazine, which produces six glossy editions each year, chock-full of tips and how-to advice on each of Adobe's Creative Suite applications, including InDesign. The companion Web site also has lots of tutorials available.

Macworld magazine

www.macworld.com

Macworld magazine remains a spectacular resource for publishers of all skill levels, providing graphics guidance as well as general news and advice about the Mac platform that most designers use.

Recommended Books

Wiley Publishing, Inc., the publisher of this book, also offers a wide range of other books to help layout artists and publication designers exploit publishing tools to the fullest. The following four books — the first two I wrote — can help you expand your InDesign knowledge and related areas of expertise:

- My *Adobe InDesign CS5 Bible* gives you extensive insight and tips on using the newest versions of InDesign in professional publishing environments.

- My *QuarkXPress to InDesign: Face to Face* shows you how to make the move from QuarkXPress to InDesign. You'll be running at full speed in no time, leveraging your knowledge of QuarkXPress and translating it into InDesign's approach. Although this book was written using the CS2 version, its techniques apply to the CS3 through CS5 editions as well.

- *Adobe Creative Suite 5 Bible,* by Ted Padova and Kelly L. Murdock, provides a great resource on how to user Adobe's cornerstone tools (Photoshop, Illustrator, Acrobat Professional, and InDesign) together. This is not a compendium of mini-books on each product, but a guide on how the products work together — from production workflows to file exchange, from using Adobe Bridge as the central view of your projects to distributing your final results.

- *Digital Photography: Top 100 Simplified Tips & Tricks,* by Gregory Georges, provides clear, illustrated instructions for 100 tasks that reveal cool secrets, teach timesaving tricks, and explain great tips to make you a better digital photographer. To help you understand the implications of digital photography on the production process, *Total Digital Photography: The Shoot to Print Workflow Handbook,* by Serge Timacheff and David Karlins, offers complete, end-to-end workflow advice from shoot to print in a full-color presentation.

Index

• D •

• E •

Internet
Blogging For Dummies,
2nd Edition
978-0-470-23017-6

eBay For Dummies,
6th Edition
978-0-470-49741-8

Facebook For Dummies
978-0-470-26273-3

Google Blogger
For Dummies
978-0-470-40742-4

Web Marketing
For Dummies,
2nd Edition
978-0-470-37181-7

WordPress For Dummies,
2nd Edition
978-0-470-40296-2

Language & Foreign Language
French For Dummies
978-0-7645-5193-2

Italian Phrases
For Dummies
978-0-7645-7203-6

Spanish For Dummies
978-0-7645-5194-9

Spanish For Dummies,
Audio Set
978-0-470-09585-0

Macintosh
Mac OS X Snow Leopard
For Dummies
978-0-470-43543-4

Math & Science
Algebra I For Dummies,
2nd Edition
978-0-470-55964-2

Biology For Dummies
978-0-7645-5326-4

Calculus For Dummies
978-0-7645-2498-1

Chemistry For Dummies
978-0-7645-5430-8

Microsoft Office
Excel 2007 For Dummies
978-0-470-03737-9

Office 2007 All-in-One
Desk Reference
For Dummies
978-0-471-78279-7

Music
Guitar For Dummies,
2nd Edition
978-0-7645-9904-0

iPod & iTunes
For Dummies,
6th Edition
978-0-470-39062-7

Piano Exercises
For Dummies
978-0-470-38765-8

Parenting & Education
Parenting For Dummies,
2nd Edition
978-0-7645-5418-6

Type 1 Diabetes
For Dummies
978-0-470-17811-9

Pets
Cats For Dummies,
2nd Edition
978-0-7645-5275-5

Dog Training For Dummies,
2nd Edition
978-0-7645-8418-3

Puppies For Dummies,
2nd Edition
978-0-470-03717-1

Religion & Inspiration
The Bible For Dummies
978-0-7645-5296-0

Catholicism For Dummies
978-0-7645-5391-2

Women in the Bible
For Dummies
978-0-7645-8475-6

Self-Help & Relationship
Anger Management
For Dummies
978-0-470-03715-7

Overcoming Anxiety
For Dummies
978-0-7645-5447-6

Sports
Baseball For Dummies,
3rd Edition
978-0-7645-7537-2

Basketball For Dummies,
2nd Edition
978-0-7645-5248-9

Golf For Dummies,
3rd Edition
978-0-471-76871-5

Web Development
Web Design All-in-One
For Dummies
978-0-470-41796-6

Windows Vista
Windows Vista
For Dummies
978-0-471-75421-3